European film noir

Manchester University Press

European film noir

edited by
ANDREW SPICER

Manchester University Press
Manchester and New York

distributed exclusively in the USA by Palgrave

Copyright © Manchester University Press 2007

While copyright in the volume as a whole is vested in Manchester University Press, copyright in individual chapters belongs to their respective authors, and no chapter may be reproduced wholly or in part without the express permission in writing of both author and publisher.

Published by Manchester University Press
Oxford Road, Manchester M13 9NR, UK
and Room 400, 175 Fifth Avenue, New York, NY 10010, USA
www.manchesteruniversitypress.co.uk

Distributed exclusively in the USA by
Palgrave, 175 Fifth Avenue, New York,
NY 10010, USA

Distributed exclusively in Canada by
UBC Press, University of British Columbia, 2029 West Mall,
Vancouver, BC, Canada V6T 1Z2

British Library Cataloguing-in-Publication Data
A catalogue record for this book is available from the British Library

Library of Congress Cataloging-in-Publication Data applied for

ISBN   0 7190 6790 1 *hardback*
EAN   978 0 7190 6790 7

ISBN   0 7190 6791 X *paperback*
EAN   978 0 7190 6791 4

First published 2007

16 15 14 13 12 11 10 09 08 07   10 9 8 7 6 5 4 3 2 1

Typeset
by Action Publishing Technology Ltd, Gloucester
Printed in Great Britain
by Biddles Ltd, King's Lynn

Contents

For Tina

Illustrations

In some cases it has proved impossible to trace or contact the
copyright holders. If notified, the publishers will be pleased to rectify
any errors or omissions.

Notes on contributors

Tim Bergfelder is Professor and Head of Film Studies at the University of Southampton. He is the author of *International Adventures: Popular German Cinema and European Co-Productions in the 1960s* (Berghahn, 2005). Other publications include *The German Cinema Book* (BFI, 2002, co-edited with Erica Carter and Deniz Gökturk) and *The Titanic in Myth and Memory: Representations in Visual and Literary Culture* (I. B. Tauris, 2004, co-edited with Sarah Street).

Paul Cooke is Senior Lecturer in German Studies at the University of Leeds. He is the author of *Speaking the Taboo: A study of the work of Wolfgang Hilbig* (Editions Rodolphi BV, 2000), *Representing East Germany since Unification: From Colonization to Nostalgia* (Berg, 2005) and *The Pocket Essential Guide to German Expressionist Film* (2002). He has published widely on aspects of German literature, politics, media and film studies.

Ann Davies is Lecturer in Spanish at the University of Newcastle upon Tyne. She is the author of *The Metamorphoses of Don Juan's Women: Early Parity to Late Modern Pathology* (Edwin Mellen, 2004) and co-editor (with Bruce Babington and Phil Powrie) of *The Trouble with Men: Masculinities in European and Hollywood Cinema* (Wallflower Press, 2004). She has written various articles on aspects of Spanish cinema, and is currently writing a book on the Spanish film director Daniel Calparsoro, to be published by Manchester University Press.

Robert Murphy is Professor in Film Studies at De Montfort University. He is the author of *Realism and Tinsel* (Routledge, 1989), *Sixties British Cinema* (BFI, 1992) and *British Cinema and the Second World War* (Continuum, 2000), editor of *The British Cinema Book* (BFI, 2001), *British Cinema of the 90s* (BFI, 2000) and *Directors in British and Irish Cinema* (BFI, 2006).

Phil Powrie is Professor of French Cultural Studies at the University of Newcastle upon Tyne. He has published widely in French cinema studies, including *French Cinema in the 1980s: Nostalgia and the Crisis of Masculinity* (Oxford University Press, 1997), *Contemporary French Cinema: Continuity and Difference* (editor, Oxford University Press, 1999), *Jean-Jacques Beineix* (Manchester University Press, 2001), *French Cinema: An Introduction* (co-authored with Keith Reader, Arnold, 2002) and *The Cinema of France* (editor, Wallflower Press, 2006). He is the co-editor of several anthologies: *The Trouble with Men: Masculinities in European and Hollywood Cinema* (Wallflower Press, 2004), *Changing Tunes: The Use of Pre-existing Music in Film* (Ashgate, 2006), *Composing for the Screen in the USSR and Germany* (Indiana University Press, forthcoming 2007), *The Films of Luc Besson* (Manchester University Press, 2006). He is the general co-editor of the journal *Studies in French Cinema*, and co-author of a monograph on film adaptations of the Carmen story (Indiana University Press, forthcoming 2007).

Andrew Spicer is Reader in Cultural History at the Bristol School of Art, Media and Design, University of the West of England, where he is also Programme Leader for MA Film Studies and European Cinema. He has published widely on British cinema, including *Typical Men: The Representation of Masculinity in Popular British Cinema* (I. B. Tauris 2001, 2003), and is on the editorial board of the *Journal of British Cinema and Television*. He has written several articles and chapters on film noir including 'The Man Who Wasn't There: Problems of Memory and Identity in the Neo-Noir Anti-Hero', in Mark T. Conard (ed.), *The Philosophy of Neo-Noir* (University Press of Kentucky, 2006) and is the author of *Film Noir* (Longman, 2002). He has recently completed a study of Sydney Box for the British Film Makers series (Manchester University Press, 2006) and is currently working on a co-edited book *New Perspectives on Creativity* and an Historical Dictionary of Film Noir.

Rob Stone is Senior Lecturer and Head of Media and Communication at the University of Swansea, Wales. He is the author of *Spanish Cinema* (Longman, 2002), *The Wounded Throat: Flamenco in the Works of Federico García Lorca and Carlos Saura* (Edwin Mellen, 2004) and *Julio Medem* (Manchester University Press, 2007). He co-edited *The Unsilvered Screen: Surrealism on Film* (Wallflower, 2007) and has published widely on Basque, Spanish and Cuban cinema.

Ginette Vincendeau is Professor of Film Studies at King's College, London. She has written widely on popular French and European cinema. She is the editor of *The Encyclopedia of European Cinema* (BFI/Cassell, 1995) and co-editor, with Susan Hayward, of *French Film: Texts and Contexts* (Routledge, 1990 and 2000) and, with Alastair Phillips, of *Journeys of Desire, European Actors in Hollywood* (BFI, 2006). She is the author of *Pépé le Moko* (BFI, 1998); *Stars and Stardom in French Cinema* (Continuum, 2000; shortly to be published in French by L'Harmattan); *Jean-Pierre Melville: An American in Paris* (BFI, 2003); and *La Haine* (I. B. Tauris, 2005).

Mary P. Wood is Reader in European Cinema at Birkbeck, University of London, where she is Course Director of the undergraduate and Continuing Education programmes in Film and Media Studies. She is the author of *Italian Cinema* (Berg, 2005) and *Contemporary European Cinema* (forthcoming, Arnold, 2007). She teaches film and her research, conference papers and recent publications in the field of Italian cinema have been on the *femme fatale* in Italian film noir, representations of violence and terrorism, visual style and contested space, women and representations of prosperity in post-war cinema – for Penny Morris (ed.) *Women in Italy 1945–61*, (Palgrave, 2006), on 'pink neorealism' in Phil Powrie, Ann Davies and Bruce Babington (eds), *The Trouble with Men: Masculinities in European and Hollywood Cinema* (Wallflower Press, 2004), and on the director, Francesco Rosi, *Projections 8* (Faber, 1998); Rosi's *Carmen* in Ann Davies and Chris Perriam (eds), *Carmen* (Rodopi, 2005); *Le Mani sulla citta*, in 'Laboratorio Cinema Città', no 1, 2005; and on Rosi as intellectual activist in *Intellettuali italiani* for a German publication, 2006). She has also written on the intrusion of representations of the Balkans into mainstream cinema, and on the European quality film.

Acknowledgements

I should like to offer my sincere thanks to the contributors of this volume for responding so generously to my editorial suggestions, for their patience in what must have seemed an interminable wait for this work to be completed, and for the depth and rigour of their scholarship from which I learned so much. A particular word of gratitude is due to Tim Bergfelder who kindly and most ably stepped into the breach when the original contributor on German noir dropped out, and also to Mary Wood who agreed to extend her chapter to a chapter-and-a-half when we both realised the richness of the Italian film noir.

I am indebted to Brian McFarlane and Robert Murphy for their helpful comments on my own chapter; Brian McFarlane also kindly commented on the Introduction, as did Brian Neve, and I am grateful for their advice. Thanks too, to Matthew Frost at Manchester University Press for agreeing to this volume, and to Jonathan Bevan for seeing it through the final stages. I should also like to thank the Research Committee of the Bristol School of Art, Media and Design for approving a request for some teaching relief to complete the editing and to Professor Paul Gough, Dean of the School and Angela Partington, Head of Visual Culture, for their backing. As ever, I am conscious that this book could not have been produced without the love and support of my partner Joyce Woolridge; her perceptive comments on my own contributions sharpened their argument and her help in preparing the ms and the index was invaluable.

Parts of Mary Wood's chapter on Italian film noir first appeared in her book, *Italian Cinema* (Berg, 2005), and I am grateful to Berg for agreeing to its use here.

I

Introduction

Andrew Spicer

European film noir aims to provide an overview of the history and development of film noir and neo-noir in five major European cinemas – France, Britain, Germany, Spain and Italy – written by leading authorities in their respective fields. Each chapter contains a bibliography and extensive filmography. Occasional brief considerations of various European film noirs have emerged – and one impressionistic book-length account of French film noir – but *European film noir* is the first systematic attempt to map out the territory and to identify the key films.[1] The collection begins with France, the most widely recognised film noir outside America, and ends with a single, longer, chapter on Italy where film noir has rarely been discussed as such because the problems of defining it are so pervasive. Each chapter describes the distinctiveness of film noir or neo-noir within its respective national cinema at particular moments, but also discusses its interaction with American film noir and neo-noir. As each contributor argues, although European film noirs have characteristics that are specific to their national cultural formation, each has been profoundly affected, in various ways, by American noir, in a complex, two-way dialogue that ranges from imitation to radical originality via all shades of hybridity. This Introduction reflects on the significant similarities and differences that emerge in these accounts of the various European film noirs, and on the nature of this dialogue, which suggests the need to understand film noir as a transnational cultural phenomenon. But it begins by examining some necessary preliminaries: the problems of defining film noir and the reasons why it has almost always been regarded solely as an American form.

A 'conceptual black hole'?

Attempting to define film noir's necessary and sufficient characteristics is notoriously problematic. Although frequently referred to as a genre, film noir is not a genre in the conventional sense that the musical and the western are genres, partly because it was defined retrospectively and therefore did not operate as an industrial category whose existence and features can be established and checked through reference to contemporaneous documentation.[2] Nor can film noir be classified as a movement in the customary usage of that term, as its creators were unaware of the label and not affiliated to each other ideologically or aesthetically. Film noir has also often been defined historically as a group or series of films made between 1940 and 1959.[3] But, as with a generic label, this is a retrospective categorisation that bears little relationship to the actual conditions of the production and reception of these films, to the particular and diverse cycles of films (crime thrillers, detective thrillers, gangster films, gothic romances, semi-documentaries, social problem films, horror) to which they belonged. It is also notoriously the case that the film noir 'canon' remains an object of dispute and estimates of its size vary considerably.[4]

Part of the problem is the lack of agreement as to what are the common, shared features that mark out film noir. Film noir has often been defined in terms of a particular look or visual style: low-key or strongly opposing patterns of light, unconventional camera angles and movements, asymmetrical compositions.[5] However, these conventions are clearly used in other types of film and many films that are frequently referred to as film noir do not exhibit these features. Similar problems occur if noir is defined through its particular narrative patterns and devices including voice-overs, flashbacks and various forms of complex, disruptive chronologies.[6] The themes and subject matter of film noirs are also diverse, and it is far from the case that all are crime films or contain a crime. Indeed, any attempt to define film noir as a set of 'essential' or 'irreducible' formal components – stylistic, narratological or thematic – tends to be reductive and even misleading. Some commentators have sought to unify film noir through its prevailing mood or tone, one that can be characterised as cynical, pessimistic, paranoid, morally ambivalent, with a strong sense of alienation and that existence is meaninglessness and absurd.[7] This is seductively vague, but only encompasses certain types of film noirs (the darkest) not all of them, as many have upbeat or redemptive endings, which reinscribe the forces of law and order or romantic love as triumphant.

In the light of these problems of definition, is film noir therefore a confusing and unhelpful category, in Thomas Elsaesser's words, a 'conceptual black hole'?[8] A sharper understanding of the term, if not a solution to the problems of its definition, can be gained from a brief consideration of its evolution as an ideologically charged, discursive construction. The term was employed in late summer 1946 by French film reviewers, startled and fascinated by a group of American thrillers – *The*

Maltese Falcon (1941), *Double Indemnity* (1944), *Murder, My Sweet* (1944) and *Laura* (1944) – that indicated a new direction for the crime film. Film noir was used through its analogy with Gallimard's *Série Noire*, the label given to French translations of American 'hard-boiled' crime fiction from which several of those films had been adapted. As Charles O'Brien notes, these critics were simply extending a pre-war tradition in which the term was used to describe sombre, bleak French films that have been retrospectively classified as poetic realism.[9] However, in the post-war period, film noir became an important component of a French intellectual climate dominated by existentialism and surrealism, eager to find aspects of American culture that embodied these ideas and attitudes.[10] The French espousal of film noir was the celebration of popular cinema elevated to art, and, moreover, an art that presented a devastating critique of American values. As Marc Vernet summarises '[film noir] allows one to love the United States while criticizing it, or more exactly to criticize it in order to be able to love it'.[11] Indeed, as the present volume makes clear, this ambivalent attitude to American culture is a vital component of European film noir. The first full-length study of film noir, Raymond Borde and Etienne Chaumeton's *Panorama du film noir américain*, published in 1955, was the culmination of over a decade of French commentary on American film noir.[12] Borde and Chaumeton chose to emphasise noir's surrealist credentials, the 'note of confusion [that] is at the very heart of the oneiric quality specific to the series'.[13]

When Anglo-American criticism belatedly embraced film noir – notably in Paul Schrader's seminal 1972 essay 'Notes on *Film Noir*', originally written to accompany a major retrospective at the Los Angeles Museum – it took over a concept and a corpus of films that had been culturally validated by Europe, with the concomitant high status and cachet.[14] The many academic studies that have followed, however they defined film noir, collectively served to reinforce the significance of these films and the validity of the term. Alain Silver and Elizabeth Ward's *Film Noir: An Encyclopedic Reference to the American Style*, first published in 1980, was enormously influential in defining the noir 'canon' through its commentaries on over 250 films, both noir and neo-noir.[15] Film noir now occupies a privileged, if contested, place within film studies, and numerous course modules are devoted to it, in America and in Europe.

Complementing and extending this academic interest has been noir's espousal within the American film industry. Schrader was already conscious, in 1972, that noir spoke to a new generation of Americans disillusioned by Vietnam, becoming part of the vocabulary and thinking of young American filmmakers increasingly aware of the corruption and inequalities of American society. This impulse led to the development of neo-noirs that draw upon the putative conventions of film noir as a means of addressing these issues, including Martin Scorsese's *Taxi Driver* (1976) with a screenplay by Schrader. Twenty years on, Borde and Chaumeton recognised that a 'new series' had emerged, 'a flourishing renaissance of film noir', again specifically American, and with 'a new kind of morbid hardheartedness'.[16] Film noir has become an important part of contemporary film-makers' cultural heritage and neo-noirs are characteristically highly intertextual and allusive, full of knowing references to previous noirs that their creators know modern audiences will both recognise and enjoy. This allusiveness further reinforces the status and significance of classic noir by constant reference back to the canonical films that have become part of popular consciousness. Both film noir and neo-noir are now regularly used by the film industry itself as marketing devices. As Rick Altman observes, film noir has shifted from adjective to noun, from descriptive term to category, becoming an accepted and unexceptionable label habitually used by critics and reviewers, 'as much part of film journalism as biopic, sci-fi and docudrama'.[17] In several ways this has been a decisive shift in the history of the term because neo-noir implies an understanding and acceptance of the concept of film noir. Film noir has now become a generic term and the canonical or classic film noirs 'are now viewed generically as *noirs* in a way they never were when initially released'.[18]

In *More Than Night*, the most important work on film noir in the last decade, James Naremore argues that film noir should be understood not as a set of 'definitive traits' but as a 'discursive construct with heuristic value', which is both 'an important cinematic legacy and an idea we have projected onto the past'.[19] This formulation is extremely helpful because it retains the double sense of film noir as a body of American films from a particular period ('classical noir') and a shaping discourse that constantly redefines the meaning of those films, a discourse which has significance within the academy – the history of ideas, film history – and within the industry itself in the production and marketing of neo-noirs and their classical avatars now re-released on DVD. According to Naremore, film noir has become an imprecise but necessary intellectual category, comparable to 'romantic' or 'classic', whose use helps to make sense of diverse but important phenomena and has become an indispensable part of film criticism.

An 'indigenous American form'?

If this argument is accepted – that noir is an imprecise but indispensable category – and justifies the continued use of the term, it does not follow that it is an exclusively American phenomenon. This is another aspect of the discursive construction of film noir that goes back to its earliest usage. In their *Panorama*, Borde and Chaumeton were again typical of French commentators in understanding film noir as a solely American 'series': 'a group of *nationally identifiable* films sharing certain common features (style, atmosphere, subject) sufficiently strong to mark them unequivocally and give them, with time, an inimitable quality'.[20] They played down the European influences on the evolution of film noir, raising the possibility that poetic realism was a forerunner to film noir only to dismiss it: 'Did *Pépé le Moko*, *Quai des brumes* [sic], and *La Bête humaine* announce American film noir? We think not. In the first instance, oneirism and strangeness are completely lacking'.[21] They devote a chapter to French film noir, but its main focus is a scathing attack on the then current (1954–55) fashion for film noirs aimed at young audiences, which are judged as being inauthentic, a pastiche of American noir that constitutes a 'caricature of the noir series'.[22] As Ginette Vincendeau explains in this volume, the reason behind this dismissal is that the orientation of French film noirs is social rather than generic: 'This would explain why the critics who defined film noir as uniquely American turned their back on it. Rather than the aesthetic glamour and emotional excitement of American films noirs, genuine French films noirs offered, instead, a dystopian sometimes hellish vision of French society'.[23] Intriguingly, Borde and Chaumeton also concede that there has been 'the development of an authentic British noir series', but do not develop that *aperçu* at any length.[24]

When film noir was taken up in Anglo-American criticism, the tendency to regard noir as purely American was even more pronounced.[25] In his 'Notes on *Film Noir*', Schrader saw film noir as essentially the inevitable development of the American gangster film that had been delayed by the war. He conceded that there were 'foreign off-shoots of *film noir*', but did not elaborate this point beyond naming one or two films.[26] To have developed this strand of thinking would have weakened Schrader's case that film noir was the product of a number of particular social and cultural factors that produced the definitive American noir cycle of 1941–53 that constituted a 'specific period of film history'.[27] Silver and Ward in their *Encyclopedia* were even more emphatic: 'With the Western, film noir shares the distinction of being an indigenous American form ... It is a self-contained reflection of American cultural preoccupations in film form. In short, it is a unique example of a wholly American film style'.[28] In the extensive literature on film noir that has appeared in the subsequent quarter century, there has been little fundamental questioning of this position.

Writing in 1997, Nicholas Christopher, for instance, argued that 'film noir is an utterly homegrown modern American form'.[29] Although Naremore acknowledges that film noir 'is not a specifically American form' and that its 'remarkable flexibility, range, and mythical force' allows it to operate as 'something like an international genre', he does little to substantiate this interesting notion, being concerned only with developments within American noir and neo-noir.[30]

This exclusion or marginalisation of the possibility of a European film noir is curious because American film noir has always been seen as strongly influenced by European culture; in particular, the importance of German expressionism is acknowledged by almost every commentator. Expressionism – or, more generally Weimar Cinema to include the *Strassenfilm* ('street film') and urban thrillers notably Fritz Lang's *M* (1931) – is usually cited as the principal stimulus for noir's visual style, its narrative complexity, and also, with Weimar cinema's emphasis on alienation, paranoia, dream-states, compulsive behaviour and the instability of identity, noir's central themes and subject matter. This influence was carried directly into the production of classic film noir through the extensive involvement of German (or Austrian) émigrés, that included directors Fritz Lang, Otto Preminger, Robert Siodmak, Edgar Ulmer and Billy Wilder, cinematographers John Alton, Karl Freund and Rudolph Maté, as well as actors, set designers, scriptwriters and composers. Indeed, as Tim Bergfelder notes in this volume, some commentators have gone so far as to see American film noir as German national cinema in exile, the cinema that 'might have been' but for Nazism.[31] Thomas Elsaesser has cautioned against a simple notion of direct influence, arguing that one should regard the relationship between the two cinemas as reciprocal, part of a series of 'cross-cultural compliments' paid by one national cinema to another, which could be represented as much by the term 'interference' as influence.[32] But the substantial impact of Weimar cinema and its personnel on American noir is inescapable.

More recently there has been a greater recognition, *pace* Borde and Chaumeton, of the influence of French poetic realism on film noir. The romantic and pessimistic narratives of *Le Quai des brumes* (*Port of Shadows*, 1938) or *Le Jour se lève* (*Daybreak*, 1939), set in a working-class milieu but with a 'poetic' sense of unrealised aspirations through their doomed heroes (played by Jean Gabin), were thematically, stylistically and historically close to film noir. Several were remade in Hollywood, including *Le Jour se lève*, which became *The Long Night* (1947) starring Henry Fonda. The gangster film *Pépé le Moko* (1937), also starring Gabin, acts as a bridge or missing link between German expressionism and film noir.[33] American neo-noir directors from Martin

Scorsese through to Quentin Tarantino have acknowledged their indebtedness to French cinema in particular. *Pulp Fiction* (1994) was partly inspired by the Jean-Pierre Melville's crime thriller *Le Doulos* (1962), which Tarantino described as 'my favorite screenplay of all time. You don't have any idea of what is going on until the last 20 minutes'.[34]

However, acknowledgement of the influence of European cinema on the development of film noir is not the same thing as establishing that there was such a thing as a European film noir, and I want to turn now to a brief consideration to the arguments of each contributor to this volume in support of this contention.

European film noirs

Ginette Vincendeau argues that there are several key differences between French film noir and its American counterpart. French film noir has its roots in French crime fiction extending back to the mid-nineteenth century and continues for a longer period than American, stretching from the 1930s through to the early 1970s. Its key characteristic is what she terms 'social voyeurism', a concentration on atmosphere, character and place rather than action, as exemplified in pre-war poetic realism. As has been noted, these anticipate the style, characterisation and themes of American film noir, but their trajectory is often more pessimistic, indeed fatalistic than film noir, making these films darker than their American counterparts with a greater moral ambiguity. Their post-war successors were even bleaker, retaining the quotidian realism and topographical precision that marked them as particularly French, but the poetry had disappeared in films that were marked by a strong sense of disillusionment in the aftermath of the war and the Nazi Occupation.

If French film noir was initially clearly separate from American noir, later developments show its strong influence, but in different ways. The 1950s' gangster thrillers that Borde and Chaumeton derided were generic rather than sociological, a highly stylised masculine world of conspicuous consumption riddled with corruption, but, Vincendeau argues, still retaining a distinctive French idiom. New Wave directors, notably Jean-Luc Godard and François Truffaut, appropriated American noir quite differently, incorporating its conventions affectionately, even nostalgically, but also critically, as part of their complex and innovative explorations of rebellion and alienation in an absurd world. The use of American noir conventions by Jean-Pierre Melville was much more extended (1956–72). His impressive body of work – 'sombre portrayals of criminals who inhabit eerily abstract Franco-American locations' (p. 43) – was a complex melding of both traditions, gradually evolving an expressive minimalism that was highly distinctive, creating a modern urban myth. Melville's noirs display the characteristically French self-reflexivity and stylistic self-consciousness, its consistent marginalisation of women and continue the cynical and morally ambiguous worldview that was tolerated by a less puritanical censorship system than the American Hays Code.

Phil Powrie argues that French neo-noir differs from its native antecedents stylistically and tends to be more genre based, essentially a series of developments of the *polar* (police thriller) and the political thriller, and with a clear, if complex, relationship to American neo-noir. Bob Swaim's *La Balance* (*The Nark*, 1982) was representative, set in a carefully evoked Parisian underworld, with an American-style fast-paced narrative and explosive action, but containing a doomed love affair that evoked poetic realism and the French noir tradition. The highly artificial style of the *cinéma du look* thrillers signalled a return to the visual conventions of classic American noir, but with a postmodern playfulness, though these films could still engage with serious issues, notably ethnicity. They retained a quintessential Frenchness in their quirky references to high culture, familiar Parisian landmarks, intertextual echoes to poetic realism, and an oneiric atmosphere redolent of the French surrealists.

Powrie also locates an intermittent strain of blacker French neo-noirs, which unsettle the spectator in their stark portrayals of a dystopian society (a strong continuity with the earlier French noirs), permeated with a sense of tragic inevitability, fatalism and entrapment, and populated by dysfunctional males. Examples such as Alain Corneau's *Série noire* (1979) show the influence of American noir – it was based on Jim Thompson's *A Hell of a Woman* – but the action was relocated to dismal, nondescript Parisian suburbs, and the characters recognisably French. Powrie suggests that a further development of this dystopian strain has taken place into what he terms 'hyper-noir', which 'plunges us into excessive embodiment via the abject and the repulsive' (p. 71) in films that are complex hybrids, visceral and disorientating, 'adult and knowing fairy tales' (p. 76), that have only a passing relationship to American cinema.

British cinema is often accused of being a pale reflection of American cinema, but Robert Murphy reveals a British film noir that is 'tantalisingly similar but fundamentally different from [its] American counterpart' (p. 103). As in France, British noir also began to develop before the war, drawing on American and indigenous hard-boiled crime writing, but also strongly influenced by the extensive gothic-macabre tradition in British fiction, with its emphasis on sadism and irrational violence. Its main development occurred afterwards in films that often featured maladjusted veterans, exhibiting the moral ambivalence, psychological complexity and paranoia lacking from their pre-war antecedents. British film noir makes less use of expressionist lighting than American noir, showing a greater debt to French poetic realism with its emphasis on atmosphere, fatalism and existentialism. *Temptation Harbour* (1947), a representative example, was adapted from a Georges Simenon novella. As in France, British noirs typically intertwine noir conventions with social realism, creating a cast of characters and a class-consciousness that are culturally specific, where weak, ambivalent males are the dominant focus with correspondingly less interest in *femme fatales*.

There were significant changes in the 1950s when the influence of American noir was stronger and included the use of imported second division American stars, as well as the presence of American directors, notably Cy Endfield and Joseph Losey, fleeing the blacklist. But British noirs retained an emphasis on ordinary people, not a detached underworld and melded the pace and action of American films with the depiction of resonantly British milieux. There was, in a development that paralleled the British New Wave, an increased emphasis in the late 1950s on provincial locations and a new brutalism in the violence of the action. The visual style became correspondingly bleak, with cold, hard naturalistic lighting that fitted these chilling tales of existential despair and alienation. Throughout its development, British film noir had to struggle against repressive censorship and a critical prejudice for sober realism that obscured its recognition, compounded by a strong distaste for violent British crime films that was bound up with a long-standing hostility to American popular culture.[35]

Because British film noir had never received critical recognition, Andrew Spicer argues that British neo-noir had to reinvent itself anew, with little, if any, explicit continuity with its predecessors. British neo-noirs are highly intertextual and allusive, but – with the exception of a period in the 1980s when the influence of European art cinema was strong – drawing upon American noir, the cinema that *is* known to British filmmakers and their audiences. However, the key noirs, including *Get Carter* (1971), combined American narrative pace and violence with a critical social realism, evincing a strong continuity with their predecessors, albeit an unacknowledged one. Early examples of British neo-noir were stylistically very different from classic American noir, with a bleak, uninflected modernist style, but later examples used noir visual conventions selectively, betraying a somewhat uneasy and ambiguous commerce with a seductively glamorous

American culture that the noir style both embodied and critiqued, often through the creation of a liminal space between ordinary life and a nightmare netherworld.

Spicer argues that contemporary British neo-noirs are often hybrids spanning several genres, but the majority continue to be variations of the crime thriller, differentiated from more conventional examples by their stylistic inventiveness, emphasis on moral ambiguity and psychological complexity. The central focus is on masculine identity, portraying misfits, marginal figures, damaged men or the quintessentially British figure of the man-out-of-his-time, and therefore women tend to be marginal figures. In the most recent examples, Spicer identifies a bleak, fatalistic existentialism in which the value of any action is questioned and where masculinity is in crisis. Despite some celebrated films, including *Get Carter* and *Performance* (1970), British neo-noir has been critically neglected, and the films discussed in this chapter often subject to lazy or vitriolic reviewing, indicating the continued preference for social realism and an enduring mistrust of American-inspired crime fiction.

As has been mentioned, Weimar cinema has always had a special relationship with American film noir, but, as Tim Bergfelder demonstrates, there was no critical climate in post-war Germany that acknowledged this relationship, nor was there any understanding of the concept of film noir or a celebration of the American films, as there was in France. Even the film noirs of German exiles were met with scorn or hostility as morally corrupt. Crime films, always the basis of film noir, were an insignificant category of post-war German film production. However, Bergfelder argues that there was a post-war German film noir in the 1940s and 1950s that can be retrospectively defined, one that crossed several genres or cycles of film, as the key noir theme of the inability to dwell comfortably in the present, haunted by the past and harbouring fears of the future, can be found in many post-war German films. German film noir therefore constituted a parallel development to its American counterpart, with fewer films and with less consistency of style and tone, but containing some of the same archetypal figures, including the maladjusted veteran.

There are also topographical differences; the city is often literally or metaphorically absent in a devastated country as in *Die Mörder sind unter uns* (*The Murderers Are Among Us*, 1946), the first of a short-lived cycle of *Trümmerfilme* (rubble films), that combined an expressionist heritage with topical elements, and noir conventions with the social problem film. Revealingly, this East German film was, under pressure from the Soviet authorities, made unambiguously redemptive with its doomed, self-pitying wounded and weak male protagonist nurtured by the *Trümmerfrau* to help rebuild the smashed society. It was only by the mid-1950s that German films were able to engage with the social and gender conflict that economic competition fostered, and the *femme fatale* and the delinquent appear in films that are bleak portraits of domestic life. Returning émigrés – Peter Lorre, Robert Siodmak and Fritz Lang – made the most dystopian noirs but their films were influenced less by Hollywood noir than by the dual artistic and political legacy of Weimar and the Third Reich and the need to engage with the social realities of a divided Germany.

Paul Cooke's chapter on German neo-noir delineates two periods when there was a clearly identifiable development: in the New German Cinema of the 1970s and 1980s and in the more commodified, genre-based cinema of the 1990s. As Cooke argues, the relationship of the new German cinema directors to American noir was highly complex. Not only was it filtered through the French New Wave, and used as a way of connecting a new generation of German directors with Weimar cinema through the work of the German exiles, but it was also the only language available to critique the social hypocrisies of the 'new economic miracle' and their parents' historical amnesia. New Wave directors, notably Rainer Werner Fassbinder and Wim Wenders, displayed an ambivalent attitude to American popular culture, both repelled and deeply attracted, but saw in film noir a way to explore and critique American influence and the violent authoritarianism of Germany's past. In the 1990s, Cooke argues, German filmmakers no longer felt the need to critique Hollywood, resulting in a shift from art house to more popular genre-based filmmaking that emulates the fast-paced, action-driven American mode. However, neo-noir can still be used as a critical instrument, especially for former East German film-makers anxious to explore the inequalities of the reunification, able to give marginal figures a voice and deal with the failures of integration.

As Rob Stone argues in his chapter on Spanish film noir, a *cine negro* could not develop in a country that was a predominantly rural, repressive, highly patriarchal, fascist dictatorship, underpinned by dogmatic Catholicism. There was no tradition of indigenous hard-boiled crime fiction, or even American translations, let alone critical support for film noir; American noirs were expected to be read as indexes of a corrupt and decadent nation. The low-budget urban thrillers (*policíacas*) in which, beneath the veneer of absolute moral values, a dislocated society could be glimpsed, were heavily censored, any hint of social critique highly circumscribed and with no space for the psychological development or moral ambiguity that characterise film noir. However, it was the impact of neo-realism that allowed noir themes and characterisation to emerge in Nieves Conde's *Surcos* (*Furrows*, 1951) and Juan Antonio Bardem's 'deeply subversive noir hybrid', *Muerte de un ciclista* (*Death of a Cyclist*, 1955) with its paranoid, tormented male protagonist and vengeful *femme fatale*, which shows the influence of Antonioni and the *Strassenfilm* as well as American noir. The limited reforms that were conceded in the last decade of Franco's rule allowed some dissident figures to emerge, notably Carlos Saura, whose *La caza* (1965), demonstrated the importance of film noir for Spanish filmmakers anxious to critique patriarchal culture and raise the spectre of civil war guilt.

After Franco's death in 1975 a Spanish neo-noir became possible and Ann Davies documents its powerful and substantial presence, partly based on the flourishing crime fiction boom of *novela negra*. However, its development has been impeded by declining audiences and lack of funding that have created an unstable film industry and also by lack of critical recognition and respect. In addition to being able to discuss openly sexual issues and illicit relationships, these films have acknowledged the complications of regional identities and analysed the peculiarly Spanish theme of *desencanto*, the disenchantment many felt after the hopes for democratic developments were not realised and state corruption came to light. In contradistinction to other European film noirs, Spanish neo-noir has often used female-centred narratives, which derive from American models, but with specific Spanish social and topographical concerns, a development that recognised the transformed role of women. Davies argues that retro-noir has a special place in Spanish neo-noir because it is the opportunity to explore a past that is uncomfortable and which could not be addressed at the time. These films often employ a complex flashback structure, shifting between past and present in order to examine guilt and the instabilities of memory and identity.

Recognition and discussion of Italian film noir has been trammelled by problems of definition. The word *giallo*, which entered popular vocabulary from 1929 when the publisher Mondadori brought out detective fiction in yellow covers, has subsumed noir under its extensive ambit. As Mary Wood argues, Italian film noir is characterised by its presence in a wide-range of very disparate films, representing an 'intellectual choice rather than a genre'. Its heterogeneity is partly the product of a peculiarly volatile film industry that pursues 'profitable *filoni*, strands of film themes and subjects which can be copied while public interest lasts, and then abandoned for the next fashion' (p. 263). These *filoni* have low cultural capital, which has resulted in lack of critical enquiry and definition. Italian film noir is characterised by its uses of saturated yellow tones, intense lighting contrasts, dark atmospheres, disorder and asymmetry, and performative and visual excess. As Wood contends, it is also distinguished by its highly politicised nature, critiquing an unstable, corrupt public life constantly rocked by fresh and often inexplicable scandals. Italian film noir is highly masculinist, the product of a patriarchal culture where the past and public life are conceived as male homosocial narratives in which women are marginalised.

Despite its critical obscurity, Wood reveals the deep cultural roots of Italian film noir, stretching back to silent crime serials and the proliferation of crime fiction even under Mussolini's rule. Luchino Visconti's *Ossessione* (1942), the first of two adaptations of James M. Cain's *The Postman Always Rings Twice* that preceded its American version,[36] and which transferred the action to the Po Valley, was the forerunner of the post-war *neorealismo nero* (black neo-realism) that included Alberto Lattuada's *Il bandito* (*The Bandit*, 1947), the story of returning veterans facing widespread unemployment, poverty, social and familial disruption and the questioning of accepted beliefs. Characteristically, American models influenced *Il bandito*, but its location shooting and engagement with specific issues make it topographically and socially very Italian. Although Michelangelo Antonioni made a noir – *Cronaca di un amore* (*Story of a Love Affair*, 1950) – the real development of Italian noir came through its infiltration of the interconnected popular genres: popular melodramas, crime films (translations of French *série noire* and American pulp fiction, but also indigenous sources both novels and comic books) and in horror films, especially those by Mario Bava and Dario Argento. But Italian noir's most complex and interesting reworkings, Wood argues, occurred in the *giallo politico*, an important presence in the 1970s particularly in the films of Francesco Rosi, which registered profound dissatisfactions with the exercise of power. Wood dates Italian neo-noir from the 1980s, characterised by a combination of American and Italian elements (including co-productions), which continues to be highly politicised but still lacks recognition by indigenous critics who are, ironically, quite happy to discuss American neo-noir.

The aspect of European film noir that emerges most strongly from this survey is its *national specificity*. In each country, noir and neo-noir have individual trajectories that reflect that nation's history, its political organisation, its cultural traditions, the state of its film industry and the strength of its cinematic culture. In each case, film noir and neo-noir frequently engage with social, political and cultural issues that are particular to that nation. This leads to marked variations in characterisation and in the construction of gender. There are also significant differences in visual style and aesthetics between the various countries, and also a wide variety within each separate national noir/neo-noir, which further weakens the case that it is a particular 'look' that unifies film noir. There are also clear differences of scale with France and Britain, for various reasons, able to support a larger body of films than was the case in the other three. However, in France, key developments in film noir or neo-noir were folded into more general film movements (poetic realism, the New Wave), reflecting the strength of French film culture. This was also the case with the German New Wave's embrace of film noir. In Britain and Italy, noir and neo-noir were more genre based and their development more diffuse, whereas, in Spain, noir struggled to exist at all until a regime change. European film noir/neo-noir is therefore clearly a heterogeneous phenomenon and any account of it must respect these differences and disparities.

This said, certain important similarities also emerge. In each case (with the exception of Spain) an initial, pre-war development took place that was consequent upon developments in crime fiction in the 1920s and 1930s, which explains the centrality of crime thrillers to film noir and its characteristic concern with the city and its hidden recesses. These developments, which prefigured American film noir, were interrupted by the Second World War (earlier, before it could even begin, in Germany with the rise of Nazism), which meant that film noir was therefore, almost from its inception, a discontinuous, even fugitive phenomenon. This has contributed to its 'submerged' status, lacking industrial or cultural support. This lack of recognition continues through to the present, with indigenous film noirs not honoured in their own land. Even in France, the originator of the term, its own film noir was misrecognised or scorned, while in Germany exilic film noirs were greeted with hostility.

Within this overarching resemblance between all European noirs, other similarities are noticeable. Characterisation may vary but all noirs have *femmes fatales* (though their relative importance may differ significantly) and also male archetypes including the maladjusted veteran – even if, in Spain, this figure could only be dealt with retrospectively.[37] The importance of the maladjusted veteran, as Richard Maltby has argued, goes beyond his specific delineation to encompass the general noir requirement of the central male protagonist to account for his past, 'a past that contains dark and menacing secrets that can no longer remain hidden, but must surface and find resolution'.[38] The maladjusted veteran is thus a general index of a pervasive concern across all noirs (American and European) with weak or damaged males who are socially and/or psychologically dysfunctional and who exhibit a range of neuroses and even pathologies. European film noirs may exhibit a range of visual styles and narrative strategies, but what unites them is their shared difference with the norms of classical Hollywood cinema. Characteristically, film noirs are visually, aurally and narratologically complex, often with a degree of self-reflexivity that is unusual in popular culture. European film noirs are thematically varied, but have, at their core so to speak, a dystopian sensibility that is fundamentally existential, evoking a malign and contingent universe in which existence is often seen as meaningless or absurd. European film noirs are also oppositional cinemas, often containing coruscating social and political critiques, raising uncomfortable issues about gender and sexuality, corruption and violence, and the abuse of power.

Much of what has been said above applies to European neo-noirs, but there are certain aspects that require a separate discussion. In each national cinema there was a break between noir and neo-noir, as there was in America, usually in the 1970s but occurring later in Italy. In each case, because of noir's new found generic status and widespread acceptance, neo-noir filmmakers, in Europe as in America, while they may make very different kinds of films, are conscious of the noir inheritance and draw upon it, sometimes uncritically, but often analytically (noir is a cinema of ideas as well as visual style or narrative) in a fresh attempt to unsettle viewers' perceptions. There was often a radical departure from the 'classical' noir style and the attempt to forge a new look for neo-noir. European neo-noirs also display what I have argued elsewhere is American neo-noir's characteristic shift from a revisionist modernism to a more commodified postmodernism, its seductive, instantly recognisable look part of a knowing and highly allusive postmodern culture.[39] The relationship of these postmodern European neo-noirs to their American counterpart has also changed significantly, a change that is symptomatic of a wider shift in the relationship between European and American cinema. Lacking their predecessors' sense of a European cultural heritage that must be protected and defended against Hollywood 'contamination', contemporary neo-noir filmmakers have had a more easy-going commerce with American cinema, often no longer seen as the enemy but as a potential financial partner. However, even in its postmodern form, some European neo-noirs retain, as the contributors here argue, their ability to shock and challenge, and to engage with substantive and nationally specific social and political issues.

A transnational cultural phenomenon?

The current internationalism of the film industry is nothing new –
there has always been a degree of exchange and interpenetration
between European and American cinemas.[40] However, there are
strong grounds for understanding film noir as a particular and intense
form of this general process. In their Introduction to a volume devoted
to the European precursors of film noir, Janice Morgan and Dudley
Andrew argue that film noir was 'an international popular art through
and through concentrating within itself a whole network of cross-
fertilisations that ask to be recovered', and that what particularly
characterises film noir is 'trans-Atlantic cross-cultural exchange'.[41] In
her own essay examining the relationship between Weimar cinema and
American film noir via Paris, which was a stopping of point for many
émigré personnel, Morgan argues that we need to 'view the inception
of *noir* as a multi-faceted, cross-cultural and highly intertextual
phenomenon'.[42]

In addition to the well-documented international careers of German
émigrés such as Fritz Lang and Robert Siodmak, Morgan's contention
can be supported by two rather different examples that show the
complex circulation of ideas, finance, texts and personnel that characterises noir's cross-cultural relationships. Jules Dassin, born of Russian-
Jewish parents in Hartford Connecticut before moving to Harlem where
he grew up, directed three American noirs *Brute Force* (1947), *The
Naked City* (1948) and *Thieves Highway* (1949) before being black-
listed. Dassin became one of a number of American enforced exiles
whose influence on European film noirs was considerable.[43] In an
attempt to circumvent the authorities, Darryl Zanuck at Twentieth
Century-Fox, who hated the blacklist, shuffled Dassin off to Britain to
film *Night and the City* (1950) urging him to shoot the most expensive
sequences first so that Zanuck would not be forced to fire him.[44] *Night
and the City* is an international hybrid, with American leads (Richard
Widmark and Gene Tierney), but set in London, an adaptation of the
English Gerald Kersh's 1938 novel that is more savage and macabre than
its American hard-boiled models. (It was remade in 1991, but transposed
to New York starring Robert De Niro.) Now an exile, Dassin struggled
to find work before writing (from a French source novel) and directing
Du Rififi chez les hommes (*Rififi*, 1955), ironically the one 1950s French
noir that Borde and Chaumeton admired.[45] As well as becoming a cult
film, *Rififi* was the inspiration for Tarantino's *Reservoir Dogs* (1991),
one of the icons of American neo-noir.

The American Patricia Highsmith's dark and morally ambivalent novels have cross-fertilised various film noirs. *Strangers on a Train* was adapted by Alfred Hitchcock (of course English) into one of the quintessential American classic noirs in 1951, with a screenplay by Raymond Chandler. Her novel *The Talented Mr Ripley* was adapted in France as *Plein Soleil* (*Purple Noon*, 1960), directed by René Clément and starring Alain Delon, nearly forty years before its American version directed by another Englishman, Anthony Minghella. *Ripley's Game* was the basis of Wim Wenders' *Der Amerikanische Freund* (*The American Friend*, 1977), which Paul Cooke argues was a key German neo-noir and which can be read as a metaphor for the shifting relationship between Europe and Hollywood.[46] It was remade twenty-five years later by Liliana Cavani – *Il gioco di Ripley* (2002) – an international co-production starring John Malkovich as Ripley, but with a setting and style, as Mary Wood shows, redolent of Italian neo-noir. *Ripley Under Ground* is the basis of an Anglo-American co-production due to be released in Britain in late 2006, showing the continued internationalism of film noir.[47]

In addition to these industrial and commercial processes, film noir, as has been argued, is a discursive construction, that was, from its beginning, transcultural, an idea that the French projected onto American cinema that the Americans later adopted and then re-exported. And, as *European Film Noir* argues, this reciprocal discursive appropriation and reappropriation unsettles the traditional conception of national cinemas as fixed and self-contained entities, showing instead, complex interwoven histories of influences and interferences, of, in Tim Bergfelder's phrase, 'tangled relationships, mismatches, and delayed echoes' across different national frontiers and historical periods.[48] In contradistinction to Naremore's (unsubstantiated) notion of an 'international genre', it makes better sense to conceive of film noir as a transnational cultural phenomenon, one that operates (commercially and conceptually) both as part of various national cinemas and as a wider cultural formation.[49]

In conclusion two salient points emerge. The first is the significance of the films gathered under the label noir/neo-noir, which, in addition to their historical importance, continue to fascinate, startle and speak powerfully to contemporary audiences. The second is the critical failure to recognise, let alone celebrate, the existence and achievements of European film noirs. My hope is that the present volume will go some way to rectifying that neglect and provide the inspiration for further work that examines other European noir and neo-noir cinemas.

Notes

1   These brief studies are referenced by the contributors in this volume; the one book-length study is Robin Buss, *French Film Noir* (London and New York: Marion Boyars, 1994). The most substantial earlier study was a special issue of *Iris*, 21 Spring 1996) entitled 'European Precursors of Film Noir', edited by Janice Morgan and Dudley Andrew.

2   See Steve Neale, *Genre and Hollywood* (London: Routledge, 2000), p. 153.

3   See, for instance, Raymond Borde and Etienne Chaumeton, *A Panorama of American Film Noir 1941–1953*, trans. from the French by Paul Hammond (San Francisco: City Lights Books, 2002).

4   See Andrew Spicer, *Film Noir* (Harlow, Essex: Longman/Pearson Education, 2002), pp. 27–9.

5   See, for instance, J. S. Place and L. S. Peterson, 'Some Visual Motifs of *Film Noir*', *Film Comment* (January–February 1974), reprinted in Alain Silver and James Ursini (eds), *Film Noir Reader* (New York: Limelight Editions, 1996), pp. 64–76.

6   See James Damico, '*Film Noir*: A Modest Proposal', in Silver and Ursini (eds), *Film Noir Reader*, pp. 95–105.

7   See, for instance, Paul Schrader, 'Notes on *Film Noir*', *Film Comment* 8:1 1972), reprinted in Silver and Ursini (eds), *Film Noir Reader*, pp. 53–64; Nathaniel Rich, *San Francisco Noir* (New York: The Little Bookroom, 2005), p. 97 *ff*.

8   Thomas Elsaesser, *Weimar Cinema and After: Germany's Historical Imaginary* (London: Routledge, 2000), p. 424.

9   Charles O'Brien, 'Film Noir in France: Before the Liberation', *Iris*, 21 (Spring 1996), 10.

10   See James Naremore, 'American Film Noir: the History of an Idea', *Film Quarterly* 49:2 (1995–96), 12–28.

11   Marc Vernet, '*Film Noir* on the Edge of Doom', in Joan Copjec (ed.), *Shades of Noir* (London: Verso, 1993), p. 6.

12   James Naremore, 'A Season in Hell or the Snows of Yesteryear?', Introduction to Borde and Chaumeton, *A Panorama*, p. xii.

13   Borde and Chaumeton, *A Panorama*, p. 11

14   Schrader, 'Notes on *Film Noir*'. Mention should be made of Martha Wolfenstein and Nathan Leites, *Movies: A Psychological Study* (Glencoe, Illinois: Free Press, 1950), which, without using the term, discusses a number of American, British and French film noirs in a more general analysis of films from the immediate post-war period (1946–49). Its comparative perspective makes this study especially valuable, but it had no discernible influence on the development of film noir criticism.

15   Alain Silver and Elizabeth Ward (eds), *Film Noir: An Encyclopedic Reference to the American Style* (New York: The Overlook Press, 1993).

16   Raymond Borde and Etienne Chaumeton, 'Twenty Years Later: *Film Noir* in the 1970s', *Ecran* 32 (1975), included in R. Barton Palmer (ed.),

Perspectives on Film Noir (New York: G. K. Hall, 1996), pp. 76–80.

17 Rick Altman, *Film/Genre* (London: BFI Publishing, 1999), p. 61.
18 Neale, *Genre and Hollywood*, p. 175.
19 Naremore, *More Than Night: Film Noir in Its Contexts* (Berkeley, Los Angeles and London: University of California Press, 1998), pp. 2–6, 276–7.
20 Borde and Chaumeton, *A Panorama*, p. 1, my emphasis.
21 *Ibid.*, p. 23.
22 *Ibid.*, pp. 127–38, at p. 130.
23 Ginette Vincendeau, 'French Film Noir', this volume, Chapter 2, p. 46.
24 Borde and Chaumeton, *A Panorama*, p. 126.
25 The exception was Raymond Durgnat, 'Paint it Black: the Family Tree of the *Film Noir*', *Cinema* 6:7 (1970), reprinted in Silver and Ursini (eds), *Film Noir Reader*, pp. 37–52.
26 Schrader, 'Notes on *Film Noir*', p. 54.
27 *Ibid.*, p. 53.
28 Silver and Ward, *Film Noir*, p. 1.
29 Nicholas Christopher, *Somewhere in the Night: Film Noir and the American City* (New York: Free Press, 1997), p. 12.
30 Naremore, *More Than Night*, pp. 5, 254–77.
31 Tim Bergfelder, 'German Cinema and Film Noir', this volume, Chapter 6, p. 138.
32 Elsaesser, *Weimar Cinema and After*, p. 423.
33 See Ginette Vincendeau, 'Noir is also a French Word: the French Antecedents of Film Noir', in Ian Cameron (ed.), *The Movie Book of Film Noir* (London: StudioVista, 1992), pp. 49–58.
34 Quoted in Paul Woods (ed.), *Quentin Tarantino: The Film Geek Files* (London: Plexus Books, 2000), p. 25.
35 See Richard Maltby, '"D" for disgusting: American culture and English criticism', in Geoffrey Nowell-Smith and Steven Ricci (eds), *Hollywood and Europe: Economics, Culture, National Identity 1945–95* (London: BFI Publishing, 1998), pp. 104–15.
36 The first was French, Pierre Chenal's *Le Dernier tournant* (1939), partly set on location in the south of France. The first American version was released in 1946.
37 For a discussion of this figure in British and French cinema see Margaret Butler, *Film and Community in Britain and France* (London: I. B. Tauris, 2004), pp. 98–124.
38 Richard Maltby, 'Film Noir: the Politics of the Maladjusted Text', *Journal of American Studies* 18 (1984), reprinted in Cameron (ed.), *The Movie Book of Film Noir*, pp. 39–48, at p. 39.
39 Spicer, *Film Noir*, pp. 130–74.
40 See Andrew Higson and Richard Maltby (eds), *'Film Europe' and 'Film America': Cinema, Commerce and Cultural Exchange 1920–1939* (Exeter: University of Exeter Press, 1999); Nowell-Smith and Ricci, *Hollywood and Europe*.

41   Janice Morgan and Dudley Andrew, 'Introduction' to 'European precur-
     sors of film noir', *Iris*, 21, 3–4.
42   Janice Morgan, 'Scarlet Streets: Noir Realism from Berlin to Paris to
     Moscow', *ibid.*, 31. See also Elsaesser, *Weimar Cinema*, pp. 361–82;
     Alastair Phillips, *City of Darkness, City of Light: Emigré Filmmakers in
     Paris 1929–1939* (Amsterdam: Amsterdam University Press, 2004).
43   For a general discussion see Brian Neve, *Film and Politics in America: A
     Social Tradition* (London: Routledge, 1992).
44   See Michael Sragow, 'Crime of the century', *Guardian* (6 December
     2000), p. 13.
45   For discussion of Dassin see Gordon Gow, 'Style and Instinct', *Films and
     Filming* 16:4 (February 1970), 22–6 and 16:6 (March 1970), 66–70;
     Colin McArthur, *Underworld USA* (London: Secker & Warburg, 1972),
     pp. 93–101; Patrick McGilligan, 'I'll Always Be an American: Jules
     Dassin Interviewed', *Film Comment* 32: 6 (November–December 1996),
     34–48; Andrew Horton, 'Jules Dassin: A Multi-National Filmmaker
     Considered', *Film Criticism*, 8:3 (Spring 1984), 21–35.
46   Elsaesser, *Weimar Cinema*, p. 422.
47   For further examples of Highsmith adaptions see John Grant *Noir
     Movies* (London: Facts, Figures & Fun, 2006), pp. 89–92.
48   Bergfelder, 'German Film Noir', this volume, Chapter 6, p. 156.
49   I am indebted here to the discussion of the Spaghetti western in Dimitris
     Eleftheriotis, *Popular Cinemas of Europe* (New York and London:
     Continuum, 2001), pp. 126–7. See also Thomas Elsaesser, *European
     Cinema: Face to Face with Hollywood* (Amsterdam: Amsterdam
     University Press, 2005).

Select bibliography

Altman, Rick, *Film/Genre* (London: BFI Publishing, 1999).
Borde, Raymond and Etienne Chaumeton, *A Panorama of American
     Film Noir 1941–1953*, trans. from the French by Paul Hammond
     (San Francisco: City Lights Books, 2002).
Borde, Raymond and Etienne Chaumeton, 'Twenty Years Later: *Film
     Noir* in the 1970s', *Ecran* 32 (1975), included in R. Barton Palmer
     (ed.), *Perspectives on Film Noir* (New York: G. K. Hall, 1996), pp.
     76–80.
Buss, Robin, *French Film Noir* (London and New York: Marion
     Boyars, 1994).
Christopher, Nicholas, *Somewhere in the Night: Film Noir and the
     American City* (New York: Free Press, 1997).
Damico, James, '*Film Noir*: A Modest Proposal', in Silver and Ursini
     (eds), *Film Noir Reader*, pp. 95–105.
Durgnat, Raymond, 'Paint it Black: the Family Tree of the *Film Noir*',

Cinema 6:7 (1970), reprinted in Silver and Ursini (eds), *Film Noir Reader*, pp. 37–52.

Eleftheriotis, Dimitris, *Popular Cinemas of Europe* (New York and London: Continuum, 2001).

Elsaesser, Thomas, *Weimar Cinema and After: Germany's Historical Imaginary* (London: Routledge, 2000).

Elsaesser, Thomas, *European Cinema: Face to Face with Hollywood* (Amsterdam: Amsterdam University Press, 2005).

Higson, Andrew and Richard Maltby (eds), *'Film Europe' and 'Film America': Cinema, Commerce and Cultural Exchange 1920–1939* (Exeter: University of Exeter Press, 1999).

Maltby, Richard, 'Film Noir: the Politics of the Maladjusted Text', *Journal of American Studies* 18 (1984), reprinted in Ian Cameron (ed.), *The Movie Book of Film Noir* (London; Studio Vista, 1992), pp. 39–48.

Morgan, Janice and Dudley Andrew (eds), 'European precursors of film noir', *Iris* 21 (Spring 1996).

Naremore, James, 'American Film Noir: the History of an Idea', *Film Quarterly* 49:2 (1995–96), 12–28.

Naremore, James, *More Than Night: Film Noir in Its Contexts* (Berkeley, Los Angeles and London: University of California Press, 1998).

Neale, Steve, *Genre and Hollywood* (London: Routledge, 2000).

Neve, Brian, *Film and Politics in America: A Social Tradition* (London: Routledge, 1992).

Nowell-Smith, Geoffrey and Steven Ricci (eds), *Hollywood and Europe: Economics, Culture, National Identity 1945–95* (London: BFI Publishing, 1998).

O'Brien, Charles, 'Film Noir in France: Before the Liberation', *Iris* 21 (1996).

Phillips, Alastair, *City of Darkness, City of Light: Emigré Filmmakers in Paris 1929–1939* (Amsterdam: Amsterdam University Press, 2004).

Place, J. S. and L. S. Peterson, 'Some Visual Motifs of *Film Noir*', *Film Comment* (January–February 1974), reprinted in Alain Silver and James Ursini (eds), *Film Noir Reader* (New York: Limelight Editions, 1996), pp. 64–76.

Rich, Nathaniel, *San Francisco Noir* (New York: The Little Bookroom, 2005).

Schrader, Paul, 'Notes on *Film Noir*', *Film Comment* 8:1 (1972), reprinted in Silver and Ursini (eds), *Film Noir Reader*, pp. 53–64.

Silver, Alain and Elizabeth Ward (eds), *Film Noir* (London: Secker & Warburg, 1980).

Spicer, Andrew, *Film Noir* (Harlow, Essex: Longman/Pearson Education, 2002).

Vernet, Marc, '*Film Noir* on the Edge of Doom', in Joan Copjec (ed.), *Shades of Noir* (London: Verso, 1993), pp. 1–31.

Vincendeau, Ginette, 'Noir Is also a French Word: the French Antecedents of Film Noir', in Ian Cameron (ed.), *The Movie Book of Film Noir* (London: Studio Vista, 1992), pp. 49–58.

Wolfenstein, Martha and Nathan Leites, *Movies: A Psychological Study* (Glencoe, Illinois: Free Press, 1950).

2

French film noir

Ginette Vincendeau

The 'official' story of film noir, enshrined in Raymond Borde and
Etienne Chaumeton's seminal *Panorama du film noir américain*
(1955), and subsequently endorsed by both French film history and
accounts of American film noir, resolutely leaves French cinema out of
the picture, dismissing any possible influence. The 'dynamism of
violent death', the 'strange, oneiric'[1] atmosphere and underlying eroticism of American film noir were apparently lacking in pre-war and
wartime French cinema – poetic realism was too realist: 'dream and
the fantastic are foreign to it'.[2] When the French produced more
recognisably noir crime films, such as the gangster movies of the
1950s, they were dismissed as belated copies of American films. In
their cursory few pages on 'French film noir', Borde and Chaumeton
ask: 'Why is French cinema taking up, ten years too late, formulas
which are out of date in the USA?'.[3]

My aim in this chapter is to question these assumptions and investigate the specificity of *French* film noir, assuming it can be said to exist.
For, in talking about 'French film noir', problems of definitions immediately arise, just as they do for American cinema. The term cannot be
applied to just any French crime films, but nor should it be restricted
to the films made during the same period as classic American film noir,
namely the 1940s and 1950s. However, as shown by the few serious
studies devoted to it,[4] the French crime film, known under the generic
term *policier* (a term which also applies to crime literature),[5] designates a huge and extremely varied production, as will be shown in the
discussion that follows. There are also many French films which are
not based on crime literature, but which contain elements recognisable
as noir: urban dramas with contrasted black and white photography,
pessimistic narratives, troubled male heroes trapped by their past
and/or a woman: in particular 1930s Poetic Realist films and 'social
noir' films of the 1940s and 1950s. Following Michael Walker's useful
reminder that in film noir 'tone is crucial' and 'visual style must work

in relation to narrative',[6] I will seek to locate French film noir in terms of the relationship between narrative, visual style and 'tone', arguing that a key mark of its 'Frenchness' is a particularly paradoxical relationship between these elements. In view of the extent of the corpus, I will isolate key moments, aiming to provide insights into the specificity of French film noir rather than an exhaustive survey.

Since so many French film noirs are adaptations, a word needs to be said about French crime literature, which as in America and Britain emerged in the mid-nineteenth century, coinciding with the rise of capitalism, urbanisation and popular literature. As André Vanoncini also suggests, the disappearance of death from public life in the nineteenth century caused it to resurface as a major theme in literature.[7] Most scholars agree that the 1828 memoirs of Vidocq (a criminal and spy who later joined the Paris police) constitute the starting point of modern crime literature. Vidocq's memoirs were highly influential, notably in the work of the 'inventor' of detective fiction proper, Edgar Allan Poe. His *Murders in the Rue Morgue* (1841) set in Paris and featuring the eccentric detective Auguste C. Dupin, has been described as 'the marriage of French influences (Vidocq and others) with an American form'.[8] Concurrently, French naturalist writers, Emile Zola principally, wrote exceedingly dark portraits of French society that, while not crime fiction as such, had important consequences for French film noir. In the early twentieth century, French crime literature moved towards the adventures of elegant *gentlemen-cambrioleurs* (gentlemen-burglars) epitomised by Pierre Souvestre and Marcel Allain's *Fantômas* (filmed by Louis Feuillade, 1913–15). The book's eponymous hero is a devilish master criminal, relentlessly pursued by Inspector Juve in a 'duel of giants' that recalls earlier criminal–policeman couples in Victor Hugo's *Les Misérables* (1862) and Fyodor Dostoevsky's *Crime and Punishment* (1866). *Fantômas* documents and fantasises about evil in the city, anticipating some features of French noir films. Nevertheless, the serials were firmly grounded in the adventure genre, and it is with the coming of sound, and with recourse to a different kind of literature, that French cinema may be said to enter its first real noir period.

The 1930s: the building blocks of French film noir

The early 1930s saw another phenomenal rise in crime literature, which the coming of sound made particularly attractive to French cinema. In the 1920s, British detective fiction (Conan Doyle, Agatha Christie, G. K. Chesterton) had dominated the crime genre. A sea change took place with the advent of 'hard-boiled' American writers – in particular Dashiell Hammett and Raymond Chandler and a new breed of French writers – among them Pierre Véry and the Belgian Stanislas-André Steeman. By far the most important of these was Georges Simenon (also Belgian born), who introduced a new dimension in French crime fiction writing. Within the framework of urban crime, Simenon played down action, suspense and violence and replaced them with the powerful evocation of a visual, aural and thematic 'atmosphere' – of dark, rain-soaked quotidian-ness, of routine lives shattered by crime or the 'derailing' of the central character. Simenon's novels were ground-breaking examples of what I will call 'social voyeurism'. His first major novel, *Pietr-le-Letton* was published in 1930. As early as 1932, three of his Maigret novels were adapted in rapid succession: Jean Renoir's *La Nuit du carrefour* (*Night at the Crossroads*), Julien Duvivier's *La Tête d'un homme* (*A Man's Neck*) and Jean Tarride's *Le Chien jaune* (*The Yellow Dog*). These three films, the first in a long series of Simenon adaptations, in my view constitute the beginning proper of French film noir.[9] In his characteristically exaggerated review of *La Nuit du carrefour*, Jean-Luc Godard pinpoints the attraction of the Simenonian universe: 'The smell of rain and fields swathed in mist ... make *La Nuit du carrefour* the only great French *policier*'.[10] Indeed, Simenon was aware of the cinematic potential of his novels: he insisted that the covers of his early novels be illustrated with black and white photographs rather than the customary garish drawings.

La Nuit du carrefour is set in a forlorn crossroads hamlet outside Paris, *La Tête d'un homme* in the seedy artistic milieu of Montparnasse and *Le Chien jaune* in a rain-swept seaside town in Brittany (as the last film is not easily available, I here concentrate on Renoir and Duvivier's films). *La Tête d'un homme* pits Inspector Maigret (played by Harry Baur with his customary heavy gruffness) against 'anarchist' criminal Radek in an explicit reference to *Crime and Punishment*, while *La Nuit du carrefour* opposes Maigret (the almost too elegant Pierre Renoir) to the louche inhabitants of the hamlet. Though Maigret is the representative of the law, he, and the films, always refrain from moral judgement; Simenon's frequent mist is an apt image of the stories' moral ambiguity. Maigret's method is to 'drink in' the atmosphere of the various locations – seedy garage, decaying mansion in *La Nuit du carrefour*, cheap hotel, cosmopolitan brasserie and art deco apartment in *La Tête d'un homme*. Where the traditional investigative methods fail, he solves the enigma through empathy. As François Guérif says, Maigret is 'neither hero, nor victim, but first of all a witness'.[11] Despite significant differences, the early Simenon adaptations establish the particularity that spectatorial pleasure in French film noir derives more from social voyeurism than processes of detection.

In their representation of gender, *La Nuit du carrefour* and *La Tête d'un homme* also set precedents. In *La Tête d'un homme*, Radek appears obsessed with both the rich Edna (silent star Gina Manès), and a singer who lives in his hotel, played by the famous *chanteuse* Damia. In *La Nuit du carrefour* all men are attracted to a beautiful Danish 'aristocrat' who lives in the mansion with her 'brother'. Both women potentially inhabit the role of the *femme fatale* as they directly or indirectly lead men to their demise. Yet Edna is a minor character played by an ageing star, while the 'aristocrat' turns out to be a prostitute who has slept with the whole village. Both are too marginal to qualify for the label of *femme fatale*; they simply echo the men's anxiety and failure.

Throughout the 1930s a large number of French *policiers* were made, but most belonged to the light adventure/comic whodunit genre – for instance Marcel L'Herbier's *Le Mystère de la chambre jaune* (*The Mystery of the Yellow Room*, 1930) and *Le Parfum de la dame en noir* (*The Perfume of the Lady in Black*, 1931), or Léon Mathot's *Chéri-Bibi* (1937) where the crime plot is distanced through humour. Frequently, though, films such as Pierre Chenal's *L'Alibi* (*The Alibi*, 1937) and Robert Siodmak's *Pièges* (*Personal Column*, 1939) mixed the light format with noir scenes, which they borrowed from the domi-nant 'dark' style of the period, poetic realism.[12] This term designates a pervasive style of dark urban dramas with pessimistic narratives infused with fatalism, usually set in working-class or underworld Paris. Poetic-realist films elicit a sense of beauty and tragedy through visual style, elevating humble characters and everyday surroundings to the level of 'poetry'. Many films of the period can be characterised as poetic realism, but the most canonical are those associated with the star Jean Gabin: *Les Bas-fonds* (*The Lower Depths*, 1936), *La Belle équipe* (*They Were Five*, 1936); *Pépé le Moko* (1937); *La Bête humaine* (*Judas Was a Woman*, 1938), *Le Quai des brumes* (*Port of Shadows*, 1938); *Le Jour se lève* (*Daybreak*, 1939).

Stylistically, Poetic-realist films are undoubtedly 'noir'. The gloom of the city streets and canal banks is illuminated by shiny cobblestones and pierced by mist-shrouded lampposts and gleaming nightclub signs. The city of poetic realism is both stylised and a meticulous reconstruc-tion of the real city derived from 1920s populist literature (Eugène Dabit, Francis Carco, Pierre MacOrlan) as well as contemporary photography, in particular the evocative photographs of Brassaï.[13] Another key influence is that of German cinematography. Contrasted lighting is used to outline and shape characters and sets, although in a softened version of 'Expressionist' lighting: Pierre Chenal, director of the first 'official' poetic-realist film, *La Rue sans nom* (*Street Without a Name*, 1934), asked his cinematographer to produce 'contrasted effects without the exaggeration of German Expressionist films'.[14] This strong connection stems in part from the fact that several prominent émigrés from the German studios worked in France before moving to the USA – in particular Robert Siodmak, Fritz Lang, Billy Wilder and Max Ophuls, together with directors of photography such as Eugene Schufftan. They, and their French colleagues, incorporated French narrative and visual features into their German work en route to Hollywood where several important poetic-realist films were remade by key film noir directors.[15]

Apart from visual style, one key characteristic of American film noir is its unstable male hero, thrown into a world of confusion or despair. Gabin's poetic-realist heroes are prey to destructive social forces internalised in his 'mythical' star persona.[16] Hence several of his films end in suicide and dreams of escape to exotic places are thwarted. *Le Jour se lève* concentrates all these features, while also anticipating American film noir in its complex flashback structure. Borde and Chaumeton nevertheless dismissed Gabin's influence because they saw 'no trace of gratuitous violence … Jean Gabin kills, but he is a sentimental criminal, an ordinary man who sees red'.[17] If indeed there is little 'gratuitous violence', Gabin is hardly an ordinary man who sees red (and certainly not sentimental). The relentlessly black outlook of these films, which often display a striking lack of conventional morality, led to negative reactions in France at the time, by rightwing and leftwing critics alike.[18] In Jean Renoir's *La Chienne* (*The Bitch*, 1931), for instance, the hero's misogynist hatred of his wife is humorously condoned and, after he brutally murders his mistress and lets her pimp take the rap for it, the ending shows him as a man broken in financial terms but otherwise 'liberated'. As Lotte Eisner put it, he then 'becomes a tramp, but it is less tragic downfall than release. The cynicism of this ending was only possible in the liberal French atmosphere'.[19] Certainly Fritz Lang's remake *Scarlet Street* (1945) tones this moral cynicism down, and punishes its hero more vigorously. In this respect poetic-realist films were more noir than film noir.

As a key poetic-realist film and the starting point of the French gangster film, *Pépé le Moko* deserves special mention. The film is set in the Casbah in Algiers (reconstructed in sets) where Pépé is in hiding from the police. Cinematographers Jules Kruger and Marc Fossard skilfully deploy Duvivier's virtuoso camera movements and softened

expressionist lighting, eroticising the star as well as the Casbah. Like
La Bête humaine and *Le Jour se lève*, *Pépé le Moko* shows how in
visual terms poetic realism is the missing link between German expressionism and Hollywood film noir. While centred on gangsters rather
than the police, *Pépé le Moko* exhibits many features noted in *La Nuit
du carrefour* and *La Tête d'un homme*, in particular their moral ambiguity and lack of action: Pépé's exploits are in the past and action is
displaced to make room for 'atmosphere'. The iconography of the
gangster movie (Gabin's sharp suits, hats and shoes, his gun) is celebrated but not adduced for narrative purpose. Rather than a *femme
fatale*, the romantic female character Gaby (Mireille Balin), as in the
Simenon adaptations, is a projection of Pépé's nostalgic desire for
Paris, and she is also duplicated by an older woman played by the
chanteuse Fréhel. This particular French gender formation is also
demonstrated in one of the clearest cases of 'French film noir' of the
1930s, *Le Dernier tournant* (*The Last Turn*).

The first film version of *The Postman Always Rings Twice*, *Le
Dernier tournant* has been ignored critically because of Pierre Chenal's
non-canonical status. Together with Visconti's *Ossessione* (1942), this
is the most socially anchored version of the story, part-shot on location in the south of France. Virtuoso camerawork constructs a classi-
cally noir space in long takes, night-time scenes and chiaroscuro. For
Dudley Andrew, Chenal's style is paradigmatic of poetic realism (and
I would add of French film noir) with its 'roving camera ... dark ambience, powerful moments rather than streamlined decoupage', its influence confirmed by the claim that Orson Welles studied Chenal's style
for *Citizen Kane* (1940).[20] Chenal kept James M. Cain's story of a
man 'lured' by a beautiful *femme fatale* to kill her much older
husband, only for the pair to descend into guilt and recrimination.
Chenal's version of noir marks its Frenchness in two ways: a greater
moral ambiguity and the lesser importance of the woman. Where the
1946 American version emphasises the erotic charge of the *femme
fatale* (Lana Turner) and Visconti's the attraction of the young male
hero (Massimo Girotti), Chenal gives weight and sympathy to the
husband, played by Michel Simon, significantly the greater star of the
French trio. The ambiguity of Simon's performance suggests that he is
a willing participant in the 'infernal trio' rather than simply a victim.

Le Dernier tournant was one of the last French films released before
the upheaval of the Second World War and the German Occupation,
which would change cinematic representations irrevocably and have a
significant impact on film noir.

Film noir of the *années noires*

Historians of French cinema of the *années noires* (the German Occupation) have identified its dominant feature as a series of paradoxes.[21] Despite the emigration of prestigious figures such as Duvivier, Renoir, Gabin and Morgan to Hollywood, the *années noires* were also a golden age, since American films were banned. The German and Vichy authorities maintained strict censorship, but following Goebbels' instructions cinema remained light entertainment. As a result, the dominant genres of the 220 films of the period were 'escapist': costume films, musicals and comedies flourished. Relevant to our investigation is the fact that the substantial *policier* production was predominantly recast as light comedy. Simenon adaptations, for example, markedly differ from their 1930s predecessors. Starring a wisecracking Albert Préjean as Maigret, films such as *Cécile est morte* (*Cecile Is Dead*, 1944), *Picpus* (1943) and *Les Caves du Majestic* (*Majestic Hotel Cellars*, 1945) take their social voyeurism frivolously and turn Maigret into a literally and metaphorically lighter figure. Similarly, Jacques Becker's first film, *Dernier atout* (*The Last Trump*, 1942), is styled as light thriller in fantasy Latin America and Henri-Georges Clouzot's first feature, the thriller *L'Assassin habite au 21* (*The Murderer Lives at Number 21*, 1942), alternates a few suspenseful noir scenes with a whodunit plot played by the actors with theatrical banter.

Perhaps the most startling example of the 'lightening' of crime films as a result of the Occupation is that of the now little-known *120 rue de la gare*, directed by Jacques Daniel-Norman (1946). This film is the adaptation of Léo Malet's first novel featuring his private detective Nestor Burma, widely regarded by historians of French crime literature as 'the prototype for the French *roman noir* to come'.[22] Published in 1943, the book explicitly casts criminality within the context of the Occupation: the novel opens in the POW camp where Burma is prisoner, as indeed Malet had been for his political opinions. At the same time the book is clearly inspired by American hard-boiled literature, in the choice of a private detective (definitively not a French tradition) and a Cain-style treacherous *femme fatale* complete with cigarette and trenchcoat. The film rewrites this doubly noir material into a comedy, in large part because of wartime censorship (even though filming was delayed and the film only came out in 1946).[23] Some scenes are treated in noir visual style, but tone and casting pull in the opposite direction: René Dary as Burma and Sophie Desmarets as his secretary play it as a cross between *The Thin Man* (1934) and French boulevard theatre, and the piling up of murdered bodies ends up in farce. Traces of such lightening of noir material during and immediately after the war can be found in a number of other films, including the intriguing *L'Impasse des deux anges* (1948), starring Simone Signoret, in which comic theatrical goings-on alternate with a noir late poetic-realist thriller, and *56 rue Pigalle* (1949) which – in a much less accomplished film – offers a hybrid mixture of noir blackmail drama with bourgeois adultery and orientalist African scenes. For genuine film noir during the Occupation, one has to turn to dramas such as Henri Decoin's adaptation of Simenon's *Les Inconnus dans la maison* (*Strangers in the House*, 1942) and to *Le Corbeau* (*The Raven*, 1943).

Based on an actual case, this story of a small provincial town torn apart by anonymous letters signed 'le corbeau' (the raven) confirmed Clouzot as a major filmmaker. The opening shot pans over a small town, leading us to a cemetery. The last shot is of an old woman covered in black veils walking away free, having just slashed the throat of Dr Vorzet (Pierre Larquey), the 'raven', with the silent blessing of the hero Docteur Germain (Pierre Fresnay). In between, *Le Corbeau* seethes with fear, loathing, disease, suicide, suspicion and madness. No wonder critics referred to its 'harsh, heavy and noir climate'.[24] The central relationship between Germain and Denise (Ginette Leclerc) is also, shockingly for the time, explicitly sexual, its eventual transformation into 'love' not altogether convincing. Nor is Germain's sudden enthusiasm after finding that Denise is pregnant, whereas he has professed dislike of children throughout the film, following the traumatic death of his wife in childbirth.[25] The entire narrative is darkly cynical and death-driven, in what became Clouzot's trademark worldview, leading the film to be perceived as *the* emblematic Occupation film. Contrasting it to Jean Grémillon's *Le Ciel est à vous* (*The Sky Is Yours*, 1944), a life-affirming melodrama considered to embody the resistant spirit of France, Bertrand Tavernier called *Le Corbeau* 'closer to truth'.[26]

The visual style of *Le Corbeau* is in perfect keeping with the story, with superb dark photography throughout, forbidding locations such as the church, the cemetery, the hospital and heavily furnished apartments, and the projection of strong and frightening shadows even – against verisimilitude – in day-time scenes. One of the most famous scenes of the film explicitly uses noir photography to make a point. As Vorzet and Germain discuss moral relativism, Vorzet swings a dangling ceiling light, projecting violently moving shadows on the walls and ceiling. The tone of the film is sardonic and pessimistic, reinforced by a soundtrack of dramatic music and ominous church bells.

Finally, as Judith Mayne argues, *Le Corbeau* is evidence of an unusual gender configuration.[27] Women initially appear as the culprits, yet their innocence is repeatedly demonstrated. Fear, disease and cowardice fall on the side of men, building up a world of unstable male identity. *Le Corbeau* thus epitomises the central features of film noir: a relentlessly pessimistic narrative, a dubious morality, dramatically contrasted lighting and masculinity in crisis.

Le Corbeau was indicted by the conservative (Vichy) right for 'scabrous' topics such as abortion (performed by Germain) and the base morals of most of the characters such as the 'tart' Denise; the Germans saw it as a damaging critique of the anonymous letters which were so useful to the Gestapo; the Communist and Resistant left saw it as a sordid and demoralising, and thus collaborationist, portrayal of France. At the Liberation Clouzot was tried by *épuration* tribunals, officially for having worked for the German-backed company Continental, but really for *Le Corbeau*. He was initially subjected to a life ban from working, though this was later revoked. If these controversies belong to the political context of the time, they also had reverberations in terms of definitions of film noir.

In the chaotic and exciting period that followed the end of the war, the strong commitment to film education led by critic André Bazin under Vichy continued apace. An explosion of new film journals reflected this commitment, led by the Communist-backed *L'Ecran français*. It is in the latter, in August 1946, that Nino Frank wrote his seminal analysis of the American film noirs now flooding French screens.[28] Frank and Jean-Pierre Chartier (who wrote a follow-up piece three months later) both saw the darkness of the American films as entirely new.[29] Neither referred to *Le Corbeau* or the poetic-realist films (only Chartier briefly noted that the American films lacked the 1930s French films' social dimension). This cultural amnesia is particularly extraordinary since, as Charles O'Brien demonstrates, not only did the term 'film noir' routinely appear in reviews of French films from 1938, but, even more extraordinarily, many of these reviews were written by those very same critics.[30] O'Brien convincingly offers two explanations. First, that since the term was generally used in France in a derogatory way, it needed to be detached from its French context in order to *celebrate* the American films – it is the case that 'film noir' as applied ever since has been a term of approval. More generally, and possibly unconsciously, the celebration of American films was designed to minimise connections to French culture; the celebration of the dreamlike, erotic and violent world of the American film noirs could more flatteringly reach back to earlier traditions, such as surrealism, untainted by the German Occupation. I would add that left-wing critics such as Frank and Chartier in 1946 would 'naturally' spurn Clouzot for political reasons and that, by 1954, Borde and Chaumeton would equally naturally marginalise him for aesthetic reasons. For by then he was part of the tradition of quality despised by *Cahiers du cinéma* (François Truffaut in particular).[31] The rest of the critical intelligentsia concurred: *Les Diaboliques* (*Diabolique*, 1954), for instance, is later dismissed by Borde and Chaumeton as a 'minor, gently sordid work'.[32] Yet Clouzot's work is a crucial link between the cinema of the Occupation and the post-war, as a key exponent of 'social noir' cinema.

Post-war 'social noir'

What I call 'social noir', because of the sociological focus of the films, runs from the mid-1940s to the early 1960s and encompasses *policiers* such as *Quai des orfèvres* (*Jenny Lamour*, 1947) and *Les Diaboliques*, but it refers mostly to a range of excessively pessimistic dramas set in contemporary milieux in which some form of crime takes place. Here I will concentrate on *Quai des orfèvres*, *Une si jolie petite plage* (*Riptide*, 1949), *Manèges* (*The Cheat*, 1949) and *Voici le temps des assassins* (*Deadlier than the Male*, 1956) as a representative cross-section (see filmography, pp. 49–52 for other titles). All these films were – usually negatively – perceived as noir: contemporary reviewers frequently used terms such as 'sombre', 'black', 'darkness', 'genre noir', 'sadism', 'bestially noir' and 'sordid'.[33] Of *Les Diaboliques*, *Combat* wrote melodramatically of 'characters who are black down to the third basement of their soul'.[34] Like their American counterparts and like poetic-realist films, social noir films were not necessarily dominant at the box office (where comedies and costume films reigned), though many were successful, and they attracted a great deal of critical attention, because of the status of their directors and their perceived realism. For Marcel Oms for instance, *Quai des orfèvres* was 'the most implacably lucid portrayal of post-war France'.[35]

Quai des orfèvres is the story of music-hall singer Jenny Lamour (Suzy Delair) and her husband Martineau (Bernard Blier). Jenny's professional ambition results in their implication in the murder of an old roué, Brignon, investigated by Inspector Antoine (Louis Jouvet). *Quai des orfèvres* marked Clouzot's triumphant return to filmmaking after the *Corbeau* affair, and it was meant to be an uncontroversial 'commercial' film. Despite its happy end (changed from the book), the film clearly displays Clouzot's visual and thematic darkness, 'the same suffocating style as in the blackest scenes of *Le Corbeau*'.[36]

Visually, *Quai des orfèvres*, like other social noir films, shows a skilful integration of generic noir features with French quotidian realism. It also pursues the social voyeurism noted in 1930s films, exploring a popular Parisian music hall and petit-bourgeois milieu, depicted with the same sociological and topographical precision that characterises other social noir films. However, unlike the convivial communities of poetic realism, these settings tend towards the sordid: the dingy boarding school of *Les Diaboliques*, the seedy hotels in *Plage* and *Voici le temps des assassins*. Social noir space is socially anchored, but this anchorage is oppressive rather than comforting. Escape is denied (*Manèges*, *Plage*, *Diaboliques*, *Quai des orfèvres*, *Voici le temps*), and faraway places are hellish (*Le Salaire de la peur*, *The Wages of Fear*) or traumatic (*Quai des orfèvres*). Claustrophobic studio sets reinforce the oppressive atmosphere (*Le Salaire de la peur* is a rare exception), as cafés, hotels, restaurants, courtyards, are closed in, isolated at the end of cul-de-sacs: there is literally no way out. Characters are obsessed with money and sexuality; there are no redeeming moral values. The overarching impression in social noir is, as one critic said of *Plage*, of 'an indelible image of hell on earth'.[37]

The distance between social noir and poetic realism comes sharply into relief when comparing, for instance, *Quai des orfèvres* to *La Bête humaine*. Both feature a cuckolded husband, but in Renoir's 1938 film Roubaud is graced with pathos, whereas Martineau in *Quai des orfèvres* is cowardly and mediocre. Both films feature a rich, corrupt bourgeois, but where Grandmorin in *La Bête humaine* is haughty, Brignon is just sleazy. Charming secondary characters have become ugly caricatures. Carette in *La Bête humaine* plays Gabin's supportive proletarian friend; in *Plage* the same actor is a vulgar travelling salesman. Even Marcel Carné and Jacques Prévert, foremost exponents of pre-war poetic realism, cannot resurrect its romanticism and warmth in their last joint venture *Les Portes de la nuit* (*The Gates of the Night*, 1946). Crucially, social noir films lack the transcendental tragic male figure incarnated by Gabin in the 1930s. Doomed hope has become cynical resignation. Although one should guard against direct 'zeitgeist' readings, as Richard Maltby warns apropos of American film noir,[38] in narrative and visual terms, the excessively sombre portrayal of the social noir films easily invites interpretations that relate to the disillusioned climate of the post-Liberation period, marked by economic harshness, social unrest and political disillusionment.

Gender is an area in which this disillusionment is particularly marked. Blunt sexuality has replaced romantic love. The ethereal young heroines played by Simone Simon in *La Bête humaine* and Michèle Morgan in *Le Quai des brumes* have become hard-headed, scheming women, like Jenny in *Quai des orfèvres*, Dora (Simone Signoret) in *Manèges* and Catherine (Danièle Delorme) in *Voici le temps* – ambitious yet too vulgar to qualify for the role of *femme fatale*. Opposite these ghastly women, men are pitiable (*Plage*) feeble (*Manèges*) or gullible (*Voici le temps*). This gender pattern is seen by Noël Burch and Geneviève Sellier as representative of a larger trend in post-war French cinema, in which vulnerable men are terrorised by aggressive *garces* ('bitches'), who are then harshly punished, which they link to the 'destabilization' of gender roles caused by the war.[39] For if masculinity in American film noir is readable in relation to the war (returning GIs confronted with emancipated women), French men in addition to witnessing the belated emancipation of women (finally given the vote in 1944), also had to contend with a sense of humiliation at their crushing defeat by the German army. Burch and Sellier's penetrating analysis can be modified in two ways. First of all, one must emphasise how the films, while aiming to punish female characters, also point an accusing finger at male mediocrity and cowardice. Despite the sympathy evoked by the male stars, whether glamorous (Philipe), charismatic (Gabin) or homely (Blier), male characters are sick or seedy. Social noir films portray a generation of men oppressed by the past and with no vision for the future. Second, the demeaning characterisation of women can be significantly complicated by performance. On the whole the *garces* are either played by young actresses, dominated by male stars like Gabin, or by mature, prestigious actresses such as Madeleine Robinson in *Plage* and Simone Renant in *Quai des orfèvres* in shockingly minor roles. But there is an important exception to this rule, and that is Simone Signoret.

Signoret possessed aura as a star and a prominent off-screen personality. As a performer, she exuded a powerful sexuality, manifested in her looks, clothes and deportment, which went some way to offset the vulgarity of her roles (thus contradicting the Burch–Sellier model, essentially based on narrative). From *Dédée d'Anvers* (*Woman of Antwerp*, 1948) to *Room at the Top* (1959) – via *Manèges* (*The Cheat*, 1949), *Thérèse Raquin* (1953), *La Ronde* (1950) and *Casque d'or* (1952) – Signoret's characters were defined in purely sexual terms, but her charisma as a star resists parts which were – with the exception of *Casque d'or* – hard schemers or vulgar sluts.[40] In *Manèges*, for instance, masculine order is re-established at the price of her terrible punishment (she is left paralysed and abandoned), but she effortlessly dominates the film; the contradictions between the narrative and her performance are obvious. Signoret could even be said to have incarnated these contradictions, suggesting a point of entry for female spectators.[41] In this respect, she represents the unique case of a genuine *femme fatale* in French film noir. However, not only would she soon fade away (until her second career as an older woman), but even the marginalised *garces* of social noir would disappear in the gangster films that arose around the middle of the 1950s.

The mid-1950s gangster film

Overlapping with the social noir tradition, the post-war period saw the extraordinary rise of new types of crime films. Many continued the light comic tradition of *120 rue de la gare*. First were humorous gangster films such as *Mission à Tanger* (*Mission to Tangier*, 1949) and *Mefiez-vous des blondes* (*Beware of Blondes*, 1950). Then came a popular series featuring the American actor Eddie Constantine as 'Lemmy Caution', the FBI agent created by Peter Cheyney – films such as *La Môme vert-de-gris* (*Poison Ivy*, 1953) – in which Constantine acts out a cartoon-like, stereotypical vision of the 'American': tall, tough, hard-liquor drinking and womanising.[42]

More pertinent to an investigation of French film noir is a group of influential gangster films from the mid-1950s which, at least on the surface, show greater similarities with American cinema: *Touchez pas au grisbi* (*Honour Among Thieves*, 1954), *Razzia sur la chnouf* (*Razzia*, 1955), *Du rififi chez les hommes* (*Rififi*, 1955), *Bob le flambeur* (*Bob the Gambler*, 1956) and *Le Rouge est mis* (*Speaking of Murder*, 1957). All, except *Bob*, were extremely popular at the box-office, though their critical reception was controversial.

Like the noir movies discussed so far in this chapter, they were attacked for their blackness and immorality, for the 'vulgarity' of the genre, but also for their 'Americanisation', evident in the names of their central characters, the narratives and iconography and jazz scores. Their directors were well versed in American cinema. Indeed (despite his name) Jules Dassin, *Rififi*'s director, was American and the author of a trilogy of celebrated film noirs: *Brute Force* (1947), *The Naked City* (1948), *Thieves Highway* (1949). Thus critical hostility was connected to anxieties over national identity, in the aftermath of fraught Franco-American relations during the cold war.

Essential to the understanding of post-war French gangster film is the literary imprint of the *Série Noire*, established in 1945 by Marcel Duhamel, a former surrealist who decided to publish translations of hard-boiled crime novels by Dashiell Hammett, Peter Cheyney and

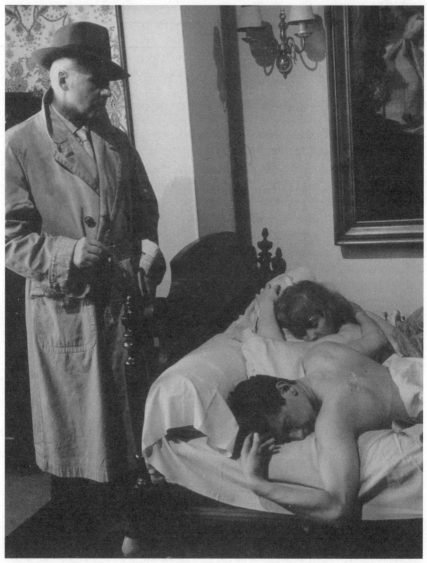

1 Bob (Roger Duchesne) looks at Paulo (Daniel Cauchy) and Anne (Isabel Corey) in bed, in *Bob le flambeur* (*Bob the Gambler*, Jean-Pierre Melville, 1956).

James Hadley Chase, among others. Duhamel was attracted by a certain vision of 'America' (Cheyney and Chase actually being British authors) as dark, violent and erotic. In his manifesto, he distances the *Série Noire* from classic detective fiction: 'Sometimes there is no mystery. And sometimes not even a detective. So what? ... Then there is action, anxiety, violence'. Raymond Queneau (also a former surrealist) adds, 'Brutality and eroticism have replaced learned deductions. The detective no longer collects cigarette ash; he kicks witnesses in the face'.[43] The *Série Noire* in its initial run published only translations, and French writers such as Boris Vian and Thomas Narcejac adopted 'American' subjects and pseudonyms. With a few exceptions, these books had initially little impact on French cinema. It is the arrival of French writers and French topics that made a difference. In 1953 Albert Simonin and Auguste Le Breton, two *Série Noire* writers who professed acquaintance with the French underworld, published, respectively, *Touchez pas au grisbi* and *Du rififi chez les hommes*, stories of Parisian gangsters written in a picturesque argot. Both were hugely successful and quickly adapted by, respectively Jacques Becker and Dassin. Following the success of *Grisbi*, other adaptations quickly followed.

While films like *Manèges* condemned the desire for consumer goods (typically styled as feminine), these gangster films present a society revelling in money and consumption – of champagne, cigarettes, smart apartments, cars, sex, alcohol, drugs, consumer goods associated with the modernity of America. While *Quai des orfèvres* celebrated French popular music, the gangster films use a hybrid 'jazzy' music that blends American and French jazz rhythms with French melodies and instruments, such as the accordion.[44] In *Grisbi*, a haunting harmonica tune is Americanised by being played on the jukebox and an automated record player, but its Frenchness is firmly anchored by the film's star – the older Jean Gabin, whose second career was thereby kick-started. Though part of the underworld, the milieu of these films is unashamedly bourgeois, mirroring the increasing wealth of the country in the 1950s – in *Grisbi*, Max (Gabin) ironically barricades his apartment against burglars, while in *Bob* the eponymous hero (Roger Duchesne) lives in a plush artist's studio. We are a long way from the down-at-heel flats and seedy hotels of social noir films. Focusing on Montmartre and Pigalle, the traditional areas of the Parisian criminal milieu, these films recast the anonymous city of American noir as a faintly nostalgic village with carefully signalled names of real streets, squares and cafés.

If social noir may be read in relation to the troubled aftermath of the war, there is a critical consensus that the 1950s gangster films are both symptoms of a new booming country and coded representations of the German Occupation, at a time when the topic had virtually disappeared from films. The gangster stories focus on underground societies and torture, and combat weapons such as grenades are occasionally used; characters often come out of a stint in jail, frequently referring to the 'good old days' before their imprisonment. The scripts develop themes of loyalty and betrayal, and whereas these existed in pre-war films, their recurrence often across the traditional law–crime divide, can be read as a metaphor of the corruption of French society by the Gestapo, which had infiltrated both the underground and the police.

As with the social noir films, gender is another aspect that can be related to the war, but here in the sense that the women's place is becoming even more marginal. Women are older barmaids, young gangster molls or 'hostesses', all types too marginal to be of consequence: when they betray it is by mistake rather than design. As in social noir, heterosexual love is absent; but now it has been replaced with virile friendship. The gangster films thus eliminate not just the *femme fatale* but the femme *tout court*, and recreate an almost entirely masculine 'family' with, at its head, a benign patriarch who is both father and mother to his brood. His mode of punishment is not the kick in the face but the infantilising slap. *Rififi*, with its harsher violence, slightly departs from this model. For Burch and Sellier, the French gangster film marks the 'return of the patriarch', replacing the vulnerable men such as we have noted in social noir. Yet, these are strangely tired patriarchs. Their power, founded on criminality, has lost the legitimacy of the pre-war figures, their advancing age and desire to 'retire' are constantly reiterated. Thus these figures may be seen as a covert critique of a generation of men who compromised with the enemy during the war and betrayed the younger generation: the young acolytes are the ones who tend to die.

The gangster films of the 1950s are emphatically black and white, deploying the traditional noir visual style. They use to the full the aesthetic possibilities of the city at night, increasingly on location (especially in *Bob*, and a little in *Rififi*, while *Grisbi* and *Chnouf* are studio bound): glistening cobblestones, dark streets and alleyways, light shining on black cars, headlights piercing the night. Yet, unlike social noir films where visual style, content and tone went hand in hand to create a sordid, oppressive atmosphere, here visual style is often divorced from narrative and tone, creating a secure, cosy world (which in most cases significantly tones down the more bitter and violent source novels). For instance in *Bob*, Bob's entrance in his local café early on in the film is shot with Bob a bold silhouette in hat and trenchcoat against a smoke-filled background, with emphatic music; yet he is only performing a routine, harmless, activity. In *Chnouf*, when Henri visits a chemist making illegal drugs, an air ventilator is used as a pretext to project huge rotating shadows over the room, although at this point neither of the characters is in danger. While *Rififi* shows a greater consistency between style and narrative, on the whole the noir visuals of the French gangster films of the 1950s do not transmit a threatening or paranoid atmosphere (as they did in *Le Corbeau* and *Plage* among others). There is no sense of oppression or malaise, rather the noir *mise-en-scène* acts as generic shorthand, purely stylistic flourish or authorial mark.

Roland Barthes talked of the French gangster film as 'the world of understatement',[45] and indeed in the films there is little action (except in *Rififi*, with its celebrated twenty-minute silent heist sequence). In this, the French gangster films of the 1950s are heirs to the 1930s films, displaying a French taste for minimalist intimate realism over action. They also display a high degree of self-consciousness towards the codes of the genre. For example, in *Rififi* a musical number includes a dancer parodying the clothes and gestures of a gangster. As well as a reference to Fred Astaire and Cyd Charisse's 'Girl Hunt ballet' in *The Band Wagon* (1953), the dance in *Rififi* comments on the sartorial narcissism at the core of the genre.

The mainstream gangster films of the 1950s in this way take on the American noir heritage and self-consciously display it, especially in visual terms, and yet they appropriate it to French narrative and ideological ends. As we will see, New Wave filmmakers make very different use of *Série Noire* material. Before moving on to them, brief mention must be made of Louis Malle's *Ascenseur pour l'échafaud* (*Lift to the Scaffold*, 1958). Whereas the gangster films 'tame' exotic material into a French idiom, Louis Malle's film performs the reverse operation, accentuating the exoticism of a banal crime story set among 'normal' people: a wealthy woman, Florence Carala (Jeanne Moreau), asks her lover Julien (Maurice Ronet) to kill her husband. After a perfect murder, he gets stuck in the office lift; while he is thus marooned his car is stolen, leading to his downfall. Malle uses on-location shooting in the streets and office blocks of modern Paris, but abstracts them through noir photography (by Henri Decaë), for instance in the tense scenes with Julien in the lift. But the most original noir scenes are those featuring Florence walking the streets of Paris at night to the – semi-improvised – music of Miles Davis. The direct overlaying of a truly modern jazz score was another way *Ascenseur* distinguished itself from the mainstream. This, his location shooting and his different use of noir material are the main reasons Malle's film was seen as a precursor to the New Wave.

New Wave tributes, mainstream rewritings

Starting as film critics, the future filmmakers of the New Wave, especially Jean-Luc Godard, François Truffaut, Claude Chabrol, Eric
Rohmer and Jacques Rivette were avid cinephiles. Love of American
cinema was the cement of their generation, and in their cinematic landscape, film noir occupied a special place.[46] Crime films were both
'very American' and easily adaptable to a French context (unlike the
western or the musical), and the Young Turks admired noir B-thrillers,
which appealed to them as cheap, 'authentic' films, with desperate,
romantic narratives. *Gun Crazy* (1949) was the supreme example,
although their own films would replace couples on the run with troubled male heroes, in this respect continuing the French tradition of
marginalising women. The attraction of American film noir was also
that it combined the prestige of 1940s American movies – with glamorous stars like Humphrey Bogart, Alan Ladd, Lauren Bacall and
Gene Tierney – with great modernist themes, such as alienation, solitude and social fragmentation.

Godard's *A bout de souffle* (*Breathless*, 1960) is universally
acknowledged as one of the manifesto films of the New Wave. It stars
Jean-Paul Belmondo as Michel Poiccard, cynical crook and
'modernist' hero rolled into one: charismatic, always on the move and
yet anomic. His trajectory predictably ends in more or less self-
inflicted death. Godard's celebrated jagged editing (echoing Martial
Solal's syncopated jazz soundtrack) traces Michel's trajectory from
Marseille to Paris. Despite Raoul Coutard's luminous photography
(the film was shot on location in the summer), and the breakneck pace
of the film, *A bout de souffle* strives to create an existentially dark
vision, through its overt tribute to film noir. As Chris Darke argues,
Godard would pursue this visual homage also in *Alphaville* (1965), a
film which 'summons forth from the history of cinema the "haunted"
light of German Expressionism and film noir'.[47] Nostalgia for 1940s
and 1950s Hollywood is also ostentatiously displayed in *A bout de
souffle* through verbal references, posters, clothes, quotations, visits to
the cinema, borrowings from genre narratives (Michel on the run after
shooting a policeman), and in a famous scene, worship of a world-
weary Bogart in *The Harder They Fall* (1958). As Belmondo, in rever-
ential silence, gazes at Bogart and rubs his lips in imitation, a romantic
and nostalgic vision of film noir is called forth – Godard directly
addressing the spectator through his alter ego. With less conviction, *A
bout de souffle* resurrects the *femme fatale* with the American Patricia
(Jean Seberg, whose casting is itself an homage to Otto Preminger),

Michel's love object, betraying him to the police. As Patricia in the last shot rubs her lips after Michel's death, she merely imitates the imitator.

A bout de souffle was an original script (by Truffaut). Later Godard, Truffaut and Chabrol drew directly on American *Série Noire* novels: Truffaut adapted David Goodis (*Tirez sur le pianiste/Shoot the Piano Player*) and William Irish (*La Mariée était en noir/The Bride Wore Black* and *La Sirène du Mississippi/Mississippi Mermaid*); Chabrol adapted Stanley Ellin (*A double tour/Web of Passion*, 1959); and Godard – distantly – D. and B. Hitchens (*Bande à part/Band of Outsiders*) and Lionel White (*Pierrot le fou*). In choosing Goodis, Truffaut opted for the darkest, most 'paranoid' type of hard-boiled literature.[48] Like many French intellectuals before him (such as Duhamel), his taste for Goodis' sad, dark vision was linked to existentialism, to the concept of rebellion and alienation in an absurd world.

Tirez sur le pianiste is the story of Charlie, a former concert pianist (under the name of Edouard), now playing in a low dive, whose past as in classic film noir catches up with him, while he gets embroiled in his brothers' criminal activities. A sensitive figure, Charlie/Edouard, as played by vulnerable-looking Charles Aznavour, exudes angst, his split identity signified by a modernist voice-over (read by another actor, in the second person). His world-weary attempt to escape his past, in which he provoked his wife's suicide, is foiled by the love of Lena (Marie Dubois), women forever acting as obstacles to male freedom. Truffaut shot *Tirez sur le pianiste* entirely on location in noir style (Raoul Coutard), deploying a run-down yet poetic noir iconography of night, rain, cars and guns and men in trenchcoats (as well as snow, a twist on classic noir iconography). Goodis's narrative serves as a frame in which Truffaut inserts his autobiographical preoccupations. Crime film tropes – rival gangsters, a shoot-out, a kidnapping – vie with the love story and New-Wave style *temps morts*.

Godard's tribute to American film noir – like that of New Wave filmmakers in general – was designed to make popular American cinema intellectually respectable. Although *A bout de souffle* was very successful at the box office, no doubt on account of its infectious freshness and energy, Belmondo's performance and its romantic vision of Paris, other New Wave film noir adaptations – including *Tirez sur le pianiste* – did not fare so well. The tensions between personal authenticity and homage to American cinema, the clash between auteur cinema, the original American noir material and the French context of reception was too great. By contrast, the mainstream filmmakers, as well as 'popular auteurs' such as Jean-Pierre Melville, went predominantly for French *Série Noire* writers and, in their different ways, carefully rewrote the material to suit their French audience, leading to greater box-office success.

The mainstream *policier*, as in earlier periods, includes many subgenres. Indeed the 1960s were a golden age for French crime films. 'Between the end of the 1950s and the beginning of the 1970s, the *policier* constituted a quarter of French film production.'[49] A successful wave of comic thrillers included new versions of *Fantômas* (with Jean Marais and Louis de Funès) and a cult series of parodic gangster/spy movies: *Les Tontons flingueurs* (*Crooks in Clover*, 1963), *Les Barbouzes* (*The Great Spy Chase*, 1964), *Du rififi à Paname* (*Rififi in Paris*, 1966) and *La Métamorphose des cloportes* (*Cloportes*, 1965). The later films borrow some of the visual effects of film noir, notably dark photography and jazz scores (*La Métamorphose* features music by Jimmy Smith). Yet their parodic tone and cast are mostly comic. In the course of the decade, a new type of 'psychological' thriller also emerged, epitomised by René Clément's adaptation of Patricia Highsmith's *The Talented Mr Ripley* as *Plein Soleil* (*Purple Noon*, 1960), in which the dichotomy between visual style on the one hand, and narrative and tone on the other, is the reverse of that of the 1950s gangster films – here horrendous crime is played out in sun-drenched Mediterranean settings and glorious colour. Clément's adaptation of Sébastien Japrisot's *Le Passager de la pluie* (*Rider on the Rain*, 1969) was however closer to contemporary Hollywood (co-starring Charles Bronson). Similarly, *Le Clan des Siciliens* (*The Sicilian Clan*, 1969) harnessed heavyweight French stars (Gabin, Alain Delon) to a Mafia story. Also using colour in predominantly comic tone, and a clear reference to contemporary Hollywood, were the successful 'retro' gangster movies *Borsalino* (1970) and *Borsalino & Co.* (1974), starring Delon and Belmondo and set in Marseille. Closer to classic film noir – and still in black and white – are *Le Trou* (*The Night Watch*, 1960), *Classe tous risques* (*The Big Risk*, 1960), *Mélodie en sous-sol* (*Any Number Can Win*, 1963), and especially the work of Jean-Pierre Melville.

Forging a unique path between the mainstream and the New Wave, Melville represents both the high point of 1960s gangster filmmaking and the swansong of classic French film noir– thus justifying this chapter's final emphasis on one director, even though it has in general taken a non-auteurist approach.[50] A lifelong Americanophile, Melville loved American cinema from a tender age. His rewriting of the codes of the American gangster film and film noir falls within three periods.

First comes the era during which Melville was within the orbit of the

New Wave: the period of *Bob le flambeur* (1956), *Deux hommes dans Manhattan* (*Two Men in Manhattan*, 1959) and *L'Aîné des Ferchaux* (*Magnet of Doom*, 1963). As we saw, *Bob* belongs to the mid-1950s French gangster films. It differed from them, though, in the extent of its location shooting, its poetic vision of Paris, its loose narrative and independent production, which impressed the New Wave critics; Chabrol praised its 'quality of imperfection'[51] and Godard cast Melville as the writer 'Parvulesco' in *A bout de souffle*. With its ironic and affectionate portrayal of Bob, its gangster hero, *Bob* was a self-conscious tribute to *The Asphalt Jungle* and American noir in general. Melville pursued this tribute even more explicitly in *Deux hommes dans Manhattan*, partly shot in New York, in which the disappearance of a French diplomat is investigated by a journalist (Melville), with noir exterior photography – mostly at night – and a jazz soundtrack. Despite these credentials, the film broke from the New Wave concept of noir, both because Melville widened his remit to an open celebration of American culture and because the core mystery referred back to the French Resistance. Similarly, *L'Aîné des Ferchaux,* despite the presence of Belmondo (and a source in a Simenon novel), departed radically from both New Wave and mainstream film noir, in a striking but idiosyncratic ode to the American South.

Melville's second gangster film period, and his most deeply noir in all senses of the term, consists of two classic *policiers* based on French *Série Noire* novels: *Le Doulos* (*Doulos the Finger Man*, 1963, from Pierre Lesou) and *Le Deuxième souffle* (*Second Breath*, 1966, from José Giovanni). The books belong to a more sober and realistic vein of the *Série Noire* than the earlier picturesque books discussed above (Giovanni's novels also form the basis of *Le Trou* and *Classe tous risques*). From this material Melville fashioned two sombre portrayals of criminals who inhabit eerily abstract Franco-American locations. These two splendid noir films (*Le Doulos* is shot by Nicolas Hayer, *Le Corbeau*'s director of photography) turn their hoodlums into distilled versions of their Hollywood ancestors. Yet the familiar personae of the stars – Belmondo and Serge Reggiani in *Le Doulos*, Lino Ventura in *Le Deuxième souffle* – humanise the characters while signifying their Frenchness, explaining the success of these films despite their bleak vision and paring down of picturesque detail.

In his third and most 'mannerist' period – his *mise-en-scène* is a model of rigour and discreet virtuosity – Melville pushed this personal vision of noir even further (paradoxically these last three films are in colour, justifying his claim to have made 'black and white films in colour': *Le Samouraï* (*The Godson*, 1967), *Le Cercle rouge* (*The Red*

Circle, 1970) and *Un flic* (*Dirty Money*, 1972).[52] All three star Alain Delon, as a contract killer in *Le Samouraï*, a gangster in *Le Cercle rouge* and as a cop in *Un flic*. Whatever the role, the star inhabits the characters with the same degree of silent, minimalist precision, obsessively performing ritualistic tasks (his way of killing, of putting his hat on or looking at his watch). Delon was the perfect expression of Melville's 'autistic' concept of masculinity, a universe from which women have virtually disappeared. Melville's tribute to American film noir consists in condensing its basic elements to the point of abstraction, but within an accessible entertainment format. Suspense is maintained through a breaking down and stretching of the mechanics of action (his 'cinema of process'),[53] while the characters exist as pure mythical figures, the end point of a long line of gangster stereotypes handed down from 1940s film noir. Compare for instance the opening of *Le Samouraï* with that of its 'model', Frank Tuttle's 1942 *This Gun For Hire*. In Tuttle's film Alan Ladd's hitman is all down-to-earth purposefulness as he dons his trenchcoat and hat in his cluttered room, against honky-tonk piano music. By contrast, Delon in *Le Samouraï* almost languid, slowly rises from his bed in a bleak grey room before watching himself go through the ritualistic process of putting on coat and hat in front of a mirror.

Whereas New Wave auteurs sought to pay tribute by importing wholesale 'American' visions into a French context, the mainstream filmmakers – including Melville – either chose stories already anchored in French culture or carefully translated their material to suit French situations and audiences.

Conclusion – French film noir: how noir and how French is it?

We have seen that the long and complex history of French film noir during the classical era, can often, as in America, be traced back to both indigenous and international literature, although on the whole the more popular films have been adapted from French sources. As in American cinema, too, the overlap between French film noir and the *policier*, while significant, is imperfect: many *policiers* are deliberately 'light' (*Grisbi*); conversely some key noir films are not conventional crime films (*Le Corbeau*, *Manèges*).

French specificity in film noir does not reside in visual style, which partakes of the universal noir vocabulary of dark and chiaroscuro lighting and claustrophobic settings, although clearly this style was in widespread use in France a decade before the classic American noir period – in the early 1930s Simenon adaptations and poetic realism.

French specificity is, rather, located in narrative and gender patterns, and in the uses to which the noir idiom is put. It emerges that a systematically more cynical and morally ambiguous worldview is in operation, due in part to different censorship codes. Until its demise in 1974, French censorship was always more concerned with protecting the state's institutions (such as the military and education) than with private moral or religious matters. Thus compared with America under the Hays code or puritan Britain, French cinema from the 1930s to the 1960s 'got away' with more liberal moral and sexual mores and taboo-breaking representations, a difference clearly illustrated in the comparison of the French films of the period with their American remakes.

The forms taken by French film noir and its reception have fluctuated widely over the forty years of this investigation. Two consistent elements have emerged however. First, there is the downplaying of action and plot in favour of atmosphere, self-reflexivity, cinephile citation and stylistic flourishes which we see across all the periods examined. This should not surprise us, as it is in keeping with classical French cinema in general, which, as I have discussed elsewhere, always privileges spectacle over narrative drive.[54] Second, there is the persistent marginalising of women, who change from idealised but marginal figures in the 1930s to a more forceful, but evil, presence in 1940s and 1950s social noir – although with the notable exception of Simone Signoret, they are too vulgar to qualify as *femme fatale*. Women recede again to the background from the mid-1950s, when they become infantilised gangster molls in the *policiers*. A more discreet but arguably more insidious form of misogyny operates in New Wave noir, while Melville eliminates women almost entirely from his bleak male world. This is not the place for an exhaustive analysis of this phenomenon, but clearly the combination of a strongly patriarchal and catholic culture in the 1930s is part of the picture, as are the changes brought by the trauma of the occupation for the later films, and later still the male focus of authorship. The marked misogyny of the 1960s and the flight from femininity in Melville's films can also be read as backlash against the full arrival of women on the public scene.

But perhaps the most surprising specificity of French film noir to emerge from this scrutiny is the paradoxical relationship between visual style and narrative/ideology. French film noir appears to be at its blackest when *not* in the *policier* mould, and often at its lightest in the gangster/detective films proper. Apart from Melville's films and a few other thrillers such as *Le Trou*, the greatest coherence of noir style, narrative and tone is to be found in poetic realism and social noir (and even then, Melville's blackest film is his Resistance movie, *L'Armée des ombres* [1969]). By contrast, 'tough' gangster films predominantly use noir visual style and iconography to present a cosy, secure world diametrically opposed to American film noir which, in Borde and Chaumeton's book, must 'create a quite specific feeling of uneasiness'.[55] In France, film noir serves a social rather than a generic purpose. This would explain why the critics who defined film noir as uniquely American turned their back on it. Rather than the aesthetic glamour and emotional excitement of American film noirs, genuine French film noirs offered, instead, a dystopian, sometimes 'hellish' vision of French society.

Notes

Thanks to Tom Brown, Simon Caulkin, Mark Lane, Valerie Orpen, Victor Perkins and Andrew Spicer for their feedback on this material. I also wish to thank Jean-Loup Bourget who invited me to teach a seminar on French film noir at the Ecole Normale Supérieure, Paris, in March 2004, which led to some of the thoughts in this chapter.

1   Raymond Borde and Etienne Chaumeton, *Panorama du film noir américain* (Paris: Les Editions de Minuit, 1955), pp. 3–5.
2   *Ibid.*, p. 27.
3   *Ibid.*, p. 159.
4   The most informative – if not academic – studies of the French crime film and film noir in French are François Guérif, *Le Cinéma policier français* (Paris: Henri Veyrier, 1981) and Olivier Philippe, *Le Cinéma policier français contemporain* (Paris: Editions du Cerf, 1996). In English there is little substantial work devoted to the French crime film as a genre or indeed French film noir, apart from a special issue of the (bilingual) Franco-American journal *Iris*, 21 (Spring 1996). References can also be found in works devoted to specific directors, such as Jean-Pierre Melville and Pierre Chenal, or the American crime film (see references to Forbes, Hardy, MacArthur, Matalon *et al.* and Vincendeau in the bibliography) and work on 1930s French cinema (see references to Andrew and Phillips). Unfortunately the only book devoted to French film noir is a disappointing journalistic work: Robin Buss, *French Film Noir* (London and New York: Marion Boyars, 1994).
5   The term *policier* – '*polar*' in slang – designates all crime films, whether the police appear in them or not.
6   Michael Walker, 'Introduction', in Ian Cameron (ed.), *The Movie Book of Film Noir* (London: Studio Vista, 1992), p. 26.
7   André Vanoncini, *Le Roman policier* (Paris: Presses Universitaires de France, 1993), pp. 8–9.

8   Claire Gorrara, *The Roman Noir in Post-war French Culture: Dark Fictions* (Oxford: Oxford University Press, 2003), p. 11.
9   See Claude Gauteur, *D'après Simenon, Simenon & le cinéma* (Paris: Omnibus, 2001).
10 Jean-Luc Godard, quoted in Guérif, *Le Cinéma policier français*, p. 58.
11 Guérif, *Le Cinéma policier français*, p. 57.
12 The most authoritative discussion of poetic realism can be found in Dudley Andrew, *Mists of Regret: Culture and Sensibility in Classic French Film*(New Jersey: Princeton University Press, 1995).
13 Brassaï, *The Secret Paris of the 30s*, translated from the French by Richard Miller (London: Thames & Hudson, 2001).
14 Pierrette Matalon, Claude Guiguet and Jacques Pinturault (eds), *Pierre Chenal* (Paris: Editions Dujarric, 1987), p. 67.
15 For further details on the work of the German émigrés in France and their connection to film noir, see Thomas Elsaesser, 'Pathos and Leave-taking', *Sight and Sound*, 53:4 (Autumn 1984); Ginette Vincendeau, 'Noir Is also a French Word', in Cameron, *The Movie Book of Film Noir*, pp. 49–58; and Alastair Phillips, *City of Darkness, City of Light: Emigré Filmmakers in Paris 1929–1939* (Amsterdam: Amsterdam University Press, 2004). On the classic Franco-American remakes, see Lucy Mazdon, *Encore Hollywood: Remaking French Cinema* (London: BFI Publishing, 2000), and Tom Brown, 'French Film Remakes: the Classical Era', in Christian Viviani (ed.), *Hollywood: Les Connections françaises* (forthcoming).
16 For further details on Gabin's star persona and his role in poetic realism and the 1950s French gangster film, see Ginette Vincendeau, *Stars and Stardom in French Cinema* (London and New York: Continuum, 2000).
17 Borde and Chaumeton, *Panorama du film noir américain*, p. 27.
18 See Charles O'Brien, 'Film Noir in France: Before the Liberation', *Iris*, 21 (Spring 1996), 7–20.
19 Lotte H. Eisner, *Fritz Lang* (London: Secker & Warburg, 1976), p. 258.
20 Andrew, *Mists of Regret*, pp. 164–5.
21 Evelyn Ehrlich, *Cinema of Paradox: French Filmmaking under the German Occupation* (New York and Guildford: Columbia University Press, 1985).
22 Gorrara, *The Roman Noir in Post-war French Culture*, p. 13.
23 Claude Beylie and Philippe d'Hugues, *Les oubliés du cinéma francais* (Paris: Editions du Cerf, 1999), pp. 297–300.
24 *Le Canard enchaîné* (anonymous) review of the reissue of *Le corbeau* (10 February 1957).
25 Noël Burch and Geneviève Sellier read this moment in the film as falling in line with the Vichy government's pro-family policies; Noël Burch and Geneviève Sellier, *La Drôle de guerre des sexes du cinéma français 1930–1956* (Paris: Nathan Université, 1996), p. 196.
26 Filmed interview with Bertrand Tavernier, Criterion DVD edition of *Le Corbeau*, 2004.
27 Judith Mayne, 'Henri-Georges Clouzot's *Le Corbeau* and the Crimes of

Women', *Sites: Journal of 20th Century/Contemporary French Studies* 4:2 (Autumn 2000), 319–42.

28 Nino Frank, 'Un nouveau genre policier: l'aventure criminelle', *L'Ecran français*, 61 (August 1946).

29 Jean-Pierre Chartier, 'Les Américains aussi font des films noirs', *La Revue du cinéma*, 2 (November 1946).

30 O'Brien, 'Film Noir in France', 7–20.

31 François Truffaut, 'A Certain Tendency of the French Cinema', in Bill Nichols (ed.), *Movies and Methods*, vol. 1 (1976), pp. 224–37. Originally published in *Cahiers du cinéma*, 31 (January 1954).

32 Borde and Chaumeton, *Panorama du film noir américain,* p. 164.

33 These terms are taken from a wide selection of reviews of the films, available at the Bifi (Bibliothèque du Film) Library in Paris – where pagination is not preserved. Among others, terms are taken from reviews of *Quai des orfèvres* in *Parallèlle 50* (11 October 1947), *Jeunesse Ouvrière* (10 October 1947), *Le Canard enchaîné* (10 February 1957); of *Manèges* in *Libération* (27 January 1950), *Combat* (27 January 1950); and of *Les Diaboliques* in *Arts* (4 March 1955), *Carrefour* (2 February 1955), *Combat* (10 October 1954).

34 *Combat* (10 October 1954).

35 Marcel Oms, *Les Cahiers de la Cinémathèque*, 25 (Spring–Summer 1978), 70.

36 *Le Canard enchaîné* (anonymous) review of the reissue of *Quai des orfèvres* (10 February 1957).

37 (Anonymous critic) cited by Richard Roud in 'Introduction', in Mary Lea Bandy (ed.), *Rediscovering French Film* (New York: Museum of Modern Art, 1983), p. 34.

38 Richard Maltby, 'Film Noir: The Politics of the Maladjusted Text', in Cameron (ed.), *The Movie Book of Film Noir*, p. 41.

39 Burch and Sellier, *La Drôle de guerre des sexes du cinéma français*, pp. 224–37; and Noël Burch and Geneviève Sellier, 'Evil Women in the Post-war French Cinema', in Ulrike Sieglohr (ed.), *Heroines Without Heroes, Reconstructing Female and National Identities in European Cinema, 1945–51* (London and New York: Cassell, 2000), pp. 47–65.

40 Richard Dyer, 'Resistance through Charisma: Rita Hayworth and *Gilda*', in E. Ann Kaplan (ed.), *Women in Film Noir* (London: BFI Publishing, 1978), pp. 91–9.

41 For further work on the contradictions in Signoret's star persona, see Sarah Leahy and Susan Hayward, 'The Tainted Woman: Simone Signoret, Site of Pathology or Agent of Retribution?', in Sieglohr, *Heroines Without Heroes*, pp. 77–91. See also Susan Hayward, *Simone Signoret: The Star As Cultural Sign* (London and New York: Continuum, 2004).

42 For further views on Eddie Constantine's films and popular *policiers* of the late 1940s and 1950s, see Jill Forbes, *The Cinema in France after the New Wave* (London: BFI/Macmillan, 1992), Chapter 2, about the

policier; see also Guérif, *Le Cinéma policier français*, p. 91, for a list of little-known *policiers* of the late 1940s.
43 Marcel Duhamel, 'Le manifeste de la *Série Noire*', www.gallimard.fr; 'Marcel Duhamel, Jean Giono et Raymond Queneau témoignent', Preface to the *Série Noire*, www.gallimard.fr.
44 For an informed discussion of French jazz, see Ludovic Tournès, *New Orleans sur Seine, Histoire du jazz en France* (Paris: Librairie Arthème Fayard, 1999).
45 Roland Barthes, 'Puissance et désinvolture', *Mythologies* (Paris: Editions du Seuil, 1957), p. 67.
46 For recent work on the New Wave in English, see Michel Marie, *The French New Wave: An Artistic School*, translated by Richard John Neupert (Oxford: Blackwell, 2003) and Richard John Neupert, *A History of the French New Wave Cinema* (Madison: Wisconsin University Press, 2002).
47 Chris Darke, *Alphaville* (London: I. B. Tauris, French Film Guides, 2005).
48 Michael Walker, 'Introduction', in Cameron (ed.), *The Movie Book of Film Noir*, pp. 14–16.
49 François Guérif and Stéphane Lévy-Klein, *Les Cahiers de la cinémathèque*, 25 (Spring–Summer 1978), 75.
50 For further work on Melville, see Ginette Vincendeau, *Jean-Pierre Melville: An American in Paris* (London: BFI Publishing, 2003).
51 Claude Chabrol, 'Saluer Melville?', *Cahiers du cinéma*, 63 (October 1956), p. 51.
52 Jean-Pierre Melville, in Rui Nogueira (ed.), *Melville on Melville* (London: Secker & Warburg/BFI, 1971), p. 130.
53 Colin McArthur, '*Mise-en-scène* Degree Zero, Jean-Pierre Melville's *Le Samouraï*', in Susan Hayward and Ginette Vincendeau (eds), *French Film: Texts and Contexts* 2nd edn (London and New York: Routledge, 2000), pp. 189–201.
54 See Ginette Vincendeau, 'The Art of Spectacle: the Aesthetics of Classical French Cinema', in Michael Temple and Michael Witt (eds), *The French Cinema Book* (London: BFI Publishing, 2004), pp. 137–52.
55 Borde and Chaumeton, *Panorama du film noir américain,* pp. 13–15.

Filmography

The 1930s
Le Mystère de la chambre jaune (*The Mystery of the Yellow Room*), Marcel L'Herbier, 1930
La Chienne (*The Bitch*), Jean Renoir, 1931
Faubourg-Montmartre, Raymond Bernard, 1931
Le Parfum de la dame en noir (*The Perfume of the Lady in Black*),Marcel L'Herbier, 1931

Le Chien jaune (*The Yellow Dog*), Jean Tarride, 1932
Cœur de Lilas (*Lilac*), Anatole Litvak, 1932
La Nuit du carrefour (*Night at the Crossroads*), Jean Renoir, 1932
La Tête d'un homme (*A Man's Neck*), Julien Duvivier, 1932
Le Grand jeu (*The Big Game*), Jacques Feyder, 1933
La Rue sans nom (*Street Without a Name*), Pierre Chenal, 1934
Justin de Marseille, Maurice Tourneur, 1935
Les Bas-fonds (*The Lower Depths*), Jean Renoir, 1936
La Belle équipe (*They Were Five*), Julien Duvivier, 1936
Jenny, Marcel Carné, 1936
Abus de confiance (*Abused Confidence*), Henri Decoin, 1937
L'Alibi (*The Alibi*), Pierre Chenal, 1937
Chéri-Bibi, Léon Mathot, 1937
Gueule d'amour (*Lady Killer*), Jean Grémillon, 1937
Pépé le Moko, Julien Duvivier, 1937
Le Puritain (*The Puritan*), Jeff Musso, 1937
La Bête humaine (*Judas Was a Woman*), Jean Renoir, 1938
L'Entraîneuse (*Nightclub Hostess*), Albert Valentin, 1938
Hôtel du Nord, Marcel Carné, 1938
La Maison du Maltais (*Sirocco*), Pierre Chenal, 1938
Prisons de femmes (*Marked Girls*), Roger Richebé, 1938
Le Quai des brumes (*Port of Shadows*), Marcel Carné, 1938
Le Dernier tournant (*The Last Turn*), Pierre Chenal, 1939
Le Jour se lève (*Daybreak*), Marcel Carné, 1939
Pièges (*Personal Column*), Robert Siodmak, 1939
Remorques (*Stormy Waters*), Jean Grémillon, 1940

The Occupation years
L'Assassinat du Père Noël (*The Killing of Santa Claus*), Christian-Jaque, 1941
L'Assassin habite au 21 (*The Murderer Lives at Number 21*), Henri-Georges
     Clouzot, 1942
Dernier atout (*The Last Trump*), Jacques Becker, 1942
Les Inconnus dans la maison (*Strangers in the House*), Henri Decoin, 1942
Le Corbeau (*The Raven*), Henri-Georges Clouzot, 1943
L'Homme de Londres (*The London Man*), Henri Decoin, 1943
Picpus, Richard Pottier, 1943
Cécile est morte (*Cecile Is Dead*), Maurice Tourneur, 1944
Les Caves du Majestic (*Majestic Hotel Cellars*), Richard Pottier, 1945
120 rue de la gare, Jacques Daniel-Norman, 1946

The 1940s and 1950s 'social noir' films
Douce (*Love Story*), Claude Autant-Lara, 1943
Le Diable au corps (*Devil in the Flesh*), Claude Autant-Lara, 1946
Panique (*Panic*), Julien Duvivier, 1946
Les Portes de la nuit (*Gates of the Night*), Marcel Carné, 1946
Quai des orfèvres (*Jenny Lamour*), Henri-Georges Clouzot, 1947

Dédée d'Anvers (*Woman of Antwerp*), Yves Allégret, 1948
Manèges (*The Cheat*), Yves Allégret, 1949
Manon, Henri-Georges Clouzot, 1949
Une si jolie petite plage (*Riptide*), Yves Allégret, 1949
La Vérité sur Bébé Donge (*The Truth About Bebe Donge*), Henri Decoin, 1951
Le Salaire de la peur (*The Wages of Fear*), Henri-Georges Clouzot, 1953
Thérèse Raquin, Marcel Carné, 1953
Les Diaboliques (*Diabolique*),Henri-Georges Clouzot, 1954
Voici le temps des assassins (*Deadlier Than the Male*), Julien Duvivier, 1956
En cas de Malheur (*Love Is My Profession*), Claude Autant-Lara, 1958
La Vérité (*The Truth*), Henri-Georges Clouzot, 1960

Late 1940s and 1950s gangster/crime films
Impasse des deux anges, Maurice Tourneur, 1948
56 rue Pigalle, Willy Rozier, 1949
Mission à Tanger (*Mission in Tangier*), André Hunnebelle, 1949
Méfiez-vous des blondes (*Beware of Blondes*), André Hunnebelle, 1950
Massacre en dentelles (*Massacre in Lace*), André Hunnebelle, 1952
Les Femmes s'en balancent (*Dames Don't Care*), Bernard Borderie, 1953
La Môme vert-de-gris (*Poison Ivy*), Bernard Borderie, 1953
Touchez pas au grisbi (*Honour Among Thieves*), Jacques Becker, 1954
Du rififi chez les hommes (*Rififi*), Jules Dassin, 1955
Je suis un sentimental (*Headlines of Destruction*), John Berry, 1955
Razzia sur la chnouf (*Razzia*), Henri Decoin, 1955
Bob le flambeur (*Bob the Gambler*), Jean-Pierre Melville, 1956
Retour de manivelle (*There's Always a Price Tag*), Denys de la Patellière, 1957
Le Rouge est mis (*Speaking of Murder*), Gilles Grangier, 1957
Ascenseur pour l'échafaud (*Lift to the Scaffold*), Louis Malle, 1958
Le Gorille vous salue bien (*The Gorilla Greets You*), Bernard Borderie, 1958
Maigret tend un piège (*Maigret Lays a Trap*), Jean Delannoy, 1958

The New Wave and the 1960s
A double tour (*Web of Passion*), Claude Chabrol, 1959
Deux hommes dans Manhattan (*Two Men in Manhattan*), Jean-Pierre Melville, 1959
A bout de souffle (*Breathless*), Jean-Luc Godard, 1960
Classe tous risques (*The Big Risk*), Claude Sautet, 1960
Tirez sur le pianiste (*Shoot the Piano Player*), François Truffaut, 1960
Plein Soleil (*Purple Noon*), René Clément, 1960
Le Trou (*The Night Watch*), Jacques Becker, 1960
Le Cave se rebiffe (*Money Money Money*), Gilles Grangier, 1961
L'Aîné des Ferchaux (*Magnet of Doom*), Jean-Pierre Melville, 1963
Le Doulos (*Doulos the Finger Man*), Jean-Pierre Melville, 1963
Mélodie en sous-sol (*Any Number Can Win*), Henri Verneuil, 1963
Les Tontons flingueurs (*Crooks in Clover*), Georges Lautner, 1963

Bande à part (*Band of Outsiders*), Jean-Luc Godard, 1964
Les Barbouzes (*The Great Spy Chase*), Georges Lautner, 1964
Fantômas, André Hunnebelle, 1964
Alphaville, une étrange aventure de Lemmy Caution (*Alphaville*), Jean-Luc
    Godard, 1965
Compartiment tueurs (*The Sleeping Car Murders*), Constantin Costa-Gavras,
    1965
La Métamorphose des cloportes (*Cloportes*), Pierre Granier-Deferre, 1965
Pierrot le fou, Jean-Luc Godard, 1965
Le Deuxième souffle (*Second Breath*), Jean-Pierre Melville, 1966
Du rififi à Paname (*Rififi in Paris*), Denys de la Patellière, 1966
Le Samouraï (*The Godson*), Jean-Pierre Melville, 1967
La Mariée était en noir (*The Bride Wore Black*), François Truffaut, 1968
Que la bête meure (*This Man Must Die*), Claude Chabrol, 1968
Le Clan des Siciliens (*The Sicilian Clan*), Henri Verneuil, 1969
Le Passager de la pluie (*Rider on the Rain*), René Clément, 1969
La Sirène du Mississipi (*Mississippi Mermaid*), François Truffaut, 1969
Borsalino, Jacques Deray, 1970
Le Cercle rouge (*The Red Circle*), Jean-Pierre Melville, 1970
Un flic (*Dirty Money*), Jean-Pierre Melville, 1972
Borsalino & Co., Jacques Deray, 1974

Select bibliography

This bibliography contains works in French and in English on the
French crime film genre and French film noir (including poetic realism)
and more general works on French cinema that make substantial reference to it. I have restricted works on American crime films and film
noir to those that make substantial reference to the French context.

Andrew, Dudley, *Mists of Regret: Culture and Sensibility in Classic
    French Film* (New Jersey: Princeton University Press, 1995).
Bandy, Mary Lea (ed.), *Rediscovering French Film* (New York:
    Museum of Modern Art, 1983).
Borde, Raymond and Etienne Chaumeton, *Panorama du film noir
    américain* (Paris: Les Editions de Minuit, 1955).
Bruzzi, Stella, 'The Instabilities of the Franco-American Gangster', in
    Undressing Cinema: Clothing and Identity in the Movies (London
    and New York: Routledge, 1997).
Burch, Noël and Geneviève Sellier, *La Drôle de guerre des sexes du
    cinéma français 1930–1956* (Paris: Nathan Université, 1996).
Burch, Noël and Geneviève Sellier, 'Evil Women in the Post-war
    French Cinema', in Ulrike Sieglohr (ed.), *Heroines Without Heroes,
    Reconstructing Female and National Identities in European*

Cinema,1945–51 (London and New York: Cassell, 2000), pp. 47–65.

Buss, Robin, *French Film Noir* (London; New York: Marion Boyars, 1994).

Cameron, Ian (ed.), *The Movie Book of Film Noir* (London: Studio Vista, 1992).

Ehrlich, Evelyn, *Cinema of paradox: French Filmmaking under the German Occupation* (New York and Guildford: Columbia University Press, 1985).

Forbes, Jill, 'The *série noire*', in Nicholas Hewitt and Brian Rigby (eds), *France and the Mass Media* (Palgrave/Macmillan, 1991).

Forbes, Jill, *The Cinema in France after the New Wave* (London: BFI/Macmillan, 1992).

Gauteur, Claude, *D'après Simenon, Simenon & le cinéma* (Paris: Omnibus, 2001).

Gorrara, Claire, *The Roman Noir in Post-war French Culture: Dark Fictions* (Oxford: Oxford University Press, 2003).

Guérif, François, *Le Cinéma policier français* (Paris: Henri Veyrier, 1981).

Hardy, Phil (ed.), *The BFI Companion to Crime* (London: Cassell/BFI, 1997).

Iris, 21 (Spring 1996): special issue 'European Precursors of Film Noir'.

Leahy, Sarah and Susan Hayward, 'The Tainted Woman: Simone Signoret, Site of Pathology or Agent of Retribution?', in Ulrike Sieglohr (ed.), *Heroines Without Heroes, Reconstructing Female and National Identities in European Cinema, 1945–51* (London and New York: Cassell, 2000), pp. 77–91.

McArthur, Colin, *Underworld USA* (London: Secker & Warburg, 1972).

Matalon, Pierrette, Claude Guiguet and Jacques Pinturault, *Pierre Chenal* (Paris: Editions Dujarric, 1987).

Naremore, James, *More Than Night: Film Noir in its Contexts* (Berkeley, Los Angeles and London: University of California Press, 1998).

O'Brien, Charles, 'Film Noir in France: Before the Liberation', *Iris*, 21 (Spring 1996) 7–20.

Philippe, Olivier, *Le Cinéma policier français contemporain* (Paris: Editions du Cerf, 1996).

Sieglohr, Ulrike (ed.), *Heroines without Heroes, Reconstructing Female and National Identities in European Cinema, 1945–51* (London and New York: Cassell, 2000).

Vanoncini, André, *Le Roman policier* (Paris: Presses Universitaires de France, 1993).

Vincendeau, Ginette, 'France 1945–1965 and Hollywood: the *policier* as International Text', *Screen* 33:1 (Spring 1992), 50–80.

Vincendeau, Ginette, 'Noir Is also a French Word: the French Antecedents of Film Noir', in Ian Cameron (ed.), *The Movie Book of Film Noir* (London: Studio Vista, 1992, pp. 49–58.

Vincendeau, Ginette, *Pépé le Moko* (London: BFI Publishing, 1998).

Vincendeau, Ginette, *Jean-Pierre Melville, An American in Paris* (London: BFI Publishing, 2003).

3

French neo-noir to hyper-noir

Phil Powrie

On the face of it, French noir since the 1970s is very different from Hollywood 'neo-noir' with its reworking of familiar 1940s themes and careful colour recreations of expressionistic noir lighting, such as we find in *Body Heat* (1981), for example. This is mainly because the French form of noir is less the detective film than the police thriller, or *polar*, as explained in the previous chapter. And yet, different though it is from its Hollywood counterpart, the post-1968 *polar* is no less indebted to Hollywood than its post-1945 predecessor.

Given that the police thriller's function is to maintain order by defining who should be included in the dominant social formation, and who should be excluded, it is by nature a conservative genre. Thus, despite the events of May 1968, which brought about seismic changes in French society, many forms of noir carried on much as before. The influential director Claude Chabrol, discussed later, continued his dissections of the provincial bourgeoisie during the 1980s;[1] major anglophone or French crime writers carried on being adapted;[2] and Delon dominated police-procedural films as before.[3]

Despite the genre's conservatism, there were several major developments of the *polar* after May 1968, which show evolution in the genre, as well, often, as continued closeness to Hollywood, even when apparently the genre is at its most French-specific. It is on these that we will concentrate in the first part of this chapter. Few films demonstrate what might be considered the typical noir sensibility – the combination of expressionistic lighting and decor, seedy urban context, *femmes fatales*, world-weary private detective – even if many of them use one or two of these tropes. Some films do, however, make more use of these characteristics than most, while at the same time pushing towards a new noir sensibility in the late 1990s, which combines the characteristics we shall explore in the first half of this chapter as part of the changes in the French polar after 1968: the paranoia of the political thriller and the violence of the postmodern and naturalistic thriller. That new noir sensibility is different enough, and dark enough, from what preceded it, for us to call it 'hyper-noir'.

One thing which did not change a great deal until the 1990s is the genre's conservative nature where gender is concerned. As was the case with American film noir, the French thriller after 1968 continued to be preoccupied with masculinity threatened by immorality, corruption, change and *femmes fatales*; since it is clearly the most macho of genres, there are few women directors of the thriller. They do exist, however, two of the best being Elizabeth Rappeneau's *Fréquence meurtre* (*Frequent Death*, 1988), in which a psychopath harasses a radio psychoanalyst, and Nicole Garcia's *Place Vendôme* (1998), both starring Catherine Deneuve. Here too, though, the reference is often as much Hollywood as it is the French tradition. In *Place Vendôme*, which takes place in the Parisian jewellery world, as the title indicates (it is a square famed for its jewellers), there are many obvious references to *Vertigo* (1958). Deneuve plays Marianne, the alcoholic wife of a jeweller forced to pull herself together after he dies, and embroiled in a thriller focusing on illegal diamonds. A younger version of Marianne, Nathalie (Emmanuelle Seigner) – with blonde hair in the same coil as Madeleine/Judy in *Vertigo* – repeats an earlier part of Marianne's life, much like Judy is forced to become Madeleine by Scottie.[4] By the end of the 1990s, however, a film with Deneuve is much more obviously about Deneuve and her star trajectory than a development of the thriller genre, even if it does refer transparently to Hitchcock. As I have explained elsewhere, 'the exploration of the enigma of the stolen diamonds is also an exploration of (Deneuve) as enigma (the lost diamonds functioning as a metaphor for the effect of time on Deneuve's body)'.[5] In this sense, at least, the traditional focus of the thriller on the enigma of the depleted male body is refocused onto the female body. As we shall see at the end of the chapter, the issue of embodiment is a key turn in certain thrillers of the late 1990s, and is potentially much more productive in terms of film form than the changes in the genre in the aftermath of 1968.

The political thriller

The political thriller, starkly different from the stylised thrillers of Melville with which the previous chapter closed, is, oddly enough, closest to what we might consider to be the noir sensibility through its climate of suspicion and paranoia, even if its formal aspects do not correspond. It is exemplified principally by two directors: Constantin Costa-Gavras and Yves Boisset, who adapted the American and Italian political thriller to the French context.

The most important single event for French society in the second half of the twentieth century, socially, politically and culturally, is undoubtedly May 1968. As Jill Forbes points out, 'the Events of May 1968 led to a questioning of the exercise of power in society. They revealed the possibility that power structures could change and that political activity could alter human relations'.[6] Mistrust of the state and a tendency to conspiracy theory was one of the main effects of May 1968 on film culture, leading to the relatively short-lived development of what was called the 'fiction de gauche' (left-wing fiction), often starring well-known left-wing sympathisers.[7] This was the case, for example, with the films of Costa-Gavras. *Z* (1969), set in Greece, tells the story of the right-wing cover-up of the murder of a liberal politician, and stars Yves Montand and Jean-Louis Trintignant. Similarly, *L'Aveu* (*The Confession*, 1970) shows how a Czechoslovakian civil servant, again starring Yves Montand (as well as his partner and fellow left-wing sympathiser, Simone Signoret), is made to confess to treason through torture; and in *Etat de siege* (*State of Siege*, 1973) – which won the Louis Delluc Prize (established in 1937 for the Best French Film of the Year) – Montand plays an official of the US Agency for International Development who is kidnapped in Uruguay; the film purports to show the struggle between the US-supported Uruguay government and the Tupamaro guerrillas. These films, influenced by similar developments in the US and Italian cinemas,[8] combined political themes with the tropes of the action film,[9] which we could summarise by the formula 'stars and suspense'.

The first of such films to be set in France, was, like *L'Aveu*, based on a real scandal. Yves Boisset's *L'Attentat* (*Plot*, 1972), starring Trintignant, recounts the kidnapping and probable murder in 1965 of a dissident Moroccan, Ben Barka, by French policemen working for the Moroccan police chief, General Oufkir, and, like *L'Aveu*, involves scenes of torture, in this case of the Ben Barka character, here called Sadiel (played by the protagonist of Rosi's Italian conspiracy thriller *Il caso Mattei*, Gian Maria Volonté).[10]

The hero is a disaffected, washed-out supporter of Algerian independence, who is called a loser by the police and 'old and shrivelled' by his wife Edith (New Wave icon Jean Seberg), and who says to the man he will half-knowingly betray, resistance leader Sadiel/Volonté, that he has 'never known what home was'. He is caught between the liberal certainties of his wife and the radical certainties of Sadiel on the one hand; and the scheming politicians, lawyers and secret service on the other, who call on him to help them trap Sadiel in return for being let off ten years earlier. The film signals its radical credentials from the very start, with a credit sequence consisting of a long hand-held camera sequence of a left-wing demonstration ending in violence, recalling much broadcast newsreel footage of the May 1968 demonstrations. It settles into what on the surface looks a rather pedestrian thriller narrative. There are traditional villains, superbly played by a smirking Michel Bouquet as a crooked lawyer, and an oleaginous Philippe Noiret as a television producer, both on the secret service payroll. The direction is all too obvious: when the lawyer tells François that the end justifies the means, the camera frames them on either side of the Arc de Triomphe ironically placed in the background between them; when François, realising he has been set up, puts on a gun, he does so in front of a mirror, with only half of his face showing (oh dear, can we trust this two-faced man?). Jean-Michel Frodon's view of the film is negative, mainly because of the use of *polar* clichés and stars, which in his view negate any radical impact that the film might have had.[11]

But the heart of the film is a complex analysis, not so much of left-wing disillusion and retrenchment, as of the role of technology and the media. The film's credit sequence is accompanied by what looks like newsreel footage; it ends with a press conference whose dialogue revolves around the role of the press, which, it is solemnly affirmed by those who have been manipulating the media, is to 'tell the truth'. François, supported financially by the secret service, sets up a company called 'Multimedia'; 'What's this Multimedia?', his wife asks, 'It sounds like pigland'. Sadiel is caught because he wishes to engage in a 'real' political dialogue on the television programme set up by François, whose producer is in the pay of the secret service. All of this might seem fairly obvious, but the end of the film reserves a real surprise: the supposedly radical American journalist, Michael Howard (Roy Schneider), is the one who murders François, and who, it is implied, is a CIA operative working with the French secret service.

If the people who control the media cannot be trusted, what about the technology? Can it be appropriated so as to record the 'truth', as in the opening 'newsreel' sequence, and as Sadiel believes it can? The pre-credits sequence of the film consists of a discussion between what we understand to be a French and American politician, who are scrutinising secret footage of Sadiel as they plan his kidnapping. The contrast between these two uses of 'documentary' footage is clearly significant, establishing a dominant trope of the film between the public and only apparently free exterior, as opposed to the conspiratorial interior where no one can be trusted. The same issue of the untrustworthiness of recorded images is apparent with recorded voices.

François records his confession on a tape; but, much like *Diva* (1981) ten years later, the tape is switched by the secret services (ironically to a recording of Thomas de Quincey's *Confessions of an English Opium Eater*, 1822). Phoning happens frequently during the film, and we think nothing of it; but the film's most startling sequence changes this perception. Towards the end when François phones Howard to arrange the meeting which will lead to his death, there is a cut to Howard in front of a garish pop-art mural. Howard says that they should invite a German journalist because 'we want to make a lot of noise, don't we?'. We then cut to a tape-recorder which is recording the conversation. A man in a grey suit turns off the recorder, and walks along a grey-coloured room, the camera tracking backwards in front of him, and revealing row upon row of similarly grey-suited male phone-tappers, as he makes his way to a telephone to tip off the secret service. Pop-art colour and 'noise' are no match for the grey world of the secret services. The same phones and recorders which François had been using to shape some kind of truth for himself all the way through the film, lead only to conspiracy and death.

The film may be influenced by the American thriller, but there are ways in which it nevertheless remains very French. Despite its pop-art *mise-en-scène*, and its focus on technology, reminiscent of Coppola's *The Conversation* two years later, and the corruption of the media, the film, much like the *cinéma du look* in the 1980s, discussed later, which is also fascinated by technology, nevertheless gestures back to the poetic realism of the 1930s. Its hero, like the hero of *Le Jour se lève* (*Daybreak*, 1939) is called François, 'the Frenchman'; like him he is disaffected and lonely; like him, he dies at the end of the film. The riot police who disperse the demonstrators at the beginning of the film recall very clearly the riot police who disperse the crowd beneath François's window in *Le Jour se lève*. This more than fortuitous echo of the earlier film is significant, because it signals the same kind of political scepticism in the post-1968 period, as had occurred in the 1930s, with the rise of fascism, the collapse of left-wing dreams with the end of the Popular Front, and the approach of war. The same post-1936 scepticism pervades this post-68 period; it is a scepticism that complicates simplistic and self-righteous conspiracy theory. The message, written on Trintignant's face with its hang-dog expression occasionally lightened by an ironic smile, is clear: the radical euphoria of 1968 is no longer possible. François, the 'ordinary Frenchman', is doomed if he does, doomed if he doesn't, and he doesn't really know what it is he should be doing anyway. 'Action' is no longer possible; he can only observe the way in which his possibilities for action are being increasingly curtailed in a corrupt and media-saturated society. It is a scepticism shared by the second film we shall more briefly consider, Chabrol's *Nada* (*The Nada Gang*, 1974).

Less 'American' than *L'Attentat*, but in much the same vein, and adapted from a novel by the same crime writer, Manchette, *Nada* is about a group of terrorists who kidnap the American ambassador, the film revolving around the morality of extreme political action. Moments of farce alternate and sometimes combine with extreme violence. Michel Duchaussoy (who plays the philosophy teacher 'Treuffais', a transparent allusion to Truffaut/Resnais) pulls a switch-blade on a German tourist in a traffic-jam; the group's leader Diaz (Fabio Testi) wears clothes more likely to be found in one of Leone's spaghetti westerns; D'Arey (Lou Castel) kills a cop with a slingshot; and the psychopathic police chief Goemond (Michel Aumont) shoots one of the terrorists after she has given herself up, and finishes off another after he has told him that his back is broken, by flipping the man's legs. Chabrol's message is clear: as Treuffais the philosophy teacher points out in the film, 'leftist terrorism and state terrorism are the twin jaws of the same trap' (a theme which, depoliticised, resur-faces during the 1980s as the indistinguishability of cops and crimi-nals). It is unsurprising that we do not get a clear picture of what the terrorists are fighting for, and that the title of the film means 'nothing'. The film is much more about the relationships between the terrorists, who are an ill-assorted crew, and between the gang leader and the police chief, who eventually kill each other. To a far greater degree than *L'Attentat*, the political is in fact personal, the political merely serving as a vehicle, leading to narratives which are deeply flawed. As Tony McKibbin comments, *Nada* is 'almost a comedy of bad manners and instinctive frustrations. Chabrol indicates the political system isn't the cause of neurosis and unhappiness; it's just another area in which personal distaste can find an outlet'.[12]

Related to these flawed 'political' narratives are the films of the civic cinema, such as the social-problem thrillers by Boisset and others. In *Dupont Lajoie* (*Rape of Innocence*, 1975), Boisset addresses racism; the eponymous character (played by Jean Carmet) rapes and murders the pretty young daughter of his camping friends, hiding the body so that suspicion falls on immigrant workers who live nearby; a white lynch-mob beats one of the immigrants to death. Although criticised by many for its spectacularisation of a political problem, as Will Higbee points out, the film encourages the middle-of-the-road audi-ence, which it was made for, to question their own reactions; it 'aims to "hook" white middle-class spectators through identification with

Lajoie, causing them to question how they would respond in the same situation'.[13] Boisset's subsequent *Le Juge Fayard dit le 'Shérif' (Judge Fayard Called the Sheriff*, 1976) won the Louis Delluc Prize for its investigation of corruption in high places; a local prosecutor is assassinated when he uncovers the links between the rich and powerful and the underworld.

It is not just the man –in –the street or the local *notable* who is taken to task in these films, however. A far more frequent trope is the critique of the police. Boisset's *Un condé (Blood on My Hands*, 1970) deals with a rogue policeman who goes outside the law to avenge his colleague. Likewise, in *Max et les ferrailleurs (Max and the Junkmen*, 1971), starring the left-wing actor Michel Piccoli, a frustrated cop sets up a robbery so as to catch the criminals who have eluded him for so long. In *Deux hommes dans la ville (Two Against the Law*, 1973), a robber recently released from prison (Alain Delon) is harassed by a cop from his past (Jean Gabin). And in *Dernier domicile connu (Last Known Address*, 1970), well-intentioned policemen cannot prevent the murder of an informer whom they have brought out of anonymity. These films all have in common the theme of the individual caught in a trap set by corrupt or failing institutions, whether these are the state at the national level, or the police, judiciary, and other *notables* at the regional or local levels. *Police Python 357 (The Case Against Ferro*, 1976) is characteristic of this trend. Like the overtly political films of Costa-Gavras, it stars Montand as Marc Ferrot, charged with investigating the murder of his mistress. It turns out that she was also the mistress of his police chief; the police chief is the murderer, and he shifts the blame onto Ferrot, whose investigation, in Kafkaesque fashion, leads to his own death. The helpless individual, corrupt institutions, conspiracy and paranoia come together in this police thriller.

Unsurprisingly, given that police thrillers tended to give a very negative impression of politicians and police, attempts to censor them frequently occurred, often with high-profile media coverage. *Un condé*, for example, was banned for six months and some twelve minutes were cut.[14] The making of *L'Attentat* was fraught with obstacles: its *avance sur recettes* (the loan given to filmmakers) was retracted on the flimsiest of pretexts; authorisation for location shoots were systematically refused for the pettiest of reasons; and there was police harassment on set.[15] Such censorship only served to confirm the conspiracy theorists' views, as well as, paradoxically, to give publicity to the films concerned and their criticisms of a corrupt police, a corrupt judiciary and a repressive state.

The American turn

French commentators considered that the *polar* was in a period of renewal in the 1980s, caused in part by the decline of a readily identifiable auteur cinema, and in part to the eclipse of 1970s oppositional cinema: 'The wave of French *polars* is due to the chronic absence of subjects in the traditional fictions, as if the *polar* had inherited from the bereavement of left-wing fiction'.[16] There were the usual police procedural narratives, increasingly familiar on the small screen (*L'Inspecteur Moulin* starring Yves Rénier started in 1976), as well as on the big screen (*Garde à vue* (*Under Suspicion*), 1981), and revenge thrillers (*Parole de flic* (*Cop's Honor*), 1985, starring and part-scripted by Delon). There were some key developments in the 1980s, however.[17]

In the 1980s, the cop not only became even more indistinguishable from the criminals, as had begun to occur during the 1970s, but he also turned from the old-style French policeman to become an American-style cop. Although *Police Python 357* was in many ways American, the '357' of the title referring to the calibre of the Magnum, as Forbes reminds us, nevertheless Ferrot 'is characteristically French in the Simenon or Clouzot manner in such details as his passion for crosswords, his bachelor life, the disposition of his office and the conduct of his love affair'.[18] This is much less the case in the 1980s, however; cop types were evolving. Tesson considers that the new type of *polar* 'has turned the crime squad into a band of trendy young private detectives, both outside the police by their "look" and inside by their functions'.[19] This is clear in the immensely successful *La Balance* (*The Nark*, 1982) set in the Parisian underworld and starring Nathalie Baye as a prostitute, and with Philippe Léotard. The eighth most popular French film of 1982, it was directed by an American, and won a César (the French Oscar) for best film. Tesson's comments refer to the team of police headed by Palouzi/Richard Berry. The bad guy is played by Maurice Ronet, veteran of the New Wave and 1960s thrillers such as *L'Ascenseur pour l'échafaud* (*Lift to the Scaffold*, 1958), *Plein Soleil* (*Purple Noon*, 1960), *Le Meurtrier* (*Enough Rope*, 1963), *La Piscine* (*The Sinners*, 1968). Although his career took a downturn in the 1970s, he nevertheless acted in a typical conspiracy thriller as described in the previous section, alongside Alain Delon, *Mort d'un pourri* (*Death of a Corrupt Man*, 1977). Casting Ronet as the villain in *La Balance* who gets his comeuppance (he is shot in the mouth by his rival Dédé/Léotard in a particularly bloody scene set in outside toilets), was thus arguably a significant gesture signalling the death of the old-style thriller, and heralding the new Americanised thriller. Dédé is caught, similarly suggesting the end of the lone 1970s hero; Léotard was a familiar face of 1970s cinema, with small parts in thrillers by Sautet and Boisset among others.

If commentators in the 1980s were concerned about the 'American turn' taken by the *polar*, it is partly because of the precarious situation of French cinema in relation to American cinema more generally during the 1980s, with French audiences steadily abandoning French films for American films; in the 1986–87 season there were more French spectators going to see American films than the national product for the first time since the end of the Second World War. In the specific case of the thriller, at the beginning of the 1970s, 50 per cent of those distributed were French, but by the end of the 1980s this had dropped to 20 per cent to 30 per cent, with American thrillers climbing up to claim 60 per cent of the French market.[20] Small wonder then that the trendy Americanised cops of *La Balance* in a fast-paced narrative replete with the kind of car chase familiar to spectators of American thrillers, such as *The French Connection* (1971), gave rise to concern.

The postmodern thriller

The second key development in the 1980s was the 'postmodern' thriller of the *cinéma du look*, made by Jean-Jacques Beineix, Luc Besson and Léos Carax. Less interested in issues of politics and morality than in style, these films, with their frequently ostentatious quirkiness, increasingly resemble *Blade Runner* (1981) and *Blue Velvet* (1986) more than they do the 'typical' French *polar*. Many of the *look* directors' films are thrillers, starting with *Diva*, labelled the first French postmodern film by Fredric Jameson because of its fascination with technology and its attachment to style – as the name *cinéma du look* might suggest – at the expense of a 'message'.[21] Like *L'Attentat*, however, the thrillers of the *cinéma du look* are only superficially American. They are not just French in flavour, but also dark in tone, if not in narrative. This is not just because their characters are gangsters, prostitutes or low-lifes, set in appropriate urban locations, but because the lighting is often low-key, and the combination of camerawork and soundtrack provocatively oneiric; that oneirism foreshadows late 1990s hyper-noir.

Diva is one of the few films of the *cinéma du look* which has led to very extensive academic enquiry, ranging across a variety of theoretical paradigms (ideological in the case of Jameson, but also feminist and psychoanalytical), suggesting its primacy as one of the key films of the 1980s. Two features of the film are worth stressing. First, it is a playful *polar* in that it comprises two strands, one the seedy low-culture noir strand of corrupt cops, murder, prostitution, drugs; the other the high-culture world of the opera. These strands criss-cross and intertwine throughout the film, emblematised by constant doublings and splittings (there are two tapes, two Taiwanese business-men, two thugs, two cars, and so on). The film's playfulness might lead us to assume that there is no critical weight to it; that it is, to reprise Jameson's characterisation of postmodern style, merely depthless pastiche;[22] that unlike the normal noir, which implicitly or explicitly deals with what is right and what is wrong (albeit in a doom-laden context which suggests that deciding between right and wrong is impossible), *Diva* makes no attempt to engage with such issues; rather it displays them as surface effects.

However, and this is the second feature, as Will Higbee has pointed out,[23] the film does engage with what we have seen is a key issue of the 1970s civic cinema, and which was to assume increasing impor-tance in the 1980s as riots in the major cities showed cracks in Republicanism's facile and colour-blind assumptions about what was meant by being 'French': race. One of the more extraordinary aspects of the film is that the focal figure is American, black, an opera singer, and that all the other main characters meet each other, but the diva stays isolated while still being the focal figure around whom all the others revolve. The film thereby manages to key into the issue of race by placing blackness at the heart of this particular noir; while at the same time it keeps that blackness separate from the grubby white busi-ness going on elsewhere (the white cops with their prostitution ring); and, finally, it manages to give blackness a voice, indeed an overpow-eringly emotional voice as the diva sings Catalani's *La Wally*, while at the same time making her 'other' (an American who speaks English when we first see her talking to Jules), and also making the focus of the narrative the fact that her voice is not her own, because the little Frenchman, Jules, has stolen it. The diva may be a goddess, as that appellation suggests; but she is the focus of the film, without really being the focus; she has a voice, without really having a voice; she is black, but dressed in white, singing white men's songs in a white man's noir. The paradoxes, like the film's narrative, multiply as if noir had lost its way, pointing this way and that, lost in the labyrinths of its own making.

Despite the American woman at the heart of the film, and its similarities to American postmodern thrillers, *Diva*, unlike *La Balance*, whose visual style is more that of the American action film (location shooting, chase films, high key lighting), shares with the other films of the *cinéma du look* a quintessential Frenchness. This is partly because of its high-cultural quirkiness, as well as through its main characters: a typical thriller police chief; an emphasis on familiar Parisian landmarks; Jules as a representative of 'traditional French left populism', as Jameson points out.[24] But it is also because, like *L'Attentat* a decade earlier, there are intertextual echoes, as Naomi Greene has shown, of 1930s poetic realism in *Diva* and in *La Lune dans le caniveau* (*The Moon in the Gutter*, 1983).[25]

The other thrillers of the *look* are similarly ambiguous. Beineix's *La Lune dans le caniveau*, although based on a novel by the American writer David Goodis, makes no attempt to locate its characters in a believable environment, American or French. It is set in a port which could be anywhere, the props (drinks, cigarette packets, and so on) especially designed for the film to give a sense of dislocation; and the *mise-en-scène* is to some extent at odds with the seediness of Goodis's novel. Beineix's purpose is to create a dream atmosphere suffused with the stuff of paranoia and nightmares, a preoccupation of the French surrealists. Besson's *Subway* (1985) takes place, despite its American title, in the Parisian metro system, its set designed by the veteran 1930s designer, Alexandre Trauner, designer of *Le Jour se lève*.

Retrospectively, then, the Americanisation of the French thriller during the 1950s and 1960s (with Melville the prime example), can be seen as a tangent, reflecting the French obsession with all things American in the immediate post-war period, symbolised by the limo and jazz in the thrillers of the time. The thrillers of the 1970s and the 1980s, despite the 'American turn' identified above, return us to the French cinema of the 1930s, either by their scepticism where political commitment is concerned (the 1970s), or by their nostalgic attachment to what has been called the golden age of French cinema (the 1980s).

The naturalistic thriller

By the 1990s, the *look* films had evolved into the ultra-violence which was to be associated with Tarantino's films in the USA, where 'style' means excessive and stylised violence above all else. *Nikita* (Besson, 1990), and *Dobermann* (Jan Kounen, 1997) are films where spectacular violence is more important than the probing of society and issues of law and order familiar to most police or thriller genres. Even Bertrand Tavernier experimented with the amoral youth genre in his

L'Appât (*The Bait*, 1995), where a young woman, Nathalie/Marie Gillain, and her two accomplices plan to lure businessmen to their flat and kill them in cold blood for money to go to the USA. It was a film made all the more gruesome by its documentary style and the fact that it was based on a true story.

Much like the comedy thriller counterbalances the paranoid political thriller in the 1970s, so too the ultra-violence of the youth-oriented thriller is counterbalanced by a fixation on the humdrum and the everyday, the very opposite of spectacular violence. Philippe remarks how television crime thrillers in France in the 1990s changed.[26] Whereas the focus had previously been on the resolution of the mystery, the focus now became, as in soap operas, day-to-day life, and more particularly the relationship between the *patron* (the chief) and his *mulets* (literally the 'mules', meaning his team). This is the case of the long-running and successful *Navarro*, starring Roger Hanin (François Mitterrand's brother-in-law), who had appeared in many (second-rate) thrillers since the late 1950s, as well as directing some; the series was directed by Gilles Béhat, who had also directed several episodes of the 1970s series already mentioned, *Commissaire Moulin*. As Philippe points out, whereas TV thrillers tended to imitate film thrillers, the reverse occurred during the 1990s. This is very much the case with Tavernier's documentary-style *L.627* (1992), with relative unknowns in a story that concentrates more on the tedium and frustration of a cop's daily life. This film raises an issue which has rumbled beneath the surface in many of the films we have mentioned: that of racism.

In *L.627*, as in many post-1968 *polars* – such as *La Balance* and *Police* among those already mentioned – the criminals are *beurs* (second-generation immigrants), and are usually uncritically linked to the dope scene (*Dupont Lajoie* is a particularly honourable exception in that its message is specifically anti-racist). This has led to debates in France about the validity of such representations. As Philippe argues, the omnipresence of such representations across so many films has a cumulative effect where it becomes impossible to dissociate blackness and criminality. This is exacerbated, Philippe suggests, by the fact that the petty criminals are habitually undeveloped as characters, so that their defining characteristic becomes the colour of their skin; add to this that the criminals are often seen in a street context mingling with other non-white walk-on characters, and the spectator can be led to assume that 'criminality is everywhere and is gradually invading the city'.[27]

In an increasingly atomised and amoral society, it is hardly surprising that audiences should be attracted to the televisual day-in-the-life genre, since watching it replaces the need to be part of society, while giving the impression that social problems are under control (because neatly packaged as a recognisable story). This process is underlined by the police thriller genre: like the contemporary spectator, the cop is part of society, but he is also distanced from it; he watches over it (just like the spectator watches it), he attempts to regulate it, disabused and sceptical that the rule of law can ever be implemented. Claude Zidi, in interview with Philippe, suggests that the turn away from thrillers which aim to resolve mysteries has to do with this scepticism: 'There are not many films where the guilty man is pursued to the bitter end ... It is as though people are not really concerned about arresting the guilty man. ... People don't believe in the immanence of justice, in divine justice'.[28]

Arguably, then, it is only in films where that sense of distance is broken down through fantasy, oneirism, voyeurism, excess, that the noir sensibility and the disquiet it engenders, the sense of threat, can be reintroduced into the experience of the spectator. In such cases, the film is no longer a symptom of social unease for the self-satisfied armchair moralist ('look at those drug-dealers; thank God I don't live in that part of town!'), but a dark trap where brooding fantasies unsettle the spectator. It is useful to recall that the word crime is etymologically linked to the word crisis: in the crime thriller, the spectator is potentially incriminated by being placed in a moment of crisis where the normal rules do not apply; hence the peculiar emptiness, but also the neutralising attraction of the naturalist thriller or the soap-opera crime series with their emphasis on the everyday, as if the ritualised and anarchic apocalypse of the criminal event could somehow be contained within quotidian exchange, and the temporality of the banal. The object of the typical thriller is, mundanely but paradoxically, to fantasise that chaos can be orderly. The best noir destroys that utopian fantasy and replaces it with dystopia. It is to some of these darker films that we now turn in the final part of this chapter to show that the noir sensibility is, despite the blandness of many French *polars*, still a feature of French cinema, and still capable of unsettling audiences.

The blackest of noir

The films we are about to explore all have in common marginal characters, which we might argue is a feature of the *polar* more generally; but they also have a sense of tragic noir inevitability, which is not

always the case with the *polar*, their doomed, deranged or obsessive
characters caught in a trap often of their own making, their obsession
born of something other than the detective's quest for truth. These
dark films occur as much in the 1970s and 1980s as they do in the
1990s.

It is perhaps appropriate to start with Corneau's *Série noire* (1979),
given that its title is that of the thriller novel series which defined the
post-war *polar*. It is based on another hard-boiled American novel,
Jim Thompson's *A Hell of a Woman*, published in that series in 1967.
Thompson's Kentucky is transposed to dismal, nondescript Parisian
suburbs, and muddy wasteland swept by rain and snow. Patrick
Dewaere plays a door-to-door salesman, Frank Poupard, with the gift
of the gab; but he is a loser who cannot make sales and whose wife has
left him. He falls in with an almost mute teenager (Marie Trintignant)
who pushes him to murder her aunt for her money. As his fantasies of
escape and the prospect of the good life gather pace, so too does his
sense of estrangement and alienation from those around him. He
murders his best friend and his wife, but his boss, who suspects him,
blackmails him for the stolen money, and he is left with nothing for his
pains at the end of the film. This brief synopsis cannot do justice to the
most startling aspect of the film: Dewaere's 'Method' performance as
a man slowly and unconsciously becoming a schizophrenic murderer,
coupled with the Georges Pérec script and its fantasmagoric mixture
of 'backslang (*le verlan*) and streetslang, combined with Anglicisms
and spoonerisms'.[29] Dewaere, who committed suicide in 1982,
confided in interview that 'the film marked me. I was never the same
again. It did something psychological in my head'.[30] As Forbes
explains, the film's social context is 'the world of violence, alienation
and racism produced by the rapid modernisation of the 1960s ... The
sense of community and belonging ... is exploded'.[31] The film
contains many features which will recur, exacerbated, in films of the
1980s and 1990s: the dysfunctional hero, the enigmatic and deranged
femme fatale, escalating violence, set in seedy urban streets where
community is a thing of the past.

We find the same combination of fantasy world and alienation in
Poussière d'ange (*Angel Dust*, 1987), where the Dewaere figure is
replaced by a world-weary cop Simon Blount/Bernard Giraudeau with
a drink problem who is fascinated by two women: his wife who has
left him, and a dreamy-eyed young woman who lives in a fantasy-
world. He witnesses the murder of his wife's lover while spying on her
and in the course of the investigation discovers that his wife's lover is
linked to his superior, and that the young woman is not only his supe-

rior's daughter, but has embarked on a carefully organised plan of revenge for her prostitute mother's death for which his wife's lover and his superior are partly responsible. In one of the more fantastical sequences, the young woman plays out an elaborate fantasy, setting up a dinner party with actors to persuade the cop that she has a family. With its world-weary detective, replete with raincoat and voice-over, with its *femme fatale* and dark *mise-en-scène* (night scenes, rain, empty streets), *Poussière d'ange* is arguably much closer to film noir than *Série noire*. As Austin points out, however, the moody tone of the film changes towards the end, turning more into a combination of action film and violent youth thriller: the crooked lawyer of the murdered man (New Wave veteran Gérard Blain) has his throat gruesomely slit by the daughter's young accomplice, who is killed as he drives off in a car.[32]

Alienation and obsessive fantasy recur in *Monsieur Hire* where the eponymous hero is a scapegoat for more general social problems. Hire (Michel Blanc) is a lonely voyeur feared by the community for his otherness. *Vertigo*-like, he spies on a young woman, Alice (Sandrine Bonnaire), and as a result knows that Alice's boyfriend has committed a murder for which he himself is suspected by an equally lonely cop. Hire puts pressure on Alice to escape with him, but she betrays him, and he falls to his death, watched by the assembled community, although not before having left evidence which will incriminate Alice's boyfriend and Alice for being an accessory. Most of Leconte's films since the early 1970s comedies have lonely men as their heroes, captivated by enigmatic women, but this film unusually also has all the hallmarks of noir, as Jean Duffy points out: 'the hard-boiled detective and the *femme fatale*; the bleak urban exterior and the claustrophobic interior; chiaroscuro lighting, and the use of confining and visually marginalising camerawork'.[33] The film, however, is not a stylistic exercise like those of Pialat and Godard mentioned above. Its purpose is rather, as Duffy points out, to investigate 'the fragility of the distinctions between deviant voyeurism, "legitimate" surveillance and persecution and ... the violence, alienation and confinement that lie at the heart of contemporary society'.[34]

In that respect, the several sequences which focus on community activities and watching are key to an understanding of the film. Hire is watched by a community not just when he falls to his death, but when he is forced by the detective to re-enact his movements on the night of Pierrette's murder, and is tripped up by a malevolent bystander, and also when he falls in the icerink where he has gone to spy on Alice. This trope of watching, being watched and falling –

surveillance inevitably leading to death – is problematised by another sequence where Hire, at the bowling alley, is this time the positive centre of attention. As the skilled habitué, he is admired by the assembled group; instead of falling or being knocked over as people watch him, he knocks over the skittles blindfolded. The contradiction between being the despised voyeuristic outsider coupled with the admired exhibitionist insider is something he points out to the detective who has watched him perform. But it is precisely this contradiction (among other features of the film, such as Hire's sensuality, or the pathos generated by the combination of Brahms and Michael Nyman for the score),[35] which attracts us to him as a character – he is not all bad – and thus allows us to identify with him. We are (insidiously) much more like Hire than we are like the schizophrenic Poupard (Dewaere) or the crumpled Blount (Giraudeau).

It is particularly interesting to note that *Monsieur Hire* is a remake of a film noir made in the wake of the Second World War, *Panique* (1947), a film criticised for its bleak view of society, but which was clearly alluding to issues of collaboration and persecution during and immediately after the war. By choosing to remake this film, Leconte is suggesting that the same climate of suspicion and alienation is rife in contemporary France, where communities define themselves by creating outsiders. Oddly, though, the real and most pressing contemporary social issue of immigrant communities in the major French cities, an issue which had had considerable media coverage after riots in Lyon in the early 1980s, is sidestepped and displaced, as though it is too difficult an issue to probe; the outsider is not the immigrant or a group of immigrants, as in *Dupont Lajoie*, but a white male with Jewish origins, cast as a harmless but disquieting voyeur. That sense of disquiet is not created in *Panique*, which, although based on a Simenon novel, is, like so many of the thrillers we have mentioned, not really a film noir in its *mise-en-scène* or cinematography; there are no empty streets or sequences with expressionist chiaroscuro lighting. In *Monsieur Hire*, however, disquiet is constantly striven for. This begins with the casting: Michel Blanc is a comic actor, creating an uneasy undercurrent in what is a serious exploration of social issues. Then there are unsettling scenes; we first see Hire in a curious exterior scene: he is returning from work – as Duffy points out, there are many scenes which stress the banal and the everyday which have no plot function – and stops to put his hand on a little girl's head as he helps her to count so as to stop her hiccoughs, before walking on. The scene is shot through a blue filter, the camera jumps across the 180–degree line, and the shots are cross-edited in relation to the dialogue, giving an unsettling feeling exacerbated by little Marie's stare as Hire walks off. In the sequence at the boxing match, Hire follows Alice and Emile into the changing rooms as Emile tries to escape; he is, ghost-like, shot with stark key over-lighting, resembling the vampire in *Nosferatu, eine Symphonie des Grauens* (*Nosferatu*, 1922). In *Panique*, we are given a strong sense of community at the beginning of the film: the town square, the local shops with people gossiping; in this community Hire is an oddball rather than an outsider; even the murderer is a respected member of the community who holds forth in the café. In *Monsieur Hire*, as the title suggests (no longer social panic generated in a community by the murder, but the exploration of the outsider's place in the community), we do not see the community at the start of the film: all the characters seem to be outsiders or oddballs, starting with the detective who takes photos of the dead woman voyeuristically for his personal use.

Monsieur Hire strives to show how evil can arise out of the banality of alienated everyday, humdrum lives. Whereas we might have associated that evil with the disquieting voyeur, we discover that the monster is not Hire at all, but society which wishes to make of him a scapegoat for the evil in its midst, and which it too readily attributes to difference (the lonely Jewish voyeur) than to the same (Emile, an iconic name recalling Rousseau's 'educated' Frenchman).

Série noire, *Poussière d'ange* and *Monsieur Hire* are all fairly conventional thrillers, anchored firmly in the French neo-noir tradition, even though they may be exceptional in other ways. The next two films go much further than this, and, arguably, create a new type of noir language, much more disruptive and disquieting, precisely because the body is more obviously at issue in (porno)graphic sex and murder scenes; this could be called *hyper-noir* because it plunges us into excessive embodiment via the abject and the repulsive. The films form part of what we could call the cinema of the abject, which is not confined to thrillers. A critic writing in *Le Monde Diplomatique* complained about this tendency in recent French cinema, criticising the combination the 'fascination for the abject and the sordid', referring to *L'Humanité* (*Humanity*, 1999), *Seul contre tous* (*I Stand Alone*, 1998), *Sombre* (1998) and *Romance* (1999) among others.[36] Since then, a number of other films in this vein have appeared, suggesting that the tendency is a major development in French cinema more generally. The two thrillers we shall explore here are *Sombre* (1998) and *Baise-moi* (*Kiss Me*, 2000).

Sombre is narratively a serial killer film: an itinerant puppeteer seeks out prostitutes and kills them. He meets Claire, a virgin, and his love for her 'redeems' him; she, also in love with him, apparently forgives his attempted murder of her flirtatious sister. As this *Beauty and the Beast* sketch might suggest, the film is more a fairytale, whose concern is to make the spectator experience the kind of primal fear associated with childhood. In that sense, the film is etymologically rather than generically a thriller: it aims to 'thrill' with a combination of excitement, awe and fear, just like the children in the second sequence of the film who are screaming as the puppeteer performs for them. Grandrieux achieves this by formal experimentation.

There is only one (magnificent) sequence less than two minutes long which could be associated with experimental films, as Jean drives the two sisters away from the family gathering. The countryside outside the car becomes progressively blurred as close-ups of undergrowth form *art brut* patterns that eventually segue into a close-up shot of Claire's sister's hair ruffled by the wind. But camerawork is nonetheless disorientating. The camera is not only mostly handheld, but it rarely shoots Jean frontally; there are insistent shots of the back of his neck, or the back of his victims' neck, or of him standing with his back to us staring at lakes or distant horizons, so that his face, when it is occasionally seen, strikes us all the more forcefully by its combination of the normal (Claire's sister comments on how good-looking he is), and the frightening, as the key lighting picks out its sallow gauntness, and the impenetrable grey-blue eyes. The film is quite literally dark, as many sequences occur at night, and daytime sequences (with one important exception, the lake sequence where Jean tries to kill Claire's sister and Claire 'tames' him by shouting at him to get back as if he were a dog or a big cat) are drained of sunlight, as if occurring at an abstract moment of the day, neither night nor day, but not twilight either. Even more important than the use of light is the use of sound; it is no coincidence that Grandrieux talks about the David Lynch of *Eraserhead* (1977) or *Lost Highway* (1997) as a key influence.[37] There is little dialogue; much of the soundtrack is composed of the grunts and sighs of both killer and victims, interspersed with a wind-like hum, apparently the sound of the car's interior as Jean travels around the countryside, but sometimes disorientatingly serving as background for moments when he is outside of the car.

The purpose of such formal experimentation is to return the spectator to something approximating the pre-Oedipal and the pre-linguistic; as Grandrieux points out, 'sound and image are the basis of cinema, and sight and hearing are the first two pulsions which constitute us'.[38] His aim is to create in the spectator the hypnagogic state between sleep and awakening, where, as he puts it using Deleuzian terminology, 'flows can cross through the spectator directly'.[39] *Sombre*, then, attempts to thrill the spectator by embodying affect directly; but it also poses moral issues of how we can reconcile the intensity of individual affect with social insertion. Grandrieux commented that Jean is intentionally far removed from reality and from socialisation, that he is a man who has 'no access to the other, no access to otherness, a man completely absorbed in repetition, in the obsession with the "same"'.[40] A different type of engagement with embodiment, although no less terrifying, can be found in *Baise-moi*.

Baise-moi achieved instant notoriety with its combination of gore and unfaked penetrative sex. Based on Despentes's novel of the same name, which she adapted for the screen with the help of porn actress Trinh Thi – the two leads (Manu/Raffaëla Anderson, Nadine/Karen Bach) also being porn actresses – it was shot on a small budget in grainy digital video. A punk or grunge version of *Thelma and Louise* (1991) – although crucially there is no Keitel-like sympathetic cop, because the focus is entirely on violent fantasy disconnected from any notion of measured response – *Baise-moi* tells the story of two women, one who is raped and the other whose friend has been shot dead. They meet by chance and go on a killing spree, indiscriminately slaughtering men, women and family. This culminates in a massacre at a sex club, the last survivor being forced to get on all fours before being shot

2 Karen Bach *in Baise-moi* (*Kiss Me*, Coralie Trinh Thi and Virginie Despentes, 2000).

in close-up through the rectum, his brains splattering over the walls. Manu is later shot, and Nadine is trying to drown herself in a forest lake just as the police arrest her. Various right-wing groups complained when it was released, as a result of which the government banned the film (the first time this had happened since 1973), leading to a media furore over censorship; the government rapidly reintroduced the 18 certificate for the film which meant that it was more or less relegated to porn movie theatres. Less censoriously, many saw the film as mere provocation, such as the critic of the communist daily *L'Humanité*, who complained that there was no character psychology and that the excessively visible violence left too little to the imagination; for him it merely exemplified 'the spirit of the times with their loss of values and points of reference'.[41]

Many women reviewers, on the other hand, were considerably more positive; Linda Ruth Williams considered it 'rather fun and refreshingly innocent',[42] a view echoed by Ginette Vincendeau, who pointed out that unlike many auteur films, including those by women, where sex is 'grim and joyless', in this film 'the women actually enjoy sex ... It's about girls having fun with sex and being able to laugh about it'.[43] And both reviewers make the point emphasised by many supporters of the film, that despite the fun and the humour (at one point Manu says 'Fuck, we don't even have a sense of the genre, we don't say the good lines at the right moment'), there is an underlying seriousness in that the film can be read as a response, albeit 'excessive', to male violence. As Carrie Tarr and Brigitte Rollet point out, the film 'is driven by a notion of sexual difference as unavoidable and grotesque, where the only answer to women's victimisation by men is to make men the victims'.[44] Despentes saw her film as a feminist statement, and provocatively argued that unfaked and violent penetrative sex amounted to a reappropriation by women of the normally fetishised and fragmented female body:

> To film the sex scenes 'for real', without stand-ins, was vital ... Time to finish with fragmentation. These scenes had to be real, to do that. Time to return their complete bodies to women, of which they have always been deprived ... To reclaim women's rights over their true sexuality, to seize it back from the male gaze.[45]

It is the emphasis on the body and on pleasure which makes this film a key film, more important in many ways than Grandrieux's formal exercise. First, this film, as Brenez points out, does not pathologise the women's actions.[46] They may be bad, but they are not mad. Second, their rules of engagement are sensational, in two senses of the word:

they are excessive, beyond the law, but they are so because they are entirely focused on sensation; as Despentes said of them, 'They are outlaws. No excuses, no explanations, no intellectualisation. They are close to us, because they are beyond judgement. Sensation, not thought'.[47] Third, the commitment to sensation is made less immoral (although certainly amoral – 'unsettlingly serene nihilism' as one writer puts it)[48] by the revaluation of pleasure, and most particularly female pleasure. This is the justification for the massacre in the sex club, since these pleasure-seekers might have seemed to be allies rather than enemies; but as Brenez points out, the men in the sex club are clients involved in a consumer exchange, while the lesson of the film is that *real* pleasure cannot be bought, indeed it may not exist at all (which is not a reason for abandoning the search for it):

> What is unbearable is the conversion of pleasure into a supreme capitalistic argument. We still don't know very clearly what to set against this except anger and destruction, insofar as the individual conditions of access to pleasure – so perilous in themselves (cf. *Sombre*) – can definitely not become solutions, or values, or even contradictory forces, for fear of distorting immediately their wild, socially irretrievable and anti-economical aspects.[49]

Despentes commented that 'We had to get to the heart of things, to places normally avoided. We wanted to dig deep, in order to end up right inside'.[50] That 'inside' can arguably be construed as *the inside of the body*. The film attempts to go beyond the spectacular, the surface of the body, the fetishised exterior, to begin to glimpse the possibilities of a transcendent and transparent embodiment, one where the outside, the exterior, is no longer separated from the interior, where the body is as much pure exteriority as interiority. For that to happen, old binaries must be dismantled. First, the male must not simply be role-reversed – as when one of the women's victims complains limply about their refusal of a condom – but he must be turned inside out: hence the shooting of the libertine through the anus, his insides being *shot through* quite literally so that the inside becomes the outside.[51] Second, there is the issue of community, predicated on the giving over of part of one's privacy; such a distinction disappears as private becomes public, and public (other people) become private (part of the women's fantasies). As Manu comments after being raped: 'I've left nothing precious in my pussy'.

Baise-moi is the logical development of various thriller strands; it is its inevitability which makes it stand out: the anomic outsider (Poupard, Hire), the problematisation of community, the foreground-

ing of exclusion at both the level of race (both women are *beurs*) and
gender (both are women), the matter-of-fact violence so different from
the spectacular and stylised violence of Besson's *Nikita* a decade
earlier (one of several films explicitly referred to in *Baise-moi*), the
implicit irony in the film's offhand references to American cinema, and
yet the refusal to intellectualise the kinds of social issues mentioned
here. In the more traditional thriller, the dead or threatened (female)
body is always at the heart of noir – opaque, enigmatic and therefore
threatening – but as a lure, since the thriller is really more interested
in the male. Its function is arguably to (ab)use that female body so as
to reconfigure a less lonely place/space for the failing male, who can
culpabilise the female and her body as part of the deal to renegotiate
his position in relation to the community and the rules which govern
that relationship: where are the limits? How far can I go? Is there an
'I' outside of community? In *Baise-moi*, the female refuses to serve as
the bracketed section of a male-driven equation. *Baise-moi* turns the
tables on genre and gender, taking neo-noir to a feminised hyper-space
where the narrative matters less than a new kind of energy: the black
hole of hyper-noir.

It is perhaps no coincidence that *Sombre* and *Baise-moi* are both
road movies as well as thrillers, suggesting – a regressive weakness we
might argue – that a combination of escape and amoral fantasy is the
only way to retrace innocence beyond the violence of the state or the
community, the only way to return to a body wrested of its moral and
social diseases. The fear of community as a repressive force takes us
back to where we started, with the paranoia of the political thriller.
Now, however, it is not only the state which is to be feared for its
corruption, but society as a whole. The logic of these last two films is,
paradoxically, that they are fairy tales, if very adult and knowing fairy
tales, to conjure the terror of adulthood. Innocence (but not necessarily freedom from guilt) can only be found far away in the stillness of a
forest, by a lake; the city is too full of prying eyes, dark streets with
dead ends, the messiness of sexuality, motion masquerading as
emotion, effect as affect. Like all black holes, matter collapses into
itself, indifferently, in violent, epiphanic stillness.[52]

Notes

1   *Poulet au vinaigre* (*Cop au Vin*, 1985), *Inspecteur Lavardin* (1986),
    Masques (*Masks*, 1987).
2   Simenon in *L'Horloger de Saint-Paul* (*The Watchmaker of St Paul*,
    Tavernier, 1973), *Les Fantômes du chapelier* (*The Hatter's Ghost*,

Chabrol, 1982), *Monsieur Hire* (Leconte, 1989); Thompson in *Coup de torchon* (*Clean Slate*, Tavernier, 1981) and *Série noire* (Corneau, 1979). Chabrol used Isabelle Huppert's distanced acting style to suggest enigma in the Ruth Rendell-based *La Cérémonie* (*A Judgement in Stone*, 1995), and *Merci pour le chocolat* (*Nightcap*, 2000), based on a novel by American crime writer Charlotte Armstrong.

3   *Un flic* (*Dirty Money*, Melville, 1972), *Flic story* (*Cop Story*, Deray, 1975); Delon directed his own *Pour la peau d'un flic* (*For a Cop's Hide*) in 1981.

4   For an extensive investigation of the links between the two films, see T. Jefferson Kline, 'Recuperating Hitchcock's Doubles: Experiencing *Vertigo* in Garcia's *Place Vendôme*', *Studies in French Cinema* 3:1 (2003), 35–46.

5   P. Powrie, 'Transtitial Woman: New Representations of Women in Contemporary French Cinema', *Esprit Créateur*, 52:3 (2002), 85.

6   J. Forbes, *The Cinema in France After the New Wave* (London: BFI/Macmillan, 1992), p. 16.

7   There was a parallel development in crime novels, labelled the *neo-polar*, whose principal exponents were Jean Amila, Francis Ryck, and, acknowledged leader in this field, Jean-Patrick Manchette.

8   For example, the conspiracy thrillers of Francesco Rosi, beginning in 1972 with *Il caso Mattei* (*The Mattei Affair*).

9   See R. Prédal, *Le Cinéma français depuis 1945* (Paris: Nathan, 1991), p. 265.

10 Manchette had published a novel based on the same event in 1971, *L'Affaire N'Gustro* in Gallimard's *Série Noire*, a series started in 1947 and which published French and American thrillers in the hard-boiled American style, many of which were subsequently adapted for the screen.

11 Jean-Michel Frodon, *L'Age moderne du cinéma français: de la Nouvelle Vague à nos jours* (Paris: Flammarion, 1995), pp. 255–6.

12 T. McKibbin, 'Slow Burn Suspense: the Films of Claude Chabrol', *Images* 9 (17 April 2001), www.imagesjournal.com/issue09 /features/chabrol/ (accessed 27 January 2004).

13 W. Higbee, 'Yves Boisset's *Dupont Lajoie* (1974): Racism, Civic Cinema and the "Immigrant Question"', *Studies in French Cinema* 2:3 (2002), 155.

14 Y. Boisset, 'Yves Boisset: Le cinéaste le plus censuré de France' (interview with Gérard Biard), *Charlie Hebdo*, 27 December 2000, www.chez.com/ezola/Docnumerises/docnumerises4.html (accessed 10 October 2003).

15 See J.-L. Douin, *Dictionnaire de la censure au cinéma* (Paris Presses Universitaires de France, 2001), pp. 60–1.

16 C. Tesson, 'Pour la peau d'un film', *Cahiers du cinéma*, 371–2 (1985), 117.

17 One relatively minor but interesting development is that a number of direc-

tors who were considered to be auteurs turned to the *polar* in the mid-1980s, their treatment of it being a formal, stylistic exercise. Truffaut's last film *Vivement Dimanche!* (*Finally, Sunday*, 1983) was the first of these, and it is also the most obvious stylistic exercise. It is based on an American film noir, Robert Siodmak's *Phantom Lady* (1944), and is in black and white with stark chiaroscuro lighting and seedy urban decor (empty rain-swept streets, a brothel). However, the film becomes increasingly and more obviously a pastiche, with several frankly comical episodes undermining the unease generated by the lawyer-villain's murders. No less stylised, though, were the ostentatiously documentary-like *Police* (Maurice Pialat, 1985) and the playful *Détective* (Jean-Luc Godard, 1985), as Godard creates an impossibly labyrinthine plot with literary characters (Ariel and Prospero), mobsters, a boxers and an airline pilot. See the chapters on these films in P. Powrie, *French Cinema in the 1980s: Nostalgia and the Crisis of Masculinity* (Oxford: Clarendon Press, 1997), pp. 84–108.

18 Forbes, *The Cinema in France*, p. 68.
19 Tesson, 'Pour la peau d'un film', p. 118.
20 O. Philippe, *La Représentation de la police dans le cinéma français (1965–1992)* (Paris: L'Harmattan, 1999), pp. 56–7.
21 Fredric Jameson, '*Diva* and French Socialism', in *Signatures of the Visible* (New York and London, Routledge, 1992), pp. 55–62. Originally published in *Social Text*, 6 (1982), 114–19. For details on the 'postmodern' aspects of this film, and the heated polemics to which it gave rise, see P. Powrie, *Jean-Jacques Beineix* (Manchester: Manchester University Press, 2001), pp. 10–19 and 33–5. For an account of Jameson's analysis, see *ibid.*, pp. 36–8.
22 Fredric Jameson, 'Postmodernism, or the Cultural Logic of Late Capitalism', in T. Docherty (ed.), *Postmodernism: A Reader* (New York and London: Harvester Wheatsheaf, 1993), pp. 62–92.
23 W. Higbee, '*Diva*', in P. Powrie (ed.), *The Cinema of France* (London: Wallflower Press, 2006), pp. 153–64.
24 Jameson, '*Diva*', p. 58.
25 N. Greene, *Landscapes of Loss: The National Past in Postwar French Cinema* (Princeton, New Jersey: Princeton University Press, 1999), pp. 168–77.
26 Philippe, *La Représentation de la police*, pp. 64–6.
27 *Ibid.*, pp. 275–6.
28 *Ibid.*, p. 412.
29 G. Austin, *Contemporary French Cinema: An Introduction* (Manchester: Manchester University Press, 1996), p. 114.
30 Interview in *France-Soir* (26 April 1979), quoted in M. Maillard, 'Loi des séries', *Jowebzine.com* (dated May 2003), www.jowebzine.com /TEMPLATES/DVD/serienoire-81.html (accessed 23 October 2003).
31 Forbes, *The Cinema in France*, p. 72.
32 Austin, *Contemporary French Cinema*, p. 111.
33 J. Duffy, 'Message Versus Mystery and *Film Noir* Borrowings in Patrice

Leconte's *Monsieur Hire*', *French Cultural Studies*, 13 (2002), 210.

34 *Ibid.*, p. 216.

35 See Austin, *Contemporary French Cinema*, pp. 103–4.

36 Carlos Pardo, 'Crime, pornographie et mépris du peuple: des films français fascinés par le sordide', *Le Monde Diplomatique* (February 2000), p. 28.

37 'Entretien avec Philippe Grandrieux' (with C. Béghin, S. Delorme and M.Lavin), dated 5 September 2000, *Balthazar* 4 (Summer 2001), http://perso.club-internet.fr/cyrilbg/grandrieux.html (accessed 11 November 2003).

38 'Au commencement était la nuit: entretien avec Philippe Grandrieux' (with N. Renaud, S. Rioux and N. L. Rutigliano), dated 14 October 1999, *Hors Champ*, www.horschamp.qc.ca/article.php3?id_article=49 (accessed 11 November 2003).

39 'Entretien', *Balthazar*.

40 'Au commencement', *Hors Champ*.

41 J. Roy, 'La douille se vide quand on tire un coup', *L'Humanité* (28 June 2000).

42 L. R. Williams, 'Sick Sisters: the Limits of Sex', *Sight and Sound*, 11:7 (July 2001), 28.

43 G. Vincendeau, '*Baise-moi*', *Sight and Sound*, 12:5 (May 2002), 38.

44 C. Tarr with Brigitte Rollet, *Cinema and the Second Sex: Women's Filmmaking in France in the 1980s and 1990s* (London: Continuum, 2001), p. 284.

45 V. Despentes, 'Director's comment', Presskit, available on the UK website of the film, www.baise-moi.co.uk/html/press.htm (accessed 6 November 2003).

46 N. Brenez, 'The Grand Style of the Epoch: *Baise-moi* – Girls Better than Maenads, Darker than Furies', *Screening the Past* (website), www.latrobe.edu.au/screeningthepast/classics/cl0703/nbcl15.html (accessed 6 November 2003). Originally published in French in *Trafic*, 39 (Autumn 2001).

47 Despentes, 'Director's Comment'.

48 M. Le Cain, 'Fresh Blood: *Baise-moi*', *Senses of Cinema* (website), dated September 2002, www.sensesofcinema.com/contents/02/22/baise-moi_max.html oi_max.html (accessed 7 November 2003).

49 Brenez, 'The Grand Style'.

50 Despentes, 'Director's Comment'.

51 It is for this reason that I disagree with Bérénice Reynaud's view that 'shooting the bad pervert in the ass is an act of covert homophobia'; see B. Reynaud, '*Baise-moi*: A Personal Angry-Yet-Feminist Reaction', *Senses of Cinema* (website), dated September 2002, www.sensesofcinema.com/contents/02/22/baise-moi.html (accessed 7 November 2003).

52 I am grateful to Andrew Spicer for his comments on an early draft of this chapter; and to Will Higbee for lending me copies of *Dupont Lajoie* and *L'Attentat*.

Filmography

French film noirs/neo-noirs

Le Jour se lève (*Daybreak*), Marcel Carné, 1939
Panique (*Panic*), Julien Duvivier, 1947
Ascenseur pour l'échafaud (*Lift to the Scaffold*), Louis Malle, 1958
Plein Soleil (*Purple Noon*), René Clément, 1960
Le Meurtrier (*Enough Rope*), Claude Autant-Lara, 1963
La Piscine (*The Sinners*), Jacques Deray, 1968
Z, Constantin Costa-Gavras, 1969
L'Aveu (*The Confession*), Constantin Costa-Gavras, 1970
Dernier domicile connu (*Last Known Address*), José Giovanni, 1970
Un condé (*Blood On My Hands*), Yves Boisset, 1970
Max et les ferrailleurs (*Max and the Junkmen*), Claude Sautet, 1971
L'Attentat (*Plot*), Yves Boisset, 1972
Un flic (*Dirty Money*), Jean-Pierre Melville, 1972
Deux hommes dans la ville (*Two Against the Law*), José Giovanni, 1973
Etat de siege (*State of Siege*), Constantin Costa-Gavras, 1973
L'Horloger de Saint-Paul (*The Watchmaker of St. Paul*), Bertrand Tavernier,
    1973
Nada (*The Nada Gang*), Claude Chabrol, 1974
Dupont Lajoie (*Rape of Innocence*), Yves Boisset, 1975
Flic story (*Cop Story*), Jacques Deray, 1975
Le Juge Fayard dit le 'Shérif' (*Judge Fayard Called the Sheriff*), Yves Boisset,
    1976
Police Python 357 (*The Case Against Ferro*), Alain Corneau, 1976
Mort d'un pourri (*Death of a Corrupt Man*), Georges Lautner, 1977
Série noire, Alain Corneau, 1979
Coup de torchon (*Clean Slate*), Bertrand Tavernier, 1981
Diva, Jean-Jacques Beineix, 1981
Garde à vue (*Under Suspicion*), Claude Miller, 1981
Pour la peau d'un flic (*For a Cop's Hide*), Alain Delon, 1981
Le Professionnel (*The Professional*), Georges Lautner, 1981
La Balance (*The Nark*), Bob Swaim, 1982
Les Fantômes du chapelier (*The Hatter's Ghost*), Claude Chabrol, 1982
La Lune dans le caniveau (*The Moon in the Gutter*), Jean-Jacques Beineix,
    1983
Vivement Dimanche! (*Finally, Sunday*), François Truffaut, 1983
Détective, Jean-Luc Godard, 1985
Parole de flic (*Cop's Honor*), José Pinheiro, 1985
Police, Maurice Pialat, 1985
Poulet au vinaigre (*Cop au Vin*), Claude Chabrol, 1985
Subway, Luc Besson, 1985
Inspecteur Lavardin, Claude Chabrol, 1986
Masques (*Masks*), Claude Chabrol, 1987
Poussière d'ange (*Angel Dust*), Edouard Niermans, 1987

Fréquence meurtre (*Frequent Death*), Elizabeth Rappeneau, 1988
Monsieur Hire, Patrice Leconte, 1989
Nikita, Luc Besson, 1990
L.627, Bertrand Tavernier, 1992
L'Appât (*The Bait*), Bertrand Tavernier, 1995
La Cérémonie (*A Judgement in Stone*), Claude Chabrol, 1995
Dobermann, Jan Kounen, 1997
Place Vendôme, Nicole Garcia, 1998
Seul contre tous (*I Stand Alone*), Gaspar Noé, 1998
Sombre, Philippe Grandrieux, 1998
L'Humanité (*Humanity*), Bruno Dumont, 1999
Romance, Catherine Breillat, 1999
Baise-moi (*Kiss Me*), Coralie Trinh Thi and Virginie Despentes, 2000
Merci pour le chocolat (*Nightcap*), Claude Chabrol, 2000

Other films mentioned
Nosferatu, eine Symphonie des Grauens (*Nosferatu*), Friedrich Wilhelm
    Murnau, 1922
Phantom Lady, Robert Siodmak, 1944
Vertigo, Alfred Hitchcock, 1958
The Conversation, Francis Ford Coppola, 1970
The French Connection, William Friedkin, 1971
Il caso Mattei (*The Mattei Affair*), Francesco Rosi, 1972
Eraserhead, David Lynch, 1977
Blade Runner, Ridley Scott, 1981
Body Heat, Lawrence Kasdan, 1981
Blue Velvet, David Lynch, 1986
Thelma and Louise, Ridley Scott, 1991
Lost Highway, David Lynch, 1997

Select bibliography

Austin, G., *Contemporary French Cinema: An Introduction* (Manchester: Manchester University Press, 1996).
Boisset, Y., 'Yves Boisset: Le cinéaste le plus censuré de France' (interview with Gérard Biard), *Charlie Hebdo* (27 December 2000), www.chez.com/ezola/Docnumerises/docnumerises4.html (accessed 10 October 2003).
Brenez, N., 'The grand style of the epoch: *Baise-moi* – girls better than maenads, darker than furies', *Screening the Past* (website), www.latrobe.edu.au/screeningthepast/classics/cl0703/nbcl15.html (accessed 6 November 2003). Originally published in French in *Trafic*, 39 (Autumn 2001).
Despentes, V., 'Director's comment', Presskit, available on the UK website of the film www.baise-moi.co.uk/html/press.htm (accessed 6 November 2003).

Dewaere, P., Interview in *France-Soir* (26 April 1979), quoted in M. Maillard, 'Loi des séries', *Jowebzine.com* (May 2003), www.jowebzine.com /TEMPLATES/DVD/serienoire-81.html (accessed 23 October 2003).

Douin, J.-L., *Dictionnaire de la censure au cinéma* (Paris Presses Universitaires de France, 2001).

Duffy, J., 'Message versus mystery and *film noir* borrowings in Patrice Leconte's *Monsieur Hire*', *French Cultural Studies*, 13 (2002), 209–24.

Forbes, J., *The Cinema in France After the New Wave* (London: BFI/Macmillan, 1992).

Frodon, J.-M., *L'Age moderne du cinéma français: de la Nouvelle Vague à nos jours* (Paris: Flammarion, 1995).

Grandrieux, P., 'Au commencement était la nuit: entretien avec Philippe Grandrieux' (with N. Renaud, S. Rioux, and N. L. Rutigliano), dated 14 October 1999, *Hors Champ*, www.horschamp.qc.ca/article. php3?id_article=49 (accessed 11 November 2003).

Grandrieux, P., 'Entretien avec Philippe Grandrieux' (with C. Béghin, S. Delorme and M. Lavin), dated 5 September 2000, *Balthazar*, 4 (Summer 2001), http://perso.club-internet.fr/cyrilbg/grandrieux.html (accessed 11 November 2003).

Greene, N., *Landscapes of Loss: The National Past in Postwar French Cinema* (Princeton, New Jersey: Princeton University Press, 1999).

Harvey, S., *May '68 and Film Culture* (London: BFI Publishing, 1978).

Higbee, W., 'Yves Boisset's *Dupont Lajoie* (1974): racism, civic cinema and the "immigrant question"', *Studies in French Cinema*, 2:3 (2002), 147–56.

Higbee, W., '*Diva*', in P. Powrie (ed.), *The Cinema of France* (London: Wallflower Press, 2006), pp. 153–64.

Jameson, F. '*Diva* and French Socialism', in *Signatures of the Visible* (New York and London: Routledge, 1992), pp. 55–62. Originally published in *Social Text*, 6 (1982), 114–19.

Jameson, F., 'Postmodernism, or the cultural logic of late capitalism', in T. Docherty (ed.), *Postmodernism: A Reader* (New York and London: Harvester Wheatsheaf, 1993), pp. 62–92.

Kline, T. Jefferson, 'Recuperating Hitchcock's doubles: experiencing *Vertigo* in Garcia's *Place Vendôme*', *Studies in French Cinema*, 3:1 (2003), 35–46.

Le Cain, M., 'Fresh Blood: *Baise-moi*', *Senses of Cinema* (website), dated September 2002, http://www.sensesofcinema.com/contents/02/22/baise-moi_max.html (accessed 7 November 2003).

Manchette, J.-P., *L'Affaire N'Gustro* (Paris: Gallimard, 1971).

Pardo, C., 'Crime, pornographie et mépris du peuple: des films français fascinés par le sordide', *Le Monde Diplomatique* (February 2000), 28.

Philippe, O., *La Représentation de la police dans le cinéma français (1965–1992)* (Paris: L'Harmattan, 1999).

Powrie, P., *French Cinema in the 1980s: Nostalgia and the Crisis of Masculinity* (Oxford: Clarendon Press, 1997).

Powrie, P., *Jean-Jacques Beineix* (Manchester: Manchester University Press, 2001).

Powrie, P., 'Transtitial Woman: New representations of women in contemporary French cinema', *Esprit Créateur*, 52:3 (2002), 81–91.

Prédal, R., *Le Cinéma français depuis 1945* (Paris: Nathan, 1991).

Reynaud, B., '*Baise-moi*: A personal angry-yet-feminist reaction', *Senses of Cinema* (website), dated September 2002, www.sensesofcinema.com /contents/02/22/baise-moi.html (accessed 7 November 2003).

Roy, J., 'La douille se vide quand on tire un coup', *L'Humanité* (28 June 2000).

Tarr, C., with Brigitte Rollet, *Cinema and the Second Sex: Women's Filmmaking in France in the 1980s and 1990s* (London: Continuum, 2001).

Tesson, C., 'Pour la peau d'un film', *Cahiers du cinéma*, 371–72 (1985), 117–19.

Vincendeau, G., *Stars and Stardom in French Cinema* (London: Continuum, 2000).

Vincendeau, G., '*Baise-moi*', *Sight and Sound*, 12:5 (May 2002), 38.

Williams, L. R., 'Sick sisters: the limits of sex', *Sight and Sound*, 11:7 (July 2001), 28–9.

4

British film noir

Robert Murphy

Critical enthusiasm for realism in British cinema, from Grierson to
Ken Loach, has obscured the fact that the majority of British films pay
little regard to a realist ethos. Melodramas and crime films have traditionally made up a significant and substantial part of British cinema
and a section of these films can be related to film noir. As film noir is
a critical category constructed to deal with a specific group of
Hollywood films, it would be surprising to find its characteristic traits
fully mirrored in British films. But if one defines noir in terms of films
that reveal the underbelly of society, expose baser emotions, concentrate on melodramatic events and represent the world as turbulent and
often unjust, than a substantial portion of British cinema falls within
its scope.

There are now a number of useful accounts of British film noir.
William K. Everson's two essays in *Films in Review* in 1987 set out the
ground, arguing that:

> British film noir is particularly fascinating, not only because it has never
> been officially acknowledged to exist, but because its peak period paral-
> lels that of American noir, but does so with several major differences, the
> key one being that it has always been influenced more by the French
> cinema of the 30s rather than the German cinema of the 20s.[1]

Laurence Miller followed up with a tantalisingly brief article,
'Evidence for a British Film Noir Cycle', which made large claims for
the significance of British noir films but did little to substantiate
them.[2] Brian McFarlane's 'Losing the Peace: Some British Films of
Postwar Adjustment', like my own chapters entitled 'The Spiv Cycle'
and 'Morbid Burrowings' in *Realism and Tinsel*, was much more
cautious.[3] McFarlane examines a cycle of films where men returning
from the war find it difficult to adjust to peacetime society. He makes
no connection with film noir, though there are distinctly noirish
elements in most of the films he mentions. Indeed, Tony Williams's

'British Film Noir', in Alain Silver and James Ursini's *Film Noir Reader*, points to 'the British representation of male trauma and insecurity' as one of the distinctive characteristics of British noir films.[4] Williams spreads his net wide, claiming that 'The fluid nature of British *film noir* may cause sleepless nights to critics preoccupied with rigidly statistical and taxonomic definitions but not to those aware of the fluid nature of generic forms'.[5] Thus he puts films as divergent as *A Canterbury Tale* (1944), *Holiday Camp* (1947) and *Blanche Fury* (1947) in the noir bag. Raymond Durgnat, a master of taxonomic definition, deals with a similar spread of films in 'Some Lines of Enquiry into Post-war British Crimes', but subdivides them into twenty different categories, including three distinct types of film noir.[6] Andrew Spicer examines British film noir alongside its American cousin, using almost as many categories and subdivisions as Durgnat; but for Spicer these all exist within the shadowy empire of film noir.[7]

A strong macabre tradition exists in British cinema, which pre-dates the critical concept of film noir. Censorship and critical neglect have compounded to mute its impact and one might agree with Williams that nit-picking over definitions is unproductive. But nevertheless, attention to its traditions and characteristic traits is important. The use of expressionist visual style – low-key lighting and extreme camera angles – and the central role of a sexually alluring but evil *femme fatale*, which are key elements in American film noir, are far less prominent in British films. Lighting and camera angles are often used to emphasise melodramatic effects, but less consistently than in American films, particularly those directed by German émigrés Fritz Lang, Robert Siodmak, Edgar G. Ulmer and Billy Wilder, all of whom had their roots in the German expressionist movement. Women in British films rarely exhibit the qualities associated with *femmes fatales*. In the 1930s, Linden Travers, Greta Gynt, Sally Gray and René Ray are attractive, plucky and resourceful but more likely to be victims in need of male assistance than scheming perpetrators. In the 1940s, scheming women do emerge, but some sympathy is allowed them given their bad luck in being married to disturbed, inadequate or emotionally shrivelled husbands.

Melodramatic precursors

The brutal traditions of British popular entertainment – bear-baiting, prize-fighting, public execution – feed into Victorian stage melodrama which in turn combined with German expressionism, pessimistic French poetic realism and American populist detective fiction to give

British cinema its own indigenous strains of noir. The Victorian melo-dramas which were transferred to the screen in the 1930s tended to be those where the villain is powerful – the dominant figure until he gets his comeuppance at the end – women are vulnerable and are made to suffer, and the hero is brought low and has an uphill struggle to right the wrong done to him. As in noir, it is a violent, unpredictable world where justice is something that has to be fought for. Right generally triumphs but only after the villain has wreaked havoc – murdering the innocent, misusing power to perpetrate injustice and enjoying the fruits of his wrongdoing – until he finally overreaches himself.

The key figure is Tod Slaughter, a charismatic stage actor who repro-duced his stage villainy in a series of low-budget British films. In *Maria Marten* (1935), Squire Corder (Slaughter) uses his power and money to seduce Maria away from the handsome young gypsy who loves her. When she insists he must fulfil his promises and marry her because she is pregnant, he murders her. Guilt brings about maddening hallucina-tions, however, and he reveals himself as the murderer. He is hanged by the gypsy, who volunteers to stand in for the temporarily indis-posed hangman. Similar ingredients make *Sweeney Todd: The Demon Barber of Fleet Street* (1936), *The Crimes of Stephen Hawke* (1936), *It's Never Too Late to Mend* (1937), *The Ticket of Leave Man* (1937), *The Face at the Window* (1939) and *Crimes at the Dark House* (1940) equally lurid.

The mysteries of Edgar Wallace

Such characteristics as a charismatic villain indulging in cruel sexual depredation were reworked into stories about contemporary society, most prolifically in the works of Edgar Wallace, whose two hundred books and plays provided the British film industry with a seemingly endless supply of lurid melodramas. According to James Chapman, some fifty British films were adapted from Wallace stories between 1925 and 1939.[8] Among the locked-door whodunits and stories cele-brating the achievements of the police, there were a number of films where criminal activity veers into the fantastic, notably *The Dark Eyes of London* (1939), the first British film to be given the 'H' (for horror) classification. The heroine (Greta Gynt) suffers multiple physical indignities, and a blind mute who tries to warn victims of their fate, is strapped to a bed and given electric shock treatment before being drowned in a water tank and tipped into the Thames. The plot is rudi-mentary and improbable – an insurance broker has his clients murdered so that he can collect on their policies – but the characters and settings are thrillingly bizarre. Dr Orloff (Bela Lugosi) the insurance broker (who is also a brilliant surgeon, barred from practising because of his unethical experiments) masquerades as Mr Dearborn, a blind philanthropist. The Dearborn Home for the Blind, a former warehouse overlooking the river, is where victims are lured to their death. Orloff/Dearborn's henchman Jake (Wilfrid Walter) is a blind, deformed giant. As in most Wallace stories, there is an intrepid Scotland Yard detective who succeeds in unmasking the villain and rescuing the heroine.

Exploring the underworld

The outlandishness of period and contemporary melodramas kept them safe from a censorship regime determined not to allow audiences to be led astray by displays of life-like criminal activity. The prohibition on the portrayal of crimes that might be imitated, of prostitutes, and scenes of prison life, meant that the reality of underworld life in Britain during this period is barely represented. Literary censorship was much less strict and there was a fashion for low-life novels in the 1930s and 1940s. James Hadley Chase and Peter Cheyney both proved surprisingly successful at mimicking American pulp fiction, but their novels were also set in the English underworld. Walter Greenwood, who had found fame with his novel about economic depression in the 1930s, *Love on the Dole*, tried his hand with *Only Mugs Work*; Richard Llewellyn, soon to be famous for *How Green Was My Valley*, wrote a screenplay – *The Silk Noose* – about pimps, prostitutes and other Soho low-life, which was condemned as unsuitable by the British Board of Film Censorship; Robert Westerby, later to become a successful scriptwriter, delved into a netherworld of stolen cars and race-fixing in *Wide Boys Never Work*; Graham Greene boldly superimposed metaphysical concerns on a particularly sordid nest of racetrack gangsters in *Brighton Rock*. But the most significant was James Curtis, whose four novels – *The Gilt Kid, You're in the Racket Too, There Ain't No Justice* and *They Drive by Night* – were published between 1936 and 1938. Two of them were immediately snapped up for films.

Penrose Tennyson's *There Ain't No Justice* (1939) is remarkable for its transformation of an unremittingly grim novel into a cheery celebration of working class life where little of Curtis's bleak worldview remains. *They Drive by Night* (1939), by contrast, although it does tone down the cynicism and the portrayal of police brutality, succeeds in capturing the spirit of Curtis's novel. It was directed by Arthur

Woods, like Tennyson a promising young director who would be killed in the war, at Warner Bros. Teddington studios. *They Drive by Night* was more ambitious than most of Warner's low-budget British quota films. Shortie Matthews (Emlyn Williams, whose play *Night Must Fall* had been filmed in Hollywood by Richard Thorpe in 1937 as a proto-noir) is a hapless man on the run, a small-time crook just out of prison who expects to be condemned for the murder of his girlfriend, whom he finds strangled with a silk stocking. He is buoyed up by Molly (Anna Konstam), a down-at-heel dance-hall hostess, who proves herself steadfast and resourceful in helping him to root out the real murderer and clear his name. Andrew Spicer claims that '*They Drive by Night* shows the passage from the macabre shocker to modern film noir, revealing a paranoid world of social and sexual corruption that exists as the dark underside to respectable British society'.[9] A not entirely innocent man accused of a crime he hasn't committed; a journey along rainswept roads at night; a liaison with a soiled but good-hearted woman; a sexually disturbed, cat-loving murderer (played by Ernest Thesiger, an English actor who had made his name in Universal's horror films) give *They Drive by Night* enough noir qualifications to justify Spicer's claim. However, it is arguable whether the film's aura of jaunty resilience encompasses 'a paranoid world of social and sexual corruption'. It would take a war to bring that about. Shortie, almost in spite of himself, acts with unselfish kindness towards Wally the lorry driver and Molly the dance-hall hostess and is rewarded by their help and trust. What is distinctive about the film is its sophistication and its realism. Woods, drawing on the well-oiled technical proficiency of Warner Bros., makes this low-life world of shadowy dives, transport cafés, the Great North Road and the glittering *palais de danse*, remarkably convincing. Thesiger's murderer might have crept in from a gothic horror film, but he is solidly rooted by the fierce class antagonism he provokes. He is sniggered at and mocked by the saloon bar regulars he tries to impress with his big ideas. Molly bristles as soon as he comes near her; Shortie quickly guesses that he is the murderer.

Ordinary lives

The attention to realistic detail shown in *They Drive by Night* was also evident in two films produced by Josef Somlo, *On the Night of the Fire* (1939) and *A Window in London* (1940). Both concern young, upwardly mobile, working-class couples whose lives become complicated by murder. In *A Window in London*, directed by Herbert

Mason, Pat (Patricia Roc) is a hotel switchboard operator married to Peter (Michael Redgrave) a crane operator working on the site of the new Waterloo Bridge. They are happy but frustrated by the fact that as she works nights and he works days they hardly see each other. When Peter witnesses what he mistakenly thinks is a murder he becomes involved with a combustible magician (Paul Lucas) and his alluring blonde wife (Sally Gray). Pat is sacked for sleeping on the job, Peter for being late, and Peter, suffering from what his workmates ribaldly call 'night starvation', is eager to commit adultery; but these are breezily dismissed problems and noirish shadows only impinge around the magician, who exudes instability and violence. A different and bleaker noir sensibility infuses Brian Desmond Hurst's *On the Night of the Fire*, a grim parable about a Newcastle barber (Ralph Richardson) and his wife (Diana Wynyard) whose attempts to better themselves lead to social ostracism and death. With Terence Fisher as editor, John Bryan as art director and Günther Krampf as cinematographer, one might expect an expressionist ethos, but as with *A Window in London*, with its convincingly evoked settings on the Waterloo Bridge construction site, melodramatic events are situated in a real world – the Newcastle shipyards and their surrounding grim terraces.

Angst-ridden films of the 1940s

American film noir borrows its milieu from the gangster film, its visual style from the horror film and its narrative structure from the detective thriller. It relies heavily on German émigrés and the expressionist heritage they bring with them. And it develops in a period of uneasy transition from war to peace to cold war and draws on the cynicism, worldliness and social and sexual disorientation of returning ex-servicemen. Britain had different traditions and a very different experience of the Second World War. The temporary but real solidarity induced by the threat of invasion and the ordeal of the Blitz, the emphasis on communal life, the drive towards greater equality between men and women, made for a more grimly down-to-earth atmosphere than in America. Nonetheless Britain suffered a heavy price for the war in terms of lives lost, property damaged, debts incurred, distorted economic development, continued austerity and a rampant black market. These traumas find an outlet in crime films, morbid melodramas and films about fugitives and men physically or mentally disturbed by the war.

During the war, the impetus to show ordinary people implicated in

murky events shifted from murder mysteries and crime thrillers to films dealing with espionage and resistance. Walter Summers' *Traitor Spy* (1939), Powell and Pressburger's *The Spy in Black* (1939) and *Contraband* (1940), Anthony Asquith's *Cottage to Let* (1941) and *Uncensored* (1942), Lawrence Huntington's *Tower of Terror* (1941), Thorold Dickinson's *Next of Kin* (1942), Harold French's *Unpublished Story* (1942) and Herbert Wilcox's *Yellow Canary* (1943) are perhaps the darkest examples.

More indicative of anxieties which would infect post-war films is *The Night Has Eyes* (1942). It tells a Wallace-like tale of young women lost on the moors who find shelter in a strange household with a sinister housekeeper (Mary Clare), her eccentric husband (Wilfrid Lawson) and their misanthropic, piano-playing master, Stephen Deremid (James Mason). Stephen is a concert pianist who has been wounded in the head while fighting in the Spanish Civil War, and there are doubts about his sanity. It turns out that there is nothing wrong with him – the housekeeper has been trying to convince him that he is mad so that she can get at his money – but he is undeniably sadistic in his treatment of the fluffy young heroine (Joyce Howard). Mason and Howard were reunited in Karel Lamac's *They Met in the Dark* (1943), a bigger budgeted film made with backing from J. Arthur Rank. This ill-matched romantic couple are set against a threatening band of fifth columnists – Karel Stepanek's womanising hypnotist, Ronald Chesney's mouth-organ virtuoso and Tom Walls's unctuous theatrical agent – and the film is atmospherically lit by the Czech cinematographer, Otto Heller. With a surer hand than that of the erratic Lamac, it would have made an extremely effective noir.

Damaged men

Men who raise a doubt over whether the damage they have suffered (sometimes psychological, sometimes accidental, but most often because of the war) has turned them into killers, become an important constituent of post-war British noir thrillers. As Martha Wolfenstein and Nathan Leites point out:

> British films in contrast to both American and French tend to see women more as possible victims of men's violence or betrayal. Correspondingly they give more emphasis to the dual potentialities of men as attackers or rescuers ... In British films the male character bears the interesting ambiguity which in American films is associated with the good-bad girl.[10]

Brian McFarlane argues that 'The returning war hero who can find no satisfying role in the post-war world is a recurring figure in British cinema of the late 1940s and the 1950s; and Andrew Spicer examines twenty-five years of 'Damaged Men' in films ranging from *I'll Turn to You* (1946) to *Demons of the Mind* (1971).[11] Along with underworld films and those films – rarer in British than in American cinema – which centre upon a man's jealous and generally murderous obsession with a woman, these 'damaged men' films constitute a rich vein of noirish cinema in the late 1940s.

Eric Portman in *Dear Murderer* (1947), Robert Newton in *Obsession* (1949), Marius Goring in *Take My Life* (1947), and, more sympathetically, Portman in *Daybreak* (1947), Mason in *The Upturned Glass* (1947) and Newton in *Temptation Harbour* (1947), are all driven to desperate measures because of unscrupulous or feck-less women.[12] Portman in *Wanted for Murder* (1946) is murderously mad, obsessed by his public hangman grandfather, but he is a victim rather than a villain and arouses our interest and concern; as does Kieron Moore in *Mine Own Executioner* (1948); he is gentle and loving to his wife, but murders her while possessed by a violent fantasy brought on by his traumatic POW camp experiences. David Farrar in *The Small Back Room* (1949) is also subject to hallucinations, but the worst he does is to smash up the furniture; he is never a threat to his stoical, supportive girlfriend (Kathleen Byron, cast against type).

Even at their worst, these are men who command a degree of sympathy. There are others whom the war has turned into irredeemable rogues. The most notable examples are Nigel Patrick's Simon Rawley in *Silent Dust* (1949) and David Farrar's Bill Glennon in *Cage of Gold* (1950). Rawley is supposed to be a dead hero, revered by his blind father who plans to erect a monument in his honour. In fact he deserted and became a black marketeer; three years after the war the film will have no truck with his supposition that it is better to be a living coward than a dead hero. Glennon is less explicably bad, a wing-commander with a good war record who prefers to exploit women and dabble in crime rather than adjust to peace.

Unlike Clem Morgan in *They Made Me a Fugitive* (1947), no excuses are made for his behaviour and he is murdered rather than redeemed. Both films have noirish undertones but firmly reject the ethos projected by their shady protagonists in favour of a couple (Sally Gray and Derek Farr in *Silent Dust*, Jean Simmons and James Donald in *Cage of Gold*) who defy him and take a harder road to peacetime adjustment.

3 Jean Simmons and David Farrar in *Cage of Gold* (Basil Dearden, 1950).

A new realism

Cage of Gold's combination of shabby realism and film noir melo-drama is evident in two earlier films, Roy Baker's *The October Man* (1947) and Ronald Neame's *Take My Life* (1947), both of which explore macabre trends within mundane austerity-ridden milieux. John Mills, the protagonist of *The October Man*, has been brain-damaged in a car crash, and mistakenly thinks he might have murdered the girl in the next room – a warm-hearted goodtime girl rather than a *femme fatale* – but it is the small-minded hostility of other lodging-house residents rather than a deliberate plot, which makes him doubt his sanity. *Take My Life* also moves away from the cruder thrills of 1930s Grand Guignol. As in *The Dark Eyes of London*, Hugh Williams and Greta Gynt have a murder mystery to solve, but here Gynt – ten years on a more formidable and resourceful heroine – has to act alone while the hapless Williams is tried for the murder committed by a more passionate and more dangerous man. Neame, making his debut as director, seems initially uncertain whether he is directing a portentous court-room drama or a scary thriller, but the final quarter of the film – thanks to John Bryan's fine production design and Guy Green's cinematography – is a tour de force of noir atmospherics.

Temptation Harbour was based on a story by Georges Simenon. Director Lance Comfort had already displayed his noirish proclivities in *Hatter's Castle* (1942), *Great Day* (1945) and *Bedelia* (1946), and he is ably abetted here by Otto Heller's cinematography; but the film is firmly rooted in the reality of post-war Britain.[13] Bert Mallinson (Robert Newton), a railway signalman, dives into Newhaven harbour to save a man but finds instead a suitcase full of money. Circumstances divert him from turning in the suitcase to the police and like Ralph Richardson's Will Kobling in *On the Night of the Fire*, he is tempted to use the money to break out of the poverty trap. Mallinson is lured along the primrose path by a fairground mermaid with 'enough atomic energy in the lobes of her ears to flatten London', and like Kobling he is driven to murder; but he remains fundamentally a decent man. Whereas Kobling despises his customers and is desperate to escape 'the stink of the street', Mallinson shares common grievances over rationing and austerity. Like Laura Jesson in *Brief Encounter* (1945), Rose Sandigate in *It Always Rains on Sunday* (1947) and the denizens of the Burgundian enclave in *Passport to Pimlico* (1949), he grasps at the chance of a more exciting and glamorous life, but when the dream turns sour, he shows a poignant regret at losing the simple, hard-working life he had shared with kindly neighbours. Though now a virtually forgotten film, in 1947 *Temptation Harbour* struck a chord with British audiences, out-grossing *Brighton Rock* at the box office.[14]

Crime and punishment

In American film noirs the characters played by Robert Mitchum, Dick Powell, Humphrey Bogart, Alan Ladd and Burt Lancaster, are tough, worldly characters who are sometimes implicated in criminal activity. But they are essentially honourable men. Private eyes, insurance investigators, former policemen, gangsters with a sense of honour, are all hard to find in British films of the late 1940s. Escaped convicts remain surprisingly popular – Trevor Howard in *They Made Me a Fugitive*, Jack Warner and George Cole in *My Brother's Keeper* (1948) and Rex Harrison in *Escape* (1948) – and they are joined by Derek Farr in *Man on the Run* (1948), who is guilty only of demobilising himself too early, not of the murder of which he is accused, and Howard's burnt-out secret service agent in *The Clouded Yellow* (1950), who is helping a disturbed girl escape the unjust murder charge levelled at her.

A cycle of films dealing with spivs and racketeers – symptomatic of a disturbing rise in black-market activity – began with John Harlow's *Appointment With Crime* in 1946 and ended with Jules Dassin's *Night and the City* in 1950.[15] *They Made Me a Fugitive*, made for Alliance, based at the small Riverside studios in Hammersmith, and distributed by Warner Bros., might seem a surprisingly low-brow choice for the respected intellectual Alberto Cavalcanti. But its source – *A Convict Has Escaped*, a stream-of-consciousness novel by Jackson Budd – couldn't have been further from pulp fiction and was adapted by Noel Langley, the young South African who had been the main scriptwriter on *The Wizard of Oz* (1939). Trevor Howard, as the maladjusted war veteran Clem Morgan, is amply matched by Griffith Jones as the vicious spiv Narcy, and highly strung Sally Gray as the chorus girl who turns against her gangster boyfriend. It was photographed by Otto Heller and designed by Andrew Mazzei, whose occasional venture from theatre into film included the ingenious *Rome Express* (1932) and the exotic *Madonna of the Seven Moons* (1944). Arthur Vesselo, writing in *Sight and Sound*, was disturbed by what he saw as 'a tale of sordidness, corruption and violence almost unrelieved', but admitted that it was 'horrifyingly well-made'.[16]

Heller's expressive lighting, Howard's lean and hungry hero, Gray's glitteringly sexy gangster's moll – like Gloria Grahame in Fritz Lang's *The Big Heat* (1953) more a helper than a *femme fatale* – make *They Made Me a Fugitive* easily identifiable as a film noir. But it remains quintessentially English. Jones' smiling villain, with his sharp awareness of class division, is a peculiarly English type, Clem Morgan, however reduced in circumstances, is still an officer and a gentleman, and Gray has a dainty sensibility which indicates her adherence to the middle-class values from which she has temporarily strayed. As in *They Drive by Night*, the conventions and concerns of film noir are shown as effective in a British as much as an American setting.

Brighton Rock, despite being marketed in the USA as 'Young Scarface', is even more parochial. Harry Waxman's cinematography brilliantly recreates Brighton as both a shadowy netherworld and a place of sunshine and fun. Structurally, it has little in common with American (or most British) film noirs. A gloomily precocious adolescent avenges the exposure of his gang leader by murdering the reporter responsible. But that only takes up the first few minutes of the film. What follows is the development of a relationship between Pinkie (Richard Attenborough) and Rose (Carol Marsh), a waitress who can invalidate his alibi, and his hunting-down by an ebullient end-of-the-pier entertainer, Ida Arnold (Hermione Baddeley). Though the metaphysical speculation is much slimmed down from Graham Greene's novel, it still dominates the relationship between Pinkie and Rose, aberrant in that it is explicitly concerned less with love than with death. Ida – who belongs to a lineage of British women detectives – is the equivalent of a hard-boiled private eye in that she is worldly and fallible but securely anchored within her own moral universe. The duel between Ida and Pinkie could be seen as a struggle between good and evil (though Greene has sympathy with the devil-like Pinkie but is wary about vulgar, bouncy Ida, the embodiment of that 'optimism which is worse than the blackest despair'). Certainly there is a contrast between dark and light. Pinkie is a creature of the shadows; he lives in a bare, dimly lit attic room in a lodging house run by a blind man; he murders a reporter on a ghost-train ride. Ida is most at home in a cheery pub or strolling along the seaside prom with the holidaymakers. Their paths cross continually but there are only fleeting moments of direct contact. It is one of the strengths of the Boultings' film that this conflict never becomes laborious and schematic. There is a remorseless logic in the way in which Ida snatches Rose back from the arms of death and causes Pinkie to hurl himself to oblivion.

Brighton Rock and *They Made Me a Fugitive* benefit from a convincing authenticity absent from two other British film noirs, *Noose* (1948) and *Night Beat* (1948). *Noose* – based on the play Richard Llewellyn had fashioned out of his banned 1930s film script – deals with racketeering and murder; the woman reporter who tries to investigate and expose them gets little help from the police and is threatened with disfigurement by the gangsters. Right only triumphs after her ex-commando fiancé rallies his demobilised men to smash up the gangs' various rackets. French director Edmond T. Greville is constantly inventive and the film has zest and panache, but *Noose* doesn't take itself seriously enough to evoke fully a noir mood.

Night Beat, less flamboyantly directed by Harold Huth, is centred on two demobilised commandos, Don (Hector Ross) and Andy (Ronald Howard) who join the police force. The script, by Guy Morgan, a *Daily Express* journalist, is topical enough: Don buckles down and becomes a CID detective, Andy falls under the spell of a prosperous spiv and goes to the bad. But Huth fails to grasp the opportunities afforded for a realistic depiction of post-war crime. Unusually, there is a proper *femme fatale*, but as played by the crude, brassy Christine Norden, she hardly rivals her American sisters in crime. Like more blatant attempts to ape American models such as *No Orchids for Miss Blandish* (1948), *Night Beat* is an unsatisfactory melange of undigested and conflicting traditions.

International interventions

That British film noir could combine glossy internationalism with an English idiom was proved decisively by Carol Reed and Graham Greene's *The Third Man* (1949). Greene had written *The Green Cockatoo* (1937), a film that has been identified as the first British film noir, but which he dismissed. However, he retained his links with Korda, who brought him together with Carol Reed to work on an adaptation of his short story 'The Basement Room' as *The Fallen Idol* (1948). Reed, who had already made the atmospherically noirish *Odd Man Out* (1946), went on to work with Greene on *The Third Man*, an international crime story for Korda and David O. Selznick.

Greene's premise is simple but intriguing. A man is invited to help a friend in a foreign city but arrives only in time for his funeral; he sticks around, unwilling to acknowledge that everything has changed because of a trivial traffic accident, and discovers that things are indeed not as they seem. Greene's story of two ex-public schoolboys finally ending their childhood friendship slips imperceptibly into that of two American buddies (played by Joseph Cotten and Orson Welles), learning to betray each other. But international stars and American co-finance make no dent on Reed and Greene's creative freedom. Reed makes skilful use of the aura of rascally charm around the unreliable and temperamental Welles. Lime is charming but he is also threatening; solid and handsome but slightly sickly – his pale round face recalling that of Hans, the moon-faced boy whose ball rolls into Lime's apartment, interrupting the concierge's revelations. Robert Krasker's cinematography consciously borrows from American film noir, but there is an element of exuberant pastiche in his use of oddly angled shots and dramatic shadowy lighting. The film takes bold risks with its narrative structure, its visual virtuosity, even its music (with its dependence on Anton Karas's solitary zither). The story of betrayal and corruption is permeated by sardonic humour, not only in Welles' performance but in the visual style of sequences such as that in which the boy Hans leads a crowd in comically threatening pursuit of Holly Martins, and the nightmare taxi drive which dumps Martins at the literary soirée where he is to deliver his lecture on literary modernism. *The Third Man* is extraordinary in the contrast between the shabby, war-torn world in which it is set (a Vienna divided, like Berlin, into zones occupied by the Allied powers) and its own artistic ambition. Like the best film noirs, it presents the world as terrible but vividly exciting.

The fusion of American and British elements is less successful in *Night and the City*, directed by Jules Dassin for Twentieth Century-Fox. Mutz Greenbaum (now anglicised to Max Greene), relishes the opportunity to recreate London as a noirish city (*The Green Cockatoo* had been confined to studio sets); but in place of Greene's sparse evocative story for *The Third Man*, Dassin has a sprawling picaresque novel by Gerald Kersh, which his scriptwriter Jo Eisinger has trouble picking her way through. His protagonist Harry Fabian is played by Richard Widmark, a key actor in American film noir, but oddly out of place as a small-time spiv in the parochial London underworld (in the novel he's a pimp). His schemes never look remotely plausible and his doom seems less an inevitable descent into tragedy than the casual swatting of a persistent bluebottle. The most interesting action happens along the sidelines particularly in the scenes between the repulsive club owner Phil Nosseros (Francis L. Sullivan) and the wife (Googie Withers) who finds she can no longer contain her physical disgust.

Legacies of the war

British cinema of the 1950s is characterised by safe, conventional comedies and celebratory war films. But as with 1950s society generally, there is a tension between the desire for security and respectability, and the dark, exciting memories of the war. The Second World War continued to haunt British culture and society throughout the 1950s. The bombed building sites that blotted the land – the source of excitement and danger for children in such films as *Hunted* (1952) and *The Yellow Balloon* (1952) – were not eradicated until the following decade. Films celebrating British achievements in the war dominated the box office, but less glorious legacies of the war continued to play a role in British film noirs.

Ralph Thomas's *The Clouded Yellow*, Basil Dearden's *Cage of Gold* and Jacques Tourneur's *Circle of Danger* (1951) all feature maladjusted war veterans. Robert Hamer's *The Spider and the Fly* (1951), set during the First World War in France, and *The Long Memory* (1952), which sidesteps the war by including it in the twelve-year period that the hero spends in prison, share the same feeling of post-war anomie. *Circle of Danger* is disadvantaged by an uninteresting love triangle. But Ray Milland's attempt to unravel the mystery of his brother's death – he was an American volunteer in a British commando unit – is intriguing. The ex-soldiers who resist his attempts to uncover what happened have nothing to be ashamed of; but their actions make the war seem like a guilty secret that needs to be shielded from prying eyes.

The commandos, though dispersed in peacetime occupations, remain a close-knit unit, prepared to kill if necessary to protect their taciturn leader. David Somers (Trevor Howard) in *The Clouded Yellow*, by contrast, is coldly expelled from his wartime network (in the more isolating, back-biting world of the Secret Intelligence Service) and betrayed by his boss when he is implicated in a murder hunt. But Somers too has friends – victims of the Nazis whom he had helped to escape to safety in England and who now in turn protect him from the authorities. Howard's Clem Morgan in *They Made Me a Fugitive*, misses the thrills of war, but Somers seeks tranquillity and a reaffirmation of his humanity. He finds salvation not with the deceptively placid English gentleman whose butterfly collection he catalogues, but with a supposedly mad girl (Jean Simmons) suspected of murder. Similarly, Philip Davidson (John Mills) in *The Long Memory* is restored to humanity by a Polish refugee whose awful wartime experiences more than match the injustice he has suffered through wrongful imprisonment.[17] The damaged, fragile but resourceful protagonists of *The Clouded Yellow* and *The Long Memory* have more in common with the heroes of pre-war French poetic realism, which *The Long Memory* consciously evokes through its strong echoes of Marcel Carné's *Le Quai des brumes* (1938) than with the tough guys of American film noir, through their central concern with the need to rebuild shattered lives grows out of the war.

The next group of films – *The Intruder* (1953), *The Ship That Died of Shame* (1955) and *Tiger in the Smoke* (1956) – has a different message concerned with the need to move on from the war and adapt to peacetime society. In *The Intruder*, ex-tank commander Wolf Merton (Jack Hawkins) disturbs a burglar and recognises him as Ginger Edwards (Michael Medwin), one of his own men. He determines to track him down, not to bring him to justice but to discover what has turned a good soldier into a thief. This necessitates Merton re-establishing contact with other men under his command, while a series of flashbacks tell the story of Ginger's honourable role in the war and the bad breaks he had suffered once returned to peacetime society. As in *Circle of Danger*, the truth eventually emerges. Merton reluctantly puts loyalty to one of his men above his deference to law and order and prepares to help Ginger escape the clutches of the police. But with his respect restored by the faith shown in him by his wartime comrades, Ginger determines to give himself up and try again to adjust to peacetime society.

Bill Randall (George Baker), wartime captain of a fast gunboat, has not sunk as low as Ginger, but his attempt to start his own business has failed and his old firm refuse to take him back. Therefore, when he meets up with Hoskins (Richard Attenborough), his rascally second-in-command, he is soon persuaded to rescue their ship from the breakers yard and use it to indulge in smuggling. But as they get more deeply involved in crime Randall, along with his faithful coxswain Birdie (Bill Owen), becomes increasingly uneasy – and the ship becomes ever more troublesome, as if it too objected to the tarnishing of its wartime exploits. During a climactic storm at sea, Hoskins is thrown overboard and the ship crashes onto the rocks. Randall and Birdie manage to swim to safety, but they have now learned their lesson and will put the war behind them and do whatever they need to do to carve themselves a niche in peacetime society.

That *Tiger in the Smoke* was based on a novel written by a woman (Margery Allingham), goes some way to explain the absence of nostalgia. The ex-servicemen of *The Intruder* and *The Ship that Died of Shame* miss the comradeship and the sense of purpose they shared during the war. To Meg Elgin (Muriel Pavlow) it is a bad memory that she had put behind her until the husband she thought killed in the war threatens to reappear on the eve of her wedding to another man. In fact this is a cruel and never satisfactorily explained trick; but her anxiety over the anticipated return of her husband is overtaken by anxiety over the disappearance of her fiancé – who has been kidnapped by a gang of war-damaged buskers. As in *Circle of Danger* and *The Intruder*, everything is rooted in the war, but here there is no sympathy for the war veterans – displayed as a pathetic bunch of misfits led by a psychopath – and the treasure they dream will transform their lives proves to be an illusion. The night and fog that dominates the first two-thirds of the film gradually dissipates and by the time the film ends Meg and her fiancé are able to take their place in the affluent society, the legacy of the war seemingly banished.

1950s B film noirs

Laurence Miller in 'Evidence for a British Film Noir Cycle', claims that 'From 1951 to 1955, 22 to 28 film noirs were released each year. The peak years were 1956 (32 films) and 1957 (41 films) followed by a decline to 25 films in 1958 and 25 in 1959'.[18] This figure might be over-optimistic, but there is undoubtedly a rich stratum of 1950s B films with noirish themes and subjects. Miller is right to point to the prolific output of crime films in the 1950s – but it is debatable how many of them can really be classified as film noirs. Low-budget thrillers like *The Blue Parrot* (1953), *The Limping Man* (1953), *The*

Black Rider (1954) and *Soho Incident* (1956) have noirish elements, but they are restricted by their low budgets to well-tried formulas and predictably conventional plots. A noirish gloom does, however, linger over many of these B crime films, especially Anglo-Amalgamated's *Scotland Yard* series of shorts and their *Edgar Wallace Presents* series of featurettes. Between 1953 and 1962 the lugubrious Edgar Lustgarten introduced forty 'stories of human weakness, of greed and envy, of cunning and stupidity', supposedly taken from the annals of Scotland Yard. The best episodes – Ken Hughes' *The Drayton Case* (1953), *The Missing Man* (1953) and *The Dark Stairway* (1954), and Paul Gherzo's *Fatal Journey* (1954), *The Mysterious Bullet* (1955) and *The Stateless Man* (1955) – are taut, atmospheric and wonderfully evocative of a world of guilty secrets, clandestine passions, suspicious landladies and mysterious happenings behind tightly drawn curtains.[19] The hour-long Edgar Wallace films made between 1960 and 1964 dwelt less on the macabre than earlier Wallace films; location shooting used to supplement the limited resources of Merton Park studios, gave them an air of brusque realism. Typical Wallace mysteries like *The Malpas Mystery* (1960) and *The Clue of the Twisted Candle* (1960) look dated, but Anglo-Amalgamated proved enterprisingly inventive in updating stories about blackmail and betrayal. Alan Bridges' *Act of Murder* (1964) and John Moxey's *Face of a Stranger* (1964), both manage to create a mood of sinister threat while eschewing noir chiaroscuro for bright, outdoor photography. *Face of a Stranger* is also remarkable in having a blind woman (Rosemary Leach) emerge as a *femme fatale*, greedily manipulating three men in her desire to get her hands on ill-gotten gains.

American influences

In the later years of the 1950s more questioning, less deferential attitudes surfaced in Britain, bringing a boost to a noir tradition that had seemed threatened by the dominant desire for law-abiding conformity. Seth Holt's *Nowhere to Go* succeeds better than *Night and the City* in integrating its American star (George Nader) into the English underworld. As an outsider who works alone, he is a plausible conman, and there is a convincing sadness in his realisation that he can trust no one, least of all his good-natured contact man (Bernard Lee). Holt and cinematographer Paul Beeson create a world of glossy surfaces that is the antithesis of noir lighting, but the cold, hard world of the film recreates the noir ethos of alienation and existential despair. *Beyond this Place* (1959), directed by cinematographer Jack Cardiff, is shot in a more conventional chiaroscuro style, and it exudes gloom and despair; the unjustly imprisoned man (Bernard Lee) seems irredeemably brutalised by his experiences. The presence of two American stars – Van Johnson and Vera Miles – brings little sense of American optimism to the gloomy Liverpool setting, where policemen are unfriendly, sour and unhelpful and an aura of corruption rules.

American stars, mostly minor or fading, were often used in British genre films of the 1950s to ease their passage into the American market, where they often played as supporting features. Films such as *The Flanagan Boy* (1953), *Marilyn* (1953) and *Impulse* (1955) deliberately copy American models, but more generally they remain distinctively British. Most intriguing are Ken Hughes' attempts at transposing Amiercan film noirs in English settings. *The House Across the Lake* (1954), based on his novel *High Wray*, begins with a washed-up American writer (Alex Nicol) confessing his involvement in a *crime passionale* on Lake Windermere. Elements of pastiche are redeemed by fine performances – particularly from Sid James as the cuckolded husband – and a satisfyingly well-constructed plot. *Confession* (1955) is less subtle but more gutsy, indeed Sydney Chaplin's hypocritical killer emulates Tod Slaughter's creations in black-hearted villainy. Often the part played by the American star is of an essentially good American/Canadian who somehow comes adrift in unfamiliar British waters. By contrast, Chaplin's character is a British man who returns from America with an attitude towards violence which is shockingly inappropriate in a quiet English backwater ('In this town we only get one murder a year – not two in two days' – an indignant policeman protests). As in *The House Across the Lake*, the mix isn't quite right, but Hughes' valiant attempts to grapple with film noir deserves more credit than they have subsequently received.[20]

Ironically, the most satisfying of Hughes' modestly stylish thrillers, *The Brain Machine* (1955), is the most English. Elizabeth Allan plays an unusually mature, intelligent heroine, a psychiatrist who leaves her work-obsessed husband only to be kidnapped by a psychopathic gangster (Maxwell Reed). The plot moves along sharply enough, and Hughes conjures up an appropriately noirish atmosphere in gloomy hospitals and bleak night-time streets; but what makes the film peculiarly resonant is the sexual and class tension that underlies the edgy relationship between this ill-matched couple. Hughes' enthusiasm for Hollywood led him to set two subsequent films in a studio-bound America. *Joe Macbeth* (1955) is a reworking of Shakespeare's Scottish play among American gangsters; *Wicked As They Come* (1956) charts the rise of a ruthlessly ambitious New York slum girl. They are less convincing than *The Long Haul* (1958), with Victor Mature slugging it out against tough British lorry drivers, and Hughes seemed most at home in the Soho milieu of *The Small World of Sammy Lee* (1963).

American exiles made a valuable contribution to British film noir. Edward Dmytryk directed *Obsession*, Jules Dassin *Night and the City*, and in the 1950s Cy Endfield made *The Limping Man* and two tough melodramas starring Stanley Baker, *Hell Drivers* (1956) and *Sea Fury* (1958). By far the most important expatriate, however, was Joseph Losey, who was responsible for a trilogy of strikingly diverse film noirs – *Time Without Pity* (1957), *Blind Date* (1959) and *The Criminal* (1960). From the lurid frenzy of its opening murder to the sacrificial suicide with which it ends, *Time Without Pity* moves with a hysterical intensity rarely seen in British cinema. Though the plot – from a play by Emlyn Williams – concerns a young man unjustly accused of murdering a young woman, Losey's concern is with three middle-aged characters: an alcoholic writer (Michael Redgrave), a psychotic egotist (Leo McKern) and a desperately unhappy woman (Ann Todd). Alongside the melodramatic race against time to save a man's life, Losey burrows beneath the surface of polite English society to reveal a world of insecurity, anxiety and injustice where the old, at best, let down, and, at worst, selfishly exploit the young.

Blind Date is calmer and less pessimistic despite its brooding settings – the overdressed apartment of a kept woman, the dingy offices of Scotland Yard – and its story of an innocent man caught in the web woven by a *femme fatale*. Stanley Baker plays Inspector Morgan, an ambitious, discontented detective whose class instincts (he is the son of a working-class chauffeur and is uncomfortably aware where power lies) cause him to crash through the barriers of deference. Though the evidence points to a young artist, Jan Van Rooyen (Hardy Kruger), as the murderer, Morgan's unwillingness to accept the obvious leads him to the real murderer. She is Jacqueline Cousteau (Micheline Presle), a rich woman who has allowed jealousy and mate-rialism to shrivel her soul. Though she denies that she knows him, Jan claims that it is she, not the murdered woman, with whom he had a passionate affair. Morgan leaves them alone together, and Jan torments her with what might have been: 'What was it? You were too old for me? Were you afraid of that? But you were young to me, all the things that should have happened to you when you were a girl I was bringing to you'. Her sophisticated façade crumbles under the onslaught of his honesty, but Jacqueline's tragedy has less weight than Jan's liberation and the film ends with him going out into the morning sunshine and jumping onto a bus, a harbinger of the optimistic, youth-dominated decade to come.

The Criminal plunges back into an unremittingly noirish milieu of treachery and death. The prison where it begins is a place of expressionist shadows, echoing sounds, moodily obsessive characters and pent up violence. Its protagonist, John Bannion (Stanley Baker), is released into a London of luxury apartments, glamorously available women and cool jazz. But the film ends in a snowy field with the dying Bannion pursued by his greedy henchmen, remorselessly searching for the haul from a racetrack robbery.[21]

The Criminal warns that affluence and modernity provided no guarantee of a brighter, happier world. Val Guest's *Hell Is a City* (1960), with its fresh-eyed approach to society and its willingness to show less-than-perfect policemen and the materialist rewards of a life of crime, is more typical of the early 1960s. Its protagonist, Inspector Martineau, again played by Baker, is a satisfyingly complex character, a hard-working and honest policeman, but one whose home life is in tatters and whose relationship to his criminal adversaries is much closer than those of more conventional Scotland Yard detectives. Despite his unhappy, childless marriage, Martineau is at home in the city and enjoys its glittering attractions. A similar hard-bitten realism permeates the Newcastle-set heist film *Payroll* (1961), and *The Informers* (1963), which centres on a charismatic police inspector (Nigel Patrick) accused of corruption in a dirty war with sophisticated criminals. *The Small World of Sammy Lee* (1963), adventurously adapts a *nouvelle-vague* style to its study of a small-time Soho operator desperately trying to raise money to avoid nemesis over his unpaid gambling debts.[22]

By the mid-1960s, as changing exhibition practices killed off the 'B' film, colour replaced black and white, and British cinema embraced the ethos of Swinging London, the era of classic film noir drew to a close, though films continued to delve into the darker side of life as the optimism of the permissive society turned to disillusion. Because they deal with the underbelly of society, British film noirs have been condemned as 'morbid' or 'sordid'; because they work within generic conventions and seek for melodramatic thrills they have been dismissed as trivial; because they borrow styles and motifs from other cinemas they have been sneered at as inauthentic. In fact they constitute a valuable and endlessly fascinating tradition of indigenous British cinema, tantalisingly similar but fundamentally different from their American counterparts. Their critiques of society might be more oblique and subdued; they are less sexualised but more closely intertwined with social reality; women are less evil but men are weaker. The rediscovery of this 'lost continent' makes British cinema seem a

richer, more exciting, and more inspiring legacy than has previously
been supposed.

Notes

1   William K. Everson, 'British Film Noir', *Films in Review*, 38:5 (May
    1987), 285; Part 2: *Films in Review*, 38:6 (June/July 1987), 341–6.
2   Laurence Miller, 'Evidence for a British Film Noir Cycle', in Wheeler
    Winston Dixon (ed.), *Re-viewing British Cinema, 1900–1992* (Albany
    NY: State University of New York Press, 1994), pp. 155–64.
3   Brian McFarlane, 'Losing the Peace: Some British Films of Postwar
    Adjustment', in Tony Barta (ed.), *Screening the Past: Film and the
    Representation of History* (Westport, Connecticut and London: Praeger,
    1998), pp. 93–107; Robert Murphy, *Realism and Tinsel: British Cinema
    and Society 1939–49* (London: Routledge, 1989).
4   Tony Williams, 'British Film Noir', in Alain Silver and James Ursini
    (eds), *Film Noir Reader 2* (New York: Limelight Editions, 1999), p. 255.
5   *Ibid.*, p. 246.
6   Raymond Durgnat, 'Some Lines of Enquiry into Post-war British
    Crimes', in Robert Murphy (ed.), *The British Cinema Book* (London:
    BFI Publishing, 2001), pp. 133–45.
7   Andrew Spicer, *Film Noir* (Harlow, Essex: Longman/Pearson Education,
    2002).
8   James Chapman, 'Celluloid Shockers', in Jeffrey Richards (ed.), *The
    Unknown 1930s* (London, I. B. Tauris, 1997), p. 82. Chapman provides
    an invaluable guide to the 350 thrillers made in Britain between 1930
    and 1939.
9   Spicer, *Film Noir*, p. 180.
10 Martha Wolfenstein and Nathan Leites, *Movies: A Psychological Study*
    (Glencoe, Illinois: Free Press, 1950), p. 23.
11 McFarlane, p. 93; Andrew Spicer, *Typical Men: The Representation of
    Masculinity in Popular British Cinema* (London: I. B. Tauris, 2001), pp.
    161–83.
12 *Great Day* (1945), *Wanted for Murder*, *Daybreak* and *Corridor of
    Mirrors* (1948), all exploit Portman's ability to portray wounded, sensi-
    tive, but slightly threatening men, and revel in oddly fantastic plots. One
    of Durgnat's noir sub-sections covers 'the Portman murders', Durgnat, p.
    136.
13 Comfort's *Squadron Leader X* (1942), *Escape to Danger* (1943) and
    Hotel Reserve (1944), on which he worked closely with cinematographer
    Max Greene/Mutz Greenbaum, all have noirish qualities. Comfort went
    on to direct *Daughter of Darkness* (1948) and *Silent Dust*, and in the
    1950s a number of proficient B film noirs, most notably *Bang! You're
    Dead* (1954). See Brian McFarlane, *Lance Comfort* (Manchester:
    Manchester University Press, 1999).

14 See Sue Harper and Vincent Porter, *British Cinema of the 1950s: The Decline of Deference* (Oxford: Oxford University Press, 2003), pp. 76, 288.

15 For more on 1940s underworld films see my 'Riff-Raff: British Cinema and the Underworld', in Charles Barr (ed.), *All Our Yesterdays* (London: BFI Publishing, 1986) (where anxious to preserve the integrity of these newly excavated films I concluded that 'Comparisons between the British spiv cycle and American film noir are inevitable but unhelpful'), 'The Spiv Cycle', Chapter 8 in Robert Murphy, *Realism and Tinsel*, and Tim Pulleine 'Spin a Dark Web' in Robert Murphy (ed.) *The British Cinema Book*.

16 Arthur Vesselo, 'The Quarter in Britain', *Sight and Sound* (Autumn 1947), 120.

17 Christine Geraghty perceptively analyses the role of Elsa, the Polish refugee in *The Long Memory* in *British Cinema in the Fifties: Gender, Genre and The 'New Look'* (London: Routledge, 2000), pp. 102–4.

18 Miller, p. 163. See also Harper and Porter, *British Cinema of the 1950s*, p. 143 and Andrew Spicer, 'Creativity and the "B" Feature: Terence Fisher's Crime Films', *Film Criticism*, xxx: 2 (Winter, 2005–6), 24–42 for Hammer's B film noirs.

19 'Paul Gherzo' was a pseudonym used by the talented documentary film-maker Paul Dickson.

20 See Allen Eyles, 'A Passion for Cinema: Ken Hughes', *Focus on Film* 6 (Spring 1971), 42–51; Spicer, *Film Noir*, pp. 191–2, 194.

21 Apart from Visconti's *Senso* (1954), *The Criminal* was Robert Krasker's most inventive achievement since *The Third Man*.

22 See Robert Murphy, *Sixties British Cinema* (London: BFI Publishing, 1992), pp. 209–10 for further discussion of *Payroll* and *The Informers*; for *The Small World of Sammy Lee*, see Steve Chibnall, 'Ordinary People: "New Wave" Realism and the British Crime Film 1959–1963', in Steve Chibnall and Robert Murphy (eds), *British Crime Cinema* (London: Routledge, 1999), p. 95.

Filmography

The Lodger, Alfred Hitchcock, 1926
Piccadilly, E. A. Dupont, 1928
Blackmail, Alfred Hitchcock, 1929
The Informer, Arthur Robison, 1929
The Frightened Lady, T. Hayes Hunter, 1933
The Ghoul, T. Hayes Hunter, 1933
The Man Who Knew Too Much, Alfred Hitchcock, 1934
Maria Marten, Milton Rosmer, 1935
The Crimes of Stephen Hawke, George King, 1936
Sabotage, Alfred Hitchcock, 1936
Sweeney Todd: The Demon Barber of Fleet Street, George King, 1936

Dark Journey, Victor Saville, 1937
The Dark Stairway, Arthur Woods, 1937
The Frog, Jack Raymond, 1937
The Green Cockatoo, William Cameron Menzies/William K. Howard, 1937
It's Never Too Late to Mend, David Macdonald, 1937
The Squeaker, William K. Howard, 1937
The Ticket of Leave Man, George King, 1937
Dead Men Tell No Tales, David Macdonald, 1938
The Gaunt Stranger, Walter Forde, 1938
Sexton Blake and the Hooded Terror, George King, 1938
Strange Boarders, Herbert Mason, 1938
The Terror, Richard Bird, 1938
They Drive by Night, Arthur Woods, 1938
The Dark Eyes of London, Walter Summers, 1939
Dead Men Are Dangerous, Harold French, 1939
The Face at the Window, George King, 1939
Murder in Soho, Norman Lee, 1939
On the Night of the Fire, Brian Desmond Hurst, 1939
Poison Pen, Paul Stein, 1939
The Spy in Black, Michael Powell, 1939
Traitor Spy, Walter Summers, 1939
A Window in London, Herbert Mason, 1939
Busman's Honeymoon, Arthur Woods, 1940
The Case of the Frightened Lady, George King, 1940
Contraband, Michael Powell, 1940
Crimes at the Dark House, George King, 1940
The Door with Seven Locks, Norman Lee, 1940
Gaslight, Thorold Dickinson, 1940
Cottage to Let, Anthony Asquith, 1941
East of Piccadilly, Harold Huth, 1941
Hatter's Castle, Lance Comfort, 1941
Tower of Terror, Lawrence Huntington, 1941
Next of Kin, Thorold Dickinson, 1942
The Night Has Eyes, Leslie Arliss, 1942
Squadron Leader X, Lance Comfort, 1942
Uncensored, Anthony Asquith, 1942
Unpublished Story, Harold French, 1942
Went the Day Well?, Cavalcanti, 1942
Escape to Danger, Lance Comfort/Max Greene, 1943
They Met in the Dark, Karel Lamac, 1943
Yellow Canary, Herbert Wilcox, 1943
Fanny by Gaslight, Anthony Asquith, 1944
Hotel Reserve, Lance Comfort/Max Greene/Victor Hanbury, 1944
Dead of Night, Robert Hamer/Cavalcanti/Charles Crichton/Basil Dearden,
      1945
Great Day, Lance Comfort, 1945

Murder in Reverse, Montgomery Tully, 1945
Pink String and Sealing Wax, Robert Hamer, 1945
Appointment with Crime, John Harlow, 1946
Bedelia, Lance Comfort, 1946
Carnival, Stanley Haynes, 1946
Daybreak, Compton Bennett, 1946
Green for Danger, Sidney Gilliat, 1946
Night Boat to Dublin, Lawrence Huntington, 1946
Wanted for Murder, Lawrence Huntington, 1946
Black Memory, John Gilling, 1947
Blanche Fury, Marc Allegret, 1947
Brighton Rock, John Boulting, 1947
Dear Murderer, Arthur Crabtree, 1947
Dual Alibi, Alfred Travers, 1947
Frieda, Basil Dearden, 1947
It Always Rains on Sunday, Robert Hamer, 1947
The Man Within, Bernard Knowles, 1947
Mine Own Executioner, Anthony Kimmins, 1947
The October Man, Roy Baker, 1947
Odd Man Out, Carol Reed, 1947
Take My Life, Ronald Neame, 1947
Temptation Harbour, Lance Comfort, 1947
They Made Me a Fugitive, Cavalcanti, 1947
Uncle Silas, Charles Frank, 1947
The Upturned Glass, Lawrence Huntington, 1947
While I Live, John Harlow, 1947
Corridor of Mirrors, Terence Young, 1948
Daughter of Darkness, Lance Comfort, 1948
Escape, Joseph Mankiewicz, 1948
The Flamingo Affair, Horace Shepherd, 1948
Good Time Girl, David Macdonald, 1948
A Gunman Has Escaped, Richard Grey, 1948
The Mark of Cain, Brian Desmond Hurst, 1948
The Monkey's Paw, Norman Lee, 1948
My Brother's Keeper, Arthur Roome, 1948
Night Beat, Harold Huth, 1948
No Orchids for Miss Blandish, St John Legh Clowes, 1948
Noose, Edmund T. Greville, 1948
Portrait from Life, Terence Fisher, 1948
Saraband for Dead Lovers, Basil Dearden, 1948
The Small Back Room, Michael Powell and Emeric Pressburger, 1948
The Small Voice, Fergus McDonnell, 1948
So Evil My Love, Lewis Allen, 1948
The Three Weird Sisters, Dan Birt, 1948
Uneasy Terms, Vernon Sewell, 1948
Forbidden, George King, 1949

For Them that Trespass, Cavalcanti, 1949
Man on the Run, Lawrence Huntington, 1949
No Way Back, Stefan Osiecki, 1949
Obsession, Edward Dmytryk, 1949
The Queen of Spades, Thorold Dickinson, 1949
Silent Dust, Lance Comfort, 1949
The Spider and the Fly, Robert Hamer, 1949
The Third Man, Carol Reed, 1949
Cage of Gold, Basil Dearden, 1950,
The Clouded Yellow, Ralph Thomas, 1950
Madeleine, David Lean, 1950
Night and the City, Jules Dassin, 1950
So Long at the Fair, Terence Fisher/Anthony Darnborough, 1950
Waterfront, Michael Anderson, 1950
Circle of Danger, Jacques Tourneur, 1951
Night Without Stars, Anthony Pelissier, 1951
Pool of London, Basil Dearden, 1951
There Is Another Sun, Lewis Gilbert, 1951
Wide Boy, Ken Hughes, 1952
The Yellow Balloon, J. Lee Thompson, 1952
The Blue Parrot, John Harlow, 1953
Black 13, Ken Hughes, 1953
The Drayton Case, Ken Hughes, short, 1953
The Flanagan Boy, Reginald LeBorg, 1953
The Intruder, Guy Hamilton, 1953
The Limping Man, Cy Endfield/Charles de la Tour, 1953
The Long Memory, Robert Hamer, 1953
The Man Between, Carol Reed, 1953
The Man Who Watched Trains Go by, Harold French, 1953
Mantrap, Terence Fisher, 1953
Marilyn, Wolf Rilla, 1953
The Missing Man, Ken Hughes, short, 1953
Street of Shadows, Richard Vernon, 1953
Bang! You're Dead, Lance Comfort, 1954
The Dark Stairway, Ken Hughes, short, 1954
Fatal Journey, Paul Gherzo, short, 1954
The Good Die Young, Lewis Gilbert, 1954
The House Across the Lake, Ken Hughes, 1954
The Passing Stranger, John Arnold, 1954
The Stranger Came Home, Terence Fisher, 1954
Thirty-Six Hours, Montgomery Tully, 1954
The Weak and the Wicked, J. Lee Thompson, 1954
The Brain Machine, Ken Hughes, 1955
Confession, Ken Hughes, 1955
Impulse, Cy Endfield/Charles de la Tour, 1955
Joe Macbeth, Ken Hughes, 1955

The Mysterious Bullet, Paul Gherzo, short, 1955
The Ship that Died of Shame, Basil Dearden, 1955
The Stateless Man, Paul Gherzo, short, 1955
The Man Who Never Was, Ronald Neame, 1956
Soho Incident, Vernon Sewell, 1956
Tiger in the Smoke, Roy Baker, 1956
Yield to the Night, J. Lee Thompson, 1956
Hell Drivers, Cy Endfield, 1957
The Flesh Is Weak, Don Chaffey, 1957
The Long Haul, Ken Hughes, 1957
Time Without Pity, Joseph Losey, 1957
The Key, Carol Reed, 1958
Nowhere to Go, Seth Holt, 1958
Tread Softly Stranger, Gordon Parry, 1958
Beyond This Place, Jack Cardiff, 1959
Blind Date, Joseph Losey, 1959
In the Wake of a Stranger, David Eady, 1959
Naked Fury, Charles Saunders, 1959
Passport to Shame, Alvin Rakoff, 1959
Circle of Deception, Jack Lee, 1960
The Criminal, Joseph Losey, 1960
Hell Is a City, Val Guest, 1960
Never Let Go, John Guillermin, 1960
The Frightened City, John Lemont, 1961
The Man in the Back Seat, Vernon Sewell, 1961
Offbeat, Cliff Owen, 1961
Payroll, Sidney Hayers, 1961
Taste of Fear, Seth Holt, 1961
Jigsaw, Val Guest, 1962
Blind Corner, Lance Comfort, 1963
Cairo, Wolf Rilla, 1963
The Informers, Ken Annakin, 1963
Nightmare, Freddie Francis, 1963
The Small World of Sammy Lee, Ken Hughes, 1963
Act of Murder, Alan Bridges, 1964
Face of a Stranger, John Moxey, 1964
Hysteria, Freddie Francis, 1964
Never Mention Murder, John Nelson Burton, 1964
The Third Secret, Charles Crichton, 1964

Select bibliography

Chapman, James, 'Celluloid Shockers', in Jeffrey Richards (ed.), *The Unknown 1930s* (London: I. B. Tauris, 1997), pp. 75–98.
Chibnall, Steve, 'Ordinary People: "New Wave" Realism and the

British Crime Film 1959–1963', in Steve Chibnall and Robert Murphy (eds), *British Crime Cinema* (London: Routledge, 1999), pp. 94–109.

Durgnat, Raymond 'Some Lines of Enquiry into Post-war British Crimes', in Robert Murphy (ed.), *The British Cinema Book* (London: BFI Publishing, 2001), pp. 135–45.

Everson, William K., 'British Film Noir', *Films in Review*, 38:5 (May 1987), 285–9; 38:6 (June/July 1987), 341–6.

Geraghty, Christine, *British Cinema in the Fifties: Gender, Genre and the 'New Look'* (London: Routledge, 2000).

Harper, Sue and Vincent Porter, *British Cinema of the 1950s: The Decline of Deference* (Oxford and New York: Oxford University Press, 2003).

McFarlane, Brian, 'Losing the Peace: Some British Films of Post-war Adjustment', in Tony Barta (ed.), *Screening the Past: Film and the Representation of History* (Westport, Connecticut and London: Praeger, 1998), pp. 93–107.

McFarlane, Brian, *Lance Comfort* (Manchester: Manchester University Press, 1999).

Miller, Laurence, 'Evidence for a British Film Noir Cycle', in Wheeler Winston Dixon (ed.), *Re-viewing British Cinema, 1900–1992* (Albany NY: State University of New York Press, 1994), pp. 155–64.

Murphy, Robert, 'Riff-Raff: British Cinema and the Underworld', in Charles Barr (ed.), *All Our Yesterdays: 90 Years of British Cinema* (London: BFI Publishing, 1986), pp. 286–305.

Murphy, Robert, *Realism and Tinsel: British Cinema and Society 1939–49* (London: Routledge, 1989).

Murphy, Robert, *Sixties British Cinema* (London: BFI Publishing, 1992).

Petley, Julian, 'The Lost Continent', in Charles Barr (ed.), *All Our Yesterdays: 90 Years of British Cinema* (London: BFI Publishing, 1986), pp. 98–119.

Pulleine, Tim, 'Spin a Dark Web', in Steve Chibnall and Robert Murphy (eds), *British Crime Cinema* (London: Routledge, 1999), pp. 27–36.

Spicer, Andrew, *Typical Men: The Representation of Masculinity in Popular British Cinema* (London: I. B. Tauris, 2001).

Spicer, Andrew, *Film Noir* (Harlow, Essex: Longman/Pearson Education, 2002).

Vesselo, Arthur, 'The Quarter in Britain', *Sight and Sound* (Autumn 1947), 120.

Williams, Tony, 'British Film Noir', in Alain Silver and James Ursini (eds), *Film Noir Reader 2* (New York: Limelight Editions, 1999), pp. 242–69.

Wolfenstein, Martha and Nathan Leites, *Movies: A Psychological Study* (Glencoe, Illinois: Free Press, 1950).

5

British neo-noir

Andrew Spicer

Because of the powerful and well-established tradition of crime films in British cinema, the vast majority of British neo-noirs are variations of the crime thriller, differentiated from more conventional films by their highly wrought visual style, an emphasis on moral ambiguity and psychological complexity, and an often deliberate blurring of the boundaries between reality and fantasy, subjectivity and objectivity. Typical of neo-noir as a whole, British neo-noirs are highly intertextual and allusive, both thematically and visually. They have a degree of visibility and recognition – even if they are often reviewed dismissively – because they are produced by filmmakers conscious of the 'tradition' of film noir. However, although they share many of the characteristics of the earlier film noirs described by Robert Murphy in the previous chapter, they draw upon, not preceding British noirs, which are virtually unknown to both filmmakers and audiences, but American film noir and neo-noir. As Antonia Bird, whose 1997 film *Face* is discussed in detail, commented, 'I'm always looking at American genre movies, and I think that's mainly because of the way our cinema is in this country, because we are raised on American thrillers and genre films. To approach it in any other way wouldn't only be foolish but unpalatable, so it's got to come through that route'.[1] *Face*'s most direct models, Bird revealed, were *The Last Boy Scout* (1991) and *Heat* (1995). As she recognises, to produce neo-noirs that can reach a broad cinema-going public necessitates British filmmakers using a shared familiarity derived from American cinema.

Although some British neo-noirs are derivative imitations of their American avatars, the majority display a strong sense of national identity and, like *Face*, engage directly with contemporary British life. They combine the observational, quasi-documentary aesthetic of social realism, a powerful and pervasive presence within British cinema, with noir conventions. As Charlotte Brunsdon has argued, the two traditions create a different sense of space and place, generic and realistic, which give these films a textual and iconographic richness.[2] With some exceptions, the most interesting British neo-noirs strive to capture the dynamism of American films combined with a detailed, and also highly critical, exploration of British social mores. They are also preoccupied with the complexities of masculinity: male violence, neuroses and unstable identities.[3]

But within these broad parameters, British neo-noirs are a remarkably heterogeneous corpus of films, with few internal connections in terms of personnel. This reflects the notorious instability of the British film industry whose volatility (shortage of production finance and chronic problems of distribution and exhibition) makes it very difficult to forge durable production teams which can sustain and develop their creative endeavour over a number of films that explore similar themes and issues. In Britain there is little sense of a community of filmmakers whose films are mutually reinforcing, or which can act as a creative influence on each other. It is much more the case that every film is a separate event, produced in isolation, with each neo-noir having to invent itself anew; it is no coincidence that many contemporary British neo-noirs are the work of first-time writer-directors. However, given these unpromising conditions, neo-noir is often an attractive option because it can be made on limited budgets without necessarily compromising its thematic and visual sophistication; deft lighting and adroit compositional devices can compensate for minimal sets and restricted settings.[4]

The one filmmaker who may be said to have a major creative presence in British neo-noir is Mike Hodges with three examples. But, even in his case, twenty-six years separated *Get Carter* (1971) from his second neo-noir, *Croupier* (1997), as Hodges, like so many talented British directors (and other creative personnel) had to seek work in Hollywood.[5] He also suffered from lack of recognition and support in his native land: *Croupier* was so poorly distributed that it had to become a word-of-mouth success in America before it gained a reasonable circuit release in Britain in the summer of 1999.[6] Critical recognition was only granted in retrospect. Even despite *Croupier*'s success, Hodges had difficulty raising finance for *I'll Sleep When I'm Dead* (2003).[7] However, *Get Carter*, a highly representative British neo-noir because of its combination of indebtedness to American gangster films and British social realism (Hodges was trained as a documentarist), has itself become a powerful model, acting as a cultural intermediary between contemporary British filmmakers and American noir. It is rare for a current neo-noir not to use some verbal or visual reference to Hodges' film. The opening shot of a railway journey in *Out of Depth*

(1998), for example, was a deliberate homage, as was the way in which the lead character was dressed.[8]

Without gainsaying the heterogeneity of British neo-noir, it is possible to identify three phases that correspond to different conditions of production and in which there are certain broad similarities in style and subject matter between the films. For reasons of space, the ensuing discussion will focus on the most representative and significant neo-noirs from each phase and concentrate on textual analysis rather than their conditions of production or reception. The filmography lists all the films that can be identified confidently as neo-noirs and includes (in brackets) those that have strong noir elements but which are not 'full' noirs.

Corruption and social transformation: 1968–72

Following the disappearance of the double bill around 1964, film noir lost what had become its production base as a variation of the second feature crime film, and the crime thriller itself was replaced temporarily as a staple genre by the spy thriller.[9] For the most part, these were conservative and morally conventional films, but the three adaptations of John le Carré novels – *The Spy Who Came in from the Cold* (1965), *The Deadly Affair* (1966) and *The Looking Glass War* (1969) – had noir elements. These films' moral ambiguity, disillusionment and sense of the intolerable pressures placed on individuals by a hypocritical establishment in a rapidly changing society, permeated into the revival of the crime film. Within that revival, neo-noir was reborn with *The Strange Affair* (1968). It occurred, as did the other neo-noirs in this phase, at the end of the period in which Hollywood majors had been prepared to finance fully British films. Filmmakers used the remarkable freedom granted them by American studios to explore the social and psychological contours of the transformation of British society in which the optimism of the mid-1960s was giving way to disenchantment.

The Strange Affair was adapted from Bernard Toms' acerbic novel that had caused a sensation by portraying policemen as cynical, careerist and occasionally corrupt, and was released amid police protests about its jaundiced view of the police force .[10] It was the first film to question overtly the conventionally admirable image of the British policeman enshrined in the television series *Dixon of Dock Green* (1955–76). Director David Greene argued that the film presented 'an authentic picture of the *modern* London police force'.[11] Greene was anxious that his film capture a city that was undergoing radical and unsettling change, filming 'on authentic locations in London, with many sequences being shot in the Edgeware Road district, where the old is giving way to the new London, with tumble-down houses and shops being torn down to make room for brand-new sky-scraper blocks of council flats and massive fly-over highways'.[12] Greene accentuates the anonymous modernity of these new buildings by shooting in extreme high or low angles, which also emphasises how they seem to press in upon the inhabitants. Odd camera angles are noir conventions, but Greene deliberately avoided chiaroscuro lighting in order to create a more modern visual style. Penelope Houston noted how *The Strange Affair*, 'entirely lacks the gloomy, responsible, wet-pavements look traditional to its type. It is filmed in scrubbed, imper-sonal, unfamiliar London – building sites, the Battersea heliport, Scotland Yard's new building – and its favourite colour is dazzling white'.[13]

The story, told in flashback after his arrest and conviction, focuses on PC Strange (Michael York), the new middle-class breed of idealis-tic policeman, determined to 'do something useful' after dropping out of university. Strange is drawn into an apparently innocuous affair with 'Fred' (Susan George), the Hampstead hippie, but their energetic lovemaking is secretly photographed by her aunt and uncle who distribute pornography. Strange becomes the classic noir victim-hero when the photographs are acquired by Detective-Sergeant Pierce (Jeremy Kemp), fixated by his vendetta against the Quinces, a ruthless and violent criminal family led by ex-Detective-Sergeant Robert Quince (Jack Watson), Pierce's *Doppelgänger*. Pierce is an ambiguous and tormented figure, verging on the psychotic, with a pent-up violence that can be unleashed at any moment; at one point he has to be restrained from strangling Quince when he evades conviction. Pierce is another noir archetype of the policeman who has absorbed too much of the city's filth and depravity to remain untainted, but also a key *British* noir figure, the man –out –of –his time. His ramrod straight walk, one hand behind his back, evince a military background (in the novel he is identified as an ex-paratrooper) and his quasi-bibli-cal turn of phrase is of a piece with the moral righteousness that has become old-fashioned, even slightly foolish, like his reliance on informers, a practice despised by his superiors. Increasingly isolated and adrift, Pierce feels his own bending of the rules is justified by the behaviour of his superiors, one a bigoted disciplinarian, the other a corrupt hypocrite in the pay of the Quinces and by the inability of the law to convict criminals. Armed with the photographs, Pierce pres-surises Strange into planting drugs on the Quinces during interrogation, but at the trial the case collapses, Pierce is removed from the force and Strange gets two years. Although the authorities condemn him, Strange is offered as a figure for identification, 'In this tangle you might have done the same as P. C. Strange', as Paramount's advertising poster expressed it. Even Pierce is not condemned, his actions understood as the intolerable pressures on a man brought up in a traditional and highly ordered world with a straightforward moral code in a society where those values seem to be crumbling or redundant.

United Artists' *The Offence* (1972) was an even more disturbing look at the modern policeman, adapted from a play by *Z Cars'* scriptwriter John Hopkins – *This Story is Yours* – in which he felt able to probe a policeman's psychology more deeply than in an episode of a long-running television series.[14] *The Offence* is also told in flashback, beginning at the moment where Detective-Sergeant Johnson (Sean Connery), stands over the body of a man he has just beaten to death during interrogation. Johnson is a veteran of over twenty years, 'ten of them stuck at detective-sergeant', a man in the throes of disillusioned middle-age and marital breakdown, shambling about in his cheap sheepskin coat, battered deerstalker rammed on his head, mouth curling under a heavy moustache. Like Pierce, Johnson is a self-righteous man –out –of –his time who has also ingested too much of the crime and depravity that has come his way in the course of numerous investigations, which makes him unstable and prone to violence. The trigger is released when he interrogates Baxter (Ian Bannen), suspected of being the child molester that the police have been searching for. As the interrogation becomes more intense, Johnson is gradually forced to recognise and confront the latent tendencies he has been suppressing, his sadism and potential paedophilia. Goaded by the ambivalent Baxter's plea, 'Don't beat me for the thoughts in your head. Things you want to do', Johnson loses control completely and pummels Baxter to death. Dismayed, but strangely relieved, Johnson recognises the appalling catharsis it has been, confiding to his superior during his own interrogation: 'I wanted what he could give me, sitting there letting me hit him. He was saying welcome home'. In an equally harrowing scene after he has returned home, Johnson confronts his wife Maureen (Vivien Merchant) with his repressed imaginings. At one point stretching his powerful body over her as if about to violate or strangle her, Johnson accuses Maureen of failing to respond to his sexual needs and as he does so he imagines the molester 'looking down on their bodies, white bodies, pressing down on them, forcing himself as she screams'.

American director Sidney Lumet, aided by Harrison Birtwhistle's discordant, unsettling score, expertly orchestrates a visual and aural correlative for Johnson's confusion and anguish. The opening scene showing Baxter's death is deliberately confusing, shot in a harsh, impenetrable white light which gradually gives way to the hazy outlines of the two figures followed by the desperate efforts of Johnson's colleagues to retrieve the situation. This explicit oneirism, blurring the boundaries between nightmare and reality, is continued in the scene after Johnson has been charged and sent home. He drives back through the neon-lit night-time streets in the heavy rain (a classic noir journey), his mind obsessively reliving the most horrific moments of the cases he has investigated, dwelling on the details of the victims' bodies. He drives from one underground car park to another then to his flat, which is so anonymous that he even goes to the wrong door. His flat's soulless interior is the domestic complement to the policestation in which much of the action takes place, whose white-walled rooms were constructed by production designer Jon Clark to be 'stark, angular, full of hard, impersonal, man-made surfaces giving the feeling of a legal Alphaville'.[15] Both are part of the deracinated environment of a Home Counties' new town (Bracknell), with its bleak, decentred landscapes, another index of a Britain in transition towards an inhuman modernity.

The other three key neo-noirs in this phase – *Performance* (1970), *Get Carter* (1971) and *Sitting Target* (1972) – all focused on the violence and psychopathologies of the professional criminal, but continued the exploration of fractured masculine identity and social dislocation. Their presentation of the 'hard man' was part of a new realism that Mike Hodges identified when he commented that before this point, 'British criminals never did anything we saw people do in American film noir; nothing really unpleasant or sadistic. Then it all changed with the Krays and the Richardson trials'.[16] The high-profile celebrity status of the Krays in particular, who were tried and sentenced in 1969, created an interest in the milieu and the psychology of the underworld villain that the films exploited. *Performance* and *Get Carter* have achieved cult status, but *Sitting Target* has been unjustly overlooked. Although its narrative of prison break-out, revenge and betrayal was somewhat conventional, it too presented London as an alien city, a world of criss-crossing railway lines and bleak, angular tower blocks. Producer Barry Kulick emphasised that it was filmed primarily in the vicinity of Clapham Junction in order to show an 'entirely different' London from the one audiences were used to seeing, which had 'a strange, nether world feeling about it'.[17]

Screenwriter Alexander Jacobs imbues the main protagonist Harry Lomart (Oliver Reed) with the implacable indestructibility and sense of futility of Lee Marvin's Walker in *Point Blank* (1969), which Jacobs co-scripted. As in the earlier film, there is a powerful suggestion that the events we witness may all have been Lomart's fantasy, a product of his disturbed mental state as he brooded in prison.

Get Carter was also a revenge drama, displaying the high degree of generic self-consciousness characteristic of neo-noir: Jack Carter (Michael Caine), a professional hitman working for London gangsters, reads *Farewell My Lovely* as he journeys north back to his hometown of Newcastle to investigate the circumstances of his brother's murder. Although clearly indebted to Hollywood gangster films, *Get Carter* was based on a British crime novel, Ted Lewis's *Jack's Return Home*, which, though borrowing from the American hard-boiled tradition, contained a detailed depiction of provincial British life. Transposing the novel's Scunthorpe to Newcastle, Hodges was determined to create a specific sense of place and time, another city in the midst of radical change, as he explained: 'Everything is in transformation. You get the sense of everything being pulled down and reconstructed. It's got a temporary feeling about it. It's a city on the cusp, a city that is going to be utterly changed'.[18] Hodges has the documentarist's keen eye for the moment at which the city's pre-war terraced housing was being cleared to make way for tower-block developments and multistorey car parks. As Steve Chibnall has shown, this rapid modernisation also embraced two of the major growth industries of the 1960s, gambling and pornography, which turned Newcastle into the Las Vegas of the north.[19] Carter's investigations reveal how civic corruption, gambling, violence and sleazy sex are intermingled in a predatory noir world.

Michael Caine's performance as the fastidious, narcissistic hitman has been justly praised. His face a blank mask, armoured by a laconic black humour and a strict professional code, Carter acts like the self-appointed scourge from a Jacobean tragedy, who seeks to cleanse the filth and corruption that lie around him and who deals to each sleazy villain their 'just' desserts. He is humanised when he sheds tears of shame and grief as he views his niece (probably daughter) appearing in a blue movie, but Hodges's presentation of Carter, more so than in the novel, is designed to be objective, not empathetic. Cinematographer Wolfgang Suschitzky's habitual use of a long lens gives much of the action a soft focus and the feeling of watching from a distance, a dispassionate observation of Carter's ruthless, often heartless actions. Although realist, *Get Carter* begins with a striking shot in which Carter is framed in a window apparently in endless space which

Hodges wanted to seem dream-like, lending him an ethereal quality, a sense that he is already an otherworldly figure.[20] The film is littered with *memento mori* that hint at Carter's inevitable death including the presence of his assassin in the same carriage in the opening train journey. He is killed by this anonymous, impersonal figure on a desolate beach punctuated by the inexorable movement of the coal hoist in which Carter has disposed of his last victim. The hoist is a symbol of a bygone age, as is Carter himself, another man out of his time whose code of conduct and loyalty to the family has become an embarrassing anachronism, part of the social corruption not its cure.

Of all the films in this phase, *Performance* made the most radical use of the extraordinary freedom offered to British filmmakers by American studios whose eyes were elsewhere. But Warner Bros. executives held up release of the film for two years, appalled at the results.[21] The inspiration for the film's extraordinary clash of lifestyles – the criminal underworld and 1960s counter-culture – came from writer and co-director Donald Cammell who, as a member of the Chelsea set, had access to both worlds.[22] For all its singularity, *Performance* has a typical sense of a swiftly changing and corrupt society being overwhelmed by pornography and violence. The main protagonist is East End hard man Chas Devlin (James Fox), the muscle for Harry Flowers (Johnny Shannon), loosely modelled on Ronnie Kray. The opening scenes establish Chas as a sexual athlete and connoisseur of the nuances of violence, armed, like Carter, with a dry wit and gallows humour and also with the type's fastidious narcissism. But his cool self-possession, 'I know who I am', is undermined by his unprofessional killing of his boyhood friend Joey Maddocks (Anthony Valentine), an act that suggests his fear of a repressed homosexuality and which also makes him an embarrassing anachronism, 'an ignorant boy, an out-of-date boy', as Flowers' sidekick intones.

Forced to hide out in what appears to be a conventional house in Notting Hill, Chas finds his other self, the reclusive rockstar Turner (Mick Jagger), who has lost his 'demon' and retreated into an alternative world of drugs and Eastern mysticism. In their encounter, each has his identity remodelled. The film's increasingly rococo, allusive and self-reflexive visual style creates a surreal, Nietzschean space in which 'all is permitted' as Chas, the sadomasochistic performer of sex and violence, is forced, through drugs and clever manipulation, to acknowledge his feminine side. In one pivotal moment, Pherber (Anita Pallenberg) holds a mirror so that her breast appears on his chest. But as Chas, now clothed in hippie attire, loses himself in drug-induced catatonia, the vampiric Turner absorbs his hard male energy and, in the performance of the song 'Message from Turner', symbolically takes over the East End gang. In the final scene, the identities of Chas and Turner have become interchangeable, suggesting the disturbing proximity, even equivalence, of these two apparently opposite worlds. *Performance*'s willingness to use fantasy to articulate the deeper recesses of male identity made it, like *Get Carter*, an inspirational film for subsequent filmmakers.

Existentialism and anti-Thatcherism: 1984–91

The first phase ended abruptly with the withdrawal of American finance.[23] Later 1970s neo-noirs, notably *The Squeeze* (1977) in which ex-policemen Jim Naboth (Stacy Keach) has become a shambling alcoholic adrift in an increasingly vicious world, were isolated films. The second phase of neo-noir's development was facilitated by a restructuring of investment finance – money from television, mainly Channel 4 and, mostly European, co-productions – that could support 'quality British films' that were not necessarily obvious box-office prospects.[24] The neo-noirs of this period were influenced powerfully by European art cinema, exhibiting the narrative indeterminacy, stylistic self-consciousness and complex, enigmatic characterisation that are its hallmarks. It was also a period in which the polarising ideology of Thatcherism galvanised the oppositional energies of British filmmakers, and neo-noir offered itself as an apposite vehicle to analyse its social and psychological impact.

Two existentialist thrillers, *The Hit* and *Parker*, both released in 1984, exemplified these characteristics. *The Hit* was set largely in Spain as a contract killer Braddock (John Hurt) and his unstable sidekick Myron (Tim Roth) take supergrass Willie Parker (Terence Stamp) from his rural villa to Paris where he is to meet his fate. Director Stephen Frears uses this simple storyline to create a meandering journey, reminiscent of Wim Wenders' films, in which the equable fatalism of Parker undermines the others' self-possession so that the action implodes. *Parker* – influenced strongly by Fassbinder (Fassbinder stalwart Kurt Raab plays the investigating policeman) – was the fruit of the long-term partnership of writer Trevor Preston and director Jim Goddard, who described this 'European film with American pacing' as about 'a middle-class mind under pressure'.[25] It concerns the obsessive efforts of Parker (Bryan Brown), a British toy salesman who disappeared for eleven days while on a routine commercial trip to Munich, to prove that he did not imagine, or fake, his abduction and incarceration in a cellar. His attempts only serve to alienate his wife Jenny (Cherie Lunghi) and exacerbate his existing confusions about his true identity.

Parker exhibits what Julian Petley aptly calls a 'persistent sense of *dépaysement*, of the curious and bizarre casually and constantly rubbing shoulders with the ordinary and the mundane'.[26] In the deliberately confusing opening scene, the cowboys that Parker meets in the forest into which he was released, turn out to be members of a German western club on a weekend outing in the Bavarian Alps. Only when he visits a medium in a perfectly ordinary British suburban location who draws a perfect picture of the cellar in which he was imprisoned and the face of one of his captors, is Parker able to uncover gradually the motivations behind his abduction, the web of crime in which he was an innocent pawn. *Parker* is a strange, disconcerting film, its protagonist both sympathetic and opaque, gripped by an existentialist angst – highly characteristic of film noir, especially *DOA* (1950) – that threatens to overwhelm him.

Hidden City (1987), written and directed by Stephen Poliakoff, had a similar sense of *dépaysement* and paranoia but marked a return to the visual style of classical noir in which London, in cinematographer Witold Stok's shimmering chiaroscuro, takes on mythical, phantasmagorical dimensions. It too was about an alienated middle-class protagonist – James Richards (Charles Dance) a successful, self-satisfied but worldweary statistician – who, against his better judgement, becomes enmeshed in the quest of a young film researcher Sharon Newton (Cassie Stuart) to find out the truth behind some disturbing scenes she has viewed in an innocuous government information film. They gradually uncover Project Magnificat, a 1950s nuclear experiment that went wrong, whose victims have been kept in a secret London hospital, now disused. However, it is their search as much as the discovery that is important, as it uncovers a strange, secret London: an old tram depot below Holborn, a vast air-raid shelter under Oxford Street where 15,000 American troops were stationed during the war and then again during the 1956 Suez crisis, the main rubbish tip in Edmonton, 'the magical world of waste' where the 'innards of London' are exposed. All are evidence of a society addicted to secrecy and evasiveness, from the older Masonic culture through classified government documentation to the emerging world of video technology which seems to have the power to visualise secret desires; at a party in a new media organisation, James is shown a pirated video of his own recurring and disturbing dream and he wakes wondering if he had imagined it. He also finds himself pursued by the Special Branch because of some medical records he had casually picked up on the tip. Despite its rather inappropriately cosy ending in which James and Cassie decide to embark on another investigation, like all good noirs, *Hidden City* reveals the disconcerting strangeness of the world we thought we knew and the blurred boundaries between dream and reality.

Mona Lisa (1987), which fused the poetic and surreal qualities of director Neil Jordan with the intimate knowledge of London and social realism of his co-screenwriter David Leland, had some similarities, but its vision of London is much darker than that of *Hidden City*, a truly noir world of underage prostitution, pornography, drug-dealing and heroin addiction. At its centre is George (Bob Hoskins), whom Jordan described as the 'utterly ordinary contemporary hero, the mug who is lost in a maze of guile, the big heart with the slow brain, the one with the child's eyes, who believes too much'.[27] In a part written specifically for him, Hoskins makes George both tough, full of inarticulate rage, and yet intensely vulnerable, naively trying to set the world to rights and be reunited with his daughter. Another man-out-of-his-time, George struggles to cope with a world that has changed radically during his seven years in prison. Returning to his old employer, Denny Mortwell (Michael Caine), George is given the job of chauffeuring Simone (Cathy Tyson), an elegant black prostitute, through whom Mortwell satisfies whatever perverted fantasy his rich clients desire. *Mona Lisa* recalls *Taxi Driver* (1976) as George and Simone drive round under the distracting glare of a neon-lit nocturnal city, but as Jordan emphasised, its characterisation is very different and specifically British, pairing a chauvinist, racist little Englander, with his opposite. As Simone's feisty independence and self-possession make George examine his attitudes even as she forces him to change his clothes, their antagonism gives way to affection and George falls in love with the enigmatic female enshrined in the smaltzy Nat King Cole song that gives *Mona Lisa* its title. As her champion, George helps Simone search for the 15–year-old prostitute Cathy (Kate Hardie), a girl who could be his daughter, and who could form part of the 'normal, ordinary family life' that George is desperate to resume.

The search for Cathy is George's entrée to a nightmare London beyond his imaginings, as the pair repeatedly revisit the street in King's Cross, the 'meat rack', where the down-and-out prostitutes gather, a street lit to resemble a hell's mouth. Jordan wanted these scenes to have a Dantean quality and for the film's look to become progressively more stylised and phantasmagorical.[28] George's purgatorial journey increases his own sense of bewilderment and further undermines his already fragile grip on his identity. His successful quest to save Cathy

shatters his own romantic delusions as he realises that she is the object
of Simone's desire. In a neatly ironic reference to the heterosexuality
of classic noir, the scene from Nicolas Ray's *They Live by Night* (1948)
where the lovers on the run walk up the garden path to the marriage
office door, is showing on the television screen in the hotel room in
Brighton to which George, Simone and Cathy have fled. After the
violent climax in which Simone shoots Mortwell, George retreats to
his surreal haven, a caravan in a warehouse owned by his friend
Thomas (Robbie Coltrane), where he is surrounded by bizarre objects
which Thomas thinks might sell. In this alternative world, reunited
with his daughter in a surrogate family of three, George's anger and
resentment, 'I sold myself for a pair of dykes', modulates into wistful,
sentimentalised compassion: 'She was trapped ... like a bird in a cage'.
He begins to see himself dispassionately as the unwitting actor in a
grotesque nightmare, that may or may not have really happened, a
story as strange as that of the novel Thomas gave him to read, John
Franklin Bardin's *The Deadly Percheron*, whose introduction of
surreal, defamiliarising qualities into the thriller world influenced
Jordan's conception of the film.[29] It is this combination of tense,
absorbing action and self-reflexivity that marks *Mona Lisa* as one of
the key British neo-noirs.

   Both *Hidden City* and *Mona Lisa* contained an implied critique of
Thatcherism in their emphasis on a secretive and acquisitive society
that thrives on inequalities, *Empire State* (1987) and *Stormy Monday*
(1989) made that critique explicit. *Empire State* was set in London's
rapidly transforming Docklands, where man –out –of his time Frank
(Ray McNally), representing the old East End gangster, clashes with
Paul (Ian Sears), a young villain who has 'crossed over' into pimping
and drug-dealing, acting as the front for the new yuppie class of property developers trying to transform the area into a second Manhattan
in alliance with American financier Chuck (Martin Landau). An ambitious film, but overloaded with too many stories and a rather shape-
less narrative, *Empire State* was highly stylised, drawing on noir
conventions but also the more lurid colours of the contemporaneous
cinéma du look, to produce a vulgarly glamorous, shimmering London
in which sex and everything else has its price.

   Empire State's critical conflation of Thatcherism and the
Americanisation of British culture was explored in a more extended
form in *Stormy Monday*. Writer-director Mike Figgis described this
process as: 'The willing take-over. We certainly haven't fought the
Americans or tried keeping them out. I think it's because we always
wanted them in our culture. It was an exciting infusion into British

music, and certainly into film'.[30] Figgis set the film in Newcastle, not in homage to *Get Carter* but because, having been brought up there, he felt Newcastle 'has a strong American industrial feel to it not unlike Brooklyn or Chicago, largely due to the immense proportions of the old 19th Century architecture'.[31] But Newcastle is undergoing another radical transformation in its huge shopping mall, American bars and diners, a change made insistently visible by 'America Week' in which the action takes place, with its marching majorettes, club bouncers in NYPD uniforms and a huge Coca-Cola bottle in the main square.

The dark face behind this transformation is shady American business-man Frank Cosmo (Tommy Lee Jones) trying to redevelop the quayside area with the help of corrupt local councillors and a notably Thatcherite mayor who welcomes him to the city. Cosmo is opposed by Finney (Sting), the owner of a club situated in the middle of that area to be rede-veloped, but who refuses to sell out. Caught between the two is the fugi-tive couple, Brendan (Sean Bean), a young drifter who becomes Finney's eyes and ears, and Kate (Melanie Griffiths) Cosmo's mistress. Figgis saw Brendan's role as pivotal, moving from 'adulation for all things American' to a more sceptical awareness of the impact of its effects on British culture.[32] His love for Kate, who has all the glamour and style he admires about America, embroils him in a noir world of violence, betrayal and death. The moment at which he shoots one of Cosmo's thugs to rescue Kate is filmed in slow-motion, allowing an audience time to recognise the impact it is having on him, how far he has now been sucked into the netherworld. *Stormy Monday* reproduces this attrac-tion–repulsion dialectic in its own visual style, drawing heavily on American noir – with numerous shots through windows or of people or things reflected in various shiny surfaces, the neon harshness alternating with Hopperesque nocturnes – but used in the service of a highly specific and critical sense of its impact on British culture.

Wasted lives: 1993 to the present

The revival of a more commercially orientated film industry in the 1990s that addressed a more expanded audience base through a renewed commitment to generic filmmaking, led to a proliferation of neo-noirs, many of which are hybrids where some noir elements are combined with various generic conventions. Such hybrids include *Shopping* (1994) – future noir; *Shallow Grave* (1995), *Darklands* (1996), *Dr Sleep* (2002) and *Trauma* (2004) – horror/psychological horror; *The Criminal* (2000) – conspiracy thriller; *Christie Malry's Own Double Entry* (2000) – black comedy; *Miranda* (2003) – comedy thriller; and *Dead Man's Shoes* (2004) – revenge melodrama. However, the overwhelming majority of neo-noirs continue to be crime films, though, as in earlier phases, they need to be distinguished from more conventional examples. Most of the current spate of British gangster films, for instance, are, visually and thematically, quite separate from neo-noir. Indeed, the neo-noirs analysed in this section are often an explicit critique of the gangster genre, focusing on petty criminals on the fringes of professional crime, on would-bes and failures, above all on those who, riddled with existentialist doubts about the purpose and meaning of their lives and who they are, wish to escape from the underworld but cannot. The five films chosen for analysis are critically reflexive, with something distinctive and important to say about British culture and society and need to be differentiated from those neo-noirs, such as *The Young Americans* (1993), which are a glossy pastiche of American noir, derivative and formulaic films that recycle noir conventions rather than using them to explore complex issues.[33] They are more typical than deliberately art-house neo-noirs such as Michael Winterbottom's *I Want You* (1998), photographed by Krzysztof Kieslowski's cameraman Slawomir Idziak, which combined a classic noir tale of the doom-laden romance between a drifter and a duplicitous *femme fatale*, with a concern for displaced persons – a brother and sister who are Balkan refugees.

Antonia Bird's *Face* (1997), was, as has been mentioned, indebted to American models, its visual style often using back-lit noir chiaroscuro, but it displays a very particular sense of place, the product of Bird's – and screenwriter Ronan Bennett's – intimate knowledge of London, particularly Bethnal Green in the East End where most of the action takes place. Scenes were often shot on location in tiny flats, or cramped terraced houses to give a sense of authenticity.[34] *Face*, made right at the end of the eighteen years of Conservative government, continues the critique of Thatcherism and its attack on the welfare state. As the bent policeman Chris (Andrew Tiernan) puts it: 'There are no public servants. There is no public service. All there is, is money and the people who have it'. The central character, Ray (Robert Carlyle), a former trades union activist, has turned to crime after the defeat of the 1983–84 miners' strike, and is now 'just chasing the money, like everyone else'. In Bird's view, his actions are logical in a society where much of the population was unemployed and disenfranchised: 'It's about the choices that you have if you come from a working-class background in inner city London and you're bright. There really are only two choices. There's no work, so either you go into crime or you give in'.[35]

However, Ray continues to be burdened by guilt at dropping out of the left's struggle for social change – there are several flashbacks to his activist past – while his mother (Sue Johnston) and girlfriend Connie (Leda Heaney) still campaign, refusing to admit that the fight is over. The storyline of *Face* is conventional – the disintegration of a gang of thieves over the proceeds of a robbery – but its characterisation has depth and subtlety. Ray's equivocations are contrasted with increasingly manic efforts of Julian (Philip Davis), trying to bring up a young family in a run-down Isle of Dogs towerblock, to recover the money, cash that has been taken by Dave (Ray Winstone), the old-fashioned 'face', another man –out –of –his time, the 'decent' villain who believes in 'looking after your own'. Dave, fading and overweight, trying to pass his middle age in suburban contentment in leafy Highgate (part of the film's richly precise geography of London), is a sympathetic figure, conscious of his failures as a criminal and a father and whose betrayal of his friends is symbolic of a wider social breakdown as he is now controlled by the bent cop Chris. In an ambivalent ending, Ray and his devoted sidekick, the simple Stevie (Steven Waddington), rejoin the loyal Connie and drive north out of London, but there is a strong sense that Ray, on the verge of a breakdown, has been irreparably damaged, a metaphor for the legacy of Thatcherism.

Writer-director Colin Teague's *Shooters* (2000) replaces Bird's overtly political agenda with the fatalistic existentialism more characteristic of this third phase of neo-noir, and the film's sense of anarchy and social breakdown is stronger. Like *Mona Lisa*, *Shooters* centres on the returning criminal. Gilly (Louis Dempsey), after serving six years for a murder committed by his friend and partner Jay (Andrew Howard), comes back to a world that has changed radically. Gilly is repulsed by the squalid and vicious nature of Jay's criminal activities on behalf of a drugs baron Max Bell (Adrian Dunbar). In one compelling scene, the drug-fuelled Jay, on the verge of disintegration, is oblivious to the irony of his savage assault on a teenager dealer outside his son's school when the drugs factory he runs for Max relies on the exploitation of child labour, including that of Jay's brother Skip. In the lugubrious voice-over that punctuates the film, Gilly reflects: 'Some people call us gangsters but that makes it sound dangerous and exciting. The fact is, it's just one deal after another, hanging around, wasting time. Jay doesn't do it because he's bad, he does it because it's the only thing he does that makes him feel important, makes him feel that he's worth something'.

Shooters was filmed within a three-mile radius of Kings Cross to give a strong sense of a squalid, decrepit London, where meetings take

place in a wasteland, or in dingy subterranean dens, including the
drugs factory, constructed under a huge polythene tent in an underground car park, in order to make it look futuristic and surreal.[36]
Accordingly, *Shooters*' presentation of violence is deliberately deglam-
orised, revealed as vicious and pointless, or ironic as in the ending. In
final attempt to redeem himself, Jay is shot rather than betray Gilly a
second time, not realising that Gilly has already made a deal with a
corrupt police inspector to set up Jay in order to buy his parole.
Gazing at the body of his friend, Gilly muses: 'We're all yesterday's
men, but I'm the only one who realises it.' In a memorable final image,
Gilly, who has always been looking for a settled family life, is shown
leaving on a ferry with Jay's wife, but rather than look at her, he gazes
at the retreating shoreline, his future hopelessly blighted.[37]

Mr In-Between (2001) was also more existential than social, an
adaptation of Neil Cross's challenging first novel that producers
Andreas Bajohra and Bob Portal thought had a 'philosophical, existential element, something beyond the norm for a thriller'.[38] Its central
character, Jon (Andrew Howard), has the typical fastidious narcissism
of the contract killer, and director Paul Sarrossy worked with cinematographer Haris Zambarlous to create a 'bleached, bypassed look'
for the sterile order of his flat, below street level where natural light
never enters, the neutral space of a living tomb.[39] Jon's flat is filled
with existentialist texts – Dostoevsky, Kafka, Sartre and Camus –
chosen for him by his employer, the Tattooed Man (John Calder), who
lives in a bizarrely lit cavernous dungeon (filmed in old railway sheds
in Bishopgate) an underground catacomb, beyond time and space,
which, like his shadowy criminal empire, is unidentifiable and fathom-
less. It is an appropriately Guignol setting for a man who is a surreal
mixture of the mundanely domesticated – making tea, cooking a meal
– and the obscene, his body decorated with the faces of all his victims,
women and children as well as men. To Jon, violence and killing are a
professional act, to the Tattooed Man they 'open the doors of perception' into a world of true creativity and understanding, beyond good
and evil. Their relationship is close and complex, father and surrogate
son, but with a homoerotic undercurrent as well as a metaphysical
dimension with the Tattooed Man acting Mephistopheles to Jon's
Faust.

Mr In-Between is clearly indebted to *Performance* in its willingness
to use the fantastic to explore the deeper recesses of Jon's identity, but
instead of moving towards a surreal space where 'all is permitted', its
trajectory is precisely the opposite as Jon begins to crave the pleasures
of ordinary life. After a chance encounter with an old schoolfriend

Andy (Andrew Tiernan), unemployed, but happily married with his wife Cathy (Geraldine O'Rawe) and their young daughter, Jon begins to understand what is missing from his life. It is his growing love for Cathy that changes Jon, opening up the feelings he has denied, making him the man in between the mundane and the macabre whose identity is beginning to dissolve. After Andy's death, for which he feels responsible, Jon, in a chilling scene, kills Cathy and her daughter in order to protect them from the Tattooed Man's vengeance before returning to his mentor to accept his fate. Like a family reunited, they go on a day out to the seaside – eating ice creams, playing football on the beach – before Jon is driven to Beachy Head where he is given the choice to jump or be pushed. He chooses to jump of his own free will, a final act that restores his autonomy – as Sartre wrote in *Being and Nothingness* 'for human reality, to be is to choose oneself' – and which makes Jon a tragic figure.

The existentialist desire to be self-created and therefore master of one's fate informs *Croupier* (1997), the fruit of Mike Hodges' collaboration with screenwriter Paul Mayersberg who had developed the script over a number of years. Mayersberg was strongly influenced by European existentialist noir, notably Robert Bresson and Jean-Pierre Melville with their sense of a contingent universe in which actions are random and inexplicable. It also draws on American noir, especially *Double Indemnity* (1944) and Nicholas Ray's *In a Lonely Place* (1950). The name of its heroine Marion is taken from Hitchcock's *Psycho*, while its anti-hero, Jack Manfred, alludes to Byron's Count Manfred, one of the central figures in English gothic literature.[40] This rich cultural heritage is moulded into a highly contemporary tale that focuses on would-be writer, Jack (Clive Owen), searching for his subject and his fictional hero, and through them his true identity. Everything changes when, at the behest of his gambler father, Jack resumes his old profession of croupier, returning to a subterranean noir world of tawdry glamour, shimmering surfaces and distorting reflections, a world obsessed with money and chance: gambling has often been a handy metaphor for an existentialist view of life. In creating the casino where much of the action takes place, production designer Jon Bunker commented: 'Mike [Hodges] wanted to convey a sense of purgatory so we made the walls out of mirrors, which gives a sense of the casino extending forever. It also has the effect that when Jack enters the casino, the reflection of the mirror conveys the idea of him walking away from himself'.[41] This separation of character and consciousness is reinforced by *Croupier*'s unconventional use of voice-over. Jack's voice-over is neither confessional nor a device to expound

4 Clive Owen in *Croupier* (Mike Hodges, 1997).

the plot, but a detached, third-person commentary on his actions. Owen was asked to learn the voice-over so that he played the scenes as if he were responding to his own thoughts. Its mode is *speculative*, allowing Jack to invoke the great existential questions: what matters? What life's about? Who am I? As Mayersberg remarked, its effect is to efface characterisation altogether making *Croupier* the story of a nobody, but one who is also Everyman.[42]

As Jack rediscovers the fascination of being a croupier, cool, professional, detached and in control, he gradually transmutes into his *Doppelgänger* Jake – symbolised as he redyes his bleached blond hair to its natural black – who understands that the object of life is to 'fuck the world over'. Jake is the ideal protagonist for Jack's novel *I, Croupier*, which becomes a number-one bestseller in a world fascinated by ruthless greed. For Hodges, Jake is a contemporary figure, the product of a post-Thatcherite world of casualised labour where everyone is on their own, struggling to succeed and caught up in forces they cannot control. It is Jake who is prepared to collude in the scheme of *femme fatale* Jani (Alex Kingston) to rob the casino, and when his girlfriend Marion (Gina McKee) – who wants him to remain the blond nice guy, to remain her romanticised image of the struggling author – is killed by a hit–and-run driver, a random act the meaning of which is unclear, Jack's conscience dies with her. Stripped of illusions, Jake settles down with worldy fellow croupier and ex-prostitute Bella (Kate Hardie), who accepts him as he is, his ruthlessness, violence and self-centredness. Thinking he is now in control of his life, Jake dedicates himself to his self-created wholeness unlike the sad gamblers who play at his table, but in a final irony, he learns that Jani was his father's mistress and he was therefore a mere pawn in his father's clever game.

Hodges' *I'll Sleep When I'm Dead* (2003) returns to the themes of *Get Carter*, but is informed by the deeper existentialism of *Croupier*. Its title evokes the later hard-boiled writers – Horace McCoy's *They Shoot Horses Don't They?*, or Cornel Woolrich's *I Married a Dead Man* – but unlike the indeterminate London of *Croupier*, *I'll Sleep* resembles *Get Carter* in its precise delineation of place, what Hodges described as the 'Dickensian' quality of squalor and decay in south London, particularly in and around Brixton, Camberwell and Peckham. But it also evokes a mythical, nocturnal London cloaked in darkness, where the flash cars of criminals, lit by the glare of the streetlights, constantly circulate like sharks waiting for their prey. But underpinning *I'll Sleep*'s noir elements was the sense of nemesis and inevitability that characterise Greek tragedy.[43]

I'll Sleep is told entirely in flashback, beginning with a surreal image of a man driving golf balls into the sea on a deserted beach, observed by Will Graham (Clive Owen) who intones: 'Most thoughts are memories. And memories deceive'. A feared hard man, Will has been living an isolated, solitary life in rural Wales following an unspecified 'breakdown', but returns to his old 'manor' after three years away in order to investigate the death of his younger brother Davey (Jonathan Rhys Meyers). Davey, abandoned by Will, had taken to making 'soft money' through selling drugs. What Will's painstaking investigations uncover is not a gangland killing, but something much more horrific: after ejaculating when he was raped, Davey had returned home to slit his own throat in shame and guilt. As Hodges commented, the rape is, 'the primary violation to the male body, the ultimate challenge to the macho braggadocios of the criminal world'.[44] Will, another indestructible revenger, finds the rapist Boad (Malcolm McDowell), only to learn that his motives were envy and petty spite. Thus despite his dramatic transformation from dishevelled 'pikey' to gleaming assassin in pin-sharp suit – the Samourai ritual of cleansing and smartening – Will gets no satisfaction from his revenge, just an inconsolable 'grief for a life wasted', like his own. Promising to leave with his ex-girlfriend Helen (Charlotte Rampling), Will, in a typical act of selfishness, drives off on his own back to his self-imposed exile. Abandoned by Will for a second time, Helen's is another life wasted, taken prisoner in her own home by the Belfast hit man whom master criminal Frank Turner (Ken Stott) has paid to kill Will, a potential rival, when he returns to her house.

Will, unlike Jack Carter, survives, but there is no redemption, as the film circles back to its opening scene. As both Hodges and screenwriter Trevor Preston argue, *I'll Sleep* is a film about futility, a study in 'lost lives, wasted lives', and about a man who tries to escape from his past, the violence and the hate within him, and create a new existence, but cannot.[45] It is a grim, bleak film, the characters occupying some morbid dream from which they cannot awaken, but also profound, the culmination of Hodges' long encounter with film noir and his efforts to diagnose the sickness of the macho hard man, his world and all that he stands for. Its existentialism is highly characteristic of the current phase of neo-noir as is its delineation of a deep crisis in masculine identity: the longing for an ordinary life by men damaged and destroyed by brutality and violence.

Hodges' three films, with their pared-down dialogue, evocative compositions and fluid camerawork, are the high point of British neo-noir, but many of the others analysed in this chapter are accomplished, challenging films that stand comparison with their American counterparts, but which are also resonantly British. Encouragingly, there is no sign that the current energies of British neo-noir are diminishing. It continues to provide both established and novice filmmakers a style and a sensibility that can engage critically with social issues as well as exploring the recesses of masculine identity. For all its heterogeneity, British neo-noir deserves to be better known and even celebrated as an important contribution to European cinema, contemporary British culture and the evolution of film noir.

Notes

The only previous analysis of British neo-noir is my own in *Film Noir* (Harlow, Essex: Longman/Pearson Education, 2002), pp. 195–202. In addition to updating that account, I have taken this opportunity to rethink and substantially revise its lines of argument, and I have consciously avoided analysis of several films (e.g. *Dance with a Stranger* or *Essex Boys*) which are discussed there.

 1 Bird, quoted in Bob McCabe, 'East End Heat', *Sight and Sound*, 7:10 (NS) (October 1997), 12.
 2 Charlotte Brunsdon, 'Space in the British Crime Film', in Steve Chibnall and Robert Murphy (eds), *British Crime Cinema* (London: Routledge, 1999), pp. 148–59.
 3 Only very rarely do British neo-noirs have a female as the central protagonist, *Dance with a Stranger* (1985) and *Another Life* (2000), both based on famous murder cases, are the exceptions – fine films, but too atypical to be included in this survey.
 4 See, among others, the remarks by writer-director Julian Simpson, in his commentary for the DVD release of *The Criminal* (2000), PHE8501.
 5 Another example is Christopher Nolan, whose micro-budgeted neo-noir *Following* (1998) became his calling card in America.
 6 See Steven Davies, *'Get Carter' and Beyond: The Cinema of Mike Hodges* (London: Batsford, 2002), pp. 167–9.
 7 Ian Nathan, 'Man Trouble', *The Times Review* (24 April, 2004), p. 23.
 8 Producer Stephen Cranny, in his commentary for the DVD release of *Out of Depth*, FMDV1065. Even the original lens used by Wolfgang Suschitzky to photograph *Get Carter* was reground for use by his grandson Adam to shoot *Out of Depth*.
 9 See Robert Murphy in this volume, Chapter 4, pp. 84–111, and his *Sixties British Cinema* (London: BFI Publishing, 1992), pp. 215–18.
10 See Sean Day-Lewis, 'Kinks and Bends in the Force', *Sunday Telegraph* (30 August 1968).
11 David Greene, quoted in the Twickenham Studios' 'Fact Sheet', included on the BFI microfiche for *The Strange Affair*; original emphasis.
12 *Ibid.*
13 Penelope Houston, *Spectator* (6 September 1968).
14 See Hopkins' comments in Tantallon Films' press release, included on the BFI microfiche for *The Offence*.
15 *Ibid.*
16 Mike Hodges, *Neon*, September 1997, quoted in Steve Chibnall, *Get Carter* (London: I. B. Tauris, 2003), pp. 42–3.
17 Twickenham Studios' press release, included on the BFI microfiche for *Sitting Target*.
18 Hodges, in his commentary for the DVD release of *Get Carter*, ZI65400.
19 Chibnall, *Get Carter*, pp. 39–47.

20   Hodges, in his commentary for the DVD release of *Get Carter*.

21   Alexander Walker, *Hollywood, England: The British Film Industry in the Sixties* (London: Harrap 1986 [1974]), pp. 417–21.

22   Colin MacCabe, *Performance* (London: BFI Publishing, 1998), pp. 13–18, 24–7.

23   Walker, *Hollywood, England*, pp. 441–65.

24   John Hill, *British Cinema in the 1980s* (Oxford: Clarendon Press, 1999), pp. 34–8, 48–51, 65–8.

25   Jim Goddard, quoted in Julian Petley, 'Travel and Rest: Jim Goddard, from theatre to TV to cinema', *Monthly Film Bulletin* 52:616 (May 1985), 144.

26   Petley, Review of *Parker, ibid.*, p. 143.

27   Neil Jordan, 'Introduction' to the screenplay of *Mona Lisa* (London: Faber & Faber, 1986), p. v.

28   Neil Jordan in his commentary for the DVD release of *Mona Lisa*, ABD4007.

29   *Ibid.*

30   Mike Figgis, 'Introduction' to *Collected Screenplays 1* (London: Faber & Faber, 2002), pp. xx.

31   Studio press release, p. 14; included on the BFI microfiche for *Stormy Monday*.

32   *Ibid.*

33   Mention should be made of *The Near Room* (1995), *Complicity* (1999), *The Debt Collector* (1999) and *Blinded* (2004), intelligent and interesting films, all funded by the Scottish Arts Council and initially released in Scotland, which almost constitute a subgenre of Scottish neo-noir.

34   See Bird's commentary for the DVD release of *Face*, PHE8504.

35   Bird, quoted in McCabe, 'East End Heat', p. 11.

36   PFG press release, p. 4; included on the BFI microfiche for *Shooters*.

37   Teague's second film, *Spivs* (2004), also co-written with Gary Young, had noir elements, including the central character Pike (Ken Stott) another man out of his time appalled by the new traffic in human flesh.

38   Portal's commentary for the DVD release of *Mr In-Between*, 8210428/RO

39   Paul Sarrossy's commentary on *ibid.*

40   Paul Mayersberg, 'Annotations, Memories and Notes for the Curious', in *Croupier* (Suffolk, ScreenPress Books, 2001), p. 132.

41   Bunker, quoted in BFI production notes, included on the BFI microfiche for *Croupier*.

42   Mayersberg, 'Annotations', p. 131.

43   See Steve Chibnall's interview with Hodges, *Sight and Sound*, 13:9 (NS) (September 2003), 13.

44   Hodges' commentary for the DVD release of *I'll Sleep When I'm Dead*, MP404D.

45   See their comments on *ibid.*

Filmography

[*The Spy Who Came in from the Cold*, Martin Ritt, 1965]
[*The Deadly Affair*, Sidney Lumet, 1966]
The Strange Affair, David Greene, 1968
[*The Looking Glass War*, Frank R. Pierson, 1969]
Fragment of Fear, Richard C. Sarafian, 1970
[*The Man Who Haunted Himself*, Basil Dearden, 1970]
Performance, Donald Cammel/Nicolas Roeg, 1970
Get Carter, Mike Hodges, 1971
[*Villain*, Mike Tuchner, 1971]
[*Frenzy*, Alfred Hitchcock, 1972]
The Offence, Sidney Lumet, 1972
Sitting Target, Douglas Hickox, 1972
Endless Night, Sidney Gilliat, 1972
Farewell, My Lovely, Dick Richards, 1975
The Squeeze, Michael Apted, 1977
The Big Sleep, Michael Winner, 1978
[*The Long Good Friday*, John Mackenzie, 1980]
The Hit, Stephen Frears, 1984
Parker, Jim Goddard, 1984
Dance with a Stranger, Mike Newell, 1985
Mona Lisa, Neil Jordan, 1986
[*Defence of the Realm*, David Drury, 1987]
Empire State, Ron Peck, 1987
Hidden City, Stephen Poliakoff, 1987
[*Scandal*, Michael Caton-Jones, 1988]
Stormy Monday, Mike Figgis, 1989
Chicago Joe and the Showgirl, Bernard Rose, 1990
[*The Krays*, Peter Medak, 1990]
Tank Malling, James Marc, 1990
['*Let Him Have It*', Peter Medak, 1991]
Under Suspicion, Simon Moore, 1991
Dirty Weekend, Michael Winner, 1993
The Young Americans, Danny Carson, 1993
Beyond Bedlam, Vadim Jean, 1994
Captives, Angela Pope, 1994
[*Shopping*, Paul Anderson, 1994]
The Near Room, David Hayman, 1995
The Innocent Sleep, Scott Michell, 1995
[*Shallow Grave*, Danny Boyle, 1995]
Crimetime, George Sluizer, 1996
Darklands, Julian Richards, 1996
Croupier, Mike Hodges, 1997
Face, Antonia Bird, 1997
[*Hard Men*, J. K. Amalou, 1997]

I Want You, Michael Winterbottom, 1998
Mojo, Jez Butterworth, 1997
[*Resurrection Man*, Marc Evans, 1997]
Following, Christopher Nolan, 1998
Killing Time, Bharat Nalluri, 1998
Out of Depth, Simon Marshall, 1998
Complicity, Gavin Millar, 1999
The Debt Collector, Anthony Neilson, 1999
Another Life, Philip Goodhew, 2000
Beautiful Creatures, Bill Eagles, 2000
[*Christie Malry's Own Double Entry*, Paul Tickell, 2000]
Circus, Rob Walker, 2000
The Criminal, Julian Simpson, 2000
Essex Boys, Terry Winsor, 2000
[*Gangster No. 1*, Paul McGuigan, 2000]
[*Sexy Beast*, Jonathan Glazer, 2000]
Shooters, Colin Teague, 2000
Alone, Philip Claydon, 2001
Mr In-Between, Paul Sarossy, 2001
Dr Sleep, Nick Willing, 2002
Killing Me Softly, Kaige Chen, 2002
Shoreditch, Malcolm Needs, 2002.
The Silent Cry, Julian Richards, 2002
This Is Not a Love Song, Bille Eltringham, 2002
I'll Sleep When I'm Dead, Mike Hodges, 2003
[*Miranda*, Marc Munden, 2003]
Asylum, David Mackenzie, 2004
Blinded, Eleanor Yule, 2004
[*Dead Man's Shoes*, Shane Meadows, 2004]
Room 36, Jim Groom, 2004
[*Spivs*, Colin Teague, 2004]
[*Trauma*, Marc Evans, 2004]

Select bibliography

Brunsdon, Charlotte, 'Space in the British Crime Film', in Steve Chibnall, and Robert Murphy (eds), *British Crime Cinema* (London: Routledge, 1999), pp. 148–59.
Chibnall, Steve, 'Travels in Ladland: the British Gangster Film Cycle, 1998–2001', in Robert Murphy (ed.), *The British Cinema Book*, 2nd edn (London: BFI Publishing, 2001), pp. 281–91.
Chibnall, Steve, *Get Carter* (London: I. B. Tauris, 2003).
Chibnall, Steve, 'Interview with Mike Hodges', *Sight and Sound* 13:9 (NS) (September 2003), 12–13.
Chibnall, Steve and Robert Murphy (eds), *British Crime Cinema*

(London: Routledge, 1999).

Davies, Steven, *'Get Carter' and Beyond: The Cinema of Mike Hodges* (London: Batsford, 2002).

Figgis, Mike, 'Introduction' to *Collected Screenplays 1* (London: Faber & Faber, 2002), pp. vii–xxviii.

Hill, John, *British Cinema in the 1980s* (Oxford: Clarendon Press, 1999).

Hill, John, 'Allegorising the Nation: British Gangster Films of the 1980s', in Steve Chibnall and Robert Murphy (eds), *British Crime Cinema* (London: Routledge, 1999), pp. 160–71.

Hodges, Mike, 'Mike Hodges Discusses *Get Carter* with the NFT Audience', in Steve Chibnall and Robert Murphy (eds), *British Crime Cinema* (London: Routledge, 1999), pp. 117–22.

Hunt, Leon, 'Dog Eat Dog: *The Squeeze* and the *Sweeney* Films', in Steve Chibnall and Robert Murphy (eds), *British Crime Cinema* (London: Routledge, 1999), pp. 134–47.

Kemp, Philip, 'English Manners', *Sight and Sound* 56:4 (Autumn 1987), pp. 288–9.

Jordan, Neil, 'Introduction' to *Mona Lisa* (London: Faber & Faber, 1986), pp. v–vi.

McCabe, Bob, 'East End Heat', *Sight and Sound* 7:10 (NS) (October 1997), 12–13.

MacCabe, Colin, *Performance* (London: BFI Publishing, 1998).

Mayersberg, Paul, 'Annotations, Memories and Notes for the Curious', in *Croupier* (Suffolk: ScreenPress Books, 2001).

Mottram, James, '"Following On": Christopher Nolan and Jeremy Theobald Interviewed', in Christopher Nolan, *Memento and Following* (London: Faber & Faber, 2001), pp. 93–102.

Murphy, Robert, *Sixties British Cinema* (London: BFI Publishing, 1992).

Murphy, Robert, 'A Revenger's Tragedy – *Get Carter*', in Steve Chibnall, and Robert Murphy (eds), *British Crime Cinema* (London: Routledge, 1999), pp. 123–33.

Murphy, Robert, *British Cinema of the 90s* (London: BFI Publishing, 2000).

Petley, Julian, 'Travel and Rest: Jim Goddard, from Theatre to TV to Cinema', *Monthly Film Bulletin* 52:616 (May 1985), 143–4.

Spicer, Andrew, *Typical Men: The Representation of Masculinity in Popular British Cinema* (London: I. B. Tauris, 2001).

Spicer, Andrew, *Film Noir* (Harlow, Essex: Longman/Pearson Education, 2002).

Spicer, Andrew, 'British Neo-Noir and the Male Anti-Hero', *Anglo*

Files 128 (September 2003), 11–19.

Walker, Alexander, *Hollywood, England: The British Film Industry in the Sixties* (London: Harrap, 1986 [1974]).

Williams, Christopher, 'The Social Art Cinema: a Moment in the History of British Film and Television Culture', in C. Williams (ed.), *Cinema: The Beginnings and the Future* (London: University of Westminster Press, 1996), pp. 192–200.

6

German cinema and film noir

Tim Bergfelder

German cinema and film noir: influence and reception

It has been suggested that the films made by German émigrés in 1940s Hollywood, including many noir classics, could be conceived of as a national cinema in exile, as the kind of German cinema 'that might have been' had Hitler not come to power.[1] More recently, however, Thomas Elsaesser has challenged this narrative of noir's German 'ancestry', and in particular the seamless continuity between Weimar cinema and Hollywood that this scenario suggests.[2] Marc Vernet, meanwhile, has demonstrated that many of the stylistic elements and narrative conventions of noir credited to German influence were used in Hollywood long before the advent of noir and the influx of émigré filmmakers, which also seems to undermine a theory of a wholesale imported aesthetic.[3] Despite such challenges, the links between the German cinema of the 1920s and early 1930s and the American film noir of the 1940s and 1950s remain a significant element in the critical construction of the latter. This chapter will focus on two questions that have so far been neglected in film historical studies, namely whether there was any reciprocal influence of American noir in the post-war German context, and whether one can identify an indigenous noir tradition in post-Second World War German cinema.

In most accounts of the special relationship between Germany and film noir the issue of noir's reception in post-war Germany barely features, as this would reveal that the genre was neither properly acknowledged until the late 1960s, nor, with very few exceptions, were its conventions consciously incorporated into domestic productions. By contrast with France, where by the 1950s noir was in common usage as a critical buzzword, and where popular indigenous genres clearly displayed an American influence, there was hardly any understanding of the concept of noir as a separate category, style or mood in either West or East Germany during the same period. Nor, perhaps more surprisingly, was the supposed special connection between American film noir and Weimar cinema much commented upon or even acknowledged by German film critics. Moreover, as I have argued elsewhere, among domestic productions in the 1950s, crime films (which form a significant part of the noir corpus) constituted a relatively negligible genre, which would have added to the lack of interest shown to American imports in this category.[4] This changed in the 1960s when West German genre production came to be dominated by a series of playfully self-reflective, homegrown Edgar Wallace adaptations, set in a quaintly gothic British netherworld. While these thrillers may in retrospect appear to display a noir influence in their visual style and narrative format, it was not Hollywood but British popular culture and an older Weimar legacy that provided the blueprints.[5]

Generally speaking, few of the now classic American noir films of the 1940s and 1950s had a significant impact on contemporary German audiences and reviewers on their initial release. In most cases, film noir, as with almost all popular Hollywood genres, was subsumed into a general suspicion towards Hollywood, which was perceived as a prime instance of an unwanted American colonisation and debasing of German high culture. At the same time, as a number of studies have shown, although American distributors had quickly established a stronghold in the German market after the war, West German audiences on the whole preferred domestic and other European products to Hollywood fare well into the late 1960s.[6] The East German reception of American noir during the same period, meanwhile, owing to cold war ideology, censorship, and politically motivated patterns of distribution and exhibition, was even more muted, to the point of being insignificant.

The fact that a great number of noir films were directed by German émigrés did not necessarily endear them any more to West German critics and, where such a link was not ignored altogether, could lead to unfavourable comparisons with their earlier work. In the late 1950s, for example, the weekly West German magazine *Der Spiegel* dismissed Fritz Lang's American œuvre with the verdict that 'Lang did not manage to establish himself as an artistically ambitious Hollywood director. He had to be content to manufacture adventure and crime films'.[7] In some cases, noir classics were rejected much more forcefully. A case in point was Robert Siodmak's gothic noir masterpiece *The Spiral Staircase* (1946), which was condemned upon its German release in 1948 as a 'typically American invitation to moral corruption';[8] it was met with calls for boycott from Germany's two main churches. As Lutz Koepnick has argued,

The hostile response to Siodmak's *The Spiral Staircase* in postwar Germany exemplifies a double process of displacement characteristic of German film culture in the 1940s and 1950s. It brings to view both the postwar failure to address the texts and meanings produced by Hitler refugees in Hollywood exile and the unwillingness to see in contemporary American film noir more than simply a harbinger of deviance and corruption.[9]

As Paul Cooke's chapter in this collection documents, a serious engagement with film noir commenced in West Germany only in the late 1960s, although even New German Cinema's reception of the concept was not necessarily motivated by noir's German legacy. Similarly, it was in the early 1970s that German audiences, primarily through television retrospectives and documentaries, became familiar with the terminology, iconography and mythology of the genre, which was initially adopted under the term *Schwarze Serie* (Black Series), from the French *Série Noire*. In terms of critical and academic writing, meanwhile, it is only within the last two decades that the role of émigrés in the noir canon has become an essential part of the discursive engagement with the phenomenon in the German-speaking context.[10]

Film noir and post-war German cinema: parallel topographies

Despite such a history of *rejecting* or seemingly failing to engage with the very concept of noir, one can identify a number of German films made in the 1940s and 1950s that show traces of what one could retrospectively term a noir style, mood or that articulate similar themes. The genres in which one is most likely to find these elements are indigenously rooted formats such as early post-war 'rubble' films, the women's melodrama, the social-problem film, and the sporadic examples of domestic crime films. It is worth noting that only in rare instances do these films display the same generic consistency as classical noir in conforming simultaneously to specific aesthetic conventions, thematic preoccupations, and socio-political perspectives. In attempting to locate an indigenous German noir tradition, it is notable that many of the films which qualify as perhaps the purest examples during the post-war period were made by returning émigrés, thus by filmmakers who were familiar with both Weimar aesthetics and the conventions of Hollywood. However, it is not my intention to identify or isolate a 'pure' German noir canon that would exactly match its American counterpart. Rather I am interested how classical noir tropes featured and were reinterpreted in German productions of the

1940s and 1950s. What I am trying to identify are German films that may have performed a similar *function* to that which classical noir offered its American audiences, even where the specific topography and iconography may have looked different.

Edward Dimendberg has cited 'the traumas of unrecoverable time and space' and 'the inability to dwell comfortably either in the present or the past' as classical noir's central preoccupations.[11] These descriptions seem to conjure up the *Zeitgeist* of post-Second World War Germany as well, and encapsulate the anxieties of a nation intent on overcoming (and repressing) both its shameful recent past and its bleak present at the same time, resulting in a strange mixture of amnesia, unfocused nostalgia and determined reconstruction. Moreover, these anxieties can be seen to inform most, if not all, of German film production from the late 1940s to the mid-1960s, not just those (relatively few) films which offer themselves either visually or in terms of narrative themes for a comparison with noir. The sense of a (collective and individual) unease about both the past and the present applies to quantitatively more dominant and financially more successful German film genres such as the 'escapist' rural melodramas (known domestically under the generic term *Heimatfilm*) or musicals and comedies. As I have argued elsewhere, all of these frequently forego straightforward temporalities for more complex narrative (and psychological) evasions and detours, which on occasion mirror the narrative strategies of classical noir.[12] These strategies are already evident in some of the earliest post-war German films, such as the strange, elliptic thriller *Epilog – Das Geheimnis der Orplid* (*Epilogue – The Orplid Mystery*, 1950), the narrative of which disappears in *Citizen Kane*-like nested flashbacks. At the level of content, meanwhile, uncertainties about both national and gender identity surface in *Das verlorene Gesicht* (*The Lost Face*, 1951), a film about a woman who assumes multiple psychological and ethnic identities.

By the 1960s, the generation of the new German cinema saw the evasions and detours of post-war cinema as markers of its political and aesthetic regression. Noir as a critical discourse can be employed to perceive and valorise the cinematic strategies and generic trajectories of German cinema in a different way. Viewing post-war German cinema through the lens of noir, through its understanding of cinema as an expression of anxieties about modernity and as a mode of simultaneously modernist and popular generic representation – what Miriam Hansen has called, with reference to classical Hollywood, 'vernacular modernism' – [13] allows one to recover the films' contexts even or indeed particularly in their narrative absences. However, while using noir as a template of interpretation can produce useful transcultural and trans-historical insights, it is also essential to remain aware of historical, cultural, and generic specificities. There are too many significant differences between Weimar cinema, Hollywood noir and post-war German film to suggest any straightforward stylistic or thematic continuity.

Dimendberg suggests that Weimar cinema and Hollywood noir should be understood not in terms of linear influences, but rather as parallel modes of representation, divided not simply by cultural differences, but by the distinctions between early and late modernity, and by different manifestations of urban experience, namely the 'centripetal' city of early modernity, and its postmodern, post-war successor, characterised by 'centrifugal' space.[14] Thus, Fritz Lang's classic about the hunt for a paedophile killer, and one of Weimar cinema's quintessential 'city' films, M – Eine Stadt sucht einen Mörder (M – A City Searches for a Murderer, 1931) may have pre-empted noir's anxieties over, and strategies to master, the experience of modern urban life. However, its specific context, the riot-torn environment of metropolitan Germany in the 1920s, differed significantly from the spatial and social determinants of late 1940s Los Angeles, something that becomes abundantly clear when one compares Joseph Losey's Hollywood remake of M (1951) with its Weimar original.[15]

If one extends this discussion of differences in urban life to post-war German cinema, one confronts an important absence in the films of the late 1940s and early 1950s, namely the absence of the city itself, initially obliterated in the ruins of the 'rubble' film, and later supplanted by either the rural landscapes of the Heimatfilm, or the interiority of domestic melodramas and thrillers. Demarcating the borders between the 'rubble film' and the Heimatfilm is the strange hybrid Wenn abends die Heide träumt (When the Heath Dreams at Night, 1952), about two bomb disposal experts who seek respite from the dangers of the urban rubble in the German countryside. Decidedly 'city' films are rare during this period, although an interesting exception can be found across the border in the Austrian thriller Abenteuer in Wien (Stolen Identity, 1952), an almost Hitchcockian 'wrong man' plot about a Viennese cab driver embroiled in a murder case, which uses the backdrop of Vienna both effectively and atmospherically. Involved in the production were a number of Hollywood exiles who had worked on noir productions, including the actor Francis Lederer, and the director Gunther von Fritsch.[16]

Discussing the relationship in the post-war years between the ruined German city (for which Berlin is the emblematic example) as a powerful cultural symbol for an architectural as well as national 'ground zero', and the reality of urban experience in Germany, Brian Ladd has suggested that after the war

> ruins were not all that remained of the old Berlin ... *most* of its buildings still stood, reparable if not intact ... In a perverse way, those who proclaimed Berlin a total loss were guilty of wishful thinking. They included reformers who had long wished to ... correct the errors of nine-teenth-century urban development. That reformist impulse was power-fully reinforced by the widespread desire to suppress all possible links to the capital of the Third Reich, whether that desire was motivated by revulsion at the Nazis or by a sense of guilt.[17]

Dimendberg identifies nostalgia for the rapidly disappearing centripetal American city, combined with a sense of agoraphobic anxiety about the new centrifugal space of post-war development as major structuring elements in the construction of Hollywood noir in the 1940s and 1950s. In Germany, the transition from centripetal to centrifugal city underwent a crucial delay of war-related destruction, while the old city carried, as Ladd observes, quite different psycholog-ical and ideological connotations than in the American context. Post-war German town-planners and architects had aspirations towards a similar kind of urban decentralisation as their American counterparts, and many old buildings that had survived the bombing raids were demolished to give way to showpiece modern estates and suburban developments. However, the transformation that German cities under-went was on the whole far less radical than in the USA, partly a result of lesser financial means and greater pressures to provide immediate accommodation for refugees and the bombed-out homeless; partly a result of a more extensive attempt by the state to regulate urban devel-opment; and partly, as in the case of Berlin, the result of an impossi-bility to expand owing to the city's political enclosure. Most German cities retained their original design, and, as Brian Ladd has pointed out, 'with the practical uses of old buildings and streets came histori-cal continuities and symbolic baggage'.[18]

Any comparison between Hollywood noir and post-war German cinema, but also any attempt to construct a German noir tradition, needs to account for the topographical differences between these two contexts, and the social anxieties and aspirations that relate to them. In this respect the either literal or metaphorical absence of the city in post-war German cinema is the foundation on which other cinematic absences that I shall discuss in greater detail are dependent. The selected tropes I shall be focusing on in the following pages are a number of noir archetypes – the war veteran, the *femme fatale*, and the figure of the serial killer. In acknowledging similarities between post-war German cinema and film noir, as well as noting significant differences, the critical discourse of noir helps sharpen our understanding of a genre's cultural and historical determinants without losing sight of prior, parallel or subsequent developments.

Haunted veterans and the absence of the femme fatale

Die Mörder sind unter uns (*The Murderers Are Among Us*, 1946) was Germany's first post-Second World War production, the first to be made under the auspices of the Soviet occupying forces, and the first of a short-lived cycle of what has been referred to as 'rubble' films (*Trümmerfilme*) on account of their setting and use of location shooting in the bombed-out ruins of German cities in the immediate aftermath of the war.[19] The rubble film is often cited as German cinema's 'answer' to Italian neo-realism, but has also been compared to film noir.[20] It is also often perceived as the first decisive break from the aesthetic legacy of the Nazi period, in other words, post-war Germany's cinematic zero hour. The reality is more complicated. Writer-director Wolfgang Staudte, who had started his career in the Nazi-controlled Ufa media empire, developed the idea for *Die Mörder sind unter uns* with cinematographer Friedl Behn-Grund during the Second World War, when both were unlikely to have had much if any contact with either Italian neo-realism or with Hollywood's emerging noir tradition. Nazi cinema, meanwhile, had its own noir elements. The bleak pessimism and determinist inevitability that pervades many Nazi melodramas, complete with matching visual aesthetics, has, whether one likes it or not, much in common with both American noir and Hollywood's gothic melodrama during the 1940s.

   Die Mörder sind unter uns thus hardly constituted a cinematic ground zero. The film betrays its cinematic legacy most notably in its quasi-mystical lighting, used to envelop characters with luminous haloes, and employed in some abstractly symbolic scenes towards the end of the film. Echoes of Weimar cinema are perceptible in the stylisation with which Germany's post-war urban ruins are depicted – the shadows and canted angles with which Behn-Grund's cinematography captures the bombed-out lodgings and black-market dives of Berlin recall the topography of *Das Cabinet des Dr. Caligari* (*The Cabinet of Dr Caligari*, 1920) and the menacing shadows of *Nosferatu* (1922) – but it also pre-dates a similar way of depicting post-war topography in international productions such as *The Third Man* (1949). Obviously, such stylistic devices served a different ideological function from both contemporary Anglo-American noir examples, and from the film's own domestic antecedents.

Apart from aesthetic similarities, it is the film's narrative where the connection to noir issues is most apparent. As in many American noir plots of the 1940s (for example, *The Blue Dahlia*, 1946, *Crossfire*, 1947, and *Act of Violence*, 1948), *Die Mörder sind unter uns* features a psychologically scarred war veteran who cannot readjust to post-war life. Hans Mertens (Ernst W. Borchert), a former surgeon, is a guilt-ridden anti-hero, haunted by an incident during the war where his platoon was responsible for the massacre of a group of innocent civilians. Like many of his American generic cousins, Mertens has turned to alcohol, is tormented by nightmares (which, as in many American noir examples, disrupt the film's narrative through flashbacks), and lives a liminal and wilfully alienated existence in an urban wasteland. Mertens' redemption comes in the form of Susanne (Hildegard Knef), a concentration camp survivor who transforms his provisional lodgings into a home. It is through Susanne's intervention that Mertens re-encounters Brueckner, his former commanding officer, who gave the execution order for the wartime massacre, and whom Mertens believed had died. Mertens is shocked to discover that Brueckner is not only alive, but has become a successful capitalist entrepreneur, with no pangs of conscience disrupting his bourgeois existence as a jovial family man. Mertens decides to punish and kill his nemesis, but is prevented at the last minute by Susanne from doing so. Brueckner is arrested for his war crimes. By the end of the film the outlook for the male protagonist looks optimistic; under Susanne's influence Mertens has already rediscovered his vocation as a doctor and saved a child's life, while his remaining psychological problems are going to be dealt with compassion and patience by the nurturing and maternal Susanne. In the didactic and visually expressionist ending of the film, the image of Brueckner behind bars, protesting his innocence, gradually recedes into the distance, and eventually gives way to views of rows of Christian crosses on war graves on which are superimposed spectral, haunted-looking German soldiers.

Die Mörder sind unter uns is clearly influenced by the historical circumstances under which it was made, and its narrative didacticism (which makes the film a close cousin of similarly issue-based post-war American noirs such as *Crossfire*, 1947) is marked by external pressures and ambivalences. The film no doubt provides a bleak portrait of its context and is infused with an eerie atmosphere and deliberately melancholy mood. There are few unambiguously positive characters in the film, and the overall impression it paints of post-war Germany is of a hostile and alienating environment. However, the film could have been far bleaker and indeed even more noir had Staudte been allowed to make the film as originally conceived, which would have ended with Mertens succeeding in killing Brueckner. Such an ending would have certainly provided a morally more ambiguous slant to the narrative, whereas the emphasis in the existing version is focused on redemption. Much of the story's emphasis on reconciliation was due to the intervention of the Soviet censors, who hardly wanted to encourage vigilante justice and revenge killings in their administrative zone.[21]

Compared with its many other ideological and social concerns and particularly the ambiguous way in which the question of Germany's war guilt is addressed, the gender politics in *Die Mörder sind unter uns* are perhaps the film's most readable aspect, and provide another useful point of comparison with American noir and particularly with the way in which Hollywood reflected its contemporary historical context. The scenario is familiar from many accounts: in the United States, the end of the Second World War and the return of the war veteran frequently precipitated a new conflict at home – as the weakened male had to resume his role in the patriarchal order, which in his absence had been temporarily occupied by women. The crisis and humiliation experienced by men in post-war America was related to the competition from women in the economic sphere (in the workplace, as consumer), and in most of Hollywood's noir narratives this social conflict became encoded in the male hero's often deadly encounter with the *femme fatale*. Barton Byg has persuasively argued for film noir's recuperative function in post-war American society:

> American film noir ... represents a successful attempt to recuperate ... masculinity: Even when it ends in hopelessness and self-destruction, the 'tough crime' thriller represents a kind of purification ritual, capable of restoring strength to the male audiences who endure it, while inspiring awe and respect in female spectators.[22]

Much of German cinema in the immediate post-war years (whether in the East or the West) certainly had its fair share of doomed, wounded, self-pitying, and weak male protagonists, as can be seen in examples such as *Blockierte Signale* (*Blocked Signals*, 1948), *Hafenmelodie* (*Harbour Melody*, 1948), *Schicksal aus zweiter Hand* (*Second-Hand Destiny*, 1949) and *Tromba* (1949). However, there is a noticeable absence of the *femme fatale* during the same period. In *Die Mörder sind unter uns*, there are occasional glimpses of hardened showgirls in the film's scenes in dingy cabarets where Mertens gets drunk, but these 'bad girls' hardly contribute to the film's main narrative, and the prime locus of female representation is the Madonna-like figure of Susanne, combining ethereal goodness with steely determination. Not only does she appear saintly in all her actions, her visual depiction also associates her with religious imagery. Susanne is the first idealised cinematic representation of one of post-war Germany's most enduring historical heroines, the *Trümmerfrau* (rubble woman), who literally sweeps away the past to rebuild a new national future, and who shields traumatised and infantilised men in their period of recuperation. Erica Carter has argued that by aligning its central female protagonist with the religious iconography of a Madonna, *Die Mörder sind unter uns* performs an act of disavowing the past, since 'as a universal symbol removed from linear narrative, the Madonna possesses neither memory nor history'.[23] In other words, to represent post-war femininity through the symbolism of the Virgin Mary, as Carter suggests, allowed the rubble film to create a myth of German women standing outside history, untainted by war guilt (of course not necessarily a given in real life), and, as such, the only viable carrier of national values and culture into the future.

After *Die Mörder sind unter uns*, Hildegard Knef forged a successful career playing similar figures in several post-war German films, before being typecast as a more orthodox vamp in Hollywood.[24] The fact that Knef is nonetheless for the late 1940s and early 1950s that the nearest German cinema would get to a *femme fatale*, is instructive in underlining the different gender politics in the United States and in Germany at the time. This is especially evident when one studies a few of Knef's subsequent films. In *Nachts auf den Strassen* (*At Night on the Streets*, 1952), she plays a motorway siren who lures an ageing truck driver into criminal activities, yet even here the narrative of the film is at pains to redeem her character. The attempt in *Alraune* (*Unnatural*, 1952), a remake of a Weimar horror classic, to fashion Knef as an *über*-vamp in the tradition of Brigitte Helm, Marlene Dietrich or Louise Brooks, proved a failure. More typical are Knef's characterisations in *Die Sünderin* (*The Sinner*, 1951) and *Illusion in Moll* (*Illusion in a Minor Key*, 1952). Both are bleak and noirish women's melodramas which feature her less as a Virgin Mary than as a Mary Magdalene figure, where her sacrifice involves prostituting herself to save or protect her man. The fact that both films value these acts of sexual transgression positively or at least with moral indifference (incidentally the cause of much public outrage and condemnation by the main German churches at the time)[25] reflects the ethical pragmatism with which many post-war Germans made their moral arrangements according to the economic conditions and necessities of the occupation period.

Given the suspended nature of both national and masculine identity in the late 1940s, it is understandable why a post-war German cinema with recuperative intentions had neither need nor place for a *femme fatale*.[26] The only appropriate female icon that could provide the promise of national renewal was the strong, maternal woman who was willing to shoulder responsibility and to sacrifice herself, even at the risk of suspending moral values, until men were once more capable of resuming their previously held role in society and domestic life. Carter and other critics have identified this historical constellation as a 'cultural interregnum'.[27] It is only by the mid- to late 1950s, when West Germany begins to consolidate its 'economic miracle', that films begin to document the kind of social and gender conflict borne out of economic competition that American noir had depicted already ten years previously, and the *femme fatale* begins to make a comeback in German cinema in increasingly bleak portraits of domestic life. Thus, in the women's melodrama *Teufel in Seide* (*Devil in Silk*, 1955), an obsessive wife (Lilli Palmer) commits suicide, and leaves her husband accused of her murder. A similarly jealous wife kills her philandering husband in G. W. Pabst's *Das Bekenntnis der Ina Kahr* (*Ina Kahr's Confession*, 1954). A number of West German productions from the mid-1950s also took up the theme of the murderous male spouse in films such as *Geständnis unter vier Augen* (*Private Confession*, 1954) and *Ein Alibi zerbricht* (*An Alibi Collapses*, 1963). The disaffected and delinquent youth that appear in films such as *Die Halbstarken* (*The Hooligans*, 1956) and *Am Tag als der Regen kam* (*The Day the Rains Came*, 1959) also demonstrated that paranoia, gender competition and intergenerational conflict had truly entered the filmic depictions of the German institutions of home and family by the mid-1950s.

The serial killer returns

Among the most negative portraits of post-war gender relations in German cinema of the 1950s is the depiction of the rancid marriage between an infantile, quietly raging child-killer (Gert Fröbe) and his taunting, intellectually and economically superior wife (Berta Drews) in *Es geschah am hellichten Tag* (*It Happened in Broad Daylight*, 1958). In this bleak thriller (directed by former émigré Ladislao Vajda, based upon a screenplay by Swiss playwright Friedrich Dürrenmatt, and remade in Hollywood by Sean Penn as *The Pledge*, 2001), the suggestion is that the killer's homicidal ventures are directly linked to the way his patriarchal authority is undermined at home. The film's depiction of society at large is as corrosive as its view of domestic life; its setting in a remote Alpine valley emphasises the claustrophobia and paranoid introspection of its rural community, while the film's notional hero, a dour and obsessive retired detective, callously uses a child as bait to catch the killer.

Apart from the *femme fatale*, the psychopathic serial killer is of course another iconic figure linking late Weimar cinema and film noir. However, there are crucial differences in which this figure was invoked in different historical and cultural contexts. In 1920s and early 1930s Germany, the motif of the serial killer had become all pervasive across all strata of aesthetic and public discourse, finding its ultimate artistic expression in *M*.[28] Fritz Lang's film invited viewers to understand the child murderer Hans Beckert (Peter Lorre) as simultaneously villain and victim. In the process, it raised questions about society's conception of good and evil, justice and vengeance (*M* was seen both as an indictment of and as promoting capital punishment), about vigilante actions (the film demonstrates the hypocrisy of mob rule by having the killer hunted down and tried in a kangaroo court by a gang of thieves), and about the role of the mass media in generating and orchestrating public outrage as social spectacle. In his analysis of the film, Anton Kaes has drawn particular attention to the historically specific interdependencies Lang develops between the national and gendered trauma of the First World War, and the ubiquity of discourses on criminal pathology, and has proposed that 'Weimar culture was a "wound culture", where serial killing and serial culture were of one piece'.[29] In other words, the figure of the serial killer was able to function in public discourse and artistic representation as a prism for several anxieties about gender, modernity, urban experience and national memory that underlined life and culture in Weimar society.

As in the case of the absent *femme fatale* in late 1940s German films, it is initially surprising that, given the figure's ubiquity during the Weimar period, the serial killer narrative is not more prominent in post-war German cinema; one is left with a handful of examples from the mid-1940s to the 1960s. Among these, apart from *Es geschah am hellichten Tag*, are *Der Verlorene* (*The Lost One*, 1951) and *Nachts, wenn der Teufel kam* (*The Devil Strikes At Night*, 1957), which I will discuss in more detail, as well as *Viele kamen vorbei* (*Many Passed By*, 1956), and, to a lesser extent, *Gestehen Sie, Dr Corda!* (*Confess, Dr Corda*, 1958). Apart from a widespread distaste among audiences and critics for genres such as crime and horror, which were seen as inappropriate in the aftermath of the war, there are other reasons why the serial killer had lost his hold on the public imagination. Some of these reasons have to do with the way in which the Nazis had instrumentalised the figure in the intervening years. Two years after *M* both its director and its star had been forced into exile following Hitler's rise to power. In 1938, excerpts of Lorre's performance in *M* were included in the anti-Semitic propaganda compilation film *Juden ohne Maske* (*Jews without a Mask*), and again in 1940 in what is perhaps the period's most notorious hate production, *Der ewige Jude* (*The Eternal Jew*). The latter held Lorre (the actor) personally responsible for promoting sympathy with the character he was portraying, thus subverting the social and moral order.[30] In both cases the films aimed at blurring the distinctions between the (Jewish) performer Lorre and the depicted character, and at conflating so-called non-Aryan ethnicity with sexual deviancy and mental illness. This, in the eyes of the Nazis, made the serial killer, given shape in Lorre's performance, a perfect hate figure in triplicate, for all three aspects were targeted for extermination, either in concentration camps or through enforced euthanasia programmes in mental hospitals.

The serial-killer narratives that emerge in post-war German cinema have to be understood against the mobilisation of this topic under the Nazis, and it is obvious why the topic elicited unease, and why few filmmakers dared to touch it. However, these films also need to be distinguished from the way in which the serial killer was activated at the same time in American noir. Antithetically to the way the motif was employed by Nazi ideology, in classical noir, as in 1940s Hollywood more generally, the serial killer frequently stood for the dangers and inherent psychosis of antidemocratic elitism and fascist ideology.[31] Thus, the killers in *Phantom Lady* (1944), *Laura* (1944), as well as in Hitchcock's contemporaneous *Rope* (1948) are upper-class snobs, while the equally upper-class villain in *The Spiral Staircase* (1946) aims to eradicate 'deficient' lives. As James Naremore has put it succinctly, 'the villains in these pictures tend to be homosexual aesthetes or homosexual Nazi sadists who threaten the values of a democratic and somewhat proletarian masculinity'.[32]

Post-war German cinema 'reclaimed' the serial killer in a radically different way. Considering how the Nazis had used his image in his years of exile (which he spent being similarly typecast as a stock villain in Hollywood),[33] it is doubly extraordinary that Peter Lorre in the early 1950s not only returned to West Germany to shoot his first (and what remained his only) film as director, but that he would personally choose to return to the subject of the serial killer. However, *Der*

Verlorene (also co-written by Lorre, and adapted by him into a novel) is not a remake of *M*.[34] Instead it provides an astute reflection of what had happened since the early 1930s, in terms of historical events, in terms of Lorre's own biography and career trajectory, and finally in terms of cinematic aesthetics on each side of the Atlantic.

Deliberately eschewing the urban topography of both classical noir and of *M*, *Der Verlorene* opens in a refugee camp, comprising isolated barracks set in a desolate wasteland on the north German plains some time after the end of the war. Lorre himself plays Dr Rothe, the quietly spoken, compassionate camp doctor who one day happens upon a face from the past, his former assistant Hoesch, on the run from the authorities as a war criminal. The two men recall their previous encounters in a flashback, which reveals that in 1943 Rothe was a scientist conducting experiments of vital importance to the Nazi war effort. Rothe discovers that Hoesch, working for the Gestapo, seduced his fiancée Inge whereupon, driven mad by jealousy and betrayal, Rothe strangles her. Hoesch and his superior, Winkler, cover up the murder as a suicide in order to safeguard Rothe's research, but they cannot stop his now awakened homicidal urges. Under cover of the wartime blackout, he murders again, stalking potential victims among prostitutes and lonely housewives. Wrecked by guilt and self-loathing, Rothe plans to kill himself alongside his Nazi masters when he stumbles by accident upon an anti-Hitler conspiracy, spearheaded by

5 Peter Lorre in *Der Verlorene* (*The Lost One*, Peter Lorre, 1951).

Winkler. Rothe unwittingly helps to foil the plot, and Hoesch has Winkler arrested. In a bombing raid, Rothe's flat is destroyed, allowing him to fake his death and disappear. Following the conclusion of the flashback narrative, Rothe calmly shoots Hoesch with the latter's revolver, and then commits suicide by stepping onto a nearby railway track in front of an oncoming train.

Already this brief synopsis, which somewhat simplifies the film's fractured narration, indicates that *Der Verlorene* offers a stark contrast to the reconciliatory tone of *Die Mörder sind unter uns*. Lorre's Dr Rothe also differs in characterisation and function from the sophisticated dandy murderers in the noir examples cited above, although he is, as Jennifer Kapczynski has pointed out, reminiscent of the timid, petit bourgeois anti-hero of Fritz Lang's Hollywood noir classic *Scarlet Street* (1945).[35] *Der Verlorene* uses the story of a serial killer to comment allegorically on the war, on Nazi rule, and on questions of individual versus collective guilt. It invites the viewer to compare and judge different forms of killing alongside each other – Rothe's 'private' homicides; the Nazis' use of torture and murder; and the random war casualties encountered on battlefields and in bombing raids. Adopting a quasi-existentialist position, Lorre's film seems to suggest that it is futile to morally differentiate between these different deaths, a stance that some critics have considered as amounting to a facile trivialisation of the Nazis' crimes.[36] The perception of a general lack of purpose and meaning is underlined by the way in which the film's plot revolves around random acts, arbitrary events and coincidences – the cruel irony of which only Rothe seems to appreciate – such as the chance encounter between Rothe and Hoesch, the former's stumbling upon Winkler's conspirators' circle, or the chance destruction of Rothe's home in an Allied bombing raid. Nevertheless, it is the serial killer's acknowledgment of his guilt that elevates him above the opportunistic rationalising of mass murder espoused by Hoesch and by the technocrats of war. This gives Rothe the moral superiority to become, in the final scenes of the film, a legitimate avenger (something that Mertens in *Die Mörder sind unter uns*, in a similar situation, was not allowed to be).

Critics have frequently seen Rothe as merely a 'reprise' of Lorre's earlier role as Beckert in *M*, but the two characters are in some respects antithetical, and the film itself as a pale shadow of Lang's classic.[37] Whereas Beckert was manic and hyperactive, Rothe is passive and depressive, where Beckert was hysterical and nervously agitated, Rothe is melancholy and lethargic, where Beckert was a social misfit, Rothe is a an existential one, and while Beckert was infantile and unreflective, Rothe exudes the resignations and disappointments of middle age, and is painfully aware of himself and his immediate environment. Moreover, whereas Beckert remained a shadowy presence in *M* almost to the end, Rothe is clearly the central protagonist of *Der Verlorene*. Gerd Gemünden has suggested that during his career in Hollywood, Lorre managed to inflect his roles with his experience as an exile, and that his portrayals 'show national and cultural identity as a site of multiple competing, often antagonistic impulses and forces, and the complex process of adapting – or not adapting – to another culture'.[38] A similar impulse can be seen to structure Lorre's performance in *Der Verlorene*, but now with the distinction that it rather poignantly documents the impossibility and failure of re-adapting to the culture Lorre was once forced to leave behind. A highly self-reflexive film, *Der Verlorene* is ultimately less about the Nazi past than about the experience of being an outsider, and it can be seen to 'stage the complex negotiations between the filmmaker's interconnected but divergent lives in exile and at home'.[39]

There are numerous film historical references in *Der Verlorene*. Rothe's somnambulist wanderings through the film, and the way in which Lorre's cinematographer Vaclav Vich captures the stark landscapes with its isolated pylons in the framing story recall *The Cabinet of Dr Caligari* more than *M*, while later sequences in the film seem to echo, and occasionally directly quote, some of Lorre's Hollywood films, including pre- or proto-noir productions such as *Mad Love* (1935), *Stranger on the Third Floor* (1940) and *The Face Behind the Mask* (1941). Although the narrative of *Der Verlorene* has been accused of being 'fuzzy' and 'confusing',[40] the film's meandering feel imposes itself more as a deliberate aesthetic choice, in correspondence with the film's fatalistic conception of a circular destiny. There are few post-war German films which are as rigorous in their stylistic and narrative construction, and few which come as close to the mood of classical noir. Vich's masterly high-contrast cinematography combines influences from both Hollywood and from Italian neo-realism, while Franz Schroedter's superb set designs convey the suffocating claustrophobia of Rothe's apartment, the menace of permanent surveillance that pervades Rothe's laboratory, and the feeling of decadence and doom that permeates Winkler's home. But what above all stays in the audience's memory are the close-ups of Lorre, employed to particular effect in the murder scenes, and at the very end of the film, where his face freezes into a mask, which, resembling Edvard Munch's famous painting *The Scream*, concentrates a psychological state of mind into a single emblematic expression of utter despair.

Der Verlorene was a failure with audiences in 1951, acknowledged in contemporary reviews as artistically ambitious but seen as ultimately too bleak.[41] Without much international acknowledgment either, Lorre returned to Hollywood, never to direct another film. Another returning émigré, Robert Siodmak, took up the subject of a serial killer in *Nachts, wenn der Teufel kam* (*The Devil Strikes at Night*, 1957). As in *Der Verlorene*, the Nazi period is its historical setting, though the serial killer is more closely related to Lang's Beckert than to Lorre's Dr Rothe. Bruno Lüdke (Mario Adorf) is infantile, a mentally retarded menial worker living on the margins of society, but with enough cunning to cover up his crimes, and also sly enough to use his apparent naivety when caught by the police. The plot of the film revolves around a police inspector's attempts to solve a series of killings, which the Nazi authorities use as a cynical propaganda exercise to garner public support for their policy of exterminating the mentally ill. Although neither as narratively consistent nor as visually compelling as *Der Verlorene* (though with frequent visual allusions to Siodmak's previous noir films in Hollywood), this film nonetheless addressed many of the former's central issues. As in Lorre's film, the figure of the serial killer provided an opportunity to discuss highly pertinent ethical questions affecting society as a whole, particularly about issues of national identity, of individual versus collective responsibilities, and of the engagement with otherness.

Noir after reconstruction

Unlike Lorre's *Der Verlorene*, Siodmak's film was a success at the German box office and received critical accolades upon its release, which to some extent highlights the changes in the national and social context Germany had experienced in between these two films.[42] A decade after the end of the war, once the rubble had been cleared, and the majority of the population had found accommodation, anxieties about the new living conditions began to emerge, which then were articulated through cinematic narratives and visual representations. Nostalgia for an unrecoverable past coupled with an increasing disaffection with contemporary urban space grew from the mid-1950s onwards, and by the early 1960s, one widely discussed study of postwar urban development was entitled 'the murdered city'.[43] It is thus no coincidence that the city resurfaced in German cinema at this particular point in time. Genres such as the 'social problem film' began to reflect the urban landscape that had gradually consolidated itself in the 1950s as a hybrid space, an awkward and alienating mixture of old and new. Films such as *Die Halbstarken* (*The Hooligans*, 1956) or *Die Frühreifen* (*The Adolescents*, 1957) dramatised the contested use of the urban environment by different generations and different lifestyles.[44] In East German films, on the other hand, the city often became a space for contesting political aspirations. As in West German cinema, noir can retrospectively function as a productive discourse to analyse aesthetic choices in DEFA productions of the time. Set on both sides of the ideological divide, *Berlin Ecke Schönhauser* (*Berlin Schönhauser Corner*, 1957), for example, uses a visual style reminiscent of noir when capturing the dangerous and hostile world of the capitalist West, while relying more on neo-realist techniques in its depiction of the Eastern sector of the city.

As in the case of Lorre's and Siodmak's films, among the visually most accomplished of these films were those made by former exiles who had worked in Hollywood on noir productions, such as Frank Wisbar's *Nasser Asphalt* (*Wet Asphalt*, 1958) and Gerd Oswald's *Am Tag als der Regen kam* (*The Day the Rains Came*, 1959). Films such as *Das Mädchen Rosemarie* (*The Girl Rosemarie*, 1958), *Die Wahrheit über Rosemarie* (*The Truth About Rosemarie*, 1959) and *Der Rest ist Schweigen* (*The Rest Is Silence*, 1959), meanwhile, explicitly employed a noir visual style to represent new urban developments and interior design as metaphors for the shallowness of West Germany's economic miracle and its attendant consumerist ethics. The depiction of provincial communities was often similarly bleak – films such as *Es geschah am hellichten Tag*, *Die goldene Pest* (*The Golden Plague*, 1954 – another film by a remigrant noir director, John Brahm), *Schwarzer Kies* (*Black Gravel*, 1960) and *Kirmes* (*Fairground*, 1960) show small towns as rife with corruption, paranoia, introspection and hidden guilt. Even in a normally lighter genre, such as the adventure film, one finds extremely bleak examples during this period, such as Georg Tressler's *Das Totenschiff* (*Ship of the Dead*, 1959).

Perhaps the most intriguing film to articulate the 'symbolic baggage' of a still present and unmastered past that accompanied the urban experience in post-war Germany is Fritz Lang's swan song *Die tausend Augen des Dr Mabuse* (*The Thousand Eyes of Dr Mabuse*, 1960). The setting of the film and to some extent its main protagonist is a hotel, and the place's architectural legacy (built by the Nazis) triggers off events in the present of the 1950s. Exploiting both its apparent and its hidden function, Lang's titular master criminal uses the hotel to project luxury and comfort to attract the new international partners of West Germany's economic miracle, while secretly spying on the same guests through intricate systems of surveillance of false mirrors and television technology. There are few films in the 1950s that offer, in the guise of a popular genre film, such an acerbic allegory on the legacy of the Nazi past and about West Germany's capitalist aspirations at the same time. Like Lorre's *Der Verlorene*, Lang's Mabuse film is highly self-reflexive, seemingly underwritten by the same compulsion to repeat the filmmaker's previous career, and acutely aware of the existential otherness of exile experience. Tom Gunning has made a very insightful comment on Lang's decision to return not just to Germany after the war, but also to pick up once again the generic template of his Dr Mabuse films of the 1920s and early 1930s:

> This return ... from exile ... yields a profound sense of the untimeliness of history, the knowledge that nothing can ever truly be repeated, and that in repetition lies not so much the promise of rebirth as the harbinger of death. Repetition involves a profound mourning for the passage of time.[45]

Gunning's haunting comment is not only astute regarding Lang's specific case – it elegantly summarises the fate of many returning exile filmmakers in post-war Germany (including Lorre and Siodmak), whose biographies, in their detours and dead ends, often charted what one might refer to as a noir trajectory. However, if one abstracts the quotation from the strictly biographical, it also provides a perfect analogy to what I have been trying to argue more generally in this chapter with respect to the tangled relationships, mismatches and delayed echoes between Weimar and post-war German cinema, and between Hollywood noir and its pre- and post-war German cousins.

Returning in conclusion to the two major questions that I posed at the outset of this chapter concerning the reception of Hollywood noir in post-war Germany and the issue of a domestic noir tradition, it is clear that as regards the former there is little evidence of a major impact until well into the 1960s. In terms of general and critical reception, noir was either ignored, or met with hostility. As far as production was concerned, a conscious cross-over of noir themes and style only happened in rare instances, most prominently in films where this influence was mediated by returning Hollywood émigrés such as Brahm, Lang, Lorre, Oswald, Siodmak and Wisbar. However, while a conscious awareness of noir as a genre may have been restricted to the films of these exiles, there is nevertheless a wider corpus of films that can be seen to amount to something of a parallel German noir tradition, with its distinctive narrative themes and visual style. This tradition was influenced less by Hollywood, but by a dual artistic and political legacy of Weimar and the 'Third Reich', and by the specific anxieties, demands and aspirations of the two post-war German societies.

Notes

1   See, for example, Jan-Christopher Horak, 'Exilfilm 1933–1945. In der Fremde', in Wolfgang Jacobsen, Anton Kaes and Hans Helmut Prinzler (eds), *Geschichte des deutschen Films* (Stuttgart and Weimar: J. B. Metzler, 1993), pp. 101–18.

2   Thomas Elsaesser, 'A German Ancestry to Film Noir?', *Iris*, 21 (1996), 129–44. See also the Chapter 'Caligari's Legacy. Film Noir as Film History's German Imaginary', in his *Weimar Cinema and After: Germany's Historical Imaginary* London and New York: Routledge, 2000), pp. 420–44.

3   Marc Vernet, 'Film Noir on the Edge of Doom', in Joan Copjec (ed.), *Shades of Noir* (London: Verso 1993), pp. 1–31.

4   Tim Bergfelder, 'Extraterritorial Fantasies: Edgar Wallace and the German Crime Film', in Tim Bergfelder, Erica Carter and Deniz Göktürk (eds), *The German Cinema Book* (London: BFI Publishing, 2002), pp. 39–47.

5   *Ibid.*, pp. 44–6.

6   See Heide Fehrenbach, *Cinema in Democratising Germany: Reconstructing National Identity after Hitler* (Chapel Hill and London: University of North Carolina Press, 1995); Joseph Garncarz, 'Populäres Kino in Deutschland. Internationalisierung einer Filmkultur, 1925–1990' (Cologne: University of Cologne, 1996); Tim Bergfelder, *International Adventure: German Popular Cinema and European Co-Productions in the 1960s* (New York and Oxford: Berghahn, 2005).

7   Cited in Bergfelder, *International Adventures*, p. 119.

8   Cited in Lutz Koepnick, *The Dark Mirror. German Cinema between Hitler and Hollywood* (Berkeley: University of California Press, 2002), p. 193.

9   Koepnick, *The Dark Mirror*, p. 194.

10   See, for example, Christian Cargnelli and Michael Omasta (eds), *Schatten. Exil. Europäische Emigranten im Film Noir*, Vienna: PVS 1997; and Barbara Steinbauer-Grötsch, *Die lange Nacht der Schatten. Film noir und Filmexil* (Berlin: Bertz, 1997).

11   Edward Dimendberg, *Film Noir and the Spaces of Modernity* (Cambridge, MA and London: Harvard University Press, 2004), p. 1.

12   Bergfelder, *International Adventures*, pp. 40–9.

13   Miriam Hansen, 'The Mass Production of the Senses: Classical Cinema as Vernacular Modernism', in Christine Gledhill and Linda Williams (eds), *Reinventing Film Studies* (London: Arnold, 2000), pp. 332–50.

14   Dimendberg, *Film Noir and the Spaces of Modernity*. See also his

'Siegfried Kracauer, "Hollywood's Terror Films", and the Spatiality of Film Noir', in *New German Critique*, 89 (Spring/Summer 2003), 113–43.

15   Dimendberg, *Film Noir and the Spaces of Modernity*, pp. 218–27.

16   See Michael Omasta, 'Ein vergessender Reisender in Sachen Film. Notizen zu Leben und Werk des Regisseurs und Cutters Gunther von Fritsch', in Christian Cargnelli and Michael Omasta (eds), *Aufbruch ins Ungewisse. Österreichische Filmschaffende in der Emigration vor 1945* (Vienna: Wespennest, 1993), pp. 175–86.

17   Brian Ladd, *The Ghosts of Berlin: Confronting German History in the Urban Landscape* (Chicago and London: University of Chicago Press, 1997), p. 177.

18   *Ibid.*, p. 178.

19   See Robert Shandley, *Rubble Films: German Cinema in the Shadow of the Third Reich* (Philadelphia: Temple University Press, 2001).

20   Thomas Brandlmeier, 'Von Hitler zu Adenauer. Deutsche Trümmerfilme', in Jürgen Berger, Hans-Peter Reichmann and Rudolf Worschech (eds), *Zwischen Gestern und Morgen. Westdeutscher Nachkriegsfilm, 1946–1962* (Frankfurt-on-Main: Deutsches Filmmuseum, 1989), pp. 32–59.

21   Sabine Hake, *German National Cinema* (London and New York: Routledge, 2002), p. 92.

22   Barton Byg, 'Nazism as *Femme Fatale*: Recuperations of Cinematic Masculinity in Postwar Berlin', in Patricia Herminghouse and Magda Müller (eds), *Gender and Germanness: Cultural Productions of Nation* (Oxford and New York: Berghahn, 1997), p. 180.

23   Erica Carter, 'Sweeping up the Past: Gender and History in the Post-war German "Rubble Film"', in Ulrike Sieglohr (ed.), *Heroines without Heroes. Reconstructing Female and National Identities in European Cinema, 1945–1951* (London and New York: Cassell, 2000), p. 104.

24   See Ulrike Sieglohr, 'Hildegard Knef: from Rubble Woman to Fallen Woman', in Sieglohr (ed.), *Heroines without Heroes*, pp. 113–27.

25   See Fehrenbach, *Cinema in Democratising Germany*, pp. 92–117.

26   One of the few striking exceptions are the two main female protagonists in Veit Harlan's very strange melodrama *Hanna Amon* (1951), in its excessiveness one of the most anomalous and bizarre films of the early 1950s, and, like some of Harlan's other post-war films, worthy of further critical attention. (*Note*: thanks to Robert Kiss for bringing the film to my attention.)

27   Carter, 'Sweeping up the Past', p. 95.

28   See Maria Tatar, *Lustmord. Sexual Murder in Weimar Germany* (Princeton, New Jersey: Princeton University Press, 1995).

29   Anton Kaes, *M* (London: BFI Publishing, 1999), p. 29.

30   *Ibid.*, p. 71.

31   Koepnick, *The Dark Mirror*, pp. 164–90.

32   James Naremore, *More Than Night: Film Noir in its Contexts* (Berkeley:

University of California Press, 1998), pp. 98–9.

33 See Gerd Gemünden, 'From "Mr. M" to "Mr Murder"': Peter Lorre and the Actor in Exile', in Margaret McCarthy and Randall Halle (eds), *Light Motives: German Popular Film in Perspective* (Detroit: Wayne State University Press, 2003), pp. 85–107.

34 Peter Lorre, *Der Verlorene* ed. Michael Farin and Hans Schmid (Munich: Belleville, 1996).

35 Jennifer M. Kapczynski, 'Homeward Bound? Peter Lorre's *The Lost Man* and the End of Exile', *New German Critique*, 89 (Spring/Summer 2003), 157.

36 Robert C. Reimer, *Nazi-Retro Film: How German Narrative Cinema Remembers the Past* (New York: Twayne, 1992), pp. 20–1.

37 *Ibid.*, p. 19.

38 Gemünden, 'From "Mr M" to "Mr Murder"', p. 99.

39 Jennifer M. Kapczynski, 'Homeward Bound?', pp. 145–6.

40 Reimer, *Nazi-Retro Film*, p. 19.

41 Brandlmeier, 'Von Hitler zu Adenauer', pp. 56–7.

42 Karl Prümm, 'Universeller Erzähler. Realist des Unmittelbaren', in Wolfgang Jacobsen and Hans Helmut Prinzler (eds), *Siodmak Bros. Berlin – Paris – London – Hollywood* (Berlin: Argon/Stiftung Deutsche Kinemathek, 1998), p. 61.

43 Cited in Hermann Glaser, *Die Kulturgeschichte der Bundesrepublik Deutschland: Band 2: Zwischen Grundgesetz und grosser Koalition 1949–1967* (Frankfurt-on-Main: Fischer, 1990), p. 142.

44 Jürgen Felix, 'Rebellische Jugend. Die 'Halbstarken'-Filme: Vorbilder und Nachbildungen', in Michael Schaudig (ed.), *Positionen deutscher Filmgeschichte* (Munich: Diskurs Film, 1996), pp. 309–28.

45 Tom Gunning, *The Films of Fritz Lang: Allegories of Vision and Modernity* (London: BFI Publishing, 2000), p. 457.

Filmography

Post-war German cinema: 1945–60

Die Mörder sind unter uns (*The Murderers Are among Us*), Wolfgang Staudte, 1946

Blockierte Signale (*Blocked Signals*), Johannes Meyer, 1948

Hafenmelodie (*Harbour Melody*), Hans Müller, 1948

Das verlorene Gesicht (*The Lost Face*), Kurt Hoffmann, 1948

Schicksal aus zweiter Hand (*Second-Hand Destiny*), Wolfgang Staudte, 1949

Tromba, Helmut Weiss, 1949

Epilog – Das Geheimnis der Orplid (*Epilogue – The Orplid Mystery*), Helmut Käutner, 1950

Der Verlorene (*The Lost One*), Peter Lorre, 1951

Die Sünderin (*The Sinner*), Willi Forst, 1951

Hanna Amon, Veit Harlan, 1951

Nachts auf den Strassen (*At Night on the Streets*), Rudolf Jugert, 1952
Illusion in Moll (*Illusion in a Minor Key*), Rudolf Jugert, 1952
Alraune (*Unnatural*), Arthur Maria Rabenalt, 1952
Wenn abends die Heide träumt (*When the Heath Dreams at Night*), Paul
    Martin, 1952
Abenteuer in Wien/Stolen Identity (Austria/USA), E. E. Reinert/Gunther von
    Fritsch, 1952
Die goldene Pest (*The Golden Plague*), John Brahm, 1954
Geständnis unter vier Augen (*Private Confession*), André Michel, 1954
Das Bekenntnis der Ina Kahr (*Ina Kahr's Confession*), G. W. Pabst, 1954
Teufel in Seide (*Devil in Silk*), Rolf Hansen, 1955
Die Halbstarken (*The Hooligans*), Georg Tressler, 1956
Viele kamen vorbei (*Many Passed By*), Peter Pewas, 1956.
Berlin Ecke Schönhauser (*Berlin Schönhauser Corner*), Gerhard Klein, 1957
Nachts wenn der Teufel kam (*The Devil Strikes at Night*), Robert Siodmak,
    1957
Die Frühreifen (*The Adolescents*), Josef von Baky, 1957
Gestehen Sie, Dr Corda! (*Confess, Dr Corda*), Josef von Baky, 1958
Das Mädchen Rosemarie (*The Girl Rosemarie*), Rolf Thiele, 1958
Es geschah am hellichten Tag (*It Happened in Broad Daylight*), Ladislao
    Vajda, 1958
Nasser Asphalt (*Wet Asphalt*), Frank Wisbar, 1958
Am Tag als der Regen kam (*The Day the Rains Came*), Gerd Oswald, 1959
Die Wahrheit über Rosemarie (*The Truth about Rosemarie*), Rudolf Jugert,
    1959
Der Rest ist Schweigen (*The Rest Is Silence*), Helmut Käutner, 1959
Das Totenschiff (*Ship of the Dead*), Georg Tressler, 1959
Die 1000 Augen des Dr Mabuse (*The Thousand Eyes of Dr Mabuse*), Fritz
    Lang, 1960
Schwarzer Kies (*Black Gravel*), Helmut Käutner, 1960
Kirmes (*Fairground*), Wolfgang Staudte, 1960

Other films cited
Das Cabinet des Dr. Caligari (*The Cabinet of Dr Caligari*), Robert Wiene,
    1920
Nosferatu, Friedrich Wilhelm Murnau, 1922
M – Eine Stadt sucht einen Mörder (*M – A City Searches for a Murderer*),
    Fritz Lang, 1931
Mad Love, Karl Freund, 1935
Juden ohne Maske, Walter Böttcher/Leo von der Schmiede, 1938
Der ewige Jude (*The Eternal Jew*), Fritz Hippler, 1940
Stranger On the Third Floor, Boris Ingster, 1940
The Face Behind the Mask, Robert Florey, 1941
Phantom Lady, Robert Siodmak, 1944
Laura, Otto Preminger, 1944
Scarlet Street, Fritz Lang, 1945

The Blue Dahlia, George Marshall, 1946
The Spiral Staircase, Robert Siodmak, 1946
Crossfire, Edward Dmytryk, 1947
Rope, Alfred Hitchcock, 1948
Act of Violence, Fred Zinnemann, 1948
The Third Man, Carol Reed, 1949
M, Joseph Losey, 1951
Ein Alibi zerbricht (An Alibi Collapses), Alfred Vohrer, 1963
The Pledge, Sean Penn, 2001

Select bibliography

Alpi, Deborah Lazaroff, *Robert Siodmak* (Jefferson: McFarland, 1998).
Berger, Jürgen, Hans-Peter Reichmann and Rudolf Worschech (eds), *Zwischen Gestern und Morgen. Westdeutscher Nachkriegsfilm, 1946–1962* (Frankfurt-on-Main: Deutsches Filmmuseum, 1989).
Bergfelder, Tim, *International Adventures: German Popular Cinema and European Co-productions in the 1960s* (New York and Oxford: Berghahn, 2005).
Bergfelder, Tim, Erica Carter and Deniz Göktürk (eds), *The German Cinema Book* (London: BFI Publishing, 2002).
Cargnelli, Christian and Michael Omasta (eds), *Aufbruch ins Ungewisse. Österreichische Filmschaffende in der Emigration vor 1945* (Vienna: Wespennest, 1993).
Cargnelli, Christian and Michael Omasta (eds), *Schatten. Exil. Europäische Emigranten im Film noir* (Vienna: PVS, 1997).
Dimendberg, Edward, 'Siegfried Kracauer, "Hollywood's Terror Films", and the Spatiality of Film Noir', in *New German Critique*, 89 (Spring/Summer 2003), 113–43.
Dimendberg, Edward, *Film Noir and the Spaces of Modernity* (Cambridge, Mass. and London: Harvard University Press, 2004).
Elsaesser, Thomas, 'A German Ancestry to Film Noir?', *Iris*, 21 (1996), 129–44.
Elsaesser, Thomas, *Weimar Cinema and After. Germany's Historical Imaginary* (London and New York: Routledge, 2000).
Fehrenbach, Heide, *Cinema in Democratising Germany: Reconstructing National Identity after Hitler* (Chapel Hill and London: University of North Carolina Press, 1995).
Garncarz, Joseph, 'Populäres Kino in Deutschland. Internationalisierung einer Filmkultur, 1925–1990' (Cologne: University of Cologne, 1996).
Glaser, Hermann, *Die Kulturgeschichte der Bundesrepublik Deutschland: Band 2: Zwischen Grundgesetz und grosser Koalition 1949–1967* (Frankfurt-on-Main: Fischer, 1990).
Gledhill, Christine and Linda Williams (eds), *Reinventing Film Studies* (London: Arnold, 2000).
Gunning, Tom, *The Films of Fritz Lang. Allegories of Vision and Modernity*

(London: BFI Publishing, 2000).

Hake, Sabine, *German National Cinema* (London and New York: Routledge, 2002).

Herminghouse, Patricia and Magda Müller (eds), *Gender and Germanness: Cultural Productions of Nation* (Oxford and New York: Berghahn, 1997).

Hofmann, Felix and Stephen D. Youngkin (eds), *Peter Lorre: Portrait des Schauspielers auf der Flucht* (Munich: Belleville, 1998).

Jacobsen, Wolfgang, Anton Kaes and Hans Helmut Prinzler (eds), *Geschichte des deutschen Films* (Stuttgart and Weimar: J. B. Metzler, 1993).

Jacobsen, Wolfgang and Hans Helmut Prinzler (eds), *Siodmak Bros. Berlin – Paris – London – Hollywood* (Berlin: Argon/Stiftung Deutsche Kinemathek, 1998).

Kaes, Anton, *M* (London: BFI Publishing, 1999).

Kapczynski, Jennifer M., 'Homeward Bound? Peter Lorre's *The Lost Man* and the End of Exile', *New German Critique*, 89 (Spring/Summer 2003), 145–72.

Koepnick, Lutz, *The Dark Mirror: German Cinema between Hitler and Hollywood* (Berkeley: University of California Press, 2002).

Ladd, Brian, *The Ghosts of Berlin: Confronting German History in the Urban Landscape* (Chicago and London: University of Chicago Press, 1997).

Loacker, Armin (ed.), *Austrian Noir. Essays zur österreichisch-amerikanischen Koproducktion Abenteur In Wien/Stolen Identity* (Vienna: Filmarchiv Austria, 2005).

Lorre, Peter, *Der Verlorene* ed. Michael Farin and Hans Schmid (Munich: Belleville, 1996).

McCarthy, Margaret and Randall Halle (eds), *Light Motives: German Popular Film in Perspective* (Detroit: Wayne State University Press, 2003).

Naremore, James, *More than Night: Film Noir in its Contexts* (Berkeley: University of California Press, 1998).

Omasta, Michael, Brigitte Mayr, Elisabeth Streit (eds), *Peter Lorre: Ein Fremder im Paradies* (Vienna: Zsolnay, 2004).

Orbanz, Eva and Hans Helmut Prinzler, *Wolfgang Staudte* (Berlin: Spiess, 1991).

Phillips, Gene D., *Exiles in Hollywood: Major European Film Directors in America* (Bethlehem: Lehigh University Press, 1998).

Reimer, Robert C., *Nazi-Retro Film: How German Narrative Cinema Remembers the Past* (New York: Twayne, 1992).

Schaudig, Michael (ed.), *Positionen deutscher Filmgeschichte* (Munich: Diskurs Film, 1996).

Shandley, Robert, *Rubble Films: German Cinema in the Shadow of the Third Reich* (Philadelphia: Temple University Press, 2001).

Sieglohr, Ulrike (ed.), *Heroines without Heroes. Reconstructing Female and National Identities in European Cinema, 1945–1951* (London and New York: Cassell, 2000).

Spicer, Andrew, *Film Noir* (Harlow, Essex: Longman/Pearson Education, 2002).

Steinbauer-Grötsch, Barbara, *Die lange Nacht der Schatten: Film noir und Filmexil* (Berlin: Bertz, 1997).

Tatar, Maria, *Lustmord. Sexual Murder in Weimar Germany* (Princeton, New Jersey: Princeton University Press, 1995).

Taylor, John Russell, *Strangers in Paradise: The Hollywood Emigrés 1933–1950* (London: Faber & Faber, 1983).

Vernet, Marc, 'Film Noir on the Edge of Doom', in Joan Copjec (ed.), *Shades of Noir* (London: Verso, 1993), pp. 1–31.

Wager, Jans B., *Dangerous Dames: Women and Representation in the Weimar Street Film and Film Noir* (Columbus: Ohio State University Press, 1999).

7

German neo-noir

Paul Cooke

The relationship between film noir and German cinema has a long history. However, the influence of this American tradition in Germany has been particularly important in the post-war period during the two moments when Germany's national cinema has gained a degree of international recognition. The first, and by far the most successful, period was that of the new German cinema. During this era, which spans the late 1960s to the early 1980s, filmmakers such as Rainer Werner Fassbinder and Wim Wenders gained huge international acclaim with their avant-garde films, in many of which we find the emergence of what Andrew Spicer terms self-reflexive 'modernist neo-noir'.[1]

The second period came after German unification in 1990, and more specifically since the release of Tom Tykwer's techno-fuelled youth movie *Lola Rennt* (*Run Lola Run*, 1998), whose success has once more put German cinema on the international map, albeit on a smaller scale. Although current directors, like their New German Cinema predecessors, are making use of the style and themes of American noir, here we see a movement away from the 'modernist neo-noir' of Wenders and Fassbinder towards what might be characterised, to return to Spicer's taxonomy, as a more commodified, 'postmodern', form.[2] Such postmodern films are often accused of simply going through the stylistic motions of noir, that is of merely aping the classical form and having nothing new to say. This characterisation of the shift between modernist and postmodernist culture as a shift from self-reflexive critique to nostalgic wallowing is, of course, a common criticism of postmodern culture, notably recalling Frederick Jameson's dichotomy between modernism, which he views as being dominated by a mode of critical 'parody', and postmodernism, in which all critical distance has been lost and we are left with an unreflective 'pastiche' of a past age.[3]

In this chapter I explore the perceived shift from a modernist to postmodernist mode in filmmaking since the late 1960s, focusing initially on the work of Fassbinder and Wenders who have made much use of neo-noir, before turning to a small number of paradigmatic neo-noir films from recent years. As we shall see, many of the films discussed here stretch Jameson's definitions. Nevertheless, I argue that, with regard to German neo-noir at least, his parody–pastiche dichotomy remains productive, while at the same time suggesting that in pastiche we can still find elements of critical engagement. In particular, I explore how this dichotomy is useful in an analysis of the complex relationship between German neo-noir and Hollywood, a relationship which, I shall suggest, is central to an understanding of much German film culture.

The new German cinema: negotiating the Nazi past and the 'Americanised' present

To understand the use of film noir in the work of the filmmakers of the New German Cinema, it is first necessary to understand the relationship of this generation both to the history of its own society and to American culture. This relationship is often summarised by reference to the line from Wim Wenders' *Im Lauf der Zeit* (*Kings of the Road*, 1976), 'the Yanks have colonised our subconscious'. In the wake of the Second World War, the influx of American aid to the Western sectors of the country (sectors which would in 1949 become West Germany) meant that the Western regions were quickly permeated by American culture. Its subsequent dominance was largely accepted, even welcomed, by the population as a necessary quid pro quo for the avoidance of awkward questions about its National Socialist past and its own tainted cultural tradition. Things started to change in the late 1960s with the emergence of New German Cinema. In society at large, those who were born with no experience or knowledge of the war years had come of age, and were beginning to attack what they saw as American cultural imperialism and the hypocrisy of their parents' acceptance of it. In 1967–68 this new generation took to the streets, bringing about a seismic shift in West Germany, forcing their parents to re-examine their relationship to National Socialism, and to expose what they saw as continuities with fascism in the Federal Republic that had never been dealt with.

As we shall see in the work of Fassbinder and Wenders, however, the only cultural language that filmmakers of this generation were able to draw on in order to critique both their parents' historical amnesia and the domination of American culture was, paradoxically, that of the

USA itself, a conundrum neatly exemplified in this generation's reworking of film noir. If we turn to Fassbinder's early gangster neo-noir cycle, *Liebe – kälter als der Tod* (*Love Is Colder than Death*, 1969), *Götter der Pest* (*Gods of the Plague*, 1970) and *Der Amerikanische Soldat* (*The American Soldier*, 1970), we see Hollywood film culture being used not only as a parodic vehicle to critique the influence of this very culture on Germany, but also as the only available means of questioning German society itself. In *Love Is Colder than Death*, a film which is paradigmatic of the whole cycle, a simplistic plot revolving around three underworld figures – a small time pimp Franz (Fassbinder), his prostitute girlfriend Joanna (Hanna Schygulla) and gangster Bruno (Ulli Lommel), who befriends Franz in order to force him to work for a major crime organisation – becomes the vehicle for an exercise in film style. Fassbinder's film contains strong echoes of Godard's *A bout de souffle* (*Breathless,* 1960), simi-larly using natural settings to parody the sinister night-time of American noir in its drab daytime representation of Germany. Furthermore, Bruno's ridiculously exaggerated trenchcoat and hat would seem to have been directly inspired by Godard's Michel, who in turn models himself on Humphrey Bogart. Throughout the film, American noir is the characters' self-conscious point of reference. As Fassbinder states, 'I don't make films about gangsters, but about people who have seen a lot of gangster films'.[4] The characters are caught up in their roles, unable to operate outside the bounds of their Hollywood cultural parameters.

As the obvious connection with *Breathless* makes clear, Fassbinder has also been influenced here by the French New Wave of the previous decade, with directors such as Godard acting as important cultural intermediaries, shaping his reception of American noir. However, in 1960s Germany there had been an important shift. While Michel in Godard's film relishes the opportunity of playing the gangster, in Fassbinder's cycle the relationship to noir has become tired and humdrum. Unlike the original American films, which relied heavily on fast-paced action and the use of suspense, Fassbinder drains his film of any narrative energy. He removes excitement and suspense by includ-ing excessively long takes in which the characters go through the motions of the gangster plot unenthusiastically. In one sequence, for example, Franz, accompanied by Bruno and Joanna, enters a café in order to confront a man who wants to kill him. All three look the part, dressed in noirish sunglasses. Fassbinder then parodies this staple of film noir both through the scene's slow pace and by the behaviour of his characters. Bruno stares coldly and firmly into the camera, which

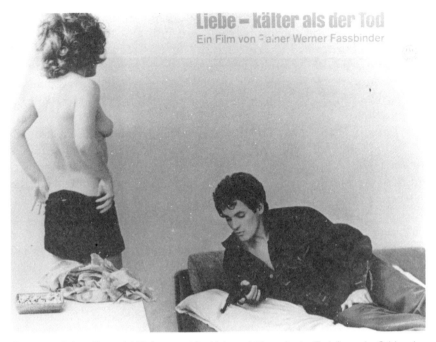

6 Hanna Schygulla and Ulli Lommel in *Liebe – kälter als der Tod (Love Is Colder than Death*, Rainer Werner Fassbinder, 1969).

stands in as Franz's would-be killer's gaze, his hand in his coat, obviously concealing a gun. Joanna, on the other hand, simply stares into space, thus avoiding the camera and undermining any potential tension. This avoidance is clearly not a result of fear of the killer. It is, rather, the spectator's gaze she wishes to evade, her body language signalling both her embarrassment at, but more importantly her boredom with, the role the film is forcing her to play.

Yet, while on one level the film parodies American film noir in order to question the influence of American culture on West Germany, this same culture also provides the necessary means to critique West German society and in particular what the filmmaker sees as its continuities with Germany's authoritarian past. Throughout his gangster cycle, Fassbinder draws parallels between the world of German postwar bourgeois respectability and the films' violent underworld milieu. As Wallace Steadman Watson notes, the Joanna–Franz–Bruno *ménage à trois* parodies bourgeois domesticity.[5] In one particularly provocative tableau of the three characters in their flat, the film's normal 'muzak' soundtrack is replaced by a soothing classical piece, seemingly pointing to the internal harmony of the scene with which we are presented. On one level this is indeed an image of domestic calm; we see Joanna lying on the bed sewing and Franz at the table doing a crossword. However, the respectability of this scene is, at the same time, ruptured both by Bruno who sits at the table with Franz, playing with his gun, thereby reminding us of his gangster credentials, and by Joanna, the prostitute, who is topless and sewing simply in order to fill the time before her next customer appears.

In *Love Is Colder than Death*, Fassbinder revisits film noir in order to critique the influence of America, and to explore continuities between West Germany of the late 1960s and the violent authoritarianism of Germany's fascist past. It is a bitter, tragic world in which the characters are caught in a soulless parody of their Hollywood models. After this first cycle, Fassbinder left the world of noir until the end of his career, when he returned to it to make his 'FRG Trilogy', *Die Ehe der Maria Braun* (*The Marriage of Maria Braun*, 1979), *Lola* (1981) and *Die Sehnsucht der Veronika Voss* (*Veronika Voss*, 1982). Here, although we find the continued use of film noir as a self-reflexive means of critique, most obviously in *Veronika Voss*, to which I now turn, the relationship to American culture becomes more ambiguous, thus suggesting a more complex reading of the relationship between Germany and Hollywood.

While Fassbinder is troubled by the 'colonisation' of Germany by American culture, he is also, ironically, deeply attracted to it. Along with the rest of his generation, Fassbinder grew up in a period in which American popular culture – in the shape of Coca-Cola, music and, above all, film – constituted a fresh and charismatic alternative to German culture, one which, unlike its homegrown equivalent, had no awkward past to conceal, and could celebrate, as he puts it, its own 'naivety':

> I would not be able to tell a film like MARNIE simply the way Hitchcock does it, because I haven't got the courage of his naivety, simply to tell a story like this and then at the end give the audience this thing, this explanation ... I wouldn't have the guts, because it also takes guts.[6]

Throughout his career, Fassbinder, as Thomas Elsaesser notes, strove to find a 'new naivety', to find a way of making 'German Hollywood' films.[7] Paradoxically, as he comes closer to achieving this in his later, more commercially successful, films, the search for 'naivety' produces a more subtle and complex use of the noir tradition.

In *Veronika Voss*, while film noir is still evoked in a highly self-reflexive manner, it is less overtly parodic than in his earlier cycle. The film reworks the central motif of Billy Wilder's *Sunset Boulevard*

(1950) telling the story of the last days in the life of a has-been star from the Nazi era, Veronika Voss (Rosel Zech). After a chance meeting on a tram, the sports reporter Robert Krohn (Hilmar Tate) follows her home, where he discovers that she is being driven to ruin by a corrupt doctor who keeps her addicted to morphine in order to rob her. *Veronika Voss*, like *Love Is Colder than Death*, is shot in black and white, but here the high-contrast film stock, along with the use of symbolically laden camera angles, seems to echo film noir of the 1940s and 1950s far more directly. That said, as in the earlier film, the noir tradition is still used to explore critically continuities between the barbaric behaviour of the National Socialist period and the institutionalised corruption of the Americanised Federal Republic of 1950s. The success of the evil doctor and her cronies in this new society highlights the continued existence of the violent behaviour inherited from Germany's authoritarian past. The film's anti-heroine is isolated by a world which superficially rejects Nazism, embracing the 'democratic' culture of its American conquerors, while in reality having done very little to overcome the fundamental societal traits that led to Hitler's takeover.

Although there are certain thematic continuities between *Love Is Colder than Death* and *Veronika Voss* there is, nevertheless, also an important development in the film's relationship to American culture. Although Fassbinder is still clearly concerned with the concept of American 'colonisation', there appears to be a redefinition in the status of film noir vis-à-vis German cinematic tradition. Now it is also presented as an integral part of Fassbinder's own film history, functioning as a kind of bridge that can reconnect him with a past to which he and his generation have been denied access. In this context, the echoes of Wilder's noir masterpiece *Sunset Boulevard* become highly significant. The roots of film noir from the 1940s and 1950s are traceable, at least in part, to the work of directors from Germany's 'Weimar' Period of the 1920s and 1930s, many of whom emigrated to America in order to escape persecution under the Nazis. In the German films of directors such as Billy Wilder and Fritz Lang we find precursors to the shadowy, liminal world of their Hollywood output. The angst-ridden, paranoid visions found in the expressionism and street realism of the Weimar period become the perfect vehicle for the portrayal of the dark underbelly of an American society recovering from the trauma of war. Although, as Elsaesser notes, one must be careful not to conflate German and American film history, many film critics in particular do, nevertheless, construct film noir as what he terms 'film history's German imaginary'.[8] Film noir, in a sense, is

viewed as the German film industry that never was, and as such stands
as the reverse side of the actual German film industry of the period, an
industry dominated by Goebbels and the Nazi propaganda machine.
In *Veronika Voss* Fassbinder indulges in this comparison, bringing the
'German–Hollywood noir' and 'Nazi' traditions together. In his allusion to Wilder's *Sunset Boulevard*, he evokes the work of the German
émigrés, those filmmakers who left Germany but to whom Fassbinder
ironically now has easier access than to those who stayed, due to the
fact that they are part of the American culture industry. Fassbinder
then uses this German–American tradition as a conduit through which
he gains access to the National Socialist period. As a result, he
produces an emotional connection to this forbidden period in the spectator, reinstating it into the historical consciousness of his generation.

   This self-reflexive use of film history is also to be found in the work
of Wim Wenders. Like Fassbinder, Wenders' ambiguous relationship
with Hollywood can be seen in his appropriation of American genres,
including film noir. Elements of noir can be found throughout his
work, from his early shorts such as *Same Player Shoots Again* (1967)
and *Alabama: 2000 Light Years from Home* (1968) to the two films
that I wish to discuss here: *Der amerikanische Freund* (*The American
Friend*, 1977) and *Hammett* (1982). *The American Friend* is an adaptation of Patricia Highsmith's novel *Ripley's Game* and explores the
descent of Jonathan Zimmerman (Bruno Ganz), a happily married,
respectable picture framer, into a world of violent crime. Initially, the
film appears to set up a dichotomy between American culture, which
is coded as 'impure' and 'inauthentic' with a morally 'purer', 'authentic' German, or more broadly speaking, European cultural tradition, a
dichotomy which clearly reflects the students' attacks on American
cultural imperialism of the 1960s. The lack of authenticity in
American culture is encompassed in the figure of Ripley (Dennis
Hopper), a shady American art dealer. Ripley is out of place in the
film's Hamburg setting, dressed incongruously as a cowboy and speaking German falteringly. The dichotomy between American and
German/European culture is further underlined through Wenders' use
of film history. All the gangsters in *The American Friend* are played by
famous directors or by other figures from the film industry. As
Wenders himself puts it 'they're the only rascals I know, and the only
ones who make life and death decisions as airily as the Mafia'.[9] The
world of contemporary film, dominated by Hollywood, is then juxtaposed with the silent era, a period when German cinema enjoyed its
golden age, not yet tainted by National Socialism. This juxtaposition
is achieved via the character of the craftsman Jonathan, who

surrounds himself with artefacts from this period of film history and thus embodies this past cinematic age. Through his encounter with Ripley, Jonathan is invited to step out of this pure, pre-Nazi tradition and enter the dangerous world of the Hollywood thriller. As Roger Bromley suggests, 'What Ripley is doing is directing Jonathan in a film noir'.[10] Jonathan leaves the boundaries of his old world, or to put it another way, the picture framer destroys his frame.[11]

The transgression of boundaries is of course a central motif of film noir and in *The American Friend* a whole series begins to break down, including the American = inauthentic/German = authentic opposition. As a result, the film also ultimately communicates the same tension between the repulsion and attraction towards Hollywood that we have already discussed with regard to Fassbinder. The breakdown of the non-authentic–authentic dichotomy is achieved predominantly through the film's representation of sexuality, and specifically through the elision of the boundaries between homosexual and heterosexual orientations. Initially, Ripley is seen as an evil 'other' to Jonathan, using his knowledge of an incurable blood disease from which Jonathan is suffering to embroil him in a world of crime. As Jonathan leaves his respectable life and his marriage breaks down, his heterosexual identity also starts to crumble, taken over by an implied homosexual desire for Ripley. The traditional homosocial milieu of the underworld we find throughout film noir steps over into one of homoerotic desire. In the process of this transformation Ripley is, to a degree, recuperated. As the men get to know each other, Ripley feels more and more guilty for involving Jonathan, eventually coming to his aid when a murder Jonathan is told to commit goes wrong. A strong bond is forged between the two men. Increasingly Jonathan's only moments of happiness in his life of crime come when he is with Ripley, and there is a poignant emotional purity in the American's plaintive wish to be, as he declares in one sequence late in the film, Jonathan's 'friend', an ambiguous term within a German context, capable of meaning both companion and lover.

The American Friend explores, as Bromley suggests, the 'seductive ambivalence' of American popular culture, articulated in the film 'around the fantasies of masculinity'.[12] Ultimately it is unclear where Wenders stands in relation to this culture. Is he, like his protagonist Jonathan, trapped by it, or do both men choose to exist within it, attracted by the excitement it promises? In Wenders' later film *Hammett*, his first experience of working in Hollywood, this question would seem to have been resolved by the filmmaker ostensibly embracing American culture, since the relationship between the two cultures seems to be far less complex than in his earlier work. Indeed, the film comes very close to commodified postmodern noir, or pastiche, to return to Jameson's term. Nevertheless, one still sees traces of the tensions that Wenders explores in *The American Friend*.

The film presents a fictionalised account of an episode in the life of 'hard-boiled' crime writer Dashiell Hammett, whose stories were frequently adapted for film noirs, including John Huston's *The Maltese Falcon* (1941). Formerly a Pinkerton detective, Hammett (Frederic Forrest) has left this old life behind him and now scrapes a living writing pulp fiction. At the start of the film he is visited by his partner from his Pinkerton days, Ryan (Peter Boyle), who calls in a favour, putting Hammett back to work as a detective to help him find a missing person. Hammett, unable to refuse, is soon once more involved in a world of violence, exploitation and pornography, a world which he thought that he would only ever have to experience again in the pages of one of his manuscripts.

In terms of plot and style, the film is more noir than the original film noirs themselves. Hammett's apartment is a darker version of the one in Huston's *The Maltese Falcon*, overloaded with the same jarring acute-angled shots. As a result, this film appears to be initially nothing more than pastiche, in Jameson's terms, an unthinking and essentially insignificant homage to the classic period. Yet this overloading of the film's noir credentials injects it with a similar, if less overt, critique of American noir to that of *The American Friend*. Again we see Wenders, the European, questioning American culture through his deconstruction of a number of noir's elements. First, as already discussed, the film ironises the visual style of the original cycle. Second, Wenders examines critically the role of storytelling in film noir. Throughout the film, he foregrounds the narrative process by playing with the status of events and blurring the lines between fact and fiction, an impulse which is even found in the name of his central protagonist. Hammett is referred to throughout as Sam, echoing the name of his own fictitious private eye, Sam Spade. By playing with levels of fiction in this way, Wenders subtly shakes us out of our usual suspension of disbelief, asking us to question the status of the narrative we are watching.

This is seen most overtly in the opening sequence in which we see Hammett finish typing one of his detective stories. As he falls asleep, he replays scenes from the story as a dream. This dream is then intercut with images of his typewriter working away. Gradually the camera probes deeper and deeper into the machine, foregrounding its mechanical nature, but more importantly the manufactured, inauthentic nature of the story it is producing. Here, the typewriter, as a literal 'dream factory', becomes a symbolic representation of the film industry, which, like the typewriter in the hands of the crime novelist, churns out inauthentic neatly tied up parcels of life. This dream factory sequence is followed, however, by the image of Hammett in his bathroom, keeling over after an extended fit of coughing, the neat, mechanical plot of his detective story thus being juxtaposed with the messy, bodily nature of 'real life'. But of course this is not real life, and this brief rupture in the dream is soon mended as the 'real' Hammett becomes embroiled in the film's own story. The sick, weak man of the bathroom sequence is replaced by the streetwise investigator who is more than capable of looking after himself with his quick wits and his fists. The film's narrative in turn produces material for Hammett to write yet another story, which we see him doing at the end of the movie as he happily bashes away once again at the keys of his typewriter. Thus one fiction begets another fiction and the dream factory rumbles on.

In *Hammett*, although we have moved from Germany to America, to a degree we come full circle in our discussion of neo-noir and the New German Cinema. As in *Love Is Colder than Death*, Wenders' characters are caught inside the conventions of noir, and his film exhibits a similar sense of the form's exhaustion to Fassbinder. The pace of the film is slightly too slow. The characters, most notably Hammett and Ryan, are shadows of their former selves in their Pinkerton days, during which time, they assure the spectator, they had the energy to act heroically, to the extent that they would even die for each other. Now all that is left is their booze-fuelled cynicism. John Barry's laconic sound track further emphasises this mood. Even the casting seems to show that the form has become weary, since Forrest appears far too old to play the 34–year-old Hammett, this instance of miscasting being underlined throughout by his partner's insistence on referring to him as 'kid'. As a result the film escapes being simply pastiche and becomes another example of Wenders' European gaze being used to engage American pop culture critically.

Post-Wall neo-noir and German 'normalisation'

Although *Hammett* comes very close to what Jameson defines as postmodern pastiche, Wenders' self-conscious engagement with the nature of storytelling retains film noir as a vehicle through which American culture can be critiqued. Since the 1980s, and particularly since the fall of the Berlin Wall in 1989, this conscious need to critique Hollywood among filmmakers seems to have dissipated. It is from this point that

we see a shift in German film production away from the overtly critical auteur cinema of Fassbinder and Wenders to more popular, mainstream genre film. As Sönke Wortmann, the director of a number of
recent hit films puts it 'when I was at film school in Munich, the great
hero was Tarkovsky. Today it's Spielberg'.[13] No longer wishing to
follow the avant-garde tradition of the previous generation, these
younger filmmakers seem to emulate unproblematically the fast-
paced, action-driven entertainment films of Hollywood.

   This shift in German film aesthetics has been greeted with a degree
of alarm by some critics. As Eric Rentschler puts it, while the auteurs
of the new German cinema produced films that 'interrogated images
of the past in the hope of refining memories and catalysing changes',
contemporary cinema, lacks 'oppositional energies and critical voices'.
It is nothing more, he suggests, than 'an emanation of an overdetermined German desire for normalcy, as well as of a marked disinclina-
tion towards any serious political reflection or sustained historical
retrospection'.[14] To a degree this is the case, particularly in the film
production of the early 1990s. At this time German cinema was dominated by the so-called 'New German Comedy', films that, although
popular at home, were largely ignored abroad.[15] However, in recent
years there has been a shift away from comedy towards other genres
and styles, including the crime film and film noir, a shift that has coin-
cided with the production of more critical films as well as a renewed
international interest in German film. Yet, before we can understand
how these films relate to earlier German neo-noir, we must first
consider more closely what Rentschler means by the 'overdetermined
German desire for normalcy'.

   The notion of German 'normalisation', evoked in Rentschler's
attack, has been perhaps *the* political buzzword in recent years, pointing to the call, initially by those on the right of the political spectrum,
for Germany's realignment as a 'normal' nation state in the wake of
unification, a state that must no longer apologise for its past and can
at last take an active role in the world's community of nations. To a
degree, normalisation can be seen as the end of the project instigated
by the students of the late 1960s, a project which had wide-ranging
implications for German society, forcing not only a coming to terms
with the past, but also bringing about a number of social revolutions,
from the Women's Movement to the Green Party. As shall be shown in
my discussion of some recent examples of German neo-noir, in
Germany today we see a society that, for better or worse, is leaving
many of the concerns for which these students took to the streets
behind them. However, in other neo-noirs we find the critical explo-

ration of what the 'normalisation' of Germany in fact means, particularly for those members of society who feel alienated within this newly unified society. Thus, while one finds a largely unproblematic use of Hollywood models in the neo-noir films that I discuss, far removed from the modernist parody of the earlier generation, nonetheless, not all such films can be dismissed, in Jameson's terms, as nothing more than nostalgic wallowing.

Since its inception, a key concern of film noir has been the nature of gender relations. This continues with German neo-noir in the 1990s, most obviously in Rainer Kaufmann's *Long Hello and Short Goodbye* (1998). To a degree, however, the exploration of gender relations in the film would seem to have more in common with the broader context of German filmmaking than with Hollywood noir. As already mentioned, the dominant trend in the early 1990s in Germany was towards comedy. Particularly influential within this trend was the *Frauenkömdie*, or 'Women's Comedy', films driven, as Dickon Copsey notes, by 'the relationship between gender construction and sexuality'.[16] To a degree this concern can be seen as a continuation of Germany's strong tradition in women's cinema. From the 1960s onwards, feminist filmmakers such as Helma Sanders-Brahms have foregrounded and questioned gender roles within patriarchy. Initially, *Long Hello and Short Goodbye* suggests that it might carry on this tradition of feminist critique. Ultimately, however, this neo-noir differs radically from the feminist project instigated by the students of the late 1960s and maintained in many of the early 1990s comedies, in that it shores up rather than subverts patriarchal norms.

In *Long Hello and Short Goodbye* we meet the policewoman Melody (Nicolette Krebitz), who is asked to go undercover by her boss in order to trick the safecracker Ben (Marc Hosemann), just released from prison, into reoffending. The film is a highly stylised neo-noir, reminiscent of Quentin Tarantino's *Pulp Fiction* (1994) in its use of non-chronological narrative, interpolated stories and reference to an eclectic range of popular culture from the world of film, advertising and fashion. The spirit of Tarantino can also be seen in Kaufmann's characterisation. Melody, like many of Tarantino's characters, is a compulsive talker, constantly telling Ben that she is a policewoman sent to trap him, a claim so outrageous that he could never believe her.

Melody is initially a confusing character. We first meet her on a drugs raid, where, unbeknown to the spectator, she is working undercover. Dressed as a coquettish schoolgirl, in a short skirt and white shirt, she flirts with the drug-dealing gangsters until she gets hold of the merchandise. Having established the quality of the drugs she suddenly spins around, takes out a gun and shoots the crooks. With the arrests complete, she then turns to the camera, flicks back her hair, pirouettes and gives the spectator a bow. Melody is the knowing *femme fatale*, this time working for the police, who is well aware of the effect that the performance of her female wiles will have on her subjects. As a result she would seem to be the ideal post-feminist woman, comfortable with her femininity, and the equal to any man.

However, as the film goes on, Melody's feminist credentials are slowly eroded as she is brought back into line with traditional patriarchal values. She falls in love with Ben, the subject of her operation, a love which eventually leads her to go against the wishes of her police boss and help her lover escape his clutches forever. As a result, her role as the film's *femme fatale* is destroyed. This apparently powerful policewoman is no match for Ben, who becomes a curiously unknowing *homme fatal*, with all the manipulative charm and suppressed violent nature of the type.[17] Indeed, Melody is not the first police officer to be seduced by Ben's charms. At the end of the film we realise that Melody's boss tried before to put Ben away using a female undercover policewoman, a woman who likewise fell in love with the criminal and so failed to carry out her mission. Finally, in the film's last shot, the return to patriarchal order is sealed. Ben lies dying, having been gunned down by Melody's boss. At last Melody stops her incessant talking, the most obvious indication of the game she has been playing with Ben. The self-conscious performance of coquettish femininity disappears and she is finally transformed completely into the supportive wife/mother that patriarchy demands its women be, standing by her man in his final hour of need.

In *Long Hello and Short Goodbye* we find the feminist project, inaugurated by the student movement of the 1960s, undermined as patriarchal values are, by the end, firmly reinstated. In its return to more traditional understandings of gender, this neo-noir film thus exemplifies a shift away from the political radicalism of the new German cinema towards a more conservative age of normalisation. The end of this earlier generation's project can similarly be seen in Dani Levy's *Meschugge* (1999). Here we return to the familiar ground from the neo-noir of new German cinema, namely dealing with the Nazi past, a past that is now revisited from the perspective of post-unification 'normalisation' debates. Set in New York, the film tells the story of David (Dani Levy), an American Jew, and Lena (Maria Schrader) the granddaughter of a rich German-Jewish businessman. The couple meet and fall in love when Lena finds David's mother dead in her own mother's hotel. The ensuing investigation, carried out by a private detective engaged by David, who worked for years for the Israeli intelligence service, reveals that Lena's family is not Jewish at all. Her grandfather was in fact an SS officer at Treblinka. Lena and David's mothers were childhood friends in Germany. When David's mother was to be taken away, Lena's mother hid the girl and helped her escape to America. After the war, Lena's grandfather, thinking that the whole of the Jewish family they had once known had been wiped out, decided to adopt their identity in order to escape prosecution for war crimes. David's mother, discovering the existence of this man in Germany, and thinking him to be her own father, makes contact with the family, at which point Lena's mother comes to New York to try to buy the woman's silence, an event which ends in Lena's mother accidentally killing her childhood friend.

The style of this film is drenched with noir clichés. Kaminski, the no-nonsense maverick PI, is a straightforward Jewish version of Sam Spade or Phillip Marlowe, even the policemen look and act as if they would be more at home in a movie from the 1940s than the New York of 1998, dressed as they are in trilby hats, and working in dark, smoke-filled offices. However, although the use of noir style might at times be slightly over the top there is no sense that this is being used to question American culture as is it in *Hammett*. This is rather an attempt by a German director to make a film that looks like a mainstream Hollywood blockbuster, even down to the fact that it was filmed mainly in English. Unlike Fassbinder and Wenders, who used the American form to critique both American culture and German society, showing, to a degree at least, the unsuitability of film noir for communicating a German identity, *Meschugge* uses the 'global brand' of Hollywood neo-noir to show that German society is now coming to terms with the past and becoming a nation that can tell its stories in a similar fashion to any other.

At the heart of this film is, therefore, the normalisation of German society and in particular the normalisation of its history, a process which is symbolised, as Stuart Taberner points out, in the central narrative of David and Lena's love affair. As Kaminski's investigation unfolds, it transpires that theirs is not a relationship between two Jews, but between the son of a Holocaust survivor and the granddaughter of a Nazi war criminal. As a result, the story takes on a wider, symbolic meaning than simply the love between two individuals. It becomes symbolic of the relationship between the German and Jewish nations and the need for reconciliation between them.[18] Initially, as both David and Lena independently suspect the truth about Lena's family, each strives to keep this news from the other,

Lena to protect her family, David to manipulate Lena into bringing her father to justice. But by the end of the film their roles have reversed. David, out of love for Lena, goes to her family in order to help to protect her grandfather from Kaminski who is determined to see the old man behind bars whatever the cost. Lena, on the other hand, having learned the whole truth about her grandfather's crimes, decides to help Kaminski catch the former Nazi, feeling that he must be made to pay for his past, no matter how long ago it happened.

In the end the film's narrative is resolved through compromise. The grandfather is brought to trial, although he is deemed too frail to be imprisoned. The zealot Kaminski, on the other hand, is put in jail. In returning to Germany he has broken the bail conditions of an earlier court case and so he must serve time. Through its denouement, the film thus gives an idealised representation of the project of normalisation. The rough justice Kaminski would mete out is not permitted in the new Germany, where the rights of all, including war criminals, must be protected. Furthermore Lena has learnt to face her family's past honestly, accepting herself for who she really is. David, for his part, realises that the world cannot keep punishing Germany for its history. The sins of the grandparents cannot be blamed on their grandchildren. David must move on; a crucial step if he, Lena and, by implication, German society as a whole are to have a future.

In *Long Hello and Short Goodbye* and *Meschugge* we see the political processes of German normalisation writ large. However, in other neo-noirs we see filmmakers exploring the limitations of this process, looking at sections of German society that highlight tensions in contemporary German self-understanding. One important area of tension in present-day society, which is taken up in Andreas Kleinert's *Paths in the Night* (*Wege in die Nacht*, 1999), is the problem of integrating the citizens of the former GDR into the new Germany. In this film we find an exploration of the alienation many East Germans feel, because they perceive that their past experience is being undervalued by a capitalist society, the rules of which many still cannot fathom.

The film depicts the psychological decline of Walter (Hilmar Thate), a man who, since unification, has been consigned to Germany's rubbish heap. During the GDR period he ran a factory, but now this business has been closed down and he is forced to live off his wife's earnings as a café waitress. Walter's world has been turned upside down. Not only has unemployment robbed him of all sense of personal self-worth, he does not understand this new society, which seems to him to have no order. In an attempt to rediscover his lost sense of self, and to recapture the order of the past, he takes to riding the Berlin underground at night with two young Easterners he recruits, a brother and sister Rene (Dirk Borchardt) and Gina (Henriette Heinze). Together they form a vigilante group, meting out rough justice to the thugs they encounter on the trains.[19]

In *Paths in the Night*, Kleinert uses aspects neo-noir to bring the experience of East Germans into the mainstream of German society, forcing the West to see this experience as part of the new 'normal' state. In the stark black and white shots of East Berlin by night, Kleinert exploits film noir style in a similar manner to Levy in *Meschugge*, that is to universalise the story of Walter. In one early sequence, for example, we see Walter getting out of his car on a dark night in the city, dressed in black and smoking his cigarette, every inch the image of the lonely, alienated investigator from the American films of the 1940s and 1950s, a man who would clearly be happy to break a few rules to see justice done. Thus, like Levy, Kleinert uses the visual style and clichés of noir to translate the experience of Walter into a film language that a Western spectator, and by extension the whole of German society, can readily understand. As Kleinert has suggested in interviews, he did not want the film simply to be an 'East West story', but a story of universal applicability.[20] However, and seeming to contradict this impulse, Kleinert also undermines this use of this film tradition. Having set Walter up as the lonely noir hero, this image is then turned on its head. Shortly afterwards, Walter attempts to confront a group of men whom he thinks is stealing a car. Yet rather than taking him seriously, as they might have Humphrey Bogart if this had been 1940s America, they ridicule him. Their refusal to respect him destroys any sense of noirish machismo the earlier sequence might have built up. Consequently, while the film's visual style creates a point of connection with the Western spectator familiar with the conventions of film noir, it also questions this point of connection. Kleinert's representation of Eastern experience might resort to the familiar tropes of film noir, but it equally reveals that the American context is not completely appropriate, since the citizens of the former GDR come from a different tradition.

This notion of Eastern difference is also suggested by the fact that film noir is not the only influence here. Most notably we find echoes of the Soviet filmmaker Andrei Tarkovsky. Kleinert's representation of Walter's disused factory as a beautiful yet disturbing post-apocalyptic vision of urban decay would, for example, seem to be deliberately reminiscent of Tarkovsky's futuristic industrial landscape in his 1979 film *The Stalker*. Consequently, Kleinert marries filmic traditions from both sides of the divide in the cold war. In so doing, he attempts both to universalise the experience of East Germans, while at the same time protecting the specificity of their present and past experience.

Finally, Fatih Akin's *Kurz und Schmerzlos* (*Short Sharp Shock*, 1998) is a film which also explores the limitations of the concept of 'normalisation', specifically in this case with regard to the relationship between Germany and its ethnic minority communities. The film revolves around three friends, Costa the Greek (Adam Bousdoukos), Bobby the Serb (Aleksandar Jovanovič) and Gabriel the Turk (Mehmet Kurtulus). Since childhood, the three have formed an inseparable gang, carrying out petty crimes on the streets of Hamburg. However, for the last two years Gabriel has been in prison. Now that he has been released he wants to go straight. But his friends, and particularly Bobby, do not make this easy for him. Bobby starts to work for the Albanian mafia but when a gun deal he tries to pull off goes wrong, he finds himself in deep trouble, which finally drags Costa and Gabriel down with him, bringing death or exile to all of them.

The film's neo-noir credentials largely lie in its evocation of the work of Martin Scorsese. Specifically, it an homage to *Mean Streets* (1973) in its performance of a destructive male friendship, swapping the Italian Americans of New York for the ethnic minorities of Hamburg. Indeed, Jovanovič's performance as Bobby owes a great deal to Robert De Niro's Johnny Boy in Scorsese's film, down to De Niro's inane grin which hides his feelings of insecurity. However, there is also at least one overt reference to *Taxi Driver* (1976), in the sequence where Bobby attempts to complete his gun deal, a moment which is strongly evocative of the meeting between Travis and the gun seller in the earlier film.

On one level, Akin, like Levy in *Meschugge*, uses the tradition of American neo-noir (in this case through reference to Scorsese) to locate his culture in the mainstream, giving voice to the stories of the German immigrant community, just as Scorsese does for his own. In so doing he attempts to show how his community's experience can fit into a 'normal' American film paradigm. However, in a similar fashion to Kleinert, and somewhat paradoxically, the film also works to problematise this aim, using that same American culture to show the specificities of the German context. For example, in order to set the seal on Bobby's newly acquired position in the underworld, he is taken out for a meal by his boss to an Italian restaurant. Here the film self-consciously uses a standard trope of the American mafia film. However, in *Short Sharp Shock* the gangsters in question are an Albanian and a Serb, who can only play at being 'real mafiosi', as Bobby proudly describes himself in this sequence, that is the kind of mobsters they see in the movies. In this way the film ultimately points to the existence of cultural differences between ethnic communities, suggesting that ethnic 'others' cannot simply be interchanged.

This call for differentiation is then tentatively linked to the project of 'multiculturalism' in German society, a mainstay of this newly 'normalised' nation, which ostensibly demands for intercultural respect but which in reality seems intent on protecting the dominance of western white culture. As Sarah Ahmed notes, the call for a multi-cultural society often masks what is actually the prioritisation of western 'liberal' values, values which preach cultural tolerance but do little actually to understand different cultures on their own terms, viewing such cultures instead as a homogeneous 'other' that remains largely excluded from mainstream society.[21] While the three friends are all from ethnic minorities in Germany, they are very different from one another. Indeed the true status of the term 'multiculturalism' in Germany is indicated by Bobby. When Gabriel returns from prison, Bobby asks his friend if he would also like to join the Albanian Mafia, an organisation that, he insists, is truly 'Multikulti' (German jargon for multicultural society), thereby implying that the only place where this concept is really at work is in the criminal underworld. Thus, by presenting his multicultural community as gangsters on the 'mean streets' of Hamburg, Akin uses a mainstream American form to high-light the continuing marginality of ethnic minorities within his society, suggesting that they can only be appreciated on the periphery of the respectable world.

In *Short Sharp Shock*, as in other films since unification, we see a shift away from the parody of the New German Cinema towards a more unproblematic pastiche of American neo-noir. In some of these films, we also find filmmakers rejecting the critical agenda of this earlier generation. However, in others the use of pastiche brings with it a new mode of critique. In the work of Fassbinder and Wenders we see film noir used as a distancing device, forcing the spectator to ques-tion the dominance of American culture within German society. In more recent films this dominance is, perhaps, a given. However, at times, noir is still used to question the way Germany is developing, examining critically the trajectory of the 'normalisation' project by giving those on the periphery of society a mainstream voice. As a result, neo-noir remains an innovative cinematic vehicle for German filmmakers.

Notes

1   Andrew Spicer, *Film Noir* (Harlow, Essex: Longman/Pearson Education, 2002), p. 132.
2   *Ibid.*, p. 149.
3   Fredric Jameson, *Postmodernism or the Cultural Logic of Late Capitalism* (London: Verso, 1990).
4   Quoted in Thomas Elsaesser, *Fassbinder's Germany: History Identity Subject* (Amsterdam: Amsterdam University Press, 1996), p. 49.
5   Wallace Steadman Watson, *Understanding Fassbinder: Films as Private and Public Art* (Columbia: University of South Carolina, 1996), p. 70.
6   Quoted in Elsaesser, *Fassbinder's Germany*, p. 47.
7   *Ibid.*, pp. 48–53.
8   Thomas Elsaesser, *Weimar Cinema and after: Germany's Historical Imaginary* (London: Routledge, 2000), p. 420.
9   Wim Wenders, *On Film: Essays and Conversations* (London: Faber & Faber, 2000), p. 178.
10 Roger Bromley, *From Alice to Buena Vista: The Films of Wim Wenders* Westport: Praeger, 2001), p. 30.
11 *Ibid.*
12 *Ibid.*, p. 32.
13 Sönke Wortmann, interview with Stephen Kinzer, quoted in Ute Lischke-McNabe and Kathryn S. Hanson, 'Introduction: Recent German Film', *Seminar*, 33:4 (1997), 284.
14 Eric Rentschler, 'From New German Cinema to the Post-Wall Cinema of Consensus', in Mette Hjort and Scott Mackenzie (eds), *Cinema and Nation* (London: Routledge, 2000), pp. 263–4.
15 For a detailed discussion of this trend, see David N. Couvy, 'From Aesthetics to Commercialism: Narration and the New German Comedy', *Seminar*, 33:4 (1997), 356–73.
16 Dickon Copsey, 'Scene Change: Pluralized Identities in Contemporary German Cinema', in Alison Phipps (ed.), *Contemporary German Cultural Studies* (London: Arnold, 2002), p. 246.
17 For further discussion, see Spicer, *Film Noir*, pp. 89–90.
18 Stuart Taberner, 'Wie kannst du mich lieben? 'Normalising' the Relationship between Germans and Jews in the 1990s' Films *Aimée und Jaguar* and *Meschugge*', in William Niven and James Jordan (eds), *Politics and Culture in Twentieth-Century Germany* (London: Camden House, 2003), pp. 227–43.
19 For a more detailed discussion of the film, see David Clarke, 'Representations of East German Masculinity in Hannes Stöhr's *Berlin is in Germany* and Andreas Kleinert's *Wege in die Nacht*', *GLL*, 55 (2002), 434–49.
20 Heinz Kersten, 'Ein Mann im freien Fal: Der Regisseur Andreas Kleinert über seinen Film "Wege in die Nacht"', *Freitag* (26 November 1999).

21 Sara Ahmed, *Strange Encounters: Embodied Others in Post Coloniality* (London: Routledge, 2000).

Filmography

Same Player Shoots Again, Wim Wenders, 1967
Alabama: 2000 Light Years from Home, Wim Wenders, 1968
Liebe – kälter als der Tod (*Love Is Colder than Death*), Rainer Werner Fassbinder, 1969
Götter der Pest (*Gods of the Plague*), Rainer Werner Fassbinder, 1970
Der amerikanische Soldat (*The American Soldier*), Rainer Werner Fassbinder, 1970
Der amerikanische Freund (*The American Friend*), Wim Wenders, 1977
Die Ehe der Maria Braun (*The Marriage of Maria Braun*), Rainer Werner Fassbinder, 1979
Lola, Rainer Werner Fassbinder, 1981
Die Sehnsucht der Veronika Voss (*Veronika Voss*), Rainer Werner Fassbinder, 1982
Hammett, Wim Wenders, 1982
14 Tage lebenslänglich (*14 Days to Life*), Roland Suso Richter, 1997
Kurz und Schmerzlos (*Short Sharp Shock*), Fatih Akin, 1998
Long Hello and Short Goodbye, Rainer Kaufmann, 1998
Meschugge, Dani Levy, 1999
Wege in die Nacht (*Paths in the Night*), Andreas Kleinert, 1999
Die Unberührbare (*No Place to Go*), Andreas Roehler, 2000

Select bibliography

Ahmed, Sara, *Strange Encounters: Embodied Others in Post Coloniality* (London: Routledge, 2000).
Bromley, Roger, *From Alice to Buena Vista: The Films of Wim Wenders* (Westport: Praeger, 2001).
Clarke, David, 'Representations of East German Masculinity in Hannes Stöhr's *Berlin is in Germany* and Andreas Kleinert's *Wege in die Nacht*', GLL, 55 (2002), 434–9.
Copsey, Dickon, 'Scene Change: Pluralized Identities in Contemporary German Cinema', in Alison Phipps (ed.), *Contemporary German Cultural Studies* (London: Arnold, 2002), pp. 241–62.
Couvy, David N., 'From Aesthetics to Commercialism: Narration and the New German Comedy', *Seminar*, 33:4 (1997), 356–73.
Elsaesser, Thomas, *Fassbinder's Germany: History Identity Subject* (Amsterdam: Amsterdam University Press, 1996).
Elsaesser, Thomas, *Weimar Cinema and After: Germany's Historical Imaginary* (London: Routledge, 2000).

Jameson, Fredric, *Postmodernism or the Cultural Logic of Late Capitalism* (London: Verso, 1990).

Kersten, Heinz, 'Ein Mann im freien Fall: Der Regisseur Andreas Kleinert über seinen Film "Wege in die Nacht"', *Freitag* (26 November 1999).

Lischke-McNabe, Ute and Kathryn S. Hanson, 'Introduction: Recent German Film', *Seminar*, 33:4 (1997), 283–9.

Rentschler, Eric, 'From New German Cinema to the Post-Wall Cinema of Consensus', in Mette Hjort and Scott Mackenzie (eds), *Cinema and Nation* (London: Routledge, 2000), pp. 260–77.

Spicer, Andrew, *Film Noir* (Harlow, Essex: Longman/Pearson Education, 2002).

Steadman Watson, Wallace *Understanding Fassbinder: Films as Private and Public Art* (Columbia: University of South Carolina, 1996).

Taberner, Stuart, 'Wie kannst du mich lieben?: 'Normalising' the Relationship between Germans and Jews in the 1990s' Films *Aimée und Jaguar* and *Meschugge*', in William Niven and James Jordan (eds) *Politics and Culture in Twentieth-century Germany* (London: Camden House, 2003), pp. 227–43.

Wenders, Wim, *On Film: Essays and Conversations* (London: Faber & Faber, 2000).

8

Spanish film noir

Rob Stone

There is no such thing as Spanish film noir. At least there is none to speak of until after the death of General Franco in 1975. During the forty years of the fascist dictatorship film noir was a *bête noire*, unable to show its face for fear of reprisals on its perpetrators. How could there have been moral ambiguity in a society in which education and entertainment were dominated by rigid Catholic doctrine? How could a *femme fatale* have existed in a country that repressed independent thought and action in women, that subjugated female desire and subjectivity to the will and ego of the patriarch? How could there have been a private detective in a land where the Civil Guard were the only law and any private enterprise was regulated to the point of extinction, especially one which suggested that the law was remiss or at least fallible in its protection of the one party, one state? How could any independent auteur have flourished in a film industry that was crippled by the distribution of foreign films, stunted by lack of investment and voided of all controversial issues by state interference and an ecclesiastical censor? To make matters worse, Spain had no tradition of hard-boiled fiction and few translations of American noir existed, so there was no possibility of film noir arising from literary adaptations, while token efforts at imitating the style of popular American successes, such as John Huston's *The Asphalt Jungle* (1950), were mostly limited to a series of low budget, urban thrillers termed *policíacas* that detailed diligent policework as tokenistic illustration of the long arm of Francoist law. There was therefore no such thing as *cine negro*. There was never any place for its seditious thematics, its demoralising aesthetics or its disruptive archetypes. Except, as this chapter will argue, film noir in the Spain of the dictatorship was never more insidious and, even by its absence, was never more relevant.

Policíacas

Whereas American noir of the 1950s could be said to hold a dark mirror to American society that questioned the fundamental optimism of the American dream, no such pessimism about the Francoist dream was permitted. This was as true of literature as much as film. Most urban tales delivered more of a Galdósian attention to empirical detail of the city than a Freudian flair with the psyche of its inhabitants, and there was no tradition of hardboiled fiction in Spain until Manuel Vázquez Montalbán published the first of his Pepe Carvalho novels in 1970. Spain was a predominantly rural nation until the disruptive urban migration of the 1950s, so there was simply no urban context for film noir to inhabit and most rural dramas with pretensions to noir would have them swamped by the established conventions of the rural melodrama or tragedy. One fascinating exception, as Jo Labanyi has demonstrated, is Serrano de Osma's 1946 adaptation of Miguel de Unamuno's *Abel Sánchez*.[1] Another was Luis Saslavsky's bizarre *La corona negra* (*The Black Crown*, 1951), a Spanish-Italian co-production, co-written by Jean Cocteau and the Spanish satirist Miguel Mihura, in which a fallen, amnesiac woman played by María Félix, a beautiful Mexican star who would work for Luis Buñuel on *La Fièvre monte à El Pao* (*Fever Mounts at El Pao*, 1959), is plagued by nightmares and drink-induced flashbacks.[2] However, there were few film studios of the stature of RKO, and fewer still willing to risk the wrath of the censor by attempting a more genuine noir, while many of the best filmmakers had either sought exile during the war or had been poached by Hollywood to make Spanish-language copies of Hollywood films for the lucrative South American market. Moreover, an industry-wide lack of support for auteurs meant that no specialist in noir could emerge, for autonomy, even in the field of Spanish B pictures, was contrary to the subjugation of cultural expression to the will of the state. Imitative *policíacas* suffered from limited resources and an even more limited understanding, for there was little available film analysis that would define the genre for filmmakers. Soviet texts on filmmaking were treated as communist propaganda and if in France critical writing on noir was part of a 'self-questioning intellectual climate';[3] no such thing would be tolerated in Spain. Thus, if classic noir inhabits 'a world where there are no values or moral absolutes', Spanish attempts dissolved in its complete antithesis.[4]

Characters and types copied from imported American films (delinquent, detective, fallen woman, etc.) did appear in the melodramas and police procedural thrillers of the Francoist film industry, though, as Marsha Kinder argues, 'these films so blatantly imitated American and French genres [that they] appeared to minimise Spanish specifity'.[5] Being at the service of Catholic and fascist doctrine, *policíacas* were grim but ultimately righteous, with moral and legalistic victories claimed for the state by their close, when judgments and sentencing were often ratified by a voice-over that was indistinguishable from that of the propagandist NO-DO newsreel which had preceded the main feature. The 'pessimistic mood which most identifies film noir'[6] was outlawed, leaving facile psychology to deliver upbeat conclusions that forestalled the potential of the *policíaca*, which would only take on noirish tones after the political transition that followed the death of Franco in 1975.

Beneath the social veneer of absolute moral values, however, was a black market, juvenile delinquency, poverty, corruption, a lack of conscience or compassion from the ruling classes and bitter grudges all round stemming from the Civil War. American noir reflected the change from a unified, collective war culture to a much more fragmented post-war society, but Spain was its opposite. Readjustment was demanded immediately, while censorship made it impossible to see alternatives onscreen: infidelities were punished, justice prevailed, escaped prisoners were recaptured, 'fallen' women saw the light and, as Elena Medina de la Viña remarks, 'as regards juvenile delinquency, it was made clear that its origin was always in neglect and the lack of a Christian family background'.[7] Whereas American film noir tried and often purposefully failed to reconcile a military definition of masculinity with peacetime and its reinscripted gender roles, in Spanish cinema 'the enforced return of [Spanish] women to the hearth after the war made such anxieties unnecessary'.[8] The only psychopaths and damaged persons onscreen were those estranged from Francoism and Catholicism, while such cases were remarkably individualistic, never indicative of a wider corruption unless it came from beyond Spanish frontiers. Indeed, if the censor passed American noir for distribution it was because it believed that its criminality and degeneracy served to point up the contrast of a rotten USA with an apparently pure Spain. The fatalism of the American features could even be exaggerated in order to play up the perils of perdition: López Reiz's Spanish poster for Billy Wilder's *Double Indemnity* (1944), for example, depicts the rejected ending of the film (retitled *Perdición* in Spanish) with Fred MacMurray in the electric chair, which was clearly more agreeable to the Spanish censor.[9] The censor also recognised and favoured the kindred paranoia about communism that underscored some film noir and therefore adjudged it educative to a Spanish audience for whom McCarthysim was a way of life. However, when the homosexual subtext of Charles Vidor's *Gilda* (1946) proved too subtle for the censors to notice and the tantalising striptease of Rita Hayworth was curtailed before their scissors could reasonably intrude (she is bundled offstage after taking off nothing more than her elbow-length gloves), the Spanish clergy took matters into its own hands by picketing cinemas and threatening to excommunicate patrons for whom tickets to see the film were a one-way journey to eternal damnation. Needless to say, due to the forbidden fruit of the film itself and the intensely delicious sinfulness of its viewing (which was heightened by the Spanishness of Hayworth, born Rita Cansino), *Gilda* became a key reference point in Spanish culture, social history, film and literature.[10]

The 1950s was a time of entrenched social divisions and frustrated communication with the rest of the world for many Spanish artists, writers and filmmakers, who suffered a dual censorship of their initial scripts and their finished films. Moreover, those filmmakers, critics and academics who sought out censored foreign films found it difficult to work out what noir was, because the church, which insistently denounced the cinema as a school for criminality, demanded moralising finales in which no crime went unresolved or unpunished and therefore altered, cut or banned many of those films that failed to reach their standards. The 'darkening stain'[11] that Schrader detects in American cinema was simply washed away by the censor, whose classification system climaxed with a rating of 4 for 'gravely dangerous'. Consequently, most Spanish academics and filmmakers failed to distinguish between *policíacas* and *cine negro* and no formal recognition of Spanish film noir was attempted until Antonio Lloréns put together a season for the 33rd Valladolid International Film Festival in 1988, though even he admitted defeat in programme notes that reasoned: 'the consolidation of a Spanish film noir is not possible except in freely democratic markets, an arena that allows for all the moral, critical and ideological implications, as well as the assertions of ambiguity and accusations of guilt that characterise the specifically noir'.[12] Nevertheless, the Valladolid season offered a clutch of films with tenuous links to noir. Most were propagandist *policíacas* with flatfoots guided by God as much as by evidence. They emphasised the process of detection but added convoluted denouements and were without the noir protagonist's characteristic psychological problems, offering only glimpses of seam-stretching angst before stabilising moral panaceas. The moral lessons of the *policíacas* extended to warnings about drugs, involvement with the get-rich-quick tourist boom and the forsaking of adult responsibilities for delinquent thrills, but at least these criminals were bona-fide contemporary gangsters instead of the cheeky rogues that featured in the picaresque works of the Golden Age, a period of great artistic achievement from 1580 to 1680, such as the anonymously authored *La vida de Lazarillo de Tormes y de sus fortunas y adversidades* (*The Life of Lazarillo de Tormes*, 1554). The best of the *policíacas* demonstrated Paul Schrader's second phase of American film noir, that of the post-war realistic period, in which 'films tended more toward the problems of crime in the streets, political corruption and police routine',[13] but without, of course, in a Spanish context, any mention of political corruption.

In a major study of *policíacas*, Medina de la Viña tallies seventy-nine such films during the 1950s alone.[14] This was a time when the escalating cold war prompted the reopening of diplomatic relations between Spain and the similarly communist-hating/fearing America, which was now seeking allies that would host American airbases on mainland Europe. A policy of *apertura* (openness) allowed for the establishment of an airbase in Torrejón de Ardoz near Barajas airport on the outskirts of Madrid, an influx of foreign investment and commercial influence, and a lessening of the more severe aspects of the Francoist regime. Yet legal and governmental reform was tightly controlled by a coalition of Catholic businessmen and technocrats, many of them members of the quasi-Masonic Opus Dei, a fundamentalist Roman Catholic prelature of twentieth-century Spanish origin with a reputation for secrecy, ultraconservatism and fidelity to the dictatorship that supported it. Of the indigenous 'adult' thrillers that did make it to the screen, *Apartado de Correos 1001* (*PO Box 1001*, 1950) from the Catalan production company Emisora Films with a script by Julio Coll and Antonio Isasi-Isasmendi, was a generic crime thriller about drug-trafficking with a grippingly staged climax in Barcelona's Tibidabo funfair, an authoritative voice-over and a couple of flashbacks that fleshed out the characters in a skeletal plot. *Brigada criminal* (*Crime Force*, 1950), meanwhile, focused on a rookie policeman, whose investigation of a small-time bank robbery leads him to the detention of a crime boss. *Brigada criminal*, also the product of Emisora films, was set in the streets of Madrid and Barcelona, and featured a gang whose unity, police detection and audience recognition of their criminality was signalled by their foreignness. This functioned as a non-specific but blatantly threatening idea of non-Spanishness that illustrated the propagandist notion of Spain as a necessarily isolated and nationalistic refuge from all the sinful elsewheres. Indeed, although 'misery and malnutrition reached large areas of society and illegal commerce favoured all sorts of frauds and deception',[15] the instigators and profiteers of such criminal activities were either identified explicitly as non-Spanish, or implicitly as remnants of indigenous enemies of Francoism for whom 'the presumption of innocence simply did not exist, for all of those who had been connected with the previous regime were systematically considered guilty'.[16] The moral abyss between good and evil, which was as wide as that between Spain and the rest of the world, meant that dramatic conflict was limited to rooftop and alleyway shoot-outs, while the inevitable victory for the forces of Francoism exalted the heroism and sacrifice of a police force that, as the prologue of *Brigada criminal* declares, 'is considered to be one of the best in the world'. The documentary feel of *Brigada criminal* is punctuated by occasional visual flourishes with many striking close-ups, some unusual off-angle shots and a voice-over narration that directs the audience's attention towards specific achievements in policing, while the villain is a sadist who kicks cats and kills his own men. The overriding theme is the inspired relentlessness of Spanish police procedure, something that was governed by the censor, who demanded, for instance, that any policeman who fired his gun would hit his target first time.[17]

Policíacas were made by directors who adhered to the conventions of the genre, though the best offered agreeably tortuous autopsies of criminality. *Los peces rojos* (*Red Fish*, 1955) featured Arturo de Córdova as a writer who creates a fantasy life about an inheritance in order to seduce a dancer and, after many convolutions, finds himself investigated for murder, while *Los ojos dejan huellas* (*Eyes Leave Their Mark*, 1955, José Luis Sáenz de Heredia) concerned itself with a once-brilliant law student, now fallen on hard times, who takes revenge for his misfortune on a troubled old schoolfriend by killing him and seducing his widow. Sáenz de Heredia was a favoured director who, unable to find suitable Spanish actors for the main role, cast the Italian actor Raf Vallone, thereby continuing the convention of a more acceptable foreign flavour to criminality. Perhaps closest to the paranoia, menace and male angst of noir was screenwriter-turned-producer/director Julio Coll's *Distrito quinto* (*Fifth Precinct*, 1957), with a plot remarkably similar to Quentin Tarantino's *Reservoir Dogs* (1991). The film begins immediately after a robbery with the band of thieves holing up and reflecting on their misbegotten paths, growing ever edgier and more mutually suspicious until their evil ways devour them in a bloody climax. Of those who made *policíacas*, Coll was arguably the most ambitious in his aspirations to noir. *Distrito quinto* stars Alberto Closas, is firmly grounded in reality and briskly directed despite the claustrophobic setting – the film is based on the play *Es peligroso hacer esperar* (*It's Dangerous to Wait*) by José María Espinás – while the thieves without honour are bitter, vicious scum, who implode with impatience and mistrust.

Each of these films has striking moments, but as proto-noir the *policíaca* would always be stunted, suffering from prescribed right-eousness where a moral vacuum was needed. Most importantly, although the Francoist censor and American film noir had in common a rigid definition of masculinity, it was there to be questioned in American cinema as opposed to the Spanish equivalent, where it was there to be celebrated. Even in 1964, Mario Camus' *Muere una mujer* (*A Woman Dies*, 1964), co-written with Carlos Saura, had the original script's criminal motive of homosexual angst replaced by the censor's more acceptable motive of professional jealousy. Once again, therefore, it is this eradication of any psychological element that denudes the pretensions of the *policíacas* and redirects this search for authentic film noir towards the more informed and responsive psychological complexity of the few examples of dissident cinema that made it past the censor. And it is this redirection which allies this study of Spanish film noir with Schrader's argument that noir is not defined 'by conventions of setting or conflict, but rather by the more subtle qualities of tone and mood'.[18]

Neo-realism

As Schrader contends, realism was key to the tone and mood for it 'succeeded in breaking film noir away from the domain of high-class melodrama, placing it where it more properly belonged, in the streets with everyday people'.[19] Although the conventions and meanings of realism were already evident, perhaps coincidentally, in a few of the rural dramas of the 1940s, Italian neo-realism reached Spain in 1950 with a week-long season of films at the Italian Institute in Madrid that was devoured by intellectuals, filmmakers and students. Here was an alternative way of seeing and representing Spanish reality that was also cheap to make. As in Rome, bombed-out ruins were still visible in Madrid, though the metro and tramlines were extending rapidly, trapping outlying villages in the unchecked urban sprawl. The tensions between urban centres and these rural spaces were also tangible and, as Alberto Mira states, could be represented in terms of a 'symbolic opposition city–countryside' with massive emigration to a supposedly thriving metropolis.[20] This was defined as 'the most painful problem of our time' in the prologue to the first Spanish neo-realist film, *Surcos* (*Furrows*, 1951), directed by José Antonio Nieves Conde, a Falangist, whose standing within the regime appears to have distracted the censors, convincing them that the film was more moral that it actually is. Described by John Hopewell as 'a curious graft of American gangster thriller and neo-realism',[21] *Surcos* recounts the tribulations of a farming family that moves to Madrid's working-class district of Lavapies, though each generation has a different ambition: the father wants to work, the eldest son wants fortune, the youngest wants a family and the daughter wants fame. Against a background of a bustling *barrio*, not quite a village, not yet a city, Nieves Conde details overcrowded slums, unemployment and crime and creates 'a simplistic Manichean opposition between the corrupt city undergoing industrialization and the innocent rural Spain being ravaged'.[22] The father joins the unemployment line, the eldest son, Pepe (played by Francisco Avenzana, who was also a dubbing actor who provided the Spanish voice for Humphrey Bogart), falls in with petty crooks as their getaway driver and the ambitions of their daughter Tonia to sing are exploited by a gangster. The film is episodic, even disjointed, but its depiction of the *estraperlo* (black market), unemployment lines, delinquency and frequent street fights is remarkable for its veracity, though the censor did bracket the film with a warning subtitle – 'this story is not symbolic but, unfortunately, an all too frequent case from real life' – that reduces the neo-realist collective to the melodramatic individual. Nevertheless, what most distinguishes *Surcos*, and brings it close to what Mira calls the 'crossroads between neo-realism and film noir'[23] is its focus on the crisis of masculinity that was tantamount to blasphemy in the patriarchal, phallocentric society in which it was made.

The family steps off the train carrying live chickens in a basket and is laughed at and insulted by the streetwise inhabitants of Madrid, once migrants themselves, now quick to distance themselves from backwardness and exploit the naivety of new arrivals. The family makes its way to an overcrowded tenement where kids run riot and a single room is criss-crossed by curtains to make sleeping quarters for all; but, where the youngsters see opportunity, the elders see only despair and a lack of solidarity in the community that appears to contrast so poignantly with what they left behind. The father should be an honourable authority figure, but is reduced to lugging a basket of sweets through the streets until he is waylaid by a throng of infants who effectively trap him for the police to arrest him for lack of a licence. He takes a job in a foundry but, in the film's one truly expressionist sequence, the distorted angles and rapid cutting between his tortured face and the hammers clanging on iron cause his breakdown and ultimate humiliation. Unable to be the breadwinner, he can only watch as his unprotected, unfed children are sucked into delinquency and dishonour. 'If you go round with scruples, you'll go hungry', the family is warned and, taking heed, Pepe graduates to robbery while Tonia takes a job as maid, only to usurp her employer, a gangster's moll, in the affections of Don Roque, a trilby-wearing gangster reminiscent of a Warner Bros.' movie of the 1930s. Pepe is double-crossed and killed, his girlfriend is dragged off into the night by his jealous killer. Tonia demeans herself for a shot at celebrity and is beaten by her furious father, whose self-loathing is expressed in violence towards his brood. The film ends with Pepe's funeral during which the father looks at his handful of earth and realises it is where his family belongs. Thus, moralistic endings are duly delivered, but at great expense to the sanity and sanctity of the father figure. Then, to remove any doubt or ambiguity, the censor cut the final scene of the daughter jumping from the train to return to her sugar-daddy gangster as her parents head back to the farm.

Here were glimpses of various crises: an urban infrastructure barely able to keep pace with human need, a breakdown in community spirit and solidarity, a sidelined older generation, aimless youth and a grasping, grafting economy that was based on a survivalist lack of scruples. Most importantly, threats to patriarchy came from all sides: from within the family, with the wife's belittlement of her husband's usefulness and their children's challenges to his authority, and from beyond, with society's lack of compassion for this honourable man's plight. Kinder notes that the film connects 'the urban migration of the poor with the corruption of women as a combined threat to the moral rigidity of the Spanish patriarchy'.[24] It is this sexualisation of the woman and the correlative foregrounding of her subjectivity and desire that brings us closer to a notion of Spanish noir. Tonia is slapped around a bit by the gangster and by her father, but her censored leap to immorality represented a choice that could not be tolerated because in Franco's Spain, as Mira argues, 'violence and crime can only exist as an extremely marginal activity, not as a symptom for the state of things'.[25]

However, important as *Surcos* is, the essential psychosexual turmoil is missing and the moral ambiguity of noir is excised; for 'film noir is characterised by a certain anxiety over the existence and definition of masculinity and normality'[26] and that which is alluded to in *Surcos* is blamed solely on the corruptive force of the city, a cynical ploy designed to keep farmers farming so that the agrarian economy of Spain could finance its industrialisation. This ploy, however, was rebuked by Luis García Berlanga and Juan Antonio Bardem, who believed that country folk were not quite as simple as they were portrayed and in *Bienvenido Mister Marshall* (*Welcome Mister Marshall*, 1953) briefly employed the film noir aesthetic in a dream sequence that disparaged the moral high ground of the clergy.

Noir aesthetics

Bienvenido Mister Marshall is a cinematic Trojan horse: a knockabout screwball farce that hides a vengeful diatribe against Francoism and its stagnating sense of Spanishness. When a commission for a folkloric musical to make Lolita Sevilla a star fell to the secretly pro-communist UNINCI production company, Bardem and Berlanga used the cash to show how all the Francoist world was a stage in a tall tale of a drab Castilian village that does itself up in Andalusian glad rags in order to attract dollars from the Marshall Plan (that is, the European Recovery Act based on American assistance and investment), but the charade of *andalucismo* – incongruous flamenco, bullfighting, frills and fans – fails to impress the Americans, whose motorcade speeds through the *plaza* without stopping. In imitating the facile concepts of Spanishness that had been force-fed to the populace though stage and screen, these villagers were only attempting to live up to the reflection of themselves that Francoist cinema had assured them was true; but at night, when the villagers dream, Bardem and Berlanga reveal how their collective subconscious has been colonised by American popular culture, most specifically by the genres of the western and the film noir, with the deaf mayor (José Isbert) dreaming himself into a saloon shoot-em-up and the priest, Don Cosme (Luis Pérez de León), dreaming himself into a grim Andalusian Holy Week procession, flanked by pointy-hatted Nazarenes, which turns a corner, breaks out the jazz and turns into a Ku Klux Klan necktie party for him. Don Cosme lowers his hands from his face to find himself in the dock of the Committee for Un-American Activities that is rendered by expressionist lighting and design, a chessboard floor, twisted perspective and jagged shadows. He is bullied by cigar-chewing G-men and denounced by a demonic judge, whose incomprehensible dialogue runs backwards, before a noose lowers and the choking priest awakens.

Briefly, therefore, the expressionist motifs that had become synonymous with the corruption and moral ambiguity of noir made their appearance in Spanish cinema in a context that criticised the

Francoist establishment and put the church on trial. The dream attested to the intertextual presence of Hollywood cinema in Spanish culture and demonstrated that 'these transitional juxtapositions ... provided a space in which to construct an oppositional imaginary of resistance, initially against attempts by an official Francoist cinema to impose a self-serving national imaginary modelled by the repressive religious and militaristic values of the regime'.[27] The perverse irony of a priest on trial for communism was tactically shrewd by Bardem, whose strategy of juxtaposing cinematic genres and their aesthetics was a visual language of subversion that would become a 'form of strategic leverage that served to liberate [filmmaking in Spain] from the Spanish commercial cinema's industrial and cultural apparatus'.[28] The censor, having scuppered its own cine literacy by its refusal to engage with film culture and theory from elsewhere, was ignorant of the challenge that Bardem concocted by sleight of hand and failed to take offence at the way in which 'the priest's own xenophobic paranoia ... was expressed in such terms'.[29] Instead, it saved its wrath for the erotic dream of the prim schoolteacher, Señorita Eloísa (Elvira Quintillá), whose ravishing at the hands of an American football team was something of a deliberate decoy, an easier, more obvious target for excision.

Bardem claims he became a filmmaker after seeing John Ford's *The Informer* (1935), about the same time as he became a member of the illegal Communist party.[30] Alongside Berlanga, he joined the first intake of the new Official Film School in 1947, going on to co-found *Objetivo*, a film journal that traded political dogma under the guise of film theory and proposed a Spanish cinema that would accept its responsibilities as mirror of reality and instigator of social change. To agitate for this, he developed the technique of matching film styles to political meanings that was tested in *Bienvenido Mister Marshall* and perfected in *Muerte de un ciclista* (*Death of a Cyclist*, aka *Age of Infidelity*, 1955). Bardem, 'worked on writing the script all summer, fully aware of the difficulties that it would have with the censor'.[31] He based the film on a contrast of the aesthetics of neo-realism with melodrama which has been expertly analysed by Marsha Kinder.[32] However, what is largely missing from this and other analyses (indeed, neither Lloréns nor Medina de la Viña include it in their surveys) is the contextualising aesthetic and psycho-sexual tension that demands the film be appreciated and analysed as noir.

The noir context

Muerte de un ciclista opens at night on the speeding black car of an adulterous couple. Racing to reach the city before dawn, Juan (Alberto Closas) and María José (Lucía Bosé) hit a cyclist and leave him to die by the roadside, but Juan is consumed with guilt for the crime and attempts to compensate the cyclist's family, resign from the privileged university post that he enjoys through family contacts and convince his lover to give herself up alongside him. Desperate to save herself from both Juan's overwhelming sense of guilt and the attempts of society hanger-on Rafa (played by Uruguayan Carlos Casaravilla) to blackmail her for adultery and possibly murder, María José turns *femme fatale* and kills Juan at the site where they hit the cyclist, but then is herself killed in a car crash when speeding back to her husband. The metaphorical scale of the trauma is expressed in the juxtaposition of the aesthetics of neo-realism and melodrama, whereby the latter apparently flatters María José and her upper-class cohorts with glamorous close-ups amid brightly lit scenes that serve to foreground their selfish emotional determinism and use up all the sentimentality that might otherwise have weakened the political impact of the neo-realist scenes of the poor. Conversely, scenes of slums are rendered in objective long shots that observe the surroundings without emotion or glamour, thereby offering a poignant contrast with the glossy melodrama of the rich. The dominant tone, however, is noir; for Juan appears at the centre of this juxtaposition as a tormented figure, crisscrossed by shadows, chain-smoking, walking the rainy streets at night, and belittled by the women in his life. Most importantly, *Muerte de un ciclista* deals in the crisis of masculinity that consumes Juan as representative of the ruling class, thereby positing a metaphorical critique of the patriarchy and phallocentrism that underpins Francoism. Juan's solitary descent into an underworld of guilt and remorse denudes Francoist society's enjoyment of the spoils of war. María José is terrified by his insistence that they give themselves up to the police, for she sees no reason to confess to the killing nor, by extension, atone for the atrocities of the civil war, but as Juan slips deeper into crisis, so the noir-affected *mise-en-scène* comes to dominate.

The film is a collage of aesthetics in which Bardem drafts in such techniques as Eisenstein's intellectual montage for a scene in a flamenco *tablado* in which Juan's paranoia is exacerbated by the rapid juxtaposition of shots of whispering lips, clapping hands, listening ears and stamping feet; suffocating zooms that indicate Hitchcockian paranoia; and the Wellesian depth of field that clarifies the interrela-

7 Matilde (Bruna Corrà) confronts Juan (Alberto Closas) in *Muerte de un ciclista* (*Death of a Cyclist,* Juan Antonio Bardem, 1955).

tionship of class and crime, of cause and consequence. This is especially clear in a scene in which Juan is confronted by Matilde (Bruna Corrà), the student who protests against his conceited suspension of her degree studies and puts the blame for her failure on his arrogance. Juan is shown in close-up, seated at the end of a long table when, at the far end of the room, Matilde enters from the left. She is also in focus and therefore both contextualised by the long shot in the neo-realist aesthetic that attests to her socialist symbolism and included by the depth of field in Juan's intensifying nightmare. Bardem pans left to keep Matilde in the widening frame as, growing in stature, she walks around the end of the table and approaches Juan. 'You failed. It's a pity', Juan tells her. 'It's an injustice', she replies, stepping out of the shadows, coming closer, taking control and compounding his misery. Juan sits down and admits, 'I should ask you to forgive me. I have no excuse'. By this point Mathilde has reached the foreground and is lit by light from an open door screen left. 'There is an excuse. Your selfishness', she declares and turns out of that door, leaving Juan in his corner, trapped by shadows, his guilt and remorse.

Increasingly, therefore, Bardem deploys film techniques like a chess master and the cryptic puzzle of *Muerte de un ciclista* may be deci-

phered by reference to film aesthetics, with the juxtaposition of neo-
realism and melodrama contained within a film noir mood that takes
hold of Juan, who walks in the rainy street at night 'for something bad
I did once' and is assailed by the sound of bicycle bells in Bardem's
most explicitly expressionist setpiece. This establishes a further link
with the German *Strassenfilm* in which a respectable, middle-class
protagonist tumbles through class and social barriers and ends up in
the gutter.[33] The increasingly fragmented figure of Juan is accompanied by an insistently discordant musical theme and, in the sense that
expressionism makes manifest the instincts which are contrary to the
'reasoned' control of Catholicism, *Muerte de un ciclista* may be appreciated as a deeply subversive noir hybrid which targets its conscience-
ridden protagonist as whipping boy for the wealthy middle class, only
to give way to a redemptive parable as Juan rebels against Francoism
in his determination to make up for the crimes of the past. Juan
decides to confess and finds salvation in his sacrifice of all that main-
tains the Francoist class in its privilege, having previously passively
accepted nepotistic placements, ill-begotten wealth and blissful igno-
rance. 'They won't give me a prize, but I'll be a kind of hero', he tells
his mother, before offering María José a choice between voluntary
confession or being swept away by his penitent's zeal: 'If you leave me
now I'd take you down with me. I couldn't help it'. When they meet at
the spot where they killed the cyclist, Juan recognises it as a battlefield
where he fought during the Civil War and implicates María José in the
greater guilt he now feels for the murder of the Republican armies:
'The trenches were right here. I always thought of you. This is the
most important place in the world for us. There's always been something of us here. Here we killed a man, and let him die because he got
in our way'. At which point, María José guns the car and kills him.

However, racing to be with her husband, the murderous María José
swerves to avoid another cyclist and drives off the side of a bridge. The
final shot of her hanging upside down and dead from her crashed car,
while, equally in focus, the cyclist stands on the bridge above, suggests
that María José has died trying to save her privileges, which are
symbolised and subverted by her final melodramatic and bloody close-
up, but is ultimately contextualised by the depth of field in the reality
of this Everyman cyclist, who goes in search of help. Amazingly, this
ending also satisfied the censors, who, though unconcerned by the
death of the first cyclist, were indignant at the killers' adultery.
Bardem concluded that 'the Francoist board of censors, in which the
representative of the Catholic Church had the right of veto, didn't
believe in heavenly justice. No divine punishment or anything like it;

the adulterers had to die in front of the audience. So I swapped the logical end for *Grand Guignol* and the script was accepted and passed by the censor'.[34]

Although it was more directly inspired by Tolstoy's 1899 novel *Resurrection*, *Muerte de un ciclista* also owes much to Antonioni's neo-realist *Cronaca di un amore* (*Story of a Love*, 1950), which featured Lucía Bosé in a similar transformation into *femme fatale*, the essential counterpoint to the crisis of masculinity that, though rife in Juan, is otherwise absent from Francoist cinema and especially lacking in the *policíacas* which upheld machismo and patriarchy. Such pressures of conformity as felt by Juan are revealed in his mother's deconstructivist approach to her photo album: 'I often look at the photo album and see my sons grow: first communion, school, military service, politics, war, death … ', while the correlative negation of instinct and concomitant bluff of respectability is skewered by Rafa, the art critic and social parasite who attempts to blackmail the lovers:

'I know your dirty deeds, the things you hide. I see your sins, I classify them, file them away, and wait for the right time, for the moment to act. All the ugly things you hide, I unearth them and lay them out in front of you. It's a kind of purification.'

'Or *chantaje*.'

'An ugly word, it's not even Spanish.'

As Rafa retorts, the fact that the Spanish word for blackmail – *chantaje* – was adopted from the French is a further indication that all crimes were supposedly foreign and, therefore, that the pretence of purity was due to the preservation of a Francoist ideal of Spanishness. Juan's crisis of masculinity is compounded by his absent father and exploited by this *femme fatale*, whose murderous actions promote an ironic reinscription of Francoist values. When María José steps outside the privileges of melodrama and assumes the proactive self-determinism of the *femme fatale*, her decision to sacrifice Juan for the sake of her marriage effectively reinstates the priorities of decorum and the family unit in the genre of melodrama which is analogous to the dominant Francoist Catholicism. Even though María José has violated Francoist law and Catholic morality by her adultery, her killing of Juan realigns her selfish desire away from sexual expression beyond marriage to the seemingly more durable rewards for conformity that her husband threatens to withhold, such as furs, jewellery and her picture in the glossy magazines and NO-DO newsreels that Juan walks

out of in disgust. The brief foregrounding of female desire and subjectivity is therefore rapidly subjugated to the cause and spoils of her
class, rendering Juan an undesirable, whose movement from guiltless
adulterer to guilt-ridden confessor has constituted a potent threat to
Francoism. By contrast, the redirection of Juan's desire, away from the
superficial, physical fulfilment of sexual union towards the more
profound, moral validation and redemption obtained by atonement, is
frustrated by the vacuum of social, political, religious and familial
support which surrounds him. Kinder states that 'Spanish *cine negro*
does not focus on erotic desire for the woman [but] expresses its
cultural specificity by operating primarily as a discourse on fathers
and sons'.[35] Indeed, Juan's estrangement from his class, workplace,
family, faith and absent father provides no intermediary or even
symbolic character between this character and the supposedly patriarchal state. The discourse on fathers and sons is thus extrapolated into
that of patriarchy and citizenship; for Juan is the product of
Francoism, and the crisis of masculinity which he suffers therefore
threatens to undermine the hegemony that is supported by the church
and the military, both exclusively male organisations which have
rendered Francoist Spain in their own likeness.

Bardem developed this discourse further in the cold-hearted melodrama *Calle mayor* (*Main Street*, 1956) which included elements of
noir, with voice-overs, a hopelessly bleak ending and a degree of paranoia about the character of the small-town spinster (played by
American actress Betsy Blair) who is wooed as a cruel prank by a
bored and ultimately weak male protagonist; but the emotional determinism of femininity was always more suited to the trappings of melodrama than the harsh aesthetic of film noir.

Following the recognition of *Muerte de un ciclista* by foreign critics,
who awarded Bardem the Grand Jury prize at the 1955 Cannes Film
Festival,[36] and his forceful criticism of Spanish cinema at the same
year's Salamanca Congress, Bardem was imprisoned without charge
for two weeks during the making of *Calle mayor* and would thereafter
struggle to raise financing for further films. Instead, he turned his
hatred of the regime towards aiding other filmmakers to acquire
funding and distribution. Subsequently, in an experiment of renewed
openness designed to show the friendly face of Francoism to American
and European investors, the liberal José María García Escudero, who
had been ousted from the post of minister for film in 1952 for attempting reform and supporting Nieves Conde's *Surcos*, was reinstated in
1962. After this, limited reforms of funding, distribution and classification allowed for the tentative emergence of a new type of cinema

classified as being 'of special interest' by the Spanish censor and as 'New Spanish Cinema' by foreign critics.

The technocrats had by now achieved prominent government positions that facilitated the passing of the Stabilisation Plan of 1959. This was a radical change of strategy which opened Spanish frontiers to foreign capital, including the investment of foreign film producers such as Samuel Bronston who exploited tax breaks, loopholes and a weak peseta to make epics in Spain that flattered Francoist Catholic 'histories' such as Nicholas Ray's *King of Kings* (1961) and Anthony Mann's *El Cid* (1961). Tourism boomed in the 1960s, though rapid growth in production and national income produced an unstable 'stop-go' economy, with stages of expansion immediately followed by periods of recession. Popular cinema, meanwhile, mostly continued with comedies and musicals and made few asides to the concomitant tourist boom and coastal development unless it was with an eye on the foreign market, with a sensationalist glance at bikinis or a passing off as progress of the unchecked cementing-over of the *costas*. International co-productions and distribution contracts for dubbed Spanish films (often with Italian leads) allowed for more expensive action setpieces in homemade thrillers, while the genre of *policíacas* neglected the pessimism of noir but broadened to include Agatha Christie type whodunits such as *Rueda de sospechosos* (*Round-up of Suspects*, 1963) and Hitchcockean essays in paranoia such as *Crimen de doble filo* (*Double Edged Crime*, 1964). Franco, meanwhile, settled into old age largely by separating himself from governmental duties in order to indulge a passion for hunting that would provide a key reference point for the metaphorical narratives of dissident filmmakers in the last decade of the dictatorship. This climaxed with *Pascual Duarte* (1975) and *Furtivos* (*Poachers*, 1975), and extended to Berlanga's *La escopeta nacional* (*The National Shotgun*, 1978) and Mario Camus' *Los santos inocentes* (*The Holy Innocents*, 1984), but began in 1965 with Carlos Saura's *La caza* (*The Hunt*).

The crisis of masculinity

Saura, like Bardem, studied at the Official Film School and, alongside Bardem, had been instrumental in negotiating the brief return of Luis Buñuel to make *Viridiana* (1961). In his low-budget and barely seen *Los golfos* (*The Delinquents*, 1961), Saura had already displayed a keen eye for the neo-realist aesthetic and a sensibility congenial to noirish themes in this bleak, pessimistic film that centres on a crisis of masculinity, in which marginalised and disgruntled youths, played by non-professionals, edge towards delinquency in the Lavapies district that had grown even more forbidding since *Surcos*. Unlike *Surcos*, however, *Los golfos* focuses not on the crisis of the older generation but on that of the equally redundant younger males and, crucially and subversively, upends the moralising *policíacas* about delinquents by rendering them blameless in their acts of desperation: these youths were not threats to the state but victims of it. Unemployed and excluded from any sense of urban progress, the youths place all their ambitions on helping one of their group achieve fame in the bullring. Thus, *Los golfos* finally redirects this search for authentic Spanish film noir away from routine crime thrillers and melodramas to a hunt for that which Schrader calls 'the most overriding noir theme: a passion for the past and present, but a fear of the future. The noir hero dreads to look ahead, but instead tries to survive by the day, and if unsuccessful at that, he retreats to the past'.[37] However, the gang's retreat to the past that is symbolised by their recourse to the bullring – the traditional arena for testing *machismo* that is arguably incongruous in both its urban location and contemporary relevance – is frustrated by the ridicule heaped on their representative's ineptitude in the film's abrupt and damning conclusion.

  Los golfos lost ten scenes to the censor and was barely seen in Spain because it received the lowest possible classification that 'signall[ed] to distributors the censor's assessment of the film as undesirable for public viewing'.[38] Consequently it had a delayed and desultory run in a *cine de barrio* (fleapit) in Madrid. However, Bardem's browbeating of the new and inexperienced government board that had been set up to select films for foreign festivals did ensure its screening in Cannes in 1960, where it was seen and adored by Luis Buñuel. Saura struggled to make a follow-up until 1965, when, newly partnered by the producer Elías Querejeta, he shot *La caza* on a budget of two million pesetas (one million from Querejeta and one million from Saura's father) with a single Arriflex camera, five metres of camera track, no lights, no make-up ('the sweat of the actors was all real' says Saura)[39] and only four weeks in production. *La caza* was celebrated at the Berlin and the New York film festivals and is therefore commonly identified as the start of the so-called 'New Spanish Cinema', though this is a tenuous label at best, which refers to a series of films made by largely dissenting filmmakers during the later years of the dictatorship, in which symbolic characters and narrative convolutions provided critical, metaphorical commentary on the state of the nation. In keeping with this confrontational intent, moreover, *La caza* offers the seeming visual antithesis of noir, for, like Roman Polanski's

Chinatown (1974), Saura swaps night, rain and the city for a baking-hot day in the desert, but keeps the noir themes simmering under a pure white sky. In this Saura was abetted by Luis Cuadrado, one of the few Spanish cinematographers with enough skill, knowledge and artistry to attempt such expressionist tactics. Here, instead of shadow, he over-exposed high-speed film to create a high-contrast, bleached look that, like an X-ray, reveals Saura's stripped-down metaphor for the cancerous growth of deceit and favours that grows at the heart of Francoism.

La caza follows three former nationalist comrades from the Civil War (and the younger nephew of one) during a day spent hunting rabbits on their former battleground. As the sun beats down, an intricate but crumbling labyrinth of favours, jealousies and debts is unearthed as the men turn against each other and against many symbolic representations of women, including a shapely mannequin, a soft-porn magazine and the rabbits themselves (where 'rabbit' is the Spanish equivalent of 'pussy') in a lashing-out that stems from the crisis of masculinity. *La caza* thereby demonstrates how too-tight male bonding results in the cathartic oppression of women, who, like Saura's rabbits, were the propitiatory victims of men who struggled to live up to the rigid definition of masculinity that was demanded by Francoism, the church and several hundred years of ingrained *machismo*. The concomitant expectation of virgin brides, procreative wives and asexual mothers also largely invalidated heterosexual eroticism unless it was linked to illicit or immoral acts such as prostitution and adultery. Thus, in the intensely patriarchal and phallocentric society of the dictatorship, it was the father–son relationship which carried the greatest and most fetishistic erotic responsibility, expressed in the exclusively male activities that constituted the rituals of Francoism, from religion and law and order to hunting.

The film builds to a bloody climax in which frustrated machismo ignites survivalist instincts and all but the nephew are killed. In this cataclysmic end the conclusion of the twisted series of events that has inverted Spain's social hierarchy following the Civil War may be recognised. *La caza* presents a world gone wrong, as if the outcome of the Spanish Civil War was not an illustration of Darwinian dictum but an unnatural cheat that has prompted the victors to appropriate and pervert the concept of survival of the fittest in order to justify the triumph of the weak and spiteful. To rectify these wrongs and realign evolution, Saura forces his ex-soldiers to retreat in time, to replay the events of the past so as to realign the future. Like Juan in *Muerte de un ciclista*, they recognise their killing ground as their battlefield from

the past (they even unearth a skeleton). The unspoken crimes of the
past that so bedevil noir archetypes thereby become those of an entire
nation in the way that the civil war and its atrocities are signified as
the buried secret of a country that was striving to play down its
fascism and present a progressive modern face to foreign investors.
Most importantly, as Maltby asserts, 'the maladjusted veteran is the
key noir protagonist of the immediate post-war period'.[40] It is here, at
last, in Spanish cinema that are found three such men with 'a range of
social and psychological problems, [being] unpredictably violent [,]
resentful, prickly and turbulent, still psychologically organised for
war'.[41] An emphatically edited scene in which they lock and load their
guns shows them, and by implication their society, still defined by, and
primed for, acts of violence. They leave their jeep and a military beat
strikes up as the hunt begins and the four strike out across the terrain
in a scene copied by Sam Peckinpah, who saw *La caza* at the Berlin
Film Festival, for the climax of *The Wild Bunch* (1969), a film that
shares Saura's Nietzchean view that men of war will never change and,
furthermore, that any peacetime society which they inhabit cannot
progress with them still in it.

What finally distinguishes *La caza* as noir, however, is not the
violence towards animals or symbolic females, but that these self-
loathing men redirect their sadistic impulses towards each other in a
final bloody scramble to reclaim the promised but ephemeral superiority of machismo. The film suggests that the triumph of patriarchy in
a phallocentric culture is a mirage of control that confounds all men,
prompting them to desperate survivalist ploys that culminate in both
the implosion and explosion of Francoist-sponsored machismo. 'You
and I are friends' pleads José (Ismael Merlo). 'Friendship's one thing,
money's another', replies Paco, who is immediately identifiable in this
metaphorical narrative as the dictator for he is played by Alfredo
Mayo, who had also played the lead in a film adaptation of Franco's
semi-autobiographical novel, *Raza* (*Race*, 1942). Ultimately, what is
crucial to Saura's diatribe against the legacy of the civil war is *La
caza*'s obsession with 'the loss of public honour, heroic conventions,
personal integrity, and, finally, psychic stability'.[42] In a grim erotic
seizure that is characteristically, nihilistically noir, the hunters finally
turn their guns on each other.

That film noir should have provided such a sympathetic context for
dissident filmmakers such as Bardem and Saura to dare to criticise the
dictatorship is entirely commensurate with Schrader's statement that
noir represents 'an irretrievable past, a predetermined fate and an all-
enveloping hopelessness'.[43] The tragic, crime-filled past of the civil

war had been erased from history books and, increasingly, public memory, while the unpunished perpetrators of those atrocities maintained a rigid, compassionless control of the present that restricted any optimism for the future. However, Franco died in 1975 and the transition to democracy allowed for a renewed interest in noir, a fresh go at playing with detectives and the appearance of the *femme fatale*, the Spanish anti-virgin. True noir, however, was not to appear until disillusionment with democracy took hold and a weary cynicism infected those who only a few years earlier had looked forward to the rebirth of Spain with optimism. But this is already neo-noir, a rebirth of something that never existed, a resurrection of something that never lived. If the exception proves the rule, the lack of Spanish film noir testifies to the subversive cynicism of noir thematics and the nihilism of its psychology, the inversion of its gender-based determinism and the deep, dark misery of its aesthetics, none of which could be tolerated during the dictatorship. Noir, as Rafa might have said, is an ugly word. It's not even Spanish.

Notes

1   J. Labanyi, 'Masculinity and the Family in Crisis: Reading Unamuno through Film Noir (Serrano de Osma's 1946 Adaptation of *Abel Sánchez*)', *Romance Studies*, 26 (1995), 21.

2   G. Dapena, '*La corona negra*: the International Face of Early Francoist Cinema', paper given at Hispanic Cinemas Conference, Institute of Romance Studies, University of London (28–29 November 2003).

3   A. Spicer, *Film Noir* (Harlow, Essex: Longman/Pearson, 2002), p. 2.

4   *Ibid.*, p. 2.

5   M. Kinder, *Blood Cinema: The Reconstruction of National Identity in Spain* (Berkeley: University of California Press, 1993), p. 60.

6   B. Crowther, *Reflections in a Dark Mirror* (London: Columbus Books, 1988), p. 8.

7   E. Medina de la Viña, *Cine negro y policíaco español de los años cincuenta* (Barcelona: Editorial Laertes, 2000), p. 34.

8   Labanyi, *Masculinity and the Family in Crisis*, p. 21.

9   www.film-noir-posters.com.

10 One pertinent example is Antonio Muñoz Molina's noirish novel *Beltenebros* (1989) which inspired Pilar Miró's pastiche film noir of the same name (1992).

11 P. Schrader, 'Notes on Film Noir', in K. Jackson (ed.), *Schrader On Schrader and Other Writings* (London: Faber & Faber, 1990), p. 80.

12 A. Lloréns, *El cine negro español* (33 semana internacional de cine de Valladolid, 1988), p. 3.

13 Schrader, 'Notes on Film Noir', p. 87.

14   Medina de la Viña, *Cine negro y policíaco español*, p. 9.
15   J. L. Castro de Paz, *Un cinema herido* (Barcelona: Paidós Sesión Continua, 2002), p. 11.
16   *Ibid.*, p. 12.
17   This convention was parodied by Luis Buñuel in *Tristana* (1970) in which a chubby, bumbling flatfoot of the Guardia Civil needs two shots to kill a rabid dog and explains away his ineptitude to onlookers (and the cinema audience) as his concern for shooting women or children.
18   Schrader, 'Notes on Film Noir', p. 81.
19   *Ibid.*, p. 82.
20   A. Mira, 'Transformation of the Urban Landscape in Spanish Film Noir', in M. Konstantarakos (ed.), *Spaces in European Cinema* (Exeter: Intellect, 2000), p. 124.
21   J. Hopewell, *Out of the Past: Spanish Cinema after Franco* (London, BFI Publishing, 1986), p. 56.
22   Kinder, *Blood Cinema*, p. 43.
23   Mira, *Transformation of the Urban Landscape*, p. 128.
24   Kinder, *Blood Cinema*, p. 44.
25   Mira, *Transformation of the Urban Landscape*, p. 130.
26   Richard Dyer, 'Resistance through Charisma: Rita Hayworth and *Gilda*', in E. A. Kaplan (ed.), *Women in Film Noir* (London: BFI Publishing, 1998), p. 115.
27   K. M. Vernon, 'Reading Hollywood in/and Spanish Cinema: from Trade Wars to Transculturalism', in M. Kinder (ed.), *Refiguring Spain: Cinema/Media/Representation* (Durham and London: Duke University Press, 1997), p. 36.
28   Vernon, *Reading Hollywood in/and Spanish Cinema*, p. 37.
29   *Ibid.*, p. 42.
30   J. A. Bardem, *Y todavía sigue: memorias de un hombre de cine* (Barcelona: Ediciones B, 2002), p. 91.
31   Bardem, *Y todavía sigue*, p. 203.
32   Kinder, *Blood Cinema*, pp. 73–86.
33   J. Morgan, 'Scarlet Streets: Noir Realism from Berlin to Paris to Hollywood', *Iris*, 21 (1996), 31–53.
34   Bardem, *Y todavía sigue*, pp. 203–4.
35   Kinder, *Blood Cinema*, p. 60.
36   Ex-aqueo with Benito Alazraki's *Raíces* (*Roots*, 1955).
37   Schrader, 'Notes on Film Noir', p. 86.
38   M. D'Lugo, *The Films of Carlos Saura: The Practice of Seeing* (New Jersey: Princeton University Press, 1991), p. 42.
39   Introduction to *La caza* by Saura on the Spanish DVD (Diario El País, Gran Vía Musical de Ediciones, S. L., 2003).
40   R. Maltby, 'Film Noir: the Politics of the Maladjusted Text', in I. Cameron (ed.), *The Movie Book of Film Noir* (London: Studio Vista, 1992), p. 46.
41   Spicer, *Film Noir*, p. 86.

42   Schrader, 'Notes on Film Noir', p. 87.
43   *Ibid.*, p. 85.

Filmography

Spanish film noirs
Raza (Race), José Luis Sáenz de Heredia, 1942
Abel Sánchez, Carlos Serrano de Osma, 1946
Apartado de correos 1001 (PO Box 1001), Julio Salvador, 1950
Brigada criminal (Crime Force), Ignacio F. Iquino, 1950
La corona negra (The Black Crown), Luis Saslavsky, 1951
Surcos (Furrows), José Antonio Nieves Conde, 1951
Bienvenido Mister Marshall (Welcome Mister Marshall), Luis García Berlanga, 1953
Muerte de un ciclista (Death of a Cyclist), Juan Antonio Bardem, 1955
Los ojos dejan huellas (Eyes Leave Their Mark), José Luis Sáenz de Heredia, 1955
Los peces rojos (Red Fish), José Antonio Nieves Conde, 1955
Calle mayor (Main Street), Juan Antonio Bardem, 1956
Distrito quinto (Fifth Precinct), Julio Coll, 1957
Los golfos (The Delinquents), Carlos Saura, 1961
Viridiana, Luis Buñuel, 1961
Rueda de sospechosos (Round-up of Suspects), Ramón Fernández, 1963
Crimen de doble filo (Double Edged Crime), José Luis Borau, 1964
Muere una mujer (A Woman Dies), Mario Camus, 1964
La caza (The Hunt), Carlos Saura, 1965
Tristana, Luis Buñuel, 1970
Furtivos (Poachers), José Luis Borau, 1975
Pascual Duarte, Ricardo Franco, 1975
La escopeta nacional (The National Shotgun), Luis García Berlanga, 1978
Los santos inocentes (The Holy Innocents), Mario Camus, 1984

Other films mentioned
Double Indemnity, Billy Wilder, 1944
Gilda, Charles Vidor, 1946
The Asphalt Jungle, John Huston, 1950
Cronaca di un amore (Story of a Love), Michelangelo Antonioni, 1950
La Fièvre monte à El Pao (Fever Mounts at El Pao), Luis Buñuel, 1959
El Cid, Anthony Mann, 1961
King of Kings, Nicholas Ray, 1961
The Wild Bunch, Sam Peckinpah, 1969
Chinatown, Roman Polanski, 1974
Reservoir Dogs, Quentin Tarantino, 1992

Select bibliography

Abajo de Pablos, Juan Julio, *Los Thrillers Españoles 2* (Valladolid: Fancy ediciones, 2002).

Bardem, Juan Antonio, *Y todavía sigue: memorias de un hombre de cine* (Barcelona: Ediciones B, 2002).

Castro de Paz, José Luis, *Un cinema herido* (Barcelona: Paidós Sesión Continua, 2002).

Crowther, Bruce, *Reflections in a Dark Mirror* (London: Columbus Books, 1988).

Dapena, Gerard, '*La corona negra*: the International Face of Early Francoist Cinema', paper given at Hispanic Cinemas Conference, Institute of Romance Studies, University of London, 28–29 November 2003.

D'Lugo, Marvin, *The Films of Carlos Saura: The Practice of Seeing* (New Jersey: Princeton University Press, 1991).

Dyer, Richard, 'Resistance through Charisma: Rita Hayworth and *Gilda*', in E. A. Kaplan (ed.), *Women in Film Noir* (London: BFI Publishing, 1998), pp. 115–22.

Hirsch, Foster, *Film Noir: The Dark Side of the Screen* (New York: Da Capo, 1981).

Hopewell, John, *Out of the Past: Spanish Cinema after Franco* (London: BFI Publishing, 1986).

Kinder, Marsha, *Blood Cinema: The Reconstruction of National Identity in Spain* (Berkeley: University of California Press, 1993).

Labanyi, Jo, 'Masculinity and the Family in Crisis: Reading Unamuno through Film Noir (Serrano de Osma's 1946 Adaptation of *Abel Sánchez*)', *Romance Studies*, 26 (1995), 7–21.

Lloréns, Antonio, *El cine negro español* (33 semana internacional de cine de Valladolid, 1988).

Maltby, Richard, 'Film Noir: the Politics of the Maladjusted Text', in I. Cameron (ed.), *The Movie Book of Film Noir* (London: Studio Vista, 1992) pp. 39–48.

Maltby Richard, with Ian Craven, *Hollywood Cinema: An Introduction* (Oxford: Blackwell, 1995).

Medina de la Viña, Elena, *Cine negro y policíaco español de los años cincuenta* (Barcelona: Editorial Laertes, 2000).

Mira, Alberto, 'Transformation of the Urban Landscape in Spanish Film Noir', in Myrto Konstantarakos (ed.), *Spaces in European Cinema* (Exeter: Intellect, 2000), pp. 124–37.

Morgan, Janice, 'Scarlet Streets: Noir Realism from Berlin to Paris to Hollywood', *Iris*, 21 (1996), 31–53.

Schrader, Paul, 'Notes on *Film Noir*', in Kevin Jackson (ed.), *Schrader*

On Schrader and Other Writings (London: Faber & Faber, 1990), pp. 80–94.

Spicer, Andrew, *Film Noir* (Harlow, Essex: Longman/Pearson Education, 2002).

Vernon, Kathleen M., 'Reading Hollywood in/and Spanish Cinema: from Trade Wars to Transculturalism', in Marsha Kinder (ed.), *Refiguring Spain: Cinema/Media/Representation* (Durham and London: Duke University Press, 1997), pp. 35–64.

9

Spanish neo-noir

Ann Davies

Many reviewers and critics argue that Spain lacks not only a noir tradition but also a convincing body of neo-noir films, and disparage many of the films that have attempted to fill the gap. Carlos F. Heredero, for example, has commented that if anything, filmmakers have been even less interested in the noir and the thriller – a major gap in the national filmography after the restrictions of the Franco era – than they had been previously.[1] Francisco María Benavent, on the other hand, perceives noir and thrillers as simple attempts to offer an international product rather than, by implication, films specific to the Spanish context.[2] This lament for a lack of effective Spanish noir pervades Spanish film criticism of the 1980s and 1990s, but such dissatisfaction seems far from justified, since the corpus of Spanish neo-noir is in fact so substantial that it is possible here only to highlight its trends.

The ability of Spanish cinema to make convincing noir films, has, however, been overshadowed by the success of Spain's flourishing *novela negra*, or noir novel, an integral part of the boom in Spanish detective fiction that emerged in the wake of Spain's transition to democracy. Film noir has not gained anything like the same success as the *novela negra*, even though the latter supplied the former with some of its plots (from authors such as Manuel Vázquez Montalbán, Juan Madrid and Andreu Martín). The overwhelming association of noir with the USA, the dominance of American films at the box office, perennial funding difficulties for the Spanish film industry and declining audiences for Spanish films (noir or otherwise), have not helped. Both film noir and the *novela negra* have nonetheless participated in the cultural negotiation of rapid political and social change, after the transition from Franco's regime to democracy in the late 1970s. The hope that this transition had inspired in many social and cultural sectors gave way in the 1980s to the *desencanto* (disenchantment), an unsurprising disillusionment with a democratic process that had not delivered quite as much as people had expected. The sense of *desen-canto* increased after Spain made its first successful transfer of govern-mental power from the centre-right Unión de Centro Democrático (Union of the Democratic Centre, UCD) to the left-wing Partido Socialista Obrero Español (Spanish Socialist Workers' Party, PSOE) in 1982. In itself, this successful democratic transfer of power was cause for celebration in a country with a violent political history, but as time passed and increasing PSOE corruption came to light, disillusionment became more entrenched. Such cynicism in the face of corruption and disappointed hopes found expression through the *novela negra* and the neo-noir film.

Neo-noir also granted Spanish culture an opportunity to explore more positive social and cultural changes. There is, for instance, an emphasis on overt sexuality that was not permissible during the Franco years. In addition, Spanish neo-noir offers strong, often posi-tive and nuanced female characters, coinciding with, and reflecting the tensions of, the drive towards equality for Spanish women, for years hemmed in by traditional Catholic ideology and Francoist laws that stressed their role as homemaker. The end of Francoism also allowed a more open acknowledgement of regional Spanish identities previ-ously suppressed by the dictatorship, particularly those of the Basque Country and Catalonia; so that some neo-noirs neglect the usual noir emphasis on the urban in favour of the regional and rural, while the Basque city of Bilbao rivals Madrid as the preferred noir city. And finally, through the use of a retro style of neo-noir, the chance had now come to explore a veiled past more openly, so that Spanish culture could acknowledge and portray the suffering of the losers in the Civil War and under Franco.

Disenchantment with the public sphere

The earliest Spanish neo-noir films tapped into anxieties about the political transition, though as that political moment passed, so concern over public institutions gave way in noir films to more private crises. *Desencanto* is apparent in *El crack* and its sequel *El crack II* (1981 and 1983), particularly through the casting of comic actor Alfredo Landa against type as protagonist Germán Areta, implying a world-weariness newly devoid of humour; and other early 1980s noirs continued this vein of disillusionment with a political transformation that seems more apparent than real. Two of the more prominent noirs of this period illustrate this particularly Spanish noir theme. *El asesinato en el Comité Central* (*Murder in the Central Committee*,

1981) deals explicitly with the new Spanish political scene, and specifically with the reintegration of a newly legalised Communist Party into political life. *El Asesinato* is an adaptation of one of the series of books by Manuel Vázquez Montalbán, featuring his private detective Pepe Carvalho.[3] Carvalho (Patxi Andón), investigating the murder of the Party's general secretary, appears alienated from all who surround him – police and Communists alike – and from the city itself, Madrid (since he lives in Barcelona).[4] He was once a Communist himself, but also worked for the CIA, which suggests a complex personality at odds with the simplistic political division of right and left that still persisted in transitional Spain. Director Aranda did not in fact like Carvalho,[5] being more interested in portraying a political moment – the transition to democracy – than a character,[6] heightening this tendency by using constant references to actual headlines in Spanish papers, photographs of real-life Spanish politicians such as Santiago Carrillo (then head of the Spanish Communist Party) and television images.[7] Carvalho seems impassive in the face of events, but nonetheless – or perhaps for this very reason – he attracts the sexual attention of Party member Carmela (Victoria Abril), though the promise of a relationship between them is ultimately frustrated. Of particular thematic significance is the scene in which a naked Carvalho is tied up and violently interrogated by a CIA agent. The reduction of the hero to this vulnerable state suggests the anxiety in a new Spain in which corruption and violence continue (in politics and in the police), but where there is no longer the sense of neat polar oppositions to make sense of the political and social landscape. However, any sense of anxiety is mitigated by Andón's deadpan approach to events, so that the malaise of the noir detective is undercut by an implied ironic stance.

Similarly *El arreglo* (*The Deal*) tapped into cynicism and anxieties about the forces of law and order, attitudes only heightened after a failed coup attempt in Spain in February 1981. (At one point, the hero is pursued down the street by an armoured car that resembles a tank.) The film was based on a true story of a woman exiled from Argentina and found dead in Madrid, though this story proves secondary to the focus on the investigation of the protagonist Perales (Eusebio Poncela) that uncovers political intrigue and police corruption. Zorrilla saw Spanish neo-noir as an opportunity to contribute to a revival of Spanish cinema, to reconnect it to its public in a new, more democratic age.[8] He argued for *El arreglo* as 'a political reading of the transition'.[9] But what the film suggests is that democracy has altered nothing, and that the endemic corruption of Franco's time had not gone away, as one reviewer acknowledged: 'the facts demonstrate that the basic institutions of society remain unchanged'.[10]

Perales resembles the tortured noir male par excellence: having returned to the police force after succumbing to drug addiction and spending a period of rehabilitation in a clinic, he still suffers from shaking and panic attacks. His sense of alienation from his surroundings, his profession and his associates, culminates in his discovery that the mastermind behind the plot is his old friend and colleague Leo (Pedro Diez del Corral). The detoxed Perales might possibly be read in terms of a renewed Spain that nonetheless retained the old cankers embedded in the heart of the national infrastructure, and as such still suffered from ill health. The film ends as Perales walks downstairs after shooting Leo dead in a lift: he passes a man trying to summon the lift, who comments 'qué desastre, como siempre' ('the same mess as usual'). Perales repeats the remark, thus implicitly confirming the institutional corruption that the democratic transition has done nothing to change.

The disenchantment with public institutions apparent in these early neo-noirs gradually became of less interest to filmmakers than the anxieties of the private sphere. By the time of *Adela* (1986), a sense of disintegration within the police persists but is now subordinated to personal crisis. Andrés (Fernando Guillén), suffering from the suicide of a police colleague and a collapsing marriage, becomes infatuated with the transvestite Adela (Yani Forner) and descends into her world of crime, becoming embroiled in corruption and murder. Andrés betrays his colleagues as well as his friends, preferring to flee with his lover, but Adela betrays him in her turn. He shoots her and then turns the gun on himself. Adela as transvestite demonstrates a new and explicit awareness of sexualities beyond the heterosexual norm, but this is undercut by the comparative sobriety of the noir style. Balagué has moved away from the *desencanto* of *El arreglo*, opting to depict police corruption as an integral part of an individual collapse rather than the persistence of apparently outmoded public infrastructures.

Women as subject and object

The films considered above figure the loss of confidence in Spanish public life as explicitly a male affair: female characters fulfil secondary and traditional roles. As political life stabilised, so tensions about the public sphere, inherently tagged as masculine, eased; and this may have facilitated the greater prominence of women as subject as well as object of noir narrative. For *Fanny Pelopaja* (*Fanny Strawhair*, 1984), director Vicente Aranda changed the sex of the protagonist of the original source novel (*Prótesis*, by Andreu Martín) from male to female, and in the process offered an interestingly complex and nuanced portrait of a woman as noir subject. Fanny Pelopaja (Fanny Cottençon) starts an affair with policeman Andrés el Gallego (Bruno Cremer) in order to protect her junkie, criminal lover; but Andrés murders him in cold blood and Fanny vows revenge, eventually stabbing him in their final sexual encounter. Critic Ramón Freixas denies the label of noir to this film.[11] Aranda himself remarked that he was more interested in blurring the elements of noir together rather than make an exemplary noir film.[12] Conversely, Carlos Alvarez noted the almost totally dark spirit of the film, which is only occasionally alleviated and nuanced.[13]

Fanny may act as subject rather than object of her story, but her empowerment proves ambiguous at best. While she demonstrates her skill in planning and executing criminal heists for money and revenge, she is also the victim of horrific violence, particularly in the incident where Andrés repeatedly hits her in the teeth with his gun, so that she must wear false teeth ever after. She returns the compliment during the principal heist sequence, but her act allows Andrés to identify her behind her disguise and seek her out for their final violent encounter. There is also the uncomfortable incident where Fanny inserts a gun into her vagina in order to smuggle it into the hospital where her lover lies guarded, implying her consent to her own violation by a hostile patriarchal order. By the end of the film she is imprisoned in an asylum, not speaking, the malevolent demands of men having silenced her forever.

The move towards more woman-centred narratives did not exclude the recycling of the traditional *femme fatale* in *La Reina del mate* (*The Maté Queen*, 1985 – *mate* is a form of tea popular in Argentina). Cabal's *fatale* Cristina (Amparo Muñoz), the 'reina del mate' of the title and an Argentinian drug dealer, is linked explicitly to an increasing social presence and power for Spanish women.[14] This implies that the long-overdue call for women's equality is a threat and the result of foreign influences – the strong woman is literally foreign to Spain. On the other hand, *Adiós, pequeña* (*Goodbye, Little Girl*, 1986) continued Aranda's emphasis on the female protagonist as subject. The plot closely resembles the American neo-noir *Jagged Edge* (1985): the central character Beatriz (Ana Belén) is a lawyer who defends Lucas (Fabio Testi) on a drug-smuggling charge – she believes him innocent but he is in fact guilty. Critics took the opportunity to note yet again that Spanish cinema had failed to establish a convincing noir tradition.[15] They did also observe, however, the use of Bilbao as a noir substitute for New York, heralding noir's infiltration into the regions, which would become more prominent in the 1990s.[16] *Todo por la pasta* (*All for the Dough*, 1991) also offers Bilbao as contemporary noir setting and women as active and ultimately successful subjects of a noir narrative, and forms part of a clutch of 1990s noir hybrids that place at their centre women as subject. In *Todo por la pasta*, an unlikely alliance of nightclub dancer Azucena (María Barranco) with Verónica (Kiti Manver), the director of an old people's home, escape with the proceeds of a robbery carried out by Azucena's boyfriend. The film details their attempts to outwit the different people pursuing them, including two different sets of corrupt police. One of the detectives pursuing them is Estrada (Antonio Resines), one of the most violent cops ever shown on a Spanish screen, but who nonetheless exposes the political corruption elsewhere in the force. Heredero perceives in Estrada the bitterness, sadness and profound solitude and isolation, as well as violence, that typify the male noir protagonist.[17] The sense of male angst, however, does not provide the film's central dilemma but is instead contrasted with the female solidarity of Azucena and Verónica. The ability of women to work together and support each other enables them to succeed, while the men – working for their own individual gain and thus at odds with each other – do not.

Another noir–thriller hybrid, *Nadie hablará de nosotras cuando hayamos muerto* (*No One Will Talk About Us Women When We're Dead*, 1995), lays claim to noirish elements of *mise-en-scène* (a run-down Madrid), subtext (hopelessness, the struggle to improve one's lot in life) and history (reminiscences of life under Franco). The focal point of the film rests, however, with the strong female protagonist Gloria Duque (Victoria Abril), an ex-prostitute trying to overcome alcoholism while pursued by a hitman (Federico Luppi). Despite the odds, Gloria manages to survive, with encouragement from her mother-in-law (Pilar Bardem), who urges Gloria to continue her education, so that again we perceive a sense of female solidarity. Despite Díaz Yanes's desire to depict the downside of Spanish urban life, and the emphasis on the familiar Spanish symbols of bullfighting (Gloria's husband is a former bullfighter, now in a long-term coma after being gored), Mark Allinson suggests that this film has 'more of a contemporary US feel than of any other aesthetic'.[18] This aesthetic clearly contributed to Díaz Yanes being hailed as a 'Spanish Tarantino' at the San Sebastián Film Festival.

Another film that arguably belongs to this group of noir hybrids is Alejandro Amenábar's *Tesis* (*Thesis*, 1995). *Tesis* features Angela (Ana

Torrent), who discovers a snuff-movie ring as a result of her research into media violence. She sets out to track down the snuff killer, only to discover that the killer is the young man Bosco (Eduardo Noriega), to whom she is sexually attracted despite herself. The film's use of the labyrinthine underbelly of a Madrid university as setting, with an emphasis on enclosed and dark spaces, draws on the slasher-thriller genre but also on the more gothic elements of noir. Angela follows the trend of strong noir heroines, although she teams up with a male friend (Chema, played by Fele Martínez) rather than a female one in the course of her investigation. But Angela also resembles the gothic heroine as potential victim: the film's climax comes as she struggles to escape from Bosco, who has tied her up and plans to use her in his latest snuff video.

Other films which featured female protagonists as victims trapped in enclosed settings, innocently caught up in intrigues in which events – and male murderers – threaten to overwhelm them, include the minor film *Una casa en las afueras* (*A House in the Suburbs*, 1994), a psychological thriller with a nod to Hitchcock. Yolanda (Emma Suárez) seeks refuge and love from Daniel (Juan Echanove) but increasingly she feels that Daniel is shutting her away in the house. Daniel begins to crack up and kills Yolanda, but then continues to live with Yolanda's daughter Patricia (Tania Henche), forbidding her to talk of what has happened. In *Gimlet* (1995), the heroine Julia (Angela Molina) is increasingly attracted to an unidentified stalker and murderer (Viggo Mortensen), who sends her video tapes in which he declares his love, until finally he traps her in the upstairs room of the bar that she owns. The interrelation between murder, violence, voyeurism and the video further links *Gimlet* to Amenábar's *Tesis*.

Director Joaquín Jordá offered a more sinister take on the female protagonist with his Catalan–Spanish language film *Cos al bosc*/*Cuerpo en el bosque* (*Body in the Woods*, 1996) noteworthy for its use of rural setting (including some gruesome segments involving boar hunting). Guardia Civil Lieutenant Cifuentes (Rossy de Palma) is not only the detective pursuing a murderer but, as we eventually discover, the manipulator of events and mastermind of the crime that she is purportedly investigating. The supposed murder victim Montse (Núria Prims) turns out not to be dead at all but in hiding, having staged her own murder with Cifuentes's connivance, thus hoping to frame the man who raped her earlier. But Montse's plans for revenge backfire, since having 'died' she can never come out of hiding, and it dawns on her that she has become Cifuentes's prisoner. Cifuentes, who for the first half of the film comes across as calm and amenable, gradually reveals herself to be a lesbian schemer with a dangerous hold over her victim. The film posits the lesbian as alien through the local Catalan community's insistence on seeing Cifuentes as an outsider, addressing her in Spanish even though she communicates comfortably in Catalan. It also posits her as monstrous through the use of de Palma, an actress perhaps best known for her rather angular facial features. With *Hazlo por mí* (*Do It for Me*, 1997), we return to a more familiar figuring of the woman as *femme fatale*. The film appears highly derivative, a blend of *Fatal Attraction* (1987) and *Basic Instinct* (1992). Andrés (Carlos Hipólito) puts his marriage to Nuria (Eulalia Ramón) and his family at risk as a result of his infatuation with the *fatale* Isabel (Cayetana Guillén Cuervo), strongly reminiscent of Sharon Stone in *Basic Instinct*. In order to raise money to buy off her drug-dealing boyfriend Reina (Nancho Novo), Isabel persuades Andrés to participate in the mock kidnapping of his son in order to obtain the ransom money. But Andrés discovers too late that he's been set up: Isabel escapes with the money after shooting Reina dead. Meanwhile the son is returned to his family, but the apparent restoration of harmony is shattered when Nuria murders Andrés as he lies in his bath.

8 Cayetana Guillén Cuervo, the 'Spanish Sharon Stone' in *Hazlo por mí* (*Do It For Me*, Angel Fernández Santos, 1997).

What is abundantly clear in this film is that men get a raw deal. Andrés' attempt to escape his claustrophobic bourgeois existence leads to his betrayal and death at the hands of two different women. Reina is betrayed and dies likewise. But perhaps the most pathetic case is the son at Andrés's funeral, left to one side, ignored, isolated and desolate. Such an ending warns of the perils to the children of endangering family life, but it also suggests the inherent suffering of men – at any age – at the hands of women. This implication is prefigured in an earlier scene of father and son at the zoo, filmed through gates like prison bars. Isabel, on the other hand, gets away with her crimes: we last see her as she smiles at a new victim buying her a drink in a bar. Nuria, too, calmly attends the funeral of her victim, without any suggestion that she will be brought to book for her husband's death. Guillén Cuervo gives a polished performance of a deceptively open *fatale* but she functions as object of a male gaze rather than active subject. According to one report, the director deliberately wanted to go against the grain of what was fashionable, thus suggesting that noir was not in style at this time.[19] But it may also imply that the return to the more traditional *fatale* deliberately played against the noir–thriller trend of woman as subject rather than object.

At any rate, Spanish neo-noir began to move away from overtly women-centred narratives to films where women were equal players with the men. *La fuente amarilla* (*The Yellow Fountain*, 1999) centres on the partnership of Lola (Silvia Abascal) and Sergio (Eduardo Noriega), who work together to avenge the death of Lola's parents, descending into the world of the Chinese Triads and gang rivalry in search of the killer of her parents. The negative portrayal of the Chinese community in Spain proved controversial in the making, drawing protests from the Chinese embassy and threats against cast and crew. Of mixed Chinese and Spanish parentage, Lola is positioned as a *femme fatale* moving through two different communities but belonging to neither and thus doubly marginalised. However, her position as subject rather than object of her own narrative grants us a more positive valuation of the *fatale*. In addition, Sergio offers her not the submission of the *amour fou* but a true partnership. Sergio dies at the end as they flee the Triads, but the film's final sequences stresses Lola's mourning for her lost lover and friend. The very last image, as Sergio waits for her at the yellow fountain, the place where the dead go to drink according to Chinese legend, offers simultaneously the ominous suggestion of Lola's fate now and the reconciliation of the lovers beyond the grave.

The ever-anxious male

The emphasis on female-centred narratives did not mean the disappearance of a traditional male noir angst, though Spanish cinema saw a move away from the earlier crisis in masculinity figured through the *desencanto*, towards more private, individual and internal male torment. *El sueño del mono loco* (*Mad Monkey*, aka *Twisted Obsession*, 1989) tells of the new, caring male's ultimately failed attempt to cope with the same old *femme fatale*. Directed by Fernando Trueba – subsequently to win an Oscar for *Belle epoque* (1992) – the Spanish–French co-production aimed to attract international audiences through the use of American actor Jeff Goldblum as the central character Dan, an American scriptwriter living in Paris. Dan succumbs to the seduction of the *fatale* Jenny Greene (Liza Walker), and subsequently is impelled to investigate her disappearance and, as it turns out, her murder. Dan's anxieties about being a good father to his son (who has the same name, Daniel, indicating rather obvious assumptions that men never grow up) adds a new dimension to the male noir protagonist, but at the expense of understanding the three women around him – his ex-wife, his agent Marilyn (Miranda Richardson) and Jenny herself. This said, Heredero praised the film as a strange and attractive synthesis of guts and mathematical precision that made it the most adult and adventurous offering in Spanish cinema in recent years.[20] Dan's longing to retreat into the childish world of his son indicates that it is the adult world, that includes sexual relations with women, with which he cannot cope. The amorphous internationalism of the film facilitates the displacement of this fear from the Spanish context, where relations between men and women had undergone rapid and sometimes painful change.

The film prefigures by some years a greater interrelation between noir narratives and the destruction of childlike innocence towards the end of the 1990s and beyond, tapping into insecurities about the bourgeois nuclear family. In these films it is the male protagonist who is responsible for safeguarding children and thus upholding the sanctity of family life. Yet simultaneously it is also the male who is the ultimate threat to it, as the serial child killer. *Reflejos* (*Reflections*, 2001), a very grim film highly reminiscent of *Se7en* (1995), offers the tag line, 'to pursue a killer can be as destructive as killing'. This suggests not only the familiar disintegrating identity of the noir detective, but also the implication that men destroy each other and the families they should protect. Inspector Narbona (Georges Corraface) is haunted by his past in which he attempted to bring to trial his wife's former lover

Lázaro (Emilio Gutiérrez Caba). When a serial child killer begins work, Narbona attempts to pin the crimes on Lázaro, but at the film's climax he discovers too late that the killer is in fact his colleague Baena (Carlos Kaniowsky). Narbona dies in a shoot-out at the end, and the closing scene shows Baena at the funeral, at the side of Narbona's daughter. The sense of masculinity destructively at odds with itself does not prevent women from taking some of the blame for their undermining infidelity, although the dysfunctional relationship between Carbona and his martyred wife Julia (Ana Fernández) proves merely exasperating rather than an insight into the dark core of male noir identity. The film's fundamental weakness is the unconvincing revelation of Baena as the killer, since the little we know of him gives us no hint of a psychopathic nature even though he kills his own son. However, this mystery also implies that men, rather than women, have now become unfathomable, Freud's dark continent.

Like *Reflejos*, Imanol Uribe's *Plenilunio* (*Full Moon*, 2000), an adaptation of the novel of the same name by Antonio Muñoz Molina, also figures noir concerns through the hunt for a child killer. Manuel (Miguel Angel Solá), a police inspector, pursues the unnamed child killer (given a truly repulsive interpretation by Juan Diego Botto); but he himself is pursued by the Basque terrorists that he previously hunted down in the Basque Country. This noir appears to climax with Manuel as the victim of a terrorist shooting, but ends in a comparatively upbeat coda with the child killer behind bars and Manuel's reunion with his relieved mistress Susana (Adriana Ozores). The final scene, however, depicts the killer's denial of responsibility for his actions, which emphasises further the increased millennial anxiety about the fate of the nuclear family which appears to lie at the bottom of the fear of the child killer. Overall, the film's different plotlines do not gel, and the terrorist subplot in particular seems superfluous, only barely justified by Uribe's previous history of films about Basque terrorism.[21] *Plenilunio* is more effective when it comes to the depiction of individual isolation. All the characters – the inspector, the killer, Susana, the friendly priest, the pathologist, Manuel's wife – appear to be trapped in their own sealed worlds, which only romantic love has any hope of piercing.

In a related vein *Entre las piernas* (*Between Your Legs*, 1999) carries a subtext of the dangers of sex outside marriage and the damage it does to family life, although this subtext is deeply submerged beneath a convoluted thriller narrative that flourishes its noir credentials through its claustrophobic nocturnal urban setting and its flawed urban hero Javier. The film relied partly on established stars – Javier

Bardem (in the role of Javier), Victoria Abril (Miranda) and Carmelo Gómez (Félix) – to support a complex noir intrigue with various interpolated narratives that eventually turn out to form one narrative whole. Javier (who works in film) and Miranda meet in a therapy session to help them overcome their compulsion to promiscuous sex, only to begin an affair. Subsequently Javier becomes prime suspect for the murder of Vega (Víctor Rueda), a scriptwriter whose scripts Javier had previously rejected, and who in the guise of a woman, Azucena, has seduced Javier by means of telephone sex. Miranda's husband Félix, a police detective, investigates the crime and in the process not only links it to Javier but discovers the latter's affair with his wife. Félix determines to nail Javier for the murder, but the subsequent confrontation at Javier's office leads Javier's partner and Vega's blackmail victim Claudio (Sergi López) to panic. He flees the scene, is knocked over in the street and killed, and the police assume him to be the murderer. But in a flashback sequence played through Javier's mind, we discover that not only are Azucena and Vega the same person but that Javier is the murderer.

Heredero compared the film to a Meccano set, and thought it too mannered, with too many intrigues, clues and mysteries that obscured plot development and any deeper understanding of the characters.[22] The complexity of the film can indeed be baffling and really requires a second viewing for all the strands to be teased out, though once this is done, the apparently unrelated narrative strands do come together to form what is a satisfying whole. The underlying message appears to be the danger of promiscuous and perverse sex, with a sense that all who succumb to it become victims, particularly Javier and Miranda, whose subsequent death is implicit from earlier narrative threads. The only true survivor is Félix, the faithful husband, who in the end simply cuts his unfaithful wife out of his private life and awaits the return of his daughter from a schooltrip, a puppy in his arms as a welcoming gift.

While these noirs situated men within intricate webs of domestic as well as sexual relations, the older noir vein of men as alienated loners persisted. José Antonio Zorrilla (*El arreglo*) returned to noir with *El invierno en Lisboa* (*Winter in Lisbon*, 1991), again from a novel by Muñoz Molina. Although vague references to events in Portugal suggest the action occurs after the country's return to democracy in 1974, the use of a traditional noir style and the stress on a jazz soundtrack (in particular, the appearance of renowned jazz trumpeter Dizzy Gillespie playing one of the characters) make *El invierno* an exercise in sheer nostalgia. This in turn suggests the timelessness of protagonist

Jim Biralbo's noir dilemma over the *fatale* Lucrecia. Christian Vadim as pianist Biralbo gives an archetypal portrait of noir male angst: the film traces his affair in San Sebastián with Lucrecia, whose husband Marco (Fernando Guillén) in turn forms part of an underworld of shady art deals and gun-running. In the film's rather convoluted plot, what stands out is the disintegration of Biralbo's world as he breaks with his band and life as a musician in order to seek out and retain Lucrecia, who disappears from and reappears into his life in a confusing fashion. Despite his increasing awareness of Lucrecia's duplicity he pursues her to Lisbon and then back to San Sebastián where the film culminates in a pier-side shoot-out in which the lovers are the only survivors. And here the film ends on an ambiguous note: as Biralbo looks at Lucrecia he recognises her as a literal *femme fatale* around whom too many people have died, but nonetheless they walk away together. As a co-production, the film uses a variety of languages, as well as actors of different nationalities, but the film retains a firm Iberian context.[23] Although *El invierno* is hampered by its overly complex plot, the result of sticking too closely to Muñoz Molina's source text – Gillespie and the jazz subtext are pleasurable in themselves but serve to complicate a storyline that is already a little too elaborate – it makes effective use of *mise-en-scène*, and in particular the use of night shots of the deserted harbour at San Sebastián, suggesting a successful transfer of noir from New York urban to an Iberian coastal location.

On the other hand, *La voz de su amo* (*His Master's Voice*, 2001) figures noir male angst as a current issue through contemporary Basque realities including terrorism and protection rackets. Charli (Eduard Fernández), a former footballer-turned-hired-muscle, experiences betrayal on all sides by his boss, his friends, his lover, the police and Basque terrorists. However, this familiar noir tale is played out not in the city as is customary with noir cinema but in the rural Basque landscape and provincial town (reminiscent of the use of the Catalan countryside in *Cos al bosc*). The protagonist's noir alienation is figured through his antagonistic relationship to the countryside around him, the lush and beautiful backdrop to murder (fake) kidnappings, extortion and corrupt deals between police and criminals. Indeed the Basque motherland appears to betray him in its turn (symbolised in microcosm by the deterioration and death of Charli's mother). Martínez-Lázaro thus offers the possibility of noir as a filter through which to perceive a crisis in Basque national identity. The terrorists become no more than part of the general lies and corruption which surround Charli: they are no better and no worse than his deceitful boss, his equivocal *fatale* lover and the corrupt police. Even terrorism, then, forms an indistinguishable part of a flattened moral landscape which Charli surveys with disgust.

In a very different vein, *El detective y la muerte* (*Death and the Detective*, 1994) combines noir with art house and the fairytale to offer a hybrid of the cynical detective and the questing hero. This detective, Cornelio (Javier Bardem), protects María (María de Medeiros), an infantile Polish drop-out, as she moves around Warsaw in search of a godlike figure to restore the life of her dead baby. Simultaneously, Cornelio is on the run from a character known simply as the Man in Black (Carmelo Gómez). The antagonism between the two men (formerly colleagues) nonetheless bears more than a trace of homosociality and even homosexuality, heightened in the opening sequence by the full frontal shot of a naked Bardem as he emerges from the sea to talk to the Man in Black standing (fully clothed) on the beach. This sequence sets from the very start the overblown tone of the whole film, not helped by Gómez's histrionic performance or the overly deliberate and eventually irritating contrast between María's naivety and the sordid noir background of nightclubs and urban dereliction through which she wanders. The film's saving grace is Bardem's nuanced performance as Cornelio that brings to the fore the element of the white knight implicit in many a noir hero.

Retro noir

The concept of retro noir has a particular resonance within contemporary Spain. Films set in the past of the Civil War and the Francoist dictatorship offer not only the nostalgic pleasure of costume drama, but also attempt to address in retrospect issues to do with Francoist history and culture that could not be addressed at the time. In particular it facilitates the recovery of the history of those who were the losers under Franco, who attempted to erase their stories from the Spanish cultural map. Thus most Spanish retro noirs span this era, although arguably the historical drama *El maestro de esgrima* (*The Fencing Master*, 1992), with its context of Spanish political upheaval in 1868, can also be read in terms of noir. Retro noir comes to negotiate a past that can at times be uncomfortable to contemplate, and in which glossy production values, *mise-en-scène* and costume come to mitigate the pain of an unpalatable history.[24] Paul Schrader observes that the romantic longing in film noir for a lost past has its corollary in a lack of hope for the future – a very ironic contrast in Spanish terms, given that the romantic lost past is here Francoism, while

democracy thus becomes the grey horizon without hope.[25] The romanticisation of Francoism implies not only its depoliticisation but also
that the Franco era itself has become a source of pleasure, indicating
the reactionary potential of retro noir. In this noir world, according to
Schrader, 'style becomes paramount; it is all that separates one from
meaninglessness'.[26] Spanish retro noir differs from Schrader's judgement in that an emphasis on style nonetheless points to a potential
recovery of lost historical meaning, although it is far from certain that
this meaning will be positive.

Arguably the most successful retro noir director is Vicente Aranda.
In *Tiempo de silencio* (*Time of Silence*, 1986), an adaptation of the
1961 literary classic of the same name by Luis Martín-Santos, Aranda
provides a portrait of life in 1950s Spain that uncovers to the full its
drab, mean spirit. While the original novel is not normally considered
to be an example of *novela negra*, the film uses its *mise-en-scène* to
suggest Madrid as an ill-lit, claustrophobic noir city with a noir-like
hero unable to escape a corrupt environment and the intrigues of its
inhabitants. Pedro Martín (Imanol Arias), a young scientist, tries
unsuccessfully to give medical assistance to Florita (Diana Peñalver),
dying as a result of a backstreet abortion. Pedro's fiancée Dorita
(Victoria Abril) is murdered in revenge by the abortion victim's lover
Cartucho (Joaquín Hinojosa), who wrongly believes that the doctor
was the father of the aborted baby. Caught up in events beyond his
control, Pedro struggles to cope with the corruption that seeps
through Madrid society at all levels. The women epitomise this
corrupt society, forming the nucleus of the sordid reality which so
distresses the hero. At all social levels they are mercenary schemers, so
that Dorita and her female relatives plotting to trap Pedro into
marriage appear no better than the film's prostitutes. This sense of
women as all equally bad is heightened by the fact that the principal
actresses play multiple roles: Abril plays not only Dorita but also an
intellectual in a café, to whom Pedro is attracted, and one of the
brothel prostitutes. Likewise, Charo López plays the mother of Pedro's
dilettante friend Matías (Juan Echanove) and also a brothel prostitute.

Aranda's *Si te dicen que caí* (*If They Tell You That I Fell*, 1989)
adapted a classic novel by Juan Marsé, a novelist noted for not only
his noir-like depictions of marginalised, working-class children and
youth in 1940s and 1950s Barcelona, but also his enthusiasm for film
that is frequently reflected in both his style and settings. Many of
Marsé's novels have been adapted for film but *Si te dicen* is arguably
the most successful, particularly when we take into account the
complexity of Marsé's text, where it is not always clear what is

happening and to whom. Though Aranda had perforce to simplify things (as indeed Marsé himself did in a later edition of the novel), some of the deliberate confusion, particularly between characters and between different levels of flashback, is still there. In particular, the difficulty in the novel of distinguishing between the principal female characters Aurora/Ramona/Menchu of the novel (they may even all be different personae of the same woman) is given extra resonance by the fact that in the film Victoria Abril plays them all (repeating the motif of *Tiempo de silencio*). The film also retains the multiple levels of betrayal between characters that place the film squarely in the noir tradition.

What is unusual for noir, though not for Spanish cinema, is the use of children as protagonists, which is characteristic not only of Marsé's work but in much of Spanish film and literature which has attempted to recuperate the memories of the losers in the Spanish Civil War and under Franco by using the point of view of a child. *Si te dicen* reveals children as active participants in the corruption, as willing to betray each other and the adults who surround them as the adults themselves are. Most strikingly, the central character Java (Jorge Sanz) betrays his brother Marcos (Antonio Banderas): one of the many notorious elements of the war was the frequent interfamily betrayals, which feature in Marsé's work. The sordidness of the struggle to survive in post-war Barcelona forms a continuum from childhood to adulthood, with no possibility of escape. In addition, Aranda's brutal filming of the novel's already graphic sex scenes reveal the degradation of the characters and of sexual relations at this time (which involve self-interest but rarely love or even pleasure), most shockingly in the early scene between Sanz and Abril, who engage in a sexual display for the voyeuristic pleasure of local Falangist Conrado (Javier Gurruchaga).

With *Amantes* (*Lovers*, 1990), Aranda created not only a classic of Spanish noir but arguably one of the truly great Spanish films regardless of genre. The film is based on a real-life story of lovers who murder the man's fiancée for her money; and was originally intended to furnish an episode of the Spanish television series *La huella del crimen* (*The Clue to the Crime*). Jorge Sanz as Paco is again paired with Abril as Luisa, Paco's landlady who corrupts her tenant, initiating him into both sex and crime. Desperate for money to pay off her former associates who are threatening her, she persuades him to murder his fiancée Trini (Maribel Verdú) in order to get hold of her savings. Trini is aware of Paco's duplicity and, in a striking scene as she and Paco shelter from the rain under his coat, she begs him masochistically to kill her, as she cannot live without his love. Paco duly complies, slashing her wrists with a razor. The film concludes with the enthusiastic embrace of Paco and Luisa after Luisa learns of Trini's death: the freeze frame of the embrace and the accompanying swell of music somewhat undercut by the overlaying caption that tells of their subsequent arrest and imprisonment in real life, followed by Luisa's death in prison and Paco's release and rehabilitation. This intertitle serves as a critical parody of the captions pasted on to American noirs somewhat desperately by the Francoist censors to persuade Spanish audiences that the villains did not get away with their crimes.

Marvin D'Lugo observes that Trini and Luisa represent, in a rather obvious way, the commonly perceived 'two Spains' of the victorious right and the defeated left: Trini stands for traditionalist, Francoist ideology and the conservative role it envisaged for women, while Luisa as *femme fatale* stands at the opposite pole.[27] Paco chooses and embraces the 'other', marginalised Spain at the end of the film, which undercuts the sense of moralistic, Francoist closure that D'Lugo observes.[28] But then arguably many noirs with *fatales* lay claim to this moral ambiguity, for though the men may regret taking up with such dangerous women there is no firm evidence that the straight and narrow would have been able to contain them. Certainly Paco falls for Luisa very easily indeed and in fact, as she caustically comments, gets the best of both worlds with two women competing for his sexual favours. The apparent reversal of sexual roles – the women as sexual initiators, the man the pursued object of desire – does not necessarily serve to reverse the power of gender roles per se. Chris Perriam has noticed how such ambiguity plays out in the sex scenes between Paco and Luisa, where the former is filmed as the object of an implicitly non-male gaze. Perriam points out that 'Luisa's domination of Paco's body and its responses . . . are by no means free of association with pornographic male fantasies'.[29] But this again may merely make overt the masculine wishful thinking that underlies the figuration of the *fatale*.

D'Lugo uses his discussion of *Amantes* to problematise the use of retro noir as a vehicle for recuperating memory. He argues that while the generic elements of noir merely emphasise the erasure of cultural specificity, our reading in the present of what seems a familiar past – using a 'future anterior' mode of perception and interpretation – means that we read these film texts in terms of a self-conscious historicity.[30] On this basis, he argues for Luisa as a contemporary challenge to the narrow patriarchal values embodied in the historical setting as well as in Trini.[31] But the emphasis on historicity neglects the demands of genre. An awareness of classic American noir facilitates not only a retro style but also a retro spectatorial stance deliberately adopting a past mode of perception as if the future had not happened; and if we adopt this, then Luisa simply re-enacts the familiar *fatale* trope of the lethal woman who must be punished.

Aranda's retro noirs heralded a penchant for noir in heritage film, and another major retro noir was not long in coming. *Beltenebros* (1991) exemplifies the glossy production values and costume drama fostered by the director herself when the PSOE government gave her responsibility for film policy. Another adaptation of a Muñoz Molina novel, *Beltenebros* uses primarily British actors in the leading roles. The protagonist Darman (Terence Stamp) originally travelled to Madrid in the 1940s to identify and execute a traitor in a clandestine communist cell. But doubts about the victim's guilt resurface when he returns to Madrid in 1962 to repeat the process, and his mind constantly flashes back to the events of the 1940s. The real traitor is the same man in both cases, known as Valdivia in the 1940s and Ugarte in the 1960s, the only main character played by a Spaniard (José Luis Gómez). On both his visits to Madrid, Darman is attracted to the woman involved with the supposed traitor: these women happen to share the name Rebeca (Geraldine James in the 1940s, Patsy Kensit in the 1960s). The film begins and ends as Darman flees Madrid in the company of the younger Rebeca after the final confrontation between Ugarte and Valdivia in which the latter dies.

Beltenebros carries at least one reminder of past Spanish history with its explicit reference to Rita Hayworth in *Gilda* (1946), when the younger Rebeca performs Hayworth's famous number 'Put the Blame on Mame' (though Rebeca strips much further than *Gilda* does). The opening of *Gilda* in Madrid caused a scandal: members of the Spanish Falange defaced posters, and priests censured parishioners who attended any theatre showing the film. Despite, or because of, these attempts to frighten off cinemagoers, *Gilda* acquired a particular resonance for Spanish audiences. In using the image of Hayworth/Gilda, *Beltenebros* explicitly refers to the classic noir genre in order to mark itself out as strongly noir. Kathleen Vernon argues that Rebeca's assumption of the Hayworth role does not aim to 'challenge conventional gender positioning but to proclaim the interchangeability of women, the woman as icon, as floating signifier but one that resists the imposition of meaning'.[32] This is fact further stressed because the two principal characters in the film carry the same name, suggesting that all woman are alike. The identity of Rebeca – as Darman himself tells us, never a real name – becomes what Vernon describes as 'the empty surface onto which men may project their desires'. Hence the younger

Rebeca spends much of her screen time assuming different costumes for the pleasure of men.[33]

Thus *Beltenebros*, as well as Aranda's three films to a greater or lesser extent, suggests that there is little or no attempt, in retro noir at least, to recuperate the lost histories of women under Francoism, who were very often its primary victims. Rather, the films indulge in the recycling of older and more malevolent stereotypes of women as indistinguishably duplicitous, while using historicity as an alibi. But this position is not inevitable, and Miró's last film (before her sudden death in 1997) demonstrates a possible alternative reading of the *fatale*. *Tu nombre envenena mis sueños* (*Your Name Poisons My Dreams*, 1996) is another adaptation, from the novel by Joaquín Leguina. The film's complex structure involves two levels of flashback, as former police detective Angel Barciela (Carmelo Gómez) in the 1950s looks back to the investigation of a series of murders of former Falange members and his relationship with murder suspect Julia Buendía (Emma Suárez) in the 1940s, while in the 1940s sequences she in turn looks back to her life during the Spanish Civil War. Barciela eventually discovers that Julia has murdered the victims as revenge for their killing of her lover of the war years. He allows her to flee the country, but resigns from his job in a move that blends yearning for a lost woman with simultaneous disgust with her.

Tu nombre offers us a beautifully nuanced portrait of Julia that implies that *femmes fatales* are made and not born. The flashbacks from Julia as a predatory type who specifically aims to ensnare her murder victims, to the younger Julia, sexually experienced but nonetheless more frank and open, concerned for her family and her lover, living for the moment, suggest that she therefore deliberately adopts the *fatale* role in order to avenge her lover. The film thus grants the potential for a more positive valuation of the *femme fatale* as certainly dangerous as well as desirable, but also as a locus for resistance to a patriarchy identified with the Francoist past, but still very much alive in the Spanish present. Of all the retro noirs discussed here, Miró's film comes the closest to recuperating specific political climates and events, although Allinson argues that 'where Leguina's novel contains a powerful historical awareness, the film version concentrates on individuals rather than contexts'.[34] Arguably a lot of retro films tend to do this, preferring to have one or two characters with which audiences can clearly identify and thus make at least some sense of historical events. Nonetheless the historicising of the *femme fatale* suggests a closer imbrication of characters with events, which becomes clearer if we compare Julia to Luisa in Aranda's *Amantes*. Luisa's *fatale*-ness may simply be her way of surviving the grim realities of Madrid in the 1950s and thus determined to some extent by circumstances. But the political and historical nature of Julia's *fatale*-ness are clearer to the extent that we can perceive her *fatale* masquerade as direct resistance to the Fascists that (at that point in time, at any rate) undergirded the Franco regime – a regime that in turn undergirds the law and order that Barciela must maintain. Thus, in contrast to Luisa as resistant from a standpoint in the 1990s, as D'Lugo posited, Julia resists within her own historical place and time; her resistance is of the historical moment.

Other retro noirs include a Galician noir, *Continental* (1989), which starred Eusebio Poncela (*El arreglo*) as well as well-known actors Marisa Paredes and Jorge Sanz. Set at the end of the 1950s, the film revolves around gang warfare over the control of the profits from drugs and prostitution. Press coverage stressed its contribution to Galician cinema rather than to Spanish noir, but Villaverde aimed to offer a renovation of the noir genre, although his comment that the enclosed world of the film represented Galicia suggests an implicit equation between the claustrophobia of noir and that of Galicia, making the latter an appropriate noir setting.[35] *Catorce estaciones* (*Fourteen Stations*, 1991), a badly received co-production, relates more directly to Spanish history. The action takes place in 1947 on the Paris–Portugal train, on which Lázaro (Juan Luis Galiardo), an exiled teacher, is returning clandestinely to Spain in order to undertake a secret mission against Franco. Simón (Jacques Penot) aims to murder him, but falls in love with Lázaro's wife Luisa (Geraldine Danon), who is on the train without her husband's knowledge. Virtually all the action takes place on the train, suggesting again the sense of claustrophobia that was endemic to Franco's regime.

El embrujo de Shanghai (*The Shanghai Enchantment*, 2002), derived from another novel by Juan Marsé, takes us back to a noir Barcelona, in which Forcat (Eduard Fernández), from the Spanish resistance, tells a young girl Susana (Aida Folch) and her friend Daniel (Fernando Tielve) of the adventures of Susana's father Kim (Antonio Resines) in Shanghai. Forcat weaves a mystery of enchantment around Kim's investigation of Madame Chen (Ariadna Gil, who also plays Susana's mother); and Trueba offers an ironic contrast between the tale and reality by shooting the former in black and white (thus positing it precisely as a noir within a noir, and underscoring it explicitly as a film text), and the latter in colour. Nonetheless, the melodrama of the interpolated tale cannot ultimately blot out the sordidness of life in Barcelona, or that the mysterious *fatale* Madame Chen is a romanticisation of Susana's tawdry, tipsy mother. Indeed, the tale of Kim and of Forcat turns out to be just as sordid in reality, as we discover when their old associate Denis (a menacing Jorge Sanz) arrives to reveal the truth. *El embrujo* again offers the doubling of women in Gil's roles, implying that the mystique of women hides a less pleasant degradation. It also offers Susana as a Lolita figure who teases and entices Daniel, initiating him into the attractions of heterosexuality but also implying – in contrast to *Tu nombre envenena* – that women are *fatale* virtually from the cradle.

Trueba emphasises glossy exoticism at the expense of an exploration of the grim realities that made fantasy all the more necessary for survival, so that real life in colour in Barcelona becomes as much a fabrication as Shanghai in black and white. The film illustrates the potentially disturbing possibilities of the retro for the romanticisation of a violent past as well as, more specifically, of more retrograde portraits of women as dangerous *fatales*. But these are possibilities rather than inevitabilities. The Spanish retro noir is more than simply an exercise in costume drama, and as a genre it is particularly effective in suggesting – *El embrujo de Shanghai* notwithstanding – how desperate were the living conditions of the time, as the powerful retro films of Aranda, in particular, illustrate. It recuperates above all a precise ambience which has been left behind by the transition to democracy (and greater prosperity), and thus at the very least acts as a trace in the Spanish cultural memory. It is nonetheless the contemporary neo-noir that has demonstrated a greater awareness of the complexities of the Spanish past and present, drawing on specifically Spanish realities without necessarily being confined to them. There can arguably have been no better film vehicle for portraying the social and political climate of the transition, given the emphasis on corruption and cynicism in both noir and the sense of *desencanto*. Neo-noir has also played a major part – generally unacknowledged – in bringing to Spanish screens images of positive and independent women able to solve problems and deal with complex realities, thus recognising the transformation of expectations for Spanish women in the last twenty years. And with its emphasis on the troubled male, neo-noir has also proved an apt tool with which to probe the anxieties surrounding male identities following the disappearance of a patriarchal dictatorship. Spanish neo-noir has also been unusually effective in moving beyond the confines of the city to feature regional, rural and coastal contexts. This has not only assisted in the cultural recuperation of the regional identities suppressed under Franco, but has also demonstrated an ability to go beyond noir's traditional parameters to say new things about rural as well as urban realities. Taking these points together, it becomes more and more surprising that Spanish critics and reviewers have been prepared to dismiss Spanish neo-noir so readily. Neo-noir is Spain's forgotten genre that has nonetheless maintained a steady presence in Spanish cinema, and which, along with the *novela negra*, has refused to allow the exploration of the past and the negotiation of the present to be ghettoised in high-brow literature and art-house cinema. It has helped to bring specifically Spanish realities, often uncomfortable ones, into the mainstream.

Notes

1   Carlos F. Heredero, '*Todo por la pasta*: un thriller de Bilbao', *Dirigido por* 194 (September 1991), 16.
2   Francisco María Benavent, *Cine español de los noventa: diccionario de películas, directores y temático* (Bilbao: Mensajero, 2000), p. 25
3   Two other Carvalho adaptations have since been made, *Los mares del sur/Els mars del sud* (*The Southern Seas*, Manuel Esteban Marquilles, 1991) and *El laberinto griego* (*The Greek Labyrinth*, Rafael Alcázar, 1992); neither film was very successful.
4   Ramón Freixas, 'Asesinato en el Comité Central', *Dirigido por* 91 (March 1982), 59–60.
5   Pascual Vera, *Vicente Aranda* (Madrid: JC, 1989), p. 133; quoted in Thomas Deveny, *Contemporary Spanish Film from Fiction* (Lanham, MD: Scarecrow Press, 1999), p. 386.
6   Rosa Alvares Hernández and Belén Frías, *Vicente Aranda, Victoria Abril: el cine como pasión* (Valladolid: 36 Semana Internacional de Cine, 1991), p. 131; quoted in Deveny, p. 386.
7   Deveny, p. 386
8   José Antonio Zorrilla, 'El cine de la libertad', *Diario 16* (3 October 1983).
9   Antonio Castro, 'Entrevista con José Antonio Zorrilla', *Dirigido por* 109 (November 1983), 57.
10 Antonio Castro, 'El Arreglo, de José Antonio Zorrilla', *Dirigido por* 110 (December 1983), 70.
11 Ramón Freixas, '*Fanny Pelopaja*', *Dirigido por* 117 (August/September 1984).
12 Ramón Freixas, 'Entrevista con Vicente Aranda', *Dirigido por* 116 (June/July 1984).
13 Carlos Alvarez, 'Sadomasoquismo y acción violenta en *Fanny Pelopaja*', *Liberación* (1 December 1984).
14 Fernando Bejarano, 'Fermín Cabal: "Las mujeres mueven el mundo, son despiadadas en sus ambiciones y afectos"', *Diario 16* (19 April 1985).
15 Review by Eduardo T. Gil de Muro in Equipo Reseña, *Cine para leer 1986* (Bilbao: Mensajero, s.d), pp. 95–8.

16 Pedro Crespo, '"Adiós pequeña", cine negro en Bilbao', *Epoca* (10 November 1986), 122.

17 Carlos Heredero, *20 nuevos directores del cine español* (Madrid: Alianza, 1999), pp. 340, 342. Heredero concludes with the usual lament that the film promised a return to quality noir that ultimately came to nothing.

18 Mark Allinson, 'Not Matadors, not Natural Born Killers: Violence in Three Films by Young Spanish Directors', *Bulletin of Hispanic Studies* LXXIV (1997), 326.

19 José Arenas, 'Se rueda "Hazlo por mí", un "thriller" español con tinte negro', *ABC* (17 April 1997).

20 Carlos F. Heredero, 'El sueño del mono loco: pesadilla de la infancia y de la muerte', *Dirigido por* 176 (January 1990), 38.

21 These earlier films were: *El proceso de Burgos* (*The Burgos Trial*, 1979), *La fuga de Segovia* (*Flight from Segovia*, 1981), *La muerte de Mikel* (*The Death of Mikel*, 1983) and somewhat later, *Días contados* (*Running Out of Time*, 1994).

22 Heredero, *20 nuevos directores*, pp. 162–3.

23 The archive version viewed at the Filmoteca Española, Madrid, was primarily in English.

24 See Rikki Morgan-Tamosunas 'Screening the Past: History and Nostalgia in Contemporary Spanish Cinema', in Barry Jordan and Rikki Morgan-Tamosunas (eds), *Contemporary Spanish Cultural Studies* (London: Arnold, 2000), pp. 111–22.

25 Paul Schrader, 'Notes on Film Noir', in Alain Silver and James Ursini (eds), *Film Noir Reader* (New York: Limelight, 1998), pp. 57–8.

26 *Ibid.*, p. 58.

27 Marvin D'Lugo, 'Vicente Aranda's *Amantes*: History as Cultural Style in Spanish Cinema', in Jenaro Talens and Santos Zunzunegui (eds), *Modes of Representation in Spanish Cinema*, Hispanic Issues 16 (Minneapolis: University of Minnesota Press, 1998), p. 295

28 D'Lugo, p. 295

29 Chris Perriam, 'Jorge Sanz: *el Galán Sumiso*: Problematising Masculinities in Mainstream Cinema in Spain', *Forum for Modern Language Studies* XXXVII/1 (2001), 31.

30 D'Lugo, pp. 292–3.

31 *Ibid.*, p. 296.

32 Kathleen Vernon, 'Reading Hollywood In/And Spanish Cinema: From Trade Wars to Transculturation', in Marsha Kinder, ed. *Refiguring Spain: Cinema/Media/Representation* (Durham: Duke University Press, 1997), p. 51.

33 *Ibid.*, p. 53.

34 Mark Allinson, 'Pilar Miró's Last Two Films: History, Adaptation and Genre', in Rob Rix and Roberto Rodríguez-Saona (eds), *Spanish Cinema: Calling the Shots* (Leeds: Trinity and All Saints, 1999), p. 44.

35   Maite Gimeno, '"Continental", visión renovadora del cine negro', *Atlántico* (24 November 1989).

Filmography

El crack, José Luis Garci, 1981
El asesinato en el Comité Central (*Murder in the Central Committee*), Vicente Aranda, 1981
El crack II, José Luis Garci, 1983
El arreglo (*The Deal*), José Antonio Zorrilla, 1983
Fanny Pelopaja (*Fanny Strawhair*), Vicente Aranda, 1984
La Reina del mate (*The Maté Queen*), Fermín Cabal, 1985
Adela, Carlos Balagué, 1986
Puzzle, Luis José Comerón, 1986
Adiós, pequeña (*Goodbye, Little Girl*), Imanol Uribe, 1986
Tiempo de silencio (*Time of Silence*), Vicente Aranda, 1986
Al acecho (*Lying in Wait*), Gerardo Herrero, 1987
Un negre amb un saxo (*Black with a Sax*), Francesc Bellmunt, 1988
El sueño del mono loco (*Mad Monkey*, aka *Twisted Obsession*), Fernando Trueba, 1989
Si te dicen que caí (*If They Tell You That I Fell*), Vicente Aranda, 1989
Una ombra al jardí/Una sombra en el jardín (*A Shadow in the Garden*), Antonio Chavarrías, 1989
Continental, Xavier Villaverde, 1989
Amantes (*Lovers*), Vicente Aranda, 1990
Beltenebros, Pilar Miró, 1991
Todo por la pasta (*All for the Dough*), Enrique Urbizu, 1991
Els mars del sud/Los mares del sur (*The Southern Seas*), Manuel Esteban Marquilles, 1991
El invierno en Lisboa (*Winter in Lisbon*), José Antonio Zorrilla, 1991
Manila, Antonio Chavarrías, 1991
Catorce estaciones (*Fourteen Stations*), Antonio Giménez-Rico, 1991
El maestro de esgrima (*The Fencing Master*), Pedro Olea, 1992
El laberinto griego (*The Greek Labyrinth*), Rafael Alcázar, 1992
Una casa en las afueras (*A House in the Suburbs*), Pedro Costa, 1994
El detective y la muerte (*Death and the Detective*), Gonzalo Suárez, 1994
Nadie hablará de nosotras cuando hayamos muerto (*No One Will Talk About Us Women When We're Dead*), Agustín Díaz Yanes, 1995
Tesis (*Thesis*), Alejandro Amenábar, 1995
Gimlet, José Luis Acosta, 1995
Cos al bosc/Cuerpo en el bosque (*Body in the Woods*), Joaquín Jordá, 1996
Susana, Antonio Chavarrías, 1996
Tu nombre envenena mis sueños (*Your Name Poisons My Dreams*), Pilar Miró, 1996
Hazlo por mí (*Do It For Me*), Angel Fernández Santos, 1997

El crimen del Cine Oriente (*The Crime at the Oriente Cinema*), Pedro Costa, 1997
La fuente amarilla (*The Yellow Fountain*), Miguel Santesmases, 1999
Entre las piernas (*Between Your Legs*), Manuel Gómez Pereira, 1999
Reflejos (*Reflections*), Miguel Angel Vivas, 2001
Plenilunio (*Full Moon*), Imanol Uribe, 2000
La voz de su amo (*His Master's Voice*), Emilio Martínez-Lázaro, 2001
El embrujo de Shanghai (*The Shanghai Enchantment*), Fernando Trueba, 2002

Select bibliography

Allinson, Mark, 'Not Matadors, not Natural Born Killers: Violence in Three Films by Young Spanish Directors', *Bulletin of Hispanic Studies* LXXIV (1997), 315–30.

Allinson, Mark, 'Pilar Miró's Last Two Films: History, Adaptation and Genre', in Rob Rix and Roberto Rodríguez-Saon (eds), *Spanish Cinema: Calling the Shots* (Leeds: Trinity and All Saints, 1999), pp. 33–45.

Alvarez, Carlos, 'Sadomasoquismo y acción violenta en *Fanny Pelopaja*', *Liberación* (1 December 1984).

Arenas, José, 'Se rueda "Hazlo por mí", un "thriller" español con tinte negro', *ABC* (17 April 1997).

Bejarano, Fernando, 'Fermín Cabal: "Las mujeres mueven el mundo, son despiadadas en sus ambiciones y afectos"', *Diario* 16 (19 April 1985).

Benavent, Francisco María, *Cine español de los noventa: diccionario de películas, directores y temático* (Bilbao: Mensajero, 2000).

Castro, Antonio, 'Entrevista con José Antonio Zorrilla', *Dirigido por* 109 (November 1983), pp. 56–9.

Castro, Antonio, 'El arreglo, de José Antonio Zorrilla', *Dirigido por* 110 (December 1983), 69–71.

Crespo, Pedro, '"Adiós pequeña", cine negro en Bilbao', *Epoca* (10 November 1986)

Deveny, Thomas, *Contemporary Spanish Film from Fiction* (Lanham, MD: Scarecrow Press, 1999).

D'Lugo, Marvin, 'Vicente Aranda's *Amantes*: History as Cultural Style in Spanish Cinema', in Jenaro Talens and Santos Zunzunegui (eds), *Modes of Representation in Spanish Cinema*, *Hispanic Issues* 16 (Minneapolis: University of Minnesota Press, 1998), pp. 289–300.

Freixas, Ramón, 'Asesinato en el Comité Central', *Dirigido por* 91 (March 1982), 59–60.

Freixas, Ramón, 'Entrevista con Vicente Aranda', *Dirigido por* 116 (June/July 1984).

Freixas, Ramón, '*Fanny Pelopaja*', *Dirigido por* 117 (August/ September 1984).

Gil de Muro, Eduardo T., 'Adiós, pequeña', in Equipo Reseña (ed.), *Cine para leer 1986* (Bilbao: Mensajero, s.d), pp. 95–8.

Gimeno, Maite, '"Continental", visión renovadora del cine negro', *Atlántico* (24 November 1989).

Heredero, Carlos F., 'El sueño del mono loco: pesadilla de la infancia y de la muerte', *Dirigido por* 176 (January 1990), 38–45.

Heredero, Carlos F., '*Todo por la pasta*: un thriller de Bilbao', *Dirigido por* 194 (September 1991), 16–17.

Heredero, Carlos F., *20 nuevos directores del cine español* (Madrid: Alianza, 1999).

Morgan-Tamosunas, Rikki, 'Screening the Past: History and Nostalgia in Contemporary Spanish Cinema', in Barry Jordan and Rikki Morgan-Tamosunas (eds), *Contemporary Spanish Cultural Studies* (London: Arnold, 2000), pp. 111–22.

Perriam, Chris, 'Jorge Sanz: *el Galán Sumiso*: Problematising Masculinities in Mainstream Cinema in Spain', *Forum for Modern Language Studies* XXXVII/1 (2001), 26–37.

Schrader, Paul, 'Notes on *Film Noir*', in Alain Silver and James Ursini (eds), *Film Noir Reader* (New York: Limelight, 1998), pp. 53–63.

Vernon, Kathleen, 'Reading Hollywood in/and Spanish Cinema: from Trade Wars to Transculturation', in Marsha Kinder (ed.) *Refiguring Spain: Cinema/Media/Representation* (Durham: Duke University Press, 1997), pp. 35–64

Zorrilla, José Antonio, 'El cine de la libertad', *Diario 16* (3 October 1983).

10

Italian film noir

Mary P. Wood

Giallo or noir?

Although Italy has hosted festivals of film noir for many years, there have been few critical attempts to define Italian film noir as a genre. The fundamental reason for the Italian difficulty with the concept of noir is undoubtedly the predominance of the word *giallo* which entered popular vocabulary to denote mystery stories from 1929 when the publisher, Mondadori, started bringing out detective fiction in yellow covers. The word *giallo* has come to be used both as a short-hand term for any type of detective fiction and, more widely, as a generic term for stories with any mystery element; hence the genres of the *giallo erotico*, the *giallo politico* and, as we shall see, the use of saturated yellow tones on film to connote hidden realities and to intro-duce the intertextual frame of generic conventions into the text.

No other country has the problem of using a term of another colour which covers film noir, several media and many genres. Moreover, the European style of filmmaking with its use of the long take rather than fast cutting, the visual flair of Italian genre films which, even in low-budget examples, can combine realism of place with spectacular *mise-en-scène* has made many critics ill at ease with Italian forms which did not seem to fit American models. Italian genres are flexible structures, reflecting the fact that the Italian film industry has always been a precarious enterprise, with a tradition of rapidly identifying successful trends and incorporating them into current production. If one then adds into the equation the complexities of a Byzantine film industry in a constant state of crisis, a bourgeois critical tradition which privileged realism and serious themes as marks of cinematic quality, the low esteem which popular film genres had until the late 1970s, and now the dominant position of American films in the Italian market, then difficulties in defining Italian film noir become more explicable.

As an example, Fabio Giovannini tackles the huge task of defining both American and Italian noirs in their literary, cinematic, pulp and cyber forms. He states that the one indisputable characteristic of American noir is the absence of supernatural elements and that, whereas the *giallo*, or crime fiction, has firm generic rules including the identification of *who* is responsible for a crime, the noir is only interested in *why* a crime has been committed. In transposing these rules to film, he therefore has problems with the work of Dario Argento.[1] Moreover, while acknowledging the contribution to Italian noir of 1970s cinematic thrillers, he neglects to analyse their visual elements. Orio Caldiron traces a history of the Italian cinematic *giallo*, acknowledging influences from France and American noir and gangster films.[2] His consideration of noir in 1950s melodramas, comic books, auteur cinema, and the spy genre, emphasises the dual strategies of using the *giallo* format of the investigation to explore aspects of Italian society, and the creative use of Italian landscape and architecture. However, he stops at the 1970s conspiracy thrillers, without teasing out a full definition of Italian film noir.

Jean Gili sees the *giallo* in terms of a field, covering many genres, whose flexible conventions enable Italian filmmakers to explore dark undercurrents in Italian society, which enables him to explain why some films are fully noir and others are merely crime fiction.[3] Massimo Sebastiani and Mario Sesti consider the hypercodability of crime fiction as the symbolic work of texts to restore order and stress the emotional investment of the reader/spectator.[4] Through their brief analyses of Italian crime films (a minority among the 500 films studied), emerges an implicit sense that Italian film noirs combine both visual excess and realism of place and period as indicators of the psychic investment and difficulty of the task of making sense of reasons behind criminal events, most of which mirror real events in contemporary Italy.

Interest in real events explains the prevalence of the journalistic enquiry as a narrative mode, reflecting 'the impossibility of attributing an incontrovertible and widely accepted notion of truth to historical events'.[5] In recent years the journalistic enquiry, rather than institutional pronouncements, has been unique in offering a plausible explanation of mysteries. Italian journalism has spawned the useful term, *dietrologia*, that is, the science of finding out what lies behind (*dietro*) events. But the writer Carlo Lucarelli perhaps suggests the key to a definition of Italian film noir in its ability to free itself from Anglo-Saxon models and to engage 'with a complex, mysterious and deeply irrational Italian reality, using a fruitful mix of cynicism and rage', that is, a combination of lucid intellectual analysis and strong emotion.[6]

Italian critics have been discussing these problems for at least twenty years, without coming to any firm definitions of Italian film noir. The main stumbling blocks to coherent definitions appear to be the simultaneous presence of visual excess and fantasy and the conventions of realist cinema. Recent work on trauma theory in the field of film studies offers helpful interpretive structures. As Susannah Radstone has argued, trauma theory is less useful as a term that 'refers' to a catastrophic event, than 'to the revised understandings of referentiality it prompts'.[7] This is especially relevant in the case of Italian cinema with its constant references to the 'real' world of Italian politics or social life. The Italian film industry's aping of successful projects in films with a fraction of the usual budget inevitably led to a high level of pastiche, parody and ironic quoting of the original. This phenomenon to a large extent explains why Italian film genres are such hybrids, and why elements considered to be characteristic of postmodernism are present from the 1950s onwards. However, as with Irish cinema, the relentless pull of referentiality to an exterior context is an indication of the psychic investment in the engagement with contemporary history. There is too much at stake not to attempt to make sense of everyday reality. This chapter will, therefore, take the view that noir conventions are used so widely that they constitute an intellectual and creative choice, rather than a genre. Noir elements are used to indicate dissatisfaction with official versions of events, and/or to evoke a dysfunctional world. This chapter will consider the development and some different manifestations of Italian noir in the context of the Italian film industry and Italian society.

Antecedents and influences

From very early on genres have been important commercially to Italian cinema, codes and conventions being established in the pre-sound era, drawing on previous cultural traditions such as the *commedia dell'arte*, epic, melodrama and opera. The prestige and success of French cinema also exerted an influence, resulting in Lumière-type productions, and in attempts to copy the *feuilleton*. The most successful attempt to establish the serial form was that of the actor/director Emilio Ghione. Gian Piero Brunetta suggests that, with his creation of the character of Za-la-Mort, Ghione attempted to combine various influences from detective fiction and the cinema such as Fantomas and Rocambole, Judex and Arsène Lupin. Ghione's strategy allowed him to use the investigative format and the figure of a transgressive hero, the *apache*, as keys to a darker world. These figures did not subvert established order but represented a refusal of the more sensational injustices of the law or social organisation.[8]

The injustices meted out by the forces of law and order, or of institutions of state or church are precisely those identified by the political and cultural commentator Antonio Gramsci as elements of popular ideology, the popularity of detective stories being a response to feelings of anxiety engendered by a sense of powerlessness, a general loss of religious faith and the narrowing of opportunities for adventure.[9] Interestingly, Brunetta mentions the lack of realism in the story world of Ghione's films, whose fantastic elements derive from the *feuilleton* tradition. Za-la-Mort is a criminal hero with a faithful female accomplice, Za-la-Vie, and the wrongs which they seek to redress are always excessive. Ghione couples excess with the use of working class exteriors in which sunlight 'has a corrosive force, giving the most poverty-stricken and socially backward image of Italy in all of silent cinema'.[10] Later comic-book heroes such as Diabolik draw on these elements and the creative use of intense light and the potential of the Italian environment is exploited with great flair in Italian noir.

The writing of detective fiction received a boost during the *ventennio nero* (the black twenty years, 1922–1944) when Mussolini initially encouraged crime literature, not perceiving the irony of doing so under a regime which maintained the fiction that crime did not exist in fascist Italy. Another irony lies in the fact that American gangster films were freely imported into Italy on the basis that they showed the decadence of US society and values of rampant individualism foreign to the corporate fascist state. Mussolini was astute enough to realise that 'black shirt cinema' would not be to his advantage so that the film industry was never under tight control.[11] However, the fact that gangster society in most of these American films of the 1930s was of Italian origin was not lost on either the viewing public or those who subsequently became filmmakers. Gili states that some detective films were made in the fascist period, but that these were mostly very anodyne affairs.[12] British cinema was despised for being in the hands of Jews, and French cinema for being decadent but Argentieri's description of debates in film journals about the moral worth of films by Renoir, Carné and Duvivier indicate that films such as *Le Quai des brumes* (1938) were in circulation.[13] American films continued to be imported into Italy until 1942, when the supply dried up, although some films captured in North Africa were analysed with great interest within the Centro Sperimentale di Cinematografia, the film school founded by Mussolini.

In the 1930s American writers such as Melville, Dos Passos,

Faulkner and Poe, fascinated intellectuals, their raw vitality and realism contrasting, as Donald Heiney has explored, with the 'cultural autarchy' of official fascist aims to create 'art and literature totally free from foreign influences'.[14]

Precursors and *Ossessione*

1930s American literature influenced Italian filmmakers as well as writers.[15] Luchino Visconti's *Ossessione*, made in 1942, was very different from other dramas of its time and is hailed both as a precursor of neo-realism, and as an early example of film noir. Although these categories seem on the surface to be mutually exclusive, they do in fact constitute the defining characteristics of Italian noir. The film was based on James M. Cain's novel *The Postman Always Rings Twice*, and, as interpreted by Visconti, is the story of adulterous passion on the Po delta.[16] Far from there being no interference by the director in the depiction of the reality of the Po marshes and some of its inhabitants, *Ossessione* shares with later neo-realist films quite careful choices of sets, locale and framings. Visconti is concerned to show his characters in their social context, so that their actions are to some extent explained, and always contextualised. Thus the opening sequences of the film contain many long shots showing characters acting and reacting in their environment, and is particularly marked by the use of the crane long shots. Early close-ups (and there are very few in the film) are used deliberately to suggest the immediate sexual attraction between Gino (Massimo Girotti) and Giovanna (Clara Calamai). Our gaze is drawn to focus on them both by the framing and, unusually, the camera lingers on Gino and his physical presence as much as Giovanna's. The editing is varied, but there is more use of the long take, a feature of European cinema, where the camera follows a protagonist as he/she moves, rather than cutting to speed up the action. Location shooting in *Ossessione* gives a sense of geographic realism, the high-angle shots from the road conveying a sense of the monotony of the environment and the stifling containment of the trattoria run by Giovanna's husband. Shots through doors and into cramped rooms stress how characters are bounded and trapped by their environment. The diegetic world contains a young drifter, a woman who explains her marriage to a fat, older man as an escape from unemployment, poverty and 'getting men to buy me dinner'. When Gino runs away from Giovanna to the port of Ferrara, he meets a young dancer who may be involved in prostitution, and stays with the sexually ambiguous Spagnolo. This is a dysfunctional world of privations, of people forced to the margins of society in order to survive, where the precarious equilibrium of 'normal' life is shaken by the arrival of strangers, or overwhelming sexual attraction. On its release in June 1943 it was severely criticised by the fascist press for its portrayal of adultery, amorality, sexual excess and murder and had a limited distribution. *Ossessione* was not more influential because, two months later, political events and the Allied invasion dominated national life.

The Italian pictorial heritage

Detailed examination of the links between painting and Italian film noir is beyond the scope of this chapter. However, since the drawing of attention to Italian landscapes and cityscapes and the use of spectacular images has already been identified as important, this section will briefly consider the pictorial and spatial elements drawn on by Italian film noir. The *mise-en-scène* of Italian films exploits the possibilities of the shape and appearance of public spaces in cities and towns, the environment being profoundly emblematic of the ideas of community and society which organised the lives of those who used them.

John White's analyses of architectural structures in hundreds of paintings and frescoes from antiquity to the Renaissance in Italy show that artists delighted in the artistic possibilities of the recreation of space, but then had difficulties in harmonising the depiction of realistic space with the demands of the visual plane of the story.[17] Strongly stressed orthogonals lead the eye into Renaissance compositions, creating a strong impression of spatial depth. White suggests that one of the techniques developed to arrest the apparent movement through the surface into depth was asymmetry, another the repetition of diagonals because both are 'more likely to destroy the spontaneous and complete acceptance of illusion'. Diagonal cinematic compositions can simultaneously indicate the presence of a real world constituted in deep space and at the same time, put a brake on the realism effect. Cinema can draw on additional, subtle brakes on realism, such as figure movement and camera movement. Manipulation of the perspectival systems is, therefore, one way of controlling both the impression of realism and the attention of the spectator. Italian film noir draws both on the realist pictorial heritage and the creative use of asymmetry.

The use of intense light contrasts, *chiaroscuro*, is a feature particularly of Italian baroque painting, which combined the use of illusionistic detail with figural construction designed to both lead the eye to significant elements and enhance the dramatic and emotional impact. Furthermore, the development of still photography and electric light encouraged young Italian artists at the beginning of the twentieth century to return to experiment with the depiction of light in order to express the modern world. Strong shadows on faces and buildings are features of the paintings of Futurist artists and the metaphysical paintings of Giorgio De Chirico. Mario Sironi's paintings of the late teens and 1920s are particularly interesting for their stark depiction of city peripheries – factories, railway lines, stark modern buildings – and for his use of insistent diagonal compositions to express feelings of solitude and urban alienation.

The flexibility of the melodramatic form

Dramatic visual compositions in Italian film noir find their counterpart in the use of melodrama in the sense of heightened and hyperbolic drama where personal issues are made to stand for social uncertainty. Peter Brooks' contention that melodrama comes into being 'in a world where the traditional imperatives of truth and ethics have been violently thrown into question, yet where the promulgation of truth and ethics, their instauration as a way of life, is of immediate, daily, political concern' offers an immediate insight into the usefulness of this form for mainstream cinema.[18] Brooks describes the narrator figure of melodrama as 'pressuring the surface of reality in order to make it yield the full, true terms of his story', which both accords with the display of doubts and the use of the investigative form in film noir, and with the use of spectacular *mise-en-scène*.[19]

Italian social and political films have frequent recourse to the codes and conventions of melodrama, within the framework of realism, because of the need to both symbolise and to make references to an actual world. An emotional response is necessary in order that the audience is fully persuaded of the truth of the world depicted. Film noir dramatises discontent with the present in the form of the excavation of the past, characterised by Marcia Landy as a search for secrets, which will not only enable a context to be set, but will also provide 'a means of regarding the past affectively in relation to the present'.[20]

Melodrama is usually considered to flourish in times of great social change, and to provide, through intensity of emotional involvement, the opportunity to rehearse safely and work through new ways of acting and being in the world, such as when war had speeded up the pace of modernisation and had mobilised and moved sectors of the population from their traditional homes. For women particularly, the angels or mothers stereotypes of fascist ideology must have been directly at odds with the lived experience of working and fending for the family in wartime.

Neorealismo nero

In September 1943 the German invaders ordered all the equipment and personnel of the Cinecittà studios to be transported north to a branch studio in Venice where they would be at the service of the fascist Republic of Salò, thus dividing Italy and Italian film production until April 1945. The painfully slow Allied invasion of Italy started in Sicily in 1943; Rome was liberated in 1944. Bombing had destroyed many cinemas in central northern Italy but Brunetta records that 5,000 cinemas were still active and were spruced up towards the end of 1945 so that American films, distributed by the PWB (Psychological Warfare Branch) could be shown.[21] The film industry very rapidly re-established itself, however, and from 1946 onwards neo-realist films were not only a minority in each year's Italian production, but also constituted a tiny proportion of the films people actually paid to see in the cinema. Italian filmmakers pressured the government for protection from American competition resulting in 1947 legislation known as the 'dubbing tax', the net result of which was that characters in all American films projected in Italy were voiced in Roman-accented Italian.[22] If British audiences flocked to American films because the actors' accents connoted a modernity and classlessness that contrasted to the clipped accents of British actors, then Italian audiences experienced American screen characters without the barrier of subtitles as both like and unlike at the same time. The Roman accent was deemed appropriate for big city stories.

On the positive side, there was an enormous sense of freedom and release in the late 1940s, and a desire on the part of filmmakers opposed to fascist ideas to record the turmoil of this period of Italian history. At this time there is a very small subgenre of neo-realism called *neorealismo nero* (black neo-realism) which dealt with social problems in a very melodramatic way. One of the best-known, *Il bandito* (*The Bandit*, Alberto Lattuada, 1946) deals with the problem of returning Italian soldiers. The gradual return to Italy of detainees from Germany, concentration camp survivors from Eastern Europe, and thousands of former soldiers from Russia, North Africa, Greece, coupled with the return to the cities of ordinary people who had fled into the countryside to avoid the fighting meant that a largely static and settled population had been shaken up, dispersed, and its ties to family and home (*paese*) severed. As a result, before the Marshall plan swung into effect, there was widespread unemployment, poverty, social and familial disruption and, not least, the questioning of traditionally held beliefs about social and gender hierarchies, about politics. These things were within the lived experience of all strata of Italian society.

The excesses of popular film melodramas indicated the difficulty of reconciling traditional Italian stories, based on a certain understanding of social and gender relations, and the lived experience of the world outside the cinema, which all neo-realist artists sought to engage with. It is not surprising that, in this period of 'supervised freedom', popular cinema provided an outlet for expressions of a desire for change and freedom.[23] The Italian film industry in this period could, for the most part, only express desires for changes in social and sexual mores in coded form. Ernesto the bandit (Amedeo Nazzari) is desperately attached to traditional values, such as protecting the family and looking after the family's honour and name, which were being called into question in the aftermath of war. He is in fact emblematic of an institutional crisis, the destruction of the family and moral turpitude of family members (male and female) representing the destruction of the nation. It has been suggested that former soldiers were an inconvenient reminder of the fascist regime, and that mistreating those who had fought far away, with the Germans, allowed Italians to deflect their own sense of guilt away from themselves.[24] A visual trope, which recurs in other noirs, is that of the staircase, which represents a boundary zone. Ernesto turns to criminality after his discovery that his sister is a prostitute and his killing of the man who shoots her, the whole sequence taking place on a dark and dirty staircase.

Il bandito is also emblematic of other tensions associated with desires in the population not to return to coercive social, political and gender relations, and it is significant that Nazzari plays many outsiders in his films between 1946 and 1949. His co-star in *Il bandito* is Anna Magnani, an actress with a great emotional range and the persona of the woman of the people, strong and sure of herself. The narratives of Magnani's post-war films indicate difficulties in reconciling strongly assertive female characters with traditional narratives. Magnani's emotionality is metonymic of the sufferings of women in the period of post-war chaos and the general desire for something different. She occupies as much screen space, and as many close-ups as Nazzari, in this film but her role as gangster's moll, Lydia, indicates a subordinate position with respect to Nazzari which is unresolved narratively. Ernesto and Lydia quarrel when she ridicules his postcard from his niece, Rosetta, and he humiliates her by throwing his drink in her face. Lydia betrays him to the police; Ernesto dies in a hail of gunfire trying to reach Rosetta's family's farm, and the final sequence shows Lydia, clothed in furs and with a smug expression on her face, boarding a train – unpunished. *Il bandito* employs the high contrast lighting and stressed camera angles of Hollywood cinema. Interior shots of Lydia's environment are reminiscent of 1930s gangster films, as are her satin housecoats and feather boas, but exterior shots predominate which draw attention to the reality of run-down, dirty staircases in damaged houses and streets, to urban poverty. Criminality and alien values are associated with the urban environment.

Two examples of *neorealismo nero*, Giorgio Ferroni's *Tombolo paradiso nero* (*Tombolo, Black Paradise*, 1947) and Lattuada's *Senza pietà* (*Without Pity*, 1948) were both set in the port of Livorno (Leghorn), 'the debarkation point for American army supplies and for this reason a centre of black-marketeering and prostitution'.[25] *Senza Pietà*, scripted by Federico Fellini and Tullio Pinelli, gives a remarkable picture of the violence of the time. Livorno is depicted as dominated by Pierluigi, a sinister racketeer who controls the port, siphons off shipments, robs convoys, corrupts American Army personnel and controls prostitution. He is played by Folco Lulli as a pale, etiolated figure in a white suit and hat, a man without pity who condemns others to death with a soft voice.[26] Pawns in his game are Marcella (Giulietta Masina) and the heroine, Angela (Carla del Poggio), both of whom end up as prostitutes and have relationships with black soldiers. Marcella uses her lover to get money to buy a passage to a better life in the USA. Angela meets Jerry (John Kitzmiller) when she saves his life after gangsters ambush her train, and their relationship starts when he takes her to a café and buys her something to eat. He falls in love with her, but his attempts to steal money for their journey to America fail. During his imprisonment, she becomes a prostitute because, as Pierluigi remarks 'she's pretty and she has no money'. In their attempt to steal from the gangsters, the lovers are caught outside a church. Angela is shot as she tries to protect Jerry, and he drives his truck over a cliff. Although Lattuada denied having a left-wing agenda, *Senza pietà* can be read as a denunciation both of the corrupt nature of the bourgeoisie and as a metaphor for the corruption of materialism and alien values. On the side of the villains are Pierluigi, his business associate, the fat, elderly, racist Argentinian gangster, and the racist, white American military police. Black soldiers are 'just like us' according to Marcella, lower class people denied a future.

Many of Pietro Germi's films contain noir visual elements as they explore the effects of social change. The most overtly influenced by American style is *Gioventù perduta* (*Lost Youth*, 1949), full of shadows and inky black streets in which a gang of young delinquents, led by student Stefano (Jacques Sernas), commit a number of violent armed robberies. Stefano, the son of a middle-class university professor, is represented as excessively cold-blooded. His heart-shaped face and fair hair are lit to stress his lack of expression and glacial beauty, echoed in the perfection of the fit of his light suit and silk tie. His motive is money and there is excess in the whims with which he stakes and loses vast wads of money in the gambling club, in the gaudiness of the gold bracelets which he gives to the club's singer, Inès, and in his murder of his childhood friend, Maria, to prevent her betraying him. As the police inspector says, 'these are respectable people who would shoot their mothers for money'. There is a suggestion that the war changed Stefano in some nebulous and unexplained way but his war is implicitly contrasted to that of Marcello (Massimo Girotti), the detective who pursues him – and who falls in love with Stefano's sister, Luisa (Carla Del Poggio) – who enrols late at the university because he was in the Army, and then North Africa. Two contrasting spatial paradigms are used in the film. The staircase with its ornate baroque ironwork is used as a boundary zone between the domestic spaces downstairs in the family home, filled with parents and siblings, and Stefano's room full of dark shadows and hidden guns upstairs. There are a number of beautifully composed, extreme high angle long shots of the modernist architecture of the university, representing the rational world of learning and knowledge. The graphic patterns of the regular panes of glass in the huge windows dwarf and contain the people within. This architecture contrasts with the inky darkness of city streets where Stefano's robberies take place, and the classical architecture of the police station where Marcello works. An uneasiness with modernity is being indicated.

Whereas the election of the Labour Party in Britain in 1945 expressed the hopes of the mass of the population for social change, in Italy the Christian Democrats won a key victory in the April 1948 elections, and absorbed many right-wing elements into their party. Through endless coalition governments, this party dominated political life until the fall of the First Republic in 1992. Although there was an opening up to centre-left coalitions at the end of the 1950s and, in the wake of the events of 1968, greater presence of left-wing political appointees to head public bodies, what marks Italian society from the period of post-war reconstruction onwards is a sense that power is wielded by unelected sections of the population, be they mafia-like criminal organisations, or socially or politically elite classes. Ginsborg suggests that the Christian Democrats' 'dark side' should not be underestimated, that is, the party's arrangement of the affairs of state to its own benefit, through client relationships 'which recognized no clear laws or limits, no boundaries to possible alliances forged in the name of power, money or votes'.[27] It is therefore the constant presence of unexplained events, massacres, spectacular crimes, scandals for which no rational explanation is found, and no-one punished, that provides such a fertile ground in which the noir thrives. The political situation and feelings of powerlessness, either in being able to influence events, or having one's views represented, can therefore be considered as a reason for the pervasive use of noir elements. The codes and conventions of noir could be adapted to the Italian style in order to allude to those responsible for crimes, or to work through social preoccupations.

Film noir style and auteur cinema

French noir style, particularly in portraits of doomed lovers in a corrupt society, is considered to have influenced films from *Senza pietà* to early films of Antonioni, who had worked as an assistant to Marcel Carné. *I vinti* (*The Vanquished*, 1952) and *Cronaca di un amore* (*Story of a Love Affair*, 1950) are full of moody atmosphere due in part to their evocation of desolate landscapes, and their structure which progressively dropped snippets of information into increasingly informative sequences. The investigation of *Cronaca di un amore* is set in motion by a jealous husband who wants information about his wife's past life. The detective's questions bring Paola (Lucía Bosé) back into contact with her former lover, Guido (Massimo Girotti), and uncovers the death of Guido's former girlfriend which they were guilty of not preventing. They start an affair and plot Paola's husband's death. Paola is a typical film noir heroine in that she constitutes the problem to be investigated. However, as Lesley Caldwell points out, Paola resembles the heroines of American film noir in that her beauty is often the focus of the look of other characters, but differs in being 'prey to terror and a persecutory guilt'.[28] Costumes emphasize Paola's sexuality and her position as a commodity which has been exchanged for money. The fur-trimmed sleeves of her negligees limit her movements; she wears a succession of spectacular, figure-hugging evening dresses of shimmering fabrics, and equally spectacular furs.

Paola's restless movements and neurotic terrors suggest her insecurity at moving into a higher social class. However, while the detective's investigation provides Paola's husband, Enrico, with evidence of her guilty affair, the investigative structure of the film reveals the bleak reality of the lifestyle of the Milanese upper classes, their banal conversations and pointless rituals. Whereas prostitute figures in Italian films set in lower-class milieux in the 1940s indicated a profound unease with rapid social change and the materialistic nature of American consumer culture, Antonioni chose to set his films among the middle classes, so that the figure of the woman who uses her sexuality to move up a class indicates the position of a nation which is losing its integrity in subscribing to economic prosperity. Elements of American film noir style, such as shadows over faces, strong shadows on interior walls, night-time streets, plangent jazz bassoon, are therefore used as the vehicle of the metaphoric transfer. What distinguishes this film as Italian is the creative use of the graphic and expressive possibilities of architecture and landscape. The lovers meet in dark streets, anonymous, modernist buildings or flat spaces, where compositions of insistent, asymmetrical straight lines or wide-angle extreme long shots suggest disturbance and alienation. Two, 180–degree tracking shots in the scene where the lovers plot the death of Paola's husband display the black, crossed struts of the bridge over the motorway, a graphic indication that they are going nowhere.

Subsequently, Antonioni used noir elements most effectively in *Blow-up* (1966), in which a photographer, Thomas (David Hemmings) investigates a (literal) *femme fatale* (Vanessa Redgrave) in 'Swinging London'. In his darkroom, significantly shot in sulphurous yellow, Thomas attempts to investigate reality, to fix and control it by obsessively blowing up detail after detail. *Blow-up*'s world is noir in that it is revealed as one of moral ambiguity, where the photographer/investigator exploits everyone around him, homeless men, supermodels, teenage girls. In Thomas's portrayal of crude gender and cultural power exercised by a newly ascendant class, Antonioni suggests that social turmoil masks a continuity of patriarchal relationships. Similarly, a noir structure and visual excess in *Professione: reporter* (*The Passenger*, 1975) are used to investigate questions of individual and collective identity and responsibility, the individual standing for the global.

At the top end of the market, noir conventions were used with great visual flair by art cinema directors as a shorthand which indicated both a socially dysfunctional world and the presence of the *auteur* in spectacular images. The reflection of the spiral staircase in the enor-

mous water cistern in Visconti's *Vaghe stelle dell'orsa* (*Sandra*, 1965);
the final scene in the dance hall in Bertolucci's *La commare secca* (*The
Grim Reaper*, 1962); and shots of Neapolitan working-class pool halls
and pelota courts in Rosi's *La sfida* (*The Challenge*, 1958) are examples. All use a mystery (a woman's past, a murder) to investigate a
problematic milieu.

Populist noirs

Antonioni's films were extremely unpopular at the box office and, for
popular expressions of noir in the 1950s and 1960s, we have to go to
mid- to low-budget genre films. With the increase in Italian film
production from 27 films in 1945 to a peak of 294 in 1968, industry
statistics of box office results by genre, geographic area and director
became crucial to identifying the potential success of new projects.[29]
Although directors became associated with a particular type of film,
producers, screenwriters and cinematographers worked across the
industry spectrum, and actors migrated from genres at the end of their
cycle of success to another. Gian Maria Volonté, for example, started
his career in mythological, peplum films, moved to westerns and from
there (like Enrico Maria Salerno and Franco Nero) into thrillers,
becoming a left-wing icon in political and art cinema. It should be no
surprise, therefore, that noir elements, such as dramatic, high-contrast
lighting, shadows, criminal milieux, an atmosphere of doomed lives,
are also present in popular melodramas, particularly those featuring
vendettas, persecution or fateful separations, as if attempting to identify who might be responsible for misfortune or family breakdown.
Renato Castellani's *Nella città l'inferno* (*And the Wild, Wild Women*,
1959) is set in a women's prison and uses the motifs of bars and cages
and noir lighting to explore the lives of the prisoners and why they
might have ended up in prison. Spy films and crime films also
borrowed noir conventions, adapting them to location shooting and
the Italian cityscape.

Italian television got off the ground in the late 1950s and detective
series very early on became a staple. Rai (Italian state television), for
example, produced a series of adaptations of Simenon's Maigret and
Rex Stout's Nero Wolfe stories, recently re-releasing them on video
and DVD. From the late 1950s onwards there was a growth of translations of French *Série Noire* novels and American pulp fiction. From
the early 1960s Italian low-budget films also had an Italian noir source
to draw on. Giorgio Scerbanenco's stories are described as more noir
than *giallo* in that his characters are abusers and the abused; perverse

practices are strongly hinted at, and his detective, Duca Lamberti, is a bitter, cynical former doctor with a past.[50] Their setting is a bleak and ugly Milan of anonymous hotels, waste ground, low-life clubs. Other homegrown authors include Laura Grimaldi and Andrea Camilleri. An important characteristic of Italian publishing is the perennial popularity of the *fumetti*, cheap, paperback comic books on sale at every corner newspaper kiosk and which are read by all social strata. Of contemporary cult *fumetti* some are translations of American noir comics, others, such as *Diabolik*, are Italian. From the 1950s, therefore, Italy possessed a rich and dense noir culture in which several media feed into and off each other.

Film *giallo* and noir horror

In the 1970s a number of low-budget films drawing on these earlier traditions acquired the label, *film giallo*. Many have achieved cult status and are marketed on video with garish illustrations on a yellow background. There is no space here to attempt a detailed discussion of these films beyond mentioning that one of their distinguishing characteristics (which is also visible in more upmarket *gialli* and the horror genre) is their misogyny and noticeable elements of sadism and sadomasochism. Stefano Della Casa has perceptively remarked that, before 1968 and sexual liberation, these low-budget *gialli* films were the staples of early evening cinema slots with a predominantly male audience.[31] In Lucio Fulci's *Non si sevizia un paperino* (*Don't Torture the Duck*, 1972) a slightly unhinged village wise woman is tortured and beaten on suspicion of luring local boys to their death when the perpetrator is actually the local priest. As Mikel Koven has observed, these pulp *gialli* are obsessed with liminal or enclosed spaces and their story worlds typically feature a culture clash, which indicates anxieties about modernity and the pluralism of city life.[32] After the heyday of the *giallo* in the 1970s, the *giallo poliziesco* migrated to television where several long-running series, such as *La piovra* (*Octopus: Power of the Mafia*) and *Inspector Montalban* attest to its continuing popularity.

Noir elements are also present in the Italian horror genre. Riccardo Freda's low-budget films were often shot back to back on sets built for other films, high contrast lighting and areas of shadow making a virtue of necessity. The films of Freda and Mario Bava used film noir conventions to give a gothic edge to tales of mystery and horror. As Freda remarked, 'vampires are around us all the time even if they don't have recognisable teeth ... they're older people who 'feed off' young people, sucking their vital spirit and ideas'.[33] The generational conflict is at the heart of the underlying concerns of Italian noir horror, that is, anxieties about the breakdown of traditional Italian gender power relationships. Italian women got the vote in 1946 and the economic boom of the late 1950s drew them into paid employment, disturbing previously held certainties about women's mental and physical limitations. Antonio Margheriti's *Danza macabra* (1963) and Bava's *La frusta e il corpo* (*The Whip and the Body*, aka *Night Is the Phantom*, 1963) make spectacular use of shadows and architectural features to create worlds in which the focus of horror constantly returns, usually associated with extreme female sexual desire. In *Danza macabra*, Alan takes a bet to stay overnight in a haunted house where he falls under the spell of the darkly beautiful Elizabeth (Barbara Steele), in spite of the fact that she tells him that she has been dead for ten years. Unbalanced and asymmetrical architectural compositions mirror the cycle of increasingly hysterical sexual couplings, and the constant return of Elizabeth's murderous former lover. Alan wins his bet but goes mad in the process, the ultimate metaphor of loss of power. *La frusta e il corpo* uses noir lighting, a colour palette of blues and yellows, visual asymmetry and dramatic excess in a narrative which sets freedom and restraint, duty and desire, in opposition. All the male characters seek to exercise patriarchal power in various degrees, Kurt (Christopher Lee) by whipping his former lover, Nevenka (Daliah Lavi) into sexual submission, the others in traditional marriage arrangements. Nevenka's apparent passivity is as excessive as the murders she is revealed to have committed.

Dario Argento's films up to 1982 are considered to be influenced by film noir and *giallo* conventions in their use of the investigative narrative and depiction of excessively dark and dysfunctional worlds. *Profondo rosso* (*Deep Red*, 1975) is typical in featuring non-detective investigators, Mark David (David Hemmings), a musician, and Gianna Brezzi, a journalist (Daria Nicolodi), and a mad murderer, the elderly Marta (Clara Calamai), an actress who murdered her husband to prevent him sending her to an asylum. The predominant colour tones are grey, black and deep blue, only relieved by deep red tones of frequently spilled blood and gaping, slashed wounds in flesh. The key to the first murder, of the clairvoyant Helga (Macha Méril), lie in an enormous, excessively art deco villa, haunted by a crying child. The *mise-en-scène* dwells on the rococo architectural curlicues and ornamentation, which contrast with the extreme high angle shots of the cold, empty, blue tones of the modern square in which Mark's apartment is situated, with its diner *à la* Hopper. Annalee Newitz locates the

narrative logic of serial killer narratives both in the economic imperatives of (American) capitalism, and in difficulties with traditional
gender roles.[34] In this respect the main female characters are emblematic of aspects of male unease with female emotional competence and
female autonomy. Helga mediates the thoughts of the killer to an audience, making her living out of hyper-intuitiveness. Gianna is a journalist whose intelligent and combative relationship with Mark is that of
an equal. The clue pointing to the haunted house is an article written
by Amanda (Giuliana Calandra). Photographs of the murderer's
youthful film roles as a *femme fatale* indicate that her exchange value
in capitalist terms, is in conflict with her role as a mother.

Male anxieties and pathologies are more overt in *Tenebre*
(*Tenebrae*, 1982), in which an American author, Peter Neil (Anthony
Franciosa)'s visit to Italy is disturbed by a series of murders, the
victims being found with pages of his latest novel stuffed in their
mouth. Graphic knife murders are found to be the work of disturbed
journalist, Cristiano Berti (Gabriele Lavi), but the novelist too is
revealed as a serial killer whose frenzied axe attacks derive from
sexual humiliations revealed by initially unmotivated flashbacks. He
fits Lynn Segal's suggestion that excessive male violence represents a
disavowel of man's feminine side.[35] His luckless fiancée, Jane
(Veronica Lario), has the misfortune to wear similar red shoes and
white dress to the girl in the flashback, and is rewarded by having her
arms cut off in a fountain of blood.[36] In effect, *Tenebre* represents the
limit of the appropriation of film noir by the horror genre in that its
metanarrative level is visible from the title sequence where a voice-off
(that of Dario Argento himself) reads a section from Peter Neil's pulp
horror novel, which effectively explains why the novelist is a serial
killer – killing is a cathartic experience to exorcise an earlier, traumatic
crime. The title of Neil's book is also the title of the film. The scene
where the lesbian journalist, Tilde, aggressively interrogates Neil
about his misogyny, his lack of respect for women, could as easily
apply to Argento. Berti, the incompetent television interviewer and
first killer, photographs his victims, eroticising their dead bodies. In
her study of the relationship between true crime and fictionalised
serial killings, Newitz suggests that the economic dimension is as
important as that of gender in understanding the impetus to kill.[37]
Thus, serial murders represent both the overproduction of late capitalism, and the desire to see oneself mass-produced in media reports. The
former indicates the individual's lack of power in the capitalist system,
and the latter an attempt to re-establish power. Argento's narratives
are mirrored by his own role as director who manufactures multiple

copies of stories of multiple deaths. He has always had production control of his films which, from *L'uccello dalle piume di cristallo* (*The Bird with the Crystal Plumage*, 1970) and *Quattro mosche di veluto grigio* (*Four Flies on Grey Velvet*, 1971) onwards, covered their costs on the Italian market alone. His name and cult status sell his films and other productions and they maintain premium prices when exploited in other media forms.

Argento's iconography as well as his narratives take *giallo* conventions into dark extremes. Both *Profondo rosso* and *Tenebre* contrast limited chromatic tones of modernist streets, regular architecture and interiors, with spaces of excessive decoration and saturated colour. Narrative, emotional and visual excess, complexity of themes and cultural allusions, virtuosity of ideas, *mise-en-scène* and camera work, all indicate the presence of instability, distrust of modernity, and the breakdown of social control of individual behaviour which is a feature both of film noir and neo-baroque texts, characteristics which *film giallo* and noir horror also share with political cinema.

Giallo politico

The most complex and technically significant re-workings of film noir can be seen in the Italian *giallo politico*. These films are most interesting in two periods, the 1970s and the 1990s. The 1970s represent a moment in which the grand metanarratives of class supremacy, of the conservative nature of power relations were being examined in response to a sense that democratic processes had been bypassed to the advantage of one class or social group. The second follows the political crisis of 1992–93 when an enormous void opened up in the Italian political classes following the *tangentopoli* (kickback city) investigations. *Tangentopoli* was the name given to institutionalised corruption in Italian political and civic life in which scales of bribes operated for the award of lucrative contracts or public appointments, payable to politicians or business men, and the collusion of a minority of politicians with the mafia.[38] In both periods, characteristics of the *giallo politico* are noir lighting, visual excess, instability and disruption – disruption expressed as asymmetry as well as narrative disruption.

There are various reasons for the popularity of the *giallo politico* genre in the 1970s, not least the inherent conservatism of the Italian film industry so that political commentary had predominantly to be expressed in genre forms. In the 1970s terrorist crime increased, marked by the 'strategy of tension' so that the ordinary citizen never knew if the far left, or Red Brigades, were behind a massacre or kidnapping, or far right terrorist groups setting up a left-style killing in order to justify their reprisals. Leonardo Sciascia's thrillers were set in this period and provided a fertile source for filmmakers. Conspiracy thrillers usually start with an event, a disruption, which disturbs the impression of normality preferred by the Establishment, and proceed to analyse the causes of the disruptions and the alliances of the powerful which sought to conceal the operation of their influence. The *mise-en-scène* of institutional space in exterior and interior sets and locations, and how figures act and exercise power within those spaces make social relationships visible. The very European use of the mobile camera and intra-sequence long take is also used as a tool to link diegetic events firmly to the world of contemporary Italy.

Italy is exceptionally rich architecturally so that the range of architectural paradigms chosen as expressive of institutional practices or values is particularly significant. Francesco Maselli's *Il sospetto* (*Suspicion*, 1975), set between Paris and Turin, provides one paradigm in its use of classical architecture. The protagonist, Emilio (Gian Maria Volonté), is an expatriate communist militant who is sent to Turin in 1934 in order to identify a spy. The film repeatedly makes use of long shots of classical pedimented windows, arches in cloister-like galleries and high angle long shots in grey, black and muted tones. The overall impression is of impenetrability. The protagonist constantly looks around, monitoring his environment, trying to penetrate his surroundings to find information. He fails in his quest, becoming one of the sacrificial activists of the communist party (which is represented as equally coercive and inhuman as fascism), when he is arrested and interrogated by OVRA, the fascist Security Police. The interrogator reveals that Emilio was himself 'penetrated', brainwashed and planted as a spy so that he would identify communist contacts in Turin. The *mise-en-scène* thus connects the two metaregimes of communism and fascism in their denial of the importance of the freedom of the individual.

Although classical architecture provides a recurring metaphor for an ordered, stable, coercive system of values, by far the most commonly evoked architectural style in 1970s conspiracy thrillers is that of the 1960s. *Indagine su un cittadino al di sopra di ogni sospetto* (*Investigation of a Citizen Above Suspicion*, Elio Petri, 1970) is one of the most interesting films of the 1970s *giallo politico*. It is almost entirely set in Rome, but chooses to ignore the better known or parliamentary monuments of the city, preferring instead long shots of grey, concrete or stone-faced modernist office blocks in the 1960s 'brutalist' style, all interplay of planes and textures, and sharp angles. Buildings

are differentiated from one another by their institutional names above
the main doors, but exteriors are uncommunicative of their function
and we only learn more about the institutions which operate within by
following the protagonist, a high-ranking policeman, il Dottore, into
the interiors. In this film we know from the very beginning that the
policeman has murdered his mistress on the day of his promotion from
Head of the Homicide section to Head of the Political section of the
police force. The film's investigation is, therefore, into the nature of
the institution of the police force through the actions of this emblematic character, and is a metaphysical exploration of the nature of
justice and power. The actions of il Dottore therefore guide the audience to another level of meaning, inviting the conclusion that 'truth'
does not necessarily reside in what seems regular, functional and open
to explanation. Modernism's claim to honesty and rationality is represented, at a metaphorical level, both as the insufficiency of modernity
to explain the complexity of the present situation, and as a sham in its
claim to truth. The forceful, violent gestures and speech of il Dottore
coerce his subordinates so that the kinetic elements add another level
of meaning, suggesting how male power provides a model for the
activity of political power.

Francesco Rosi's *Il caso Mattei* (*The Mattei Affair*, 1972), *Lucky
Luciano* (1973), *Cadaveri eccellenti* (*Illustrious Corpses*, 1975) are
generally regarded as critical realism, but like his earlier film investigating the death of the Sicilian bandit, *Salvatore Giuliano* (1961), are
also examples of the *giallo politico*. They contain many set pieces of
showy and spectacular *mise-en-scène*, and the foregrounding of architectural space in wide-angle long shots. They also have recourse to
modernist architecture and institutional spaces, which are represented
as similarly grey and uncommunicative, but also to the excesses and
decorative aspects of baroque buildings with stressed camera angles
and by strongly diagonal spatial compositions.[39] From film to film,
Rosi employs the investigative mode in order to explore the nature of
power relationships in Italian society. The disruptions which provoke
the investigations are exceptional events, violence or death, which
disturb the carefully constructed and maintained impression of
normality preferred by those in power. A baroque visual excess therefore comes to represent the tension between power and order (embodied in classical and modernist architecture), and revolt and disorder.
Internal conflicts are externalised. Omar Calabrese provides a persua-
sive explanation of the conflict of visual styles, defining as neo-
baroque the rejection of stability and a predisposition towards
elements that destabilise part of the system by creating turbulence and

fluctuations within it.[40] In this respect the neo-baroque in Italy is an expression of the postmodern undermining of the grand metanarratives. By foregrounding disruption and excess, doubt and ambiguity, value is given to other versions of social organization.

In effect, what is being made visual is the tension between two versions of politics or ideology. Fluidity, ambiguity, doubts, excess expressed visually or in monstrous characters or in the performance of violence, are all elements of the template of film noir, and can also be used by political filmmakers as techniques to visualise the tension between one system which aims to present itself as simple, natural and uncontroversial, and another which seeks to discredit it and reveal its inner workings and true nature.

A feature of all these films is the striking visual beauty of representations of the interiors and exteriors of buildings. The framing of the buildings and the lens used emphasise their monumentality, volumes and architectural planes. Thus, in *Cadaveri eccellenti*, shafts of light illuminate Judge Varga as he walks towards camera in the crypt of the baroque church, so that he appears to be walking through progressively larger frames, a visual representation of *mise-en-abîme* and the layering of versions of the truth. Varga's murder is the disruption which starts the investigation, and the ramifications of that investigation are immediately indicated in the funeral sequence. The eulogy and the representation of the powerful hierarchies (legal and illegal) who are massed within the enormous baroque cathedral for his funeral make links to other men of power who commissioned such showy and flamboyant art to celebrate the power of the church.

Architectural shots have different functions within the narrative of Rosi's films. In one way they form part of the cultural or reference

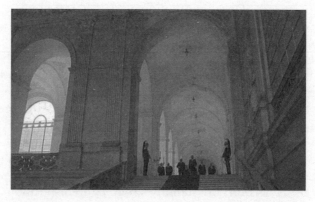

9 *Cadaveri eccelenti* (*Illustrious Corpses*, Francesco Rosi, 1975).

code of the film and relate to the audience's historical and artistic knowledge of Italy. In another way, Rosi's intention is to liberate the text from being too narrowly realist through this access to the poetic and excessive possibilities of film.[41] What Rosi calls a metaphysical dimension, and elsewhere heightened realism, has more in common with early twentieth-century *pittura metafisica*.[42] In tracing the origins of De Chirico's metaphysical painting, Robert Hughes defines it as 'a question of mood, the sense of a reality drenched in human emotion, almost pulpy with memory'.[43] This description is useful in teasing out the function of these architectural shots and how they work. These instances of heightened reality, linked to architectural space, constitute moments of excess. Calabrese suggests that, in postmodern, neo-baroque works, order and disorder, classical and baroque, coexist as signifying systems.[44] So, in these thrillers, there is an oscillation between simplicity and complexity as the disruptions disturb the equilibrium, the simple explanation. We move towards understanding in small steps, hypotactically, until the big picture is visible.

One of the most powerful tropes, for making the big picture visible, and one which occurs centrally in Rosi's *Cadaveri eccellenti* and Petri's *Indagine su un cittadino al di sopra di ogni sospetto*, is that of the panopticon. Foucault writes about prisons being designed so that the prison population (the prison heterotopia) can be under surveillance at every moment.[45] In these two films we have visual representations of the panopticon suggesting a hidden and all-powerful control of society. Rosi's panopticon is the laboratory of the head of the political police, to which the honest detective, Rogas (Lino Ventura) is assigned. Rogas' looks and questioning glances motivate the camera's showing of how the panopticon works. The scale of surveillance is indicated via repetition of television screens and the burble of tape recordings, evoking other diegetic spaces.

In Petri's film, the Political Police also operate a panopticon, with banks of tape recorders, conducting a surveillance of the unwitting citizens of Rome. The panopticon is the revelation of the ultimate level of control of the urban population, control which is unsanctioned and therefore profoundly undemocratic. The figure of the panopticon represents the intrusion into the text of the ultimate, metadiscursive, level of meaning. It makes plain how power is exercised, and the ideology of those who use it.

Social elites are targeted in a lighter vein in *La donna della Domenica* (*Sunday Woman*, Luigi Comencini, 1975) as Commissario Santamaria (Marcello Mastroianni)'s investigation of sordid architect Garrone takes him into upper class Turin society. On the way he discovers their predilection for kitsch art (a major exhibition features an enormous painting of a man having sex with a large swan) and bizarre murder weapons (a huge stone penis, manufactured with great pride in the workshop of the local stonemason). Night shooting, shadows and chases uncover a louche, amoral society of extreme wealth, sexual pluralism, exploitation and prostitution which the detective has to handle with 'silken hands in velvet gloves'.

New hero figures for the *anni di piombo*

Up to the 1970s, Italian film noir featured investigators who were not usually members of the police force, the usual reason given being the disregard in which members of the public security forces were traditionally held. The activities of the mafia from the 1960s onwards, and terrorists from the late 1970s found a response in fictional films in heroes who were honest policemen or magistrates. The *anni di piombo*, 'the years of the bullet', were profoundly disturbing to all strata of society. Many noir films of this period, such as Stefano Vanzina's *La polizia ringrazia* (*The Police Are Grateful*, 1972) display the conservative reaction of endorsing greater powers to the police.

The 1980s provided further events to persuade Italian writers, filmmakers, journalists and critics that they were living in a film noir. Prime Minister Aldo Moro was kidnapped and murdered by the Red Brigades in 1978 at a time when he was seeking closer relations between Christian Democrats and communists. Ginsborg describes how the webs of corruption gradually unravelled, culminating in the arrests of a whole raft of the political and business classes in 1992–3.[46] Investigation of the disgraced banker, Michele Sindona in March 1981 uncovered the membership of the P2 Masonic lodge, which included officers of the secret services, heads of the *carabinieri* and *Guardia di finanza*, the armed services, police, bankers, businessmen and politicians. Subsequently, the banker Roberto Calvi was found hanging under Blackfriars Bridge in London. Investigations of murders during the 'strategy of tension' years uncovered the existence of a hidden armed network called 'Gladio', part of the Italian secret services and linked to the CIA. Italian politicians were widely considered to be corrupt so that the magistrates investigating the *tangentopoli* scandals and links between mafia and politicians had wide support. At one point around 200 Italian MPs were either under investigation or in prison for corruption. A whole new institutional class, that of the magistrature, became available for hero roles. Murders of magistrates such as Giuseppe Falcone, and journalists provided rich subjects for cinema.

It is hardly surprising that these events encouraged an explosion of noir publishing both in new *giallo* collections, new authors such as Carlo Lucarelli, and new *fumetti*. Neo-noir was considered to have arrived.[47]

Social uncertainty and postmodern noir

Roberto Faenza's *L'assassino di poliziotti* (*Copkiller*, 1983) is a postmodern reworking of the noir genre and a fascinating amalgam of American and Italian style. There are quotations from the *Diabolik* comics in the figure of the hooded cop killer, Leo (John Lydon), and from Hitchcock's *Rope* (1948) in the shots of elliptical staircases and the New York skyline behind slatted blinds in the apartment of the corrupt narcotics squad cop, Watts (Harvey Keitel); slatted blinds feature anachronistically in many decors. In spite of the American setting, the use of the intra-sequence long take and the beautifully composed interior long shots are typically Italian. Not only does Faenza use the common trope of the *mise-en-abîme*, in shots down corridors framing doorway after doorway, in order to indicate layers of meaning to be investigated, but saturated yellow tones connote complicity in the *giallo* world. Decors are often divided into two, using the full graphic potential of modernist interiors, their excessive nature a mirror to the personality disorders of the two main characters. Watts has purchased the apartment with the proceeds of corruption, seeking to punish those involved in the drugs trade himself, rather than see them get off on trial. In a paranoid moment he kidnaps Leo, whom he has found taking too great an interest in the apartment, becoming enmeshed in Leo's sadomasochistic games. Watts strives for order and control; the protean Leo, the killer, thrives on disorder.

Una fredda mattina di maggio (*A Cold May Morning*, 1990) is based on an actual assassination of a journalist who stumbles on a terrorist cell. Vottorio Sindoni's highly dramatic film describes the lives of upper-middle-class students who murder the honest journalist because he endangers their plans. The film takes a critical stance towards the terrorists by contrasting the ostentatious wealth of their surroundings with the warm, cluttered domestic interiors of the journalist's home, and the ugliness and cramped home of the naive southern worker, Simone, where his family are all involved in marginal occupations of the black economy. Simone is fascinated by the terrorists' glamour and is a vehicle for ironic contrasts. He is first attracted to Niuska as she hands out leaflets, dressed in 1980s shabby-chic clothes and Palestinian scarf, during a demonstration of 'communists against the black economy'. As events progress, conversations between the terrorists are increasingly couched in the language of the business school. Falk (Matteo to his mother) wants his own faction, invents a grandiose name, and plans events which will consolidate his power. Spectacular wide-angle architectural shots of Turin create an emotional unease as much as the ultra-violent terrorist murders.

Films featuring magistrate heroes in danger of assassination by those they are investigating, constitute a revival of the *giallo politico* in the early 1990s. *Il lungo silenzio* (*The Long Silence*, Margarethe von Trotta, 1993) uses noir visuals to stress the restricted life of a doctor married to a magistrate, only able to travel with a police escort and never be able to open the slatted blinds of her apartment. *La scorta* (*The Escort*, Ricky Tognazzi, 1993), *Il muro di gomma* (*The Rubber Wall*, Marco Risi, 1991), *Il giudice ragazzino* (*The Young Judge*, Alessandro Di Robilant, 1993) and *Un eroe borghese* (*Middle Class Hero*, Michele Placido, 1994) are all examples of this subgenre.

Another interesting investigation by a magistrate reveals that the murderer of the unknown man who fell from his window is, in fact, the magistrate's wife (Valerie Kaprisky). By the end of *La fine è nota* (*The End Is Known*, Cristina Comencini, 1993) the magistrate has discovered not only the reality of southern Italian poverty and under-development, but also the falseness of his relationship with his beautiful wife and the emptiness of his perfect home. Her fatal beauty hides total self-absorption and materialism.[48] The *mise-en-scène* includes the flamboyant and spectacular use of saturated yellows, from deep ochres to acid tones, asymmetrical compositions of modernist architecture, sinuous lines of art-deco staircases and *mise-en-abîme* framings of doors and arches. The magistrate figure links two targets, suggesting that the selfishness and materialism of one is implicated in the reduced circumstances of the other.

Carla Apuzzo's *Rose e pistole* (*Roses and Guns*, 1998), featuring two characters called Rosa, is one of an interesting group of films concerned with social breakdown and the problem of Eastern European immigration into Italy. The action is set on the edge of Naples, between the run-down, working-class, industrial Bagnoli area and the Phlegrean Fields (themselves an unstable part of the earth's crust). The low-life, marginalised characters therefore inhabit a border zone and 'work' in the telephone sex industry or armed robbery. The younger Rosa and her partner are trying to leave, to start a new life for the baby they are expecting, but her ex-husband sets a hitman on their trail. The interior spaces through which these characters move are constantly coded as transgressive. In dark booths in a dark apartment, male and female 'hotliners' fake intimacy and the erotic, while filing their nails and reading magazines. A strange mathematics teacher stalks them through their habitats, appropriating a black leather mask from a 'dungeon' equipped with life-sized plastic doll, handcuffs, whips, and so on. The *mise-en-scène* quotes the stressed camera angles, high-contrast lighting, darkness and shadows of American film noir to suggest that characters are trapped in this marginal milieu. The hitman, Bosnia (who is a Serb), is the ultimate metonym for this chaotic, violent, amoral sector of society. His presence links social breakdown in Italy and the extreme violence of the Balkans, connoting fears present in Italian middle-class society at the Balkanisation of the Italian body politic. In the final sequence the camera pans over the beautiful, sunlit, Neapolitan coastline and Mediterranean pines as Rosa's voice-over brings her story up to date as she waits, free and pregnant, for the release of her lover from prison. In illustration of what Slavoj Žižek terms an 'imaginary cartography, which projects onto the real landscape its own shadowy ideological antagonisms', the outstanding beauty of the quintessentially Italian scene represents the choice of idealised national lifestyle and the narrative expulsion of the non-national regarded as aberrant.[49]

Mario Martone's *Teatro di guerra* (1998) uses dark, claustrophobic sets in an attempt to contain violence and disruption. The film follows a group of actors rehearsing Aeschylus's *Seven against Thebes*, which will be performed in Sarajevo. Rehearsals take place in the historic centre of Naples, in the Spagnoli quarter and the action never gets to Sarajevo. Martone's non-depiction of the Bosnian tragedy becomes a metonym for the disintegration of civic life in danger and moral vacuum as life outside the house where they rehearse becomes omnipresent.[50] The precarious and chaotic seep into the theatrical space. Some of the actors miss rehearsals as their outside lives impinge. One actor is drug-dependent and has to be watched. Domestic and street noises intrude from outside.

Noir conventions are again utilised in two stunningly visual recent thrillers, both of which use flamboyance, asymmetry, yellow tones and contrasting visual regimes to construct deep-level discourses about the amorality of materialism and excessive wealth. Liliana Cavani's *Il gioco di Ripley* (*Ripley's Game*, 2002), an adaptation of a Patricia Highsmith novel, contrasts the cluttered domestic and work interiors of the dying picture framer with those of Ripley (John Malkovich) into whose amoral, criminal world he is drawn by the need to provide for his family. The *mise-en-scène* of Ripley's ostentatiously architect-designed house stresses its size and hints at the expense necessary to acquire the furniture and objects within it. Ripley's beautiful partner is a musician, whose harpsichord and the occasional baroque ornamentation and paintings within the house, contrast with the modernist furniture and minimalist spaces associated with Ripley. Cavani endows Ripley's world with considerable complexity. His partner is depicted as dependent on Ripley's presence and encouragement when she performs, but it is left ambiguous whether this reflects a caring trait, or merely another level of calculating control. When Ripley attends her recording session, his reflected figure watches from the recording booth and, in the final scene, the music she plays echoes the camera's soaring through the ornate church interior in its obsessive repetition of musical phrases and curlicues.

Similar noir and *giallo* visuals structure Paolo Sorrentino's stylish *Le conseguenze dell'amore* (*The Consequences of Love*, 2004) whose protagonist, Titta Di Girolamo (Toni Servillo) lives a restricted life in a Swiss hotel, receiving mysterious suitcases full of banknotes, which he deposits regularly in a Swiss bank. From its stupendous opening diagonal long shot of the stark modernist lines of the travelator leading into the bank, the film uses the cold colour tones and orderliness of modernist architecture and bland hotels to suggest that behind order, regularity and luxury lies quite a different reality, reinforced by the number of compositions which start in mirrors or windows. Titta's bleak life is disturbed by his love for Sofia (Olivia Magnani), the young barmaid, visually associated with warmth and decoration. For Sofia he embezzles money from one of the suitcases, and is called to account by the mafia. Nothing is what it seems, or is it? As Titta's minders drive him to the conference centre occupied by his employers, the car passes the neon sign of the Hotel New Europe, and his 'trial' takes place in a conference room dominated by a projected sign announcing 'Hypertrophy of the prostate. Refresher course'!

Television has enabled the evolution of film noir and its survival on cinema screens by financing contemporary productions through pre-sales agreements. These are, however, small-scale productions, exploited rapidly and with a limited shelf life as videos or DVDs. The Italian cinema exhibition sector is dominated by American chains, or by Italian commercial interests such as Berlusconi's Fininvest empire and there are few windows of opportunity for a mid-budget, serious film to recoup most of its production costs. It is significant that much writing about film noir in Italian concentrates with huge enthusiasm on analysing American examples, as if contemporary, Italian *noirs* did not exist. If not an example of cultural cringe, one is forced to the conclusion that contemporary Italian film noirs do not exist for young critics because they simply may not have seen them.

Conclusion

Italian film noir has never been a genre on the French or Anglo-Saxon model. The presence of noir elements in very disparate films can be attributed to the Italian film industry's chase after profitable *filoni*, strands of film themes and subjects which can be copied while public interest lasts, and then abandoned for the next fashion. As we have seen, creative personnel not only work across genres and *filoni*, but also utilise noir elements when subject and time are appropriate. Above all, Italian film noir is politicised, seeking to explore a social or political context whose elements are unclear, or mysterious. A disruption usually starts the investigation which may reveal why a situation exists, rather than who is responsible. The investigation may also solve a mystery, but at the expense of giving form to anxieties about Italian society. *Giallo* conventions can be usefully evoked through the use of saturated yellow tones to indicate the presence of the mysterious. Disruptions, disturbance, anxieties, mysteries typically have a visual counterpart in intense lighting contrasts, dark atmospheres, visual disorder and asymmetry, and visual excess.

Giorgio Gosetti sees noir as still relevant as a training ground for social subjects and narrative style.[51] The constant presence of unexplained mysteries in Italian social, economic and political life has enabled noir to mutate across genres and to refresh itself at regular intervals by finding new targets to be investigated in attempts to make sense of turmoil and change in Italian civil life. This characteristic goes some way towards explaining the lack of many *femmes fatales* in Italian film noir. Between 1948 and 1968, the Censorship Commission and the Catholic Church caused problems for films which projected a pessimistic view of the Italian family. Moreover, Angela Dalle Vacche suggests that Italian patriarchal culture conceptualises the past as the father and the body politic as male. Italian cinema therefore 'employs "homosocial" narratives to represent fathers and sons in history and public life, while pushing mothers toward biology and the private sphere'.[52] Strongly autonomous female characters therefore disturb traditional gender power relationships and, although many women are active in Italian politics and institutions, fictional female bodies do not seem to be able to represent political or social power. Female power therefore becomes a sign that something is amiss, resulting in characters which constitute the disruption which starts an investigation, or transgressive models of femininity (the prostitute or hypersexual woman) which bear the blame for social malaise. In effect, Italian film noirs are male melodramas rehearsing shifting power relationships in Italian society.

As this chapter has indicated, the history of modern Italy has been marked by traumatic events and massive social change, events perceived as beyond individual control and profoundly threatening. Elsaesser suggests that 'If trauma is experienced through its forgetting, its repeated forgetting, then, paradoxically, one of the signs of the presence of trauma is the absence of all signs of it'.[53] The particular characteristics of Italian film noir, disturbing asymmetry, *chiaroscuro* lighting, showy visuals, narrative, kinetic, performative and visual excess, therefore function to draw attention to the presence of events which offend the democratic sensibilities, threats to patriarchal authority, or simple explanations which mask the abuse of power. The foregrounding of referentiality in illusionistic detail, authenticity of place and setting, lend authority to the directors' analyses and, through the realist mode, attempt to control explanations through narrative closure, while the hyperbolic emotionality of many noir films signals the importance of the mysteries and the effort that the texts are making to persuade an audience that their interpretation is the right one. Violent events still erupt through the fabric of social control in Italy, providing sources of endless conjecture and material far stranger than the vibrant fictions of Italian film noir.

Notes

All translations from the Italian are the author's own. I am grateful to the Research Fund of the Faculty of Continuing Education, Birkbeck College, University of London for financial support for this project, to Dr Umberta Brazzini of the Mediateca Regionale Toscana, Florence, and to the staff of the library of the Scuola Nazionale di Cinema, Rome for their assistance.

1   F. Giovannini, *Storia del noir: Dai fantasmi di Edgar Allan Poe al grande cinema di oggi* (Rome: Castelvecchi, 2000), p. 209.
2   O. Caldiron, *Il paradosso dell'autore* (Rome: Bulzoni, 1999), pp. 157–84.
3   J. Gili, 'Dal giallo al nero al politico-poliziesco', in G. Gosetti (ed.), *Le quattro volte del postino: il film giallo italiano: una possibile storia* (Cattolica: Mystfest, 1981), p. 43.
4   M. Sebastiani and M. Sesti, 'Il genere del misterioso e il mistero del genere', in *Delitto per delitto: 500 film polizieschi (detective story, gang-*

sterfilm, noir, thriller, spy story) (Turin: Lindau, 1998), pp. 14–15.

5 M. Fabbri, 'Per ripensare', in M. Fabbri (ed.), *Noir in Festival* (Rome: Noir in Festival, 2000), p. 7.

6 Interview in T. Dozio and C. Oliva, 'Se dieci anni vi sembran pochi … ', in M. Fabbri (ed.), *Noir in Festival* 2000, pp. 104–6.

7 S. Radstone, 'Trauma and Screen Studies: Opening the Debate', *Screen*, 42:2 (Summer 2001), 194.

8 G. P. Brunetta, *Storia del cinema italiano: Il cinema muto 1895–1929* (Rome: Editori Riuniti, 1993), pp. 208–9.

9 A. Gramsci, *Letteratura e vita nazionale* (Rome: Editori Riuniti, 1975), p. 140.

10 Brunetta, *Il cinema muto*, p. 209.

11 M. Argentieri, *Il cinema in guerra: Arte, comunicazione e propaganda in Italia 1940–44* (Rome: Editori Riuniti, 1998), p. 224.

12 J. A. Gili, 'Dal giallo al nero', p. 43. Gili is one of the few critics to speculate on the low number of Italian detective films in the 1930s, attributing it to the huge number of Hollywood films which the public flocked to see. Mervyn Leroy's *Little Caesar* (1930) was, however, banned on the grounds that Edward G. Robinson resembled Mussolini too closely!

13 M. Argentieri, *Il cinema in guerra*, pp. 30–8.

14 D. Heiney, *America in Modern Italian Literature* (New Brunswick: Rutgers University Press, 1964), p. 54.

15 Geoffrey Nowell-Smith considers that Cain's story might have appealed to Visconti precisely because it was American, rather than as a subterfuge to mislead the Fascist censor. G. Nowell-Smith, *Luchino Visconti*, 3rd edn (London: BFI, 2003), pp. 16–17.

16 Henry Bacon reports that Visconti was given a French translation of Cain's *The Postman Always Rings Twice* by Jean Renoir while filming *Une partie de campagne* (1936). H. Bacon, *Visconti: Explorations of Beauty and Decay* (Cambridge: Cambridge University Press, 1998), p. 14.

17 J. White, *The Birth and Rebirth of Pictorial Space*, 3rd edn (London: Faber & Faber, 1987).

18 P. Brooks, *The Melodramatic Imagination* (New York: Columbia University Press, 1985), pp. 13–22.

19 *Ibid.*, p. 2.

20 M. Landy, 'The Use and Abuse of History in Melodrama', paper presented to the BFI *Melodrama* Conference (July 1992).

21 G. P. Brunetta, *Cent'anni di cinema italiano, 2. Dal 1945 ai giorni nostri*, 4th edn (Rome/Bari: Laterza, 2000), pp. 7–11.

22 The politician in charge of this legislation, Giulio Andreotti, used the occasion to censor neo-realist films in particular. Andreotti went on to become six times Christian Democrat Prime Minister, and was tried in Palermo in 1993 for collusion with the Mafia.

23 M. Boneschi, *Poveri ma belli: i nostri anni cinquanta* (Milan: Oscar Mondadori, 1995), pp. 108–9.

24 G. Gubitosi, *Amedeo Nazzari* (Bologna: Il Mulino, 1998), p. 85.

25 R. Armes, *Patterns of Realism* (London: The Tantivy Press, 1971), p. 103.

26 Alberto Farassino notes that Folco Lulli was the perfect villain for *neorealismo nero*, identifying his ability to convey excessive evil, the envy of the dispossessed and a violent sensuality. A. Farassino, 'Folco Lulli, un cattivo per il neorealismo', in *Neorealismo: Cinema italiano 1945–1949* (Turin: E. D. T. Edizioni, 1989), pp. 145–6.

27 P. Ginsborg, *Italy and Its Discontents*, p. 281.

28 L. Caldwell, 'What about Women? Italian Films and Their Concerns', in U. Sieglohr (ed.), *Heroines without Heroes: Reconstructing Female and National Identities in European Cinema, 1945–51* (London: Cassell, 2000), p. 144.

29 L. Quaglietti, *Storia economico-politica del cinema italiano 1945–1980* (Rome: Editori Riuniti, 1980), pp. 245–7.

30 O. Del Buono, 'Il rosa, il nero, il giallo', introduction to G. Scerbanenco, *Milano calibro 9*, 2nd edn (Milan: Garzanti, 1970), pp. 5–12.

31 S. Della Casa, 'L'altra faccia del cinema nero italiano', in M. Fabbri (ed.), *Noir in Festival 1998* (Rome: Fahrenheit 451, 1998), p. 70.

32 M. Koven, 'La dolce morta', paper presented to the European Cinema Research Forum conference, 'Reviewing Space: Space and Place in European Cinema' (April 2003).

33 F. Faldini and G. Fofi, *L'avventurosa storia del cinema italiano raccontata dai suoi protagonisti 1960–1969* (Milan: Feltrinelli, 1981), p. 200.

34 A. Newitz, 'Serial Killers, True Crime and Economic Performance Anxiety', in C. Sharrett (ed.), *Mythologies of Violence in Postmodern Media* (Detroit: Wayne State University Press, 1999), p. 68.

35 L. Segal, *Slow Motion: Changing Masculinities, Changing Men* (New Brunswick: Rutgers University Press, 1990), p. 14.

36 Veronica Lario later became Signora Berlusconi. According to Jean-Baptiste Thoret, her husband is reported to have excised her every scene when *Tenebre* was transmitted on his television channels. In another twist, the girl in the flashback is played by a transsexual actor, Eva Robbins-Roberto Coatti, a fact which would only be known from the secondary text of reviews and articles, and which adds another dimension to the interplay of desire and revulsion in the film. J-B. Thoret, *Dario Argento: Magicien de la peur* (Paris: Cahiers du Cinéma, 2002), p. 153.

37 Newitz, 'Serial Killers', pp. 70–81.

38 See Ginsborg, *Italy and Its Discontents*, Chs 6 and 7.

39 M. Wood, 'Francesco Rosi: Heightened Realism', in J. Boorman and W. Donohue (eds), *Projections 8* (London: Faber & Faber, 1998), p. 285.

40 O. Calabrese, *Neo-Baroque: A Sign of the Times* trans. C. Lambert (New Jersey: Princeton University Press, 1992), p. 25.

41 M. Ciment, *Le dossier Rosi* (Paris: Editions Stock, 1976), pp. 168–9.

42 M. Wood, interview with Francesco Rosi, 28 July 1985.

43 R. Hughes, *The Shock of the New*, 2nd edn (London: Thames & Hudson, 1991), p. 215.
44 Calabrese, *Neo-Baroque*, p. 194.
45 M. Foucault, *Discipline and Punish* trans. A. Sheridan (Harmondsworth: Penguin, 1977), pp. 206–7.
46 See P. Ginsborg, *Italy and Its Discontents*, Chs 5–8.
47 F. Giovannini, *Storia del noir*, pp. 152–68.
48 Italian fashion and interior design have enjoyed immense prestige abroad. Domitilla Calamai has charted the interesting influence of 1940s' film noir style on men's clothing, which then feeds back into American culture in the form of the Armani and Zegna suits worn in television series.
49 S. Žižek, 'You May!', *London Review of Books* (18 March 1999), 3.
50 E. Ghezzi, 'Altrove (il disagio della regia)', in M. Martone, *Teatro di guerra: un diario* (Milan: Bompiani, 1998), pp. 12–13.
51 G. Gosetti, 'Le regole del noir', in M. Fabbri (ed.) *Noir in Festival 2002* (Rome: Noir in Festival, 2002), p. 7.
52 A. Dalle Vacche, *The Body in the Mirror: Shapes of History in Italian Cinema* (New Jersey: Princeton University Press, 1992), p. 15.
53 T. Elsaesser, 'Postmodernism as Mourning Work', *Screen*, 42:2 (Summer 2001), 199.

Select filmography

La banda delle cifre (*The Numbers Gang*), Emilio Ghione, 1915
I topi grigi (*The Grey Mice*), Emilio Ghione, 1917
Il triangolo giallo (*The Yellow Triangle*), Emilio Ghione, 1918
Ossessione, Luchino Visconti, 1942
Il bandito (*The Bandit*), Alberto Lattuada, 1946
Caccia tragica (*Tragic Pursuit*), Aldo Vergano, 1946
Tombolo, paradiso nero (*Tombolo, Black Paradise*), Giorgio Ferroni, 1947
Senza pietà (*Without Pity*), Alberto Lattuada, 1948
Gioventù perduta (*Lost Youth*), Pietro Germi, 1948
In nome della legge (*In the Name of the Law*), Pietro Germi, 1949
Cronaca di un amore (*Story of a Love Affair*), Michelangelo Antonioni, 1950
I vinti (*The Vanquished*), Michelangelo Antonioni, 1952
Processo alla città (*City on Trial*), Luigi Zampa, 1952
La signora senza camelie (*The Lady Without Camelias*), Michelangelo Antonioni, 1953
L'oro di Napoli (*The Gold of Naples*), Vittorio De Sica, 1954
Le notti bianche (*White Nights*), Luchino Visconti, 1957
La sfida (*The Challenge*), Francesco Rosi, 1958
Nella città l'inferno (*And the Wild, Wild Women*), Renato Castellani, 1959
Un maledetto imbroglio (*A Wretched Business*), Pietro Germi, 1959
Il rossetto (*Lipstick*), Damiano Damiani, 1960.

La commare secca (*The Grim Reaper*), Bernardo Bertolucci, 1961.
L'assassino (*The Ladykiller of Rome*), Elio Petri, 1962.
Salvatore Giuliano, Francesco Rosi, 1961
Lo spettro (*The Ghost*), Riccardo Freda, 1963
La frusta e il corpo (*The Whip and the Body*, aka *Night Is the Phantom*), John
     M. Old (Mario Bava), 1963.
Le mani sulla città (*Hands over the City*), Francesco Rosi, 1963
Danza macabra (*Dance Macabre*), Antonio Margheriti, 1964
Sei donne per l'assassino (*Blood and Black Lace*), Mario Bava, 1964
Vaghe stelle dell'orsa (*Sandra*), Luchino Visconti, 1965
Blow-up, Michelangelo Antonioni, 1966
A ciascuno il suo (*We Still Kill the Old Way*), Elio Petri, 1967
Banditi a Milano (*Bandits of Milan*), Carlo Lizzani, 1968
Il giorno della civetta (*The Cry of the Owl*), Damiano Damiani, 1968
Senza sapere niente di lei (*Unknown Woman*), Luigi Comencini, 1969
Indagine su un cittadino al di sopra di ogni sospetto (*Investigation of a
     Citizen Above Suspicion*), Elio Petri, 1970
L'uccello dalle piume di cristallo (*Bird With the Crystal Plumage*), Dario
     Argento, 1970
L'istruttoria è chiusa, dimentichi (*Interrogation Is Over, Forget*), Damiano
     Damiani, 1971
Milano calibro 9 (*Milan Calibre 9*), Fernando Di Leo, 1971
Quattro mosche di velluto grigio (*Four Flies on Grey Velvet*), Dario Argento,
     1971
Torino nera (*Black Turin*), Carlo Lizzani, 1972
La polizia ringrazia (*The Police Are Grateful*), Stefano Vanzina, 1972
Il caso Mattei (*The Mattei Affair*), Francesco Rosi, 1973
Lucky Luciano, Francesco Rosi, 1974
Cadaveri eccellenti (*Illustrious Corpses*), Francesco Rosi, 1975
Profondo rosso (*Deep Red*), Dario Argento, 1975
Mark il poliziotto (*Mark the Policeman*), Stelvio Massi, 1975
Mark il poliziotto spara per primo (*Policeman Mark Shoots First*), Stelvio
     Massi, 1975
Professione reporter (*The Passenger*), Michelangelo Antonioni, 1975
La donna della Domenica (*Sunday Woman*), Luigi Comencini, 1975
Il sospetto (*Suspicion*), Francesco Maselli, 1975
Non si sevizia un paperino (*Don't Torture the Duck*), Lucio Fulci, 1976
Milano violenta (*Violent Milan*), Mario Caiano, 1976
Napoli violenta (*Violent Naples*), Umberto Lenzi, 1976
Todo modo, Elio Petri, 1976
La tragedia di un uomo ridicolo (*Tragedy of a Ridiculous Man*), Bernardo
     Bertolucci, 1980
Tenebre (*Tenebrae*), Dario Argento, 1982
L'assassinio di poliziotti (*Copkiller*), Roberto Faenza, 1983
La casa del tappeto giallo (*House of the Yellow Carpet*), Carlo Lizzani, 1983
Il nome della rosa (*The Name of the Rose*), Jean Jacques Annaud, 1986

Una fredda mattina di maggio (*A Cold May Morning*), Vittorio Sindoni, 1990
Il muro di gomma (*The Rubber Wall*), Marco Risi, 1991
Il giudice ragazzino (*The Young Judge*), Alessandro Di Robilant, 1993
La fine è nota (*The End Is Known*), Cristina Comencini, 1993
Il lungo silenzio (*The Long Silence*), Margarethe von Trotta, 1993
La scorta (*The Escort*), Ricky Tognazzi, 1993
Una pura formalità (*A Pure Formality*), Giuseppe Tornatore, 1994
Un eroe borghese (*Middle Class Hero*), Michele Placido, 1994
La mia generazione (*My Generation*), Wilma Labate, 1996
La sindrome di Stendhal (*The Stendhal Syndrome*), Dario Argento, 1996
Rose e pistole (*Roses and Guns*), Carla Apuzzo, 1998
Teatro di guerra, Mario Martone, 1998
I cento passi (*The 100 Steps*), Marco Tullio Giordana, 2000
Chimera, Pappi Corsicato, 2001
Un delitto impossibile, Antonello Grimaldi, 2001
Assassini dei giorni di festa (*The Holiday Killers*), Damiano Damiani, 2002
Il gioco di Ripley (*Ripley's Game*), Liliana Cavani, 2002
Io non ho paura (*I'm Not Scared*), Gabriele Salvatores, 2002
Buongiorno notte (*Good Morning, Night*), Marco Bellocchio, 2003
La finestra di fronte (*Facing Window*), Ferzan Ozpetek, 2003
Piazza delle cinque lune (*Five Moon Square*), Renzo Martinelli, 2003
Le conseguenze dell'amore (*The Consequences of Love*, Paolo Sorrentino, 2004)

Select bibliography

Argentieri, M., *La censura nel cinema italiano* (Rome: Editori Riuniti, 1974).

Argentieri, M., *Il cinema in guerra: Arte, comunicazione e propaganda in Italia 1940–44* (Rome: Editori Riuniti, 1998).

Armes, R., *Patterns of Realism* (London: The Tantivy Press, 1971).

Bacon, M., *Visconti: Explorations of Beauty and Decay* (Cambridge: Cambridge University Press, 1998).

Baran'ski, Z. and West, R. J. (eds), *The Cambridge Companion to Modern Italian Culture* (Cambridge: Cambridge University Press, 2001).

Boneschi, M., *Poveri ma belli: I nostri anni cinquanta* (Milan: Mondadori, 1995).

Brooks, P., *The Melodramatic Imagination* (New York: Columbia University Press, 1985).

Brunetta, G. P., *Storia del cinema italiano: Il cinema muto 1895–1929* (Rome: Editori Riuniti, 1993).

Brunetta, G. P., *Cent'anni di cinema italiano, 2. Dal 1945 ai giorni nostri* (Rome: Laterza, 1998).

Calabrese, O., *Neo-Baroque: A Sign of the Times* trans. C. Lambert (New Jersey: Princeton University Press, 1992).

Caldiron, O., *Nero noir* (Udine: Centro Espressioni cinematografiche, 1992).

Caldiron, O., *Il paradosso dell'autore* (Rome: Bulzoni, 1999).

Calamai, D. and Gnomo, S., *Cento anni di stile sul Grande Schermo: Quando il noir crea la moda* (Rome: Zephiro, 1995).

Caldwell, L., 'What about Women? Italian Films and Their Concerns', in U. Sieglohr (ed.), *Heroines without Heroes: Reconstructing Female and National Identities in European Cinema, 1945–51* (London: Cassell, 2000), pp. 131–46.

Ciment, M., *Le dossier Rosi* (Paris: Editions Stock, 1976).

Cosulich, S., 'Un termometro della società', in M. P. Sutto (ed.), *Noir in Festival 1992* (Viareggio: La Meridiana Editori, 1992), pp. 96–8.

Deleuze, G., *Cinema 2: The Time Image* trans. by H. Tomlinson and R. Galeta (London: The Athlone Press, 1989).

Della Casa, S., 'L'altra faccia del cinema nero italiano', in M. Fabbri (ed.), *Noir in Festival 1998* (Rome: Fahrenheit 451, 1998).

Detassis, P. *et al.*, 'Il giallo e il nero: il cinema noir', *Ciak*, 1:8 (Supplement) 2001.

Eco, U., *The Role of the Reader* (London: Hutchinson Education, 1979).

Elsaesser, T., 'Postmodernism as Mourning Work', *Screen*, 42:2 (2001), 193–201.

Fabbri, M. (ed.), *Noir in Festival 1998* (Rome: Fahrenheit 451, 1998).

Fabbri, M. (ed.), *Noir in Festival 2000* (Rome: Noir in Festival, 2000).

Fabbri, M. (ed.), *Noir in Festival 2001* (Rome: Noir in Festival, 2001).

Fabbri, M. (ed.), *Noir in Festival 2002* (Rome: Noir in Festival, 2002).

Fabbri, M. and Resegotti, E. (eds), *I colori del nero: Cinema, letteratura noir* (Milan, Mystfest/Ubulibri, 1989).

Faldini, F. and Fofi, G., *L'avventurosa storia del cinema italiano raccontata dai suoi protagonisti 1960–1969* (Milan: Feltrinelli, 1981).

Farassino, A., *Neorealismo: Cinema italiano 1945–1949* (Turin: E. D. T. Edizioni, 1989).

Farinotti, P., *Dizionario del film giallo* (Carriago: SugarCo Edizioni, 1993).

Gandini, L., 'Il nero a colori', *Fotogenia* 1 (1994), 125–34.

Ghezzi, E., 'Altrove (il disagio della regia)', in M. Martone, *Teatro di Guerra: Un diario* (Milan: Bompiani, 1998).

Ginsborg, P., *A History of Contemporary Italy: Society and Politics 1943–1988* (Harmondsworth: Penguin Books, 1990).

Ginsborg, P., *Italy and Its Discontents 1980–2001* (London: Allen

Lane, The Penguin Press, 2001).

Giovannini, F., *Storia del noir: Dai fantasmi di Edgar Allan Poe al grande cinema di oggi* (Rome: Castelvecchi, 2000).

Giuffrida, S. and Manzoni, R. (eds), *Giallo, poliziesco, thriller e detective story* (Milan: Leonardo Arte, 1999).

Gosetti, G., 'L'occhio del diavolo', in M. Fabbri (ed.), *Noir in Festival* (Rome: Fahrenheit 451, 1998).

Gosetti, G., 'L'equivoco del nero', in M. Fabbri and E. Resegotti (eds), *I colori del nero: Cinema, letteratura, noir* (Milan: Ubulibri, 1989), pp. 10–12.

Gramsci, A., *Letteratura e vita nazionale* (Rome: Editori Riuniti, 1975).

Gubitosi, G., *Amedeo Nazzari* (Bologna: Il Mulino, 1998).

Gundle, S. and Parker, S. (eds), *The New Italian Republic: From the Fall of the Berlin Wall to Berlusconi* (London: Routledge, 1996).

Heiney, D., *America in Modern Italian Literature* (New Brunswick: Rutgers University Press, 1964).

Hughes, R., *The Shock of the New*, 2nd edn (London: Thames & Hudson, 1991).

Koven, M., 'La dolce morta', paper presented to the European Cinema Research Forum conference, *Reviewing Space and Place in European Cinema* (April 2003).

Landy, M., 'The Use and Abuse of History in Melodrama', paper presented to the BFI *Melodrama* conference (July 1992).

Lefebvre, H., *The Production of Space* trans. D. Nicholson-Smith (Oxford: Blackwell, 1991).

Livolsi, M. (ed.), *Schermi e ombre: Gli italiani e il cinema nel dopoguerra* (Florence: La Nuova Italia, 1988).

Martinelli, R., *Piazza delle cinque lune* (Rome: Gremese, 2003).

Newitz, A., 'Serial Killers, True Crime and Economic Performance Anxiety', in C. Sharrett (ed.), *Mythologies of Violence in Postmodern Media* (Detroit: Wayne State University Press, 1999).

Nowell-Smith, G., *Luchino Visconti*, 3rd edn (London: BFI Publishing, 2003).

Quaglietti, L., *Storia economico-politico del cinema italiano 1945–1980* (Rome: Editori Riuniti, 1980).

Pezzotta, A., *Mario Bava*, 2nd edn (Milan: Il Castoro, 1997).

Radstone, S., 'Trauma and Screen Studies: Opening the Debate', *Screen*, 42:2 (2001) 188–92.

Rea, L., *I colori del buio: Il cinema thrilling italiano dal 1930 al 1974* (Florence: Molino, 1999).

Restivo, A., *The Cinema of Economic Miracles: Visuality and*

Modernisation in the Italian Art Film (Durham and London: Duke University Press, 2002).

Scerbanenco, G., *Milano calibro 9*, 2nd edn (Milan: Garzanti, 1990).

Sebastiani, M. and Sesti, M., *Delitto per delitto: 500 film polizieschi (detective story, gangster film, noir, thriller, spy story)* (Turin: Lindau, 1998).

Segal, L., *Slow Motion: Changing Masculinities, Changing Men* (New Brunswick: Rutgers Univesity Press, 1990).

Sieglohr, U. (ed.), *Heroines without Heroes: Reconstructing Female and National Identities in European Cinema, 1945–51* (London: Cassell, 2000).

Thoret, J.-B., *Dario Argento: Magicien de la peur* (Paris: Cahiers du Cinéma, 2002).

Tirapelli, R., *Tracce di giallo in 201 film* (Colognola ai Colli: Dematra, 1997).

White, J., *The Birth and Rebirth of Pictorial Space*, 3rd edn (London: Faber & Faber, 1987).

Wood, M., 'Frencesco Rosi: Heightened Realism', in J. Boorman and W. Donohue (eds), *Projections 8* (London: Faber & Faber, 1998).

Wood, M., 'Revealing The Hidden City: the Cinematic Conspiracy Thriller of the 1970s', in *The Italianist* 23 (2003), 150–62.

S. Žižek, 'You May!', *London Review of Books* (18 March 1999).

Websites

http://geocities.com/Athens/Atlantis/2362/index.htm. *L'anello giallo* is the first Italian ring of *giallo* sites.

www.geocities.com/Paris/4708/giallo.html. Website of the internet magazine, *Il foglio giallo*, with links.

www.alice.it. Booksite with *giallo* link.

www.internetbookshop.it. Has a *giallo* section.

http://users.iol.it/alot/giochi.htm. All the *giallo* games.

www.fumetti.org. Details of *fumetti* old and new.

www.diabolik.it. The official website.

Index

Note: literary works can be found under authors' names; numbers in *italics* refer to illustrations.